£9

The Manchester Bantams

The Manchester Bantams

THE STORY OF A PALS BATTALION
AND A CITY AT WAR

23RD (SERVICE) BATTALION
THE MANCHESTER REGIMENT (8TH CITY)

Caroline Scott

Pen & Sword
MILITARY

First published in Great Britain in 2016 by
PEN & SWORD MILITARY
an imprint of
Pen and Sword Books Ltd
47 Church Street
Barnsley
South Yorkshire S70 2AS

Copyright © Caroline Scott, 2016

ISBN 978 1 78346 389 3

The right of Caroline Scott to be identified
as the author of this work has been asserted by her in accordance
with the Copyright, Designs and Patents Act 1988.

A CIP record for this book is available from the British Library.

All rights reserved. No part of this book may be reproduced or
transmitted in any form or by any means, electronic or mechanical
including photocopying, recording or by any information storage and
retrieval system, without permission from the Publisher in writing.

Printed and bound in England by
CPI Group (UK) Ltd, Croydon, CR0 4YY

Typeset in Times New Roman
by CHIC GRAPHICS

Pen & Sword Books Ltd incorporates the imprints of
Pen & Sword Archaeology, Atlas, Aviation, Battleground, Discovery, Family
History, History, Maritime, Military, Naval, Politics, Railways, Select, Social History,
Transport, True Crime, Claymore Press, Frontline Books, Leo Cooper, Praetorian
Press, Remember When, Seaforth Publishing and Wharncliffe.

For a complete list of Pen and Sword titles please contact
Pen and Sword Books Limited
47 Church Street, Barnsley, South Yorkshire, S70 2AS, England
E-mail: enquiries@pen-and-sword.co.uk
Website: www.pen-and-sword.co.uk

Contents

Introduction 6

CHAPTER 1   'Such Stirring, Clashing, Martial Times . . .' 8
CHAPTER 2   'Bobs' Own' 37
CHAPTER 3   'From City to Sea-side' 51
CHAPTER 4   'The Latest Methods of Making War' 98
CHAPTER 5   'The Time Had Now Come' 112
CHAPTER 6   Somme: 'The Best Type of Bantams Done In' 142
CHAPTER 7   Arras: 'City of the Dead' 185
CHAPTER 8   'De-Bantamization' 199
CHAPTER 9   'A Strange Adventure, Fantastic as a Dream': Mud and then Movement 205
CHAPTER 10   Saint-Quentin: Finding the Line 227
CHAPTER 11   Péronne and Gauche Wood: Working Parties, Cricket Matches and Plagues of Frogs 238
CHAPTER 12   'The Birdcage': Fighting for the Higher Ground 247
CHAPTER 13   Houthulst Forest: 'Practically Annihilated' 259
CHAPTER 14   'The Beginning of the End' 288
CHAPTER 15   'Honour the Dead, Remember the Living' 301

Notes 322
Index 347

Introduction

In May 1916 Major Eustace Lockhart Maxwell received a promotion. Having formerly been an officer in the Indian Cavalry, he was now given command (his first) of an infantry battalion in France. After forty-eight hours with his new unit Maxwell wrote to his family,

> The outstanding characteristic of those who belong to it seems to be their extraordinary self-complacency! *Esprit de corps* is a fine thing, but the satisfaction with which they regard themselves, their battalion, its internal economy, its gallantry, its discipline, its everything else, is almost indecent! If at the end of a month my opinion of them is half as good as their own, I shall think myself uncommonly lucky.[1]

That battalion was the 23rd Manchester 'Bantams'.

It is perhaps not entirely surprising that they were feeling pleased with themselves. Having been formed in November 1914, entirely composed of men of a height between 5ft and 5ft 3in, the battalion had spent much of 1915 training in the Lancashire seaside resort of Morecambe. There, billeted in West End boarding houses, they had been petted by landladies, were applauded by crowds as they drilled on the Promenade and had poems and songs composed about them ('See our squads along the front, / Hearts aflame to bear the brunt'). It would be some time before they made it from seafront to front line, but when the Bantams finally left Morecambe, Private Percy Gidley would write to the local paper, 'The cheerfulness, encouragement, and care of those providing the billets, and the generosity of Morecambe in general, made new men of us.'[2] Morecambe had made the Manchester men into well-polished exhibition soldiers. They looked the part (if diminutively so) and had all of the right things to say. It was now time to turn their patriotic assertions into actions.

Despite his initial concerns, by the end of that month Maxwell had developed a liking and respect for his new battalion. They were talkative, friendly, funny and bloodthirsty. 'The murderous little beasts just love their work,' Maxwell wrote.[3] He was eager, indeed impatient, to take them into the fight. His turn came on 20 July 1916. He went over the top with his murderous little beasts in an attack on enemy trenches, south of Guillemont, on the Somme. He was killed within a few yards. Maxwell was one of fifty men of the battalion who died that day; 100 more were wounded, shell-shocked or missing. The bodies of thirty-eight of those killed, Maxwell included, would never be found. Major General Sir Reginald Pinney, the commanding officer of the Division, would write in his diary at the end of that day that 'the best type of Bantams' were 'done in'.[4]

Almost half of the men involved in the attack on 20 July would eventually be counted as casualties and the 23rd Manchester Battalion would never be the same again. They would never regain the confidence that had so struck Maxwell at their first meeting. That *esprit de corps* had taken a battering. And it was about to be further tested. It simply was not possible consistently to replace casualties with recruits who had the same physique as the original Bantams, who had had the benefit of the same length of training and, perhaps most importantly, who had the same spirit – that pride to be there and hunger to prove themselves. The gaps left by short, stocky volunteers were now being filled with small, slight conscripts. The fighting quality of the Bantams was observed to be deteriorating.

At the end of 1916 the concept of the Bantam battalions would be examined, found wanting and scrapped as an unsuccessful experiment. The 23rd Manchester Battalion was officially 'De-Bantamized' in January 1917. Drafts of 6-footers now broke the tidy height uniformity of the ranks as they marched south through the icy February landscape. The Bantam battalions, so celebrated in 1915, became an embarrassing mistake. By 1917 the same journalists who had been extolling their virtues a year earlier ('the Bantams have not been long in proving that you can't measure a man's soul with a foot rule') were ridiculing them ('poor little men born of diseased civilization!'). The Bantams had become a joke. A bad joke. And something best forgotten.[5]

But the men who had called themselves Bantams remained proud (albeit now quietly so) of their achievements. On Armistice Day, in the decades after the war, they still marched through Manchester behind a banner that said '23rd Bantams'. *They* meant to be remembered. This then, in fond and respectful remembrance, is the story of Manchester's 'cock-o-doodle' Bantams.

> We are – The Bantams!
> The Cock-o-doodle Bantams:
> Morecambe breezes suit us grand.
> Firm as Heysham rocks we stand,
> Grenadiers at heart tho' small,
> Proud to answer country's call.'[6]

Chapter 1

'Such Stirring, Clashing, Martial Times . . .'

'He who believes he will reign will not reign', pronounced Madame de Thebes, the renowned Parisian prophetess. 'It is about to be accomplished. *No one can escape his fate.*'

It was 29 June 1914 – the day after the assassination of Archduke Franz Ferdinand – and the *Manchester Evening News*, reporting the predictions of Paris's 'celebrated soothsayer' alongside events in Sarajevo, had its tongue somewhat in its cheek. Though forecasting that Austria would probably now harden its line against the Slavs, the *Evening News* foresaw no significant fall-out. 'The event, tragic though it is, is not likely to have any effect on international politics,' the Manchester paper considered. The doomsaying prophecies of a Parisian astrologer were just an amusing aside.[1]

> 6——THE MANCHESTER EVENING NEWS, MONDAY, JUNE 29, 1914.
> ## HEIR TO AUSTRIAN THRONE MURDERED
> ### Archduke and His Wife Shot Dead in the Street.
> ### DETERMINED PLOT.
> Bomb First Thrown at Their Car : Second Attempt Within an Hour.
> ### BOY ASSASSIN.

Manchester Evening News, 29 June 1914.

The boy assassin's gunshot would echo loudly through international politics for the next month. Still, though, while diplomatic manoeuvres on the Continent were reported in the Manchester press, there was little expectation that Britain would become directly involved in events across the Channel. Manchester had other things to think about; it was occupied with more close-to-home concerns. In July 1914 Lancashire was preoccupied with the likelihood that a depression in the cotton trade was looming.

In 1913 Britain's cotton exports had reached an all-time high of 7.075 billion yards of cloth, worth £126.5 million. In January 1914 the *Manchester Courier* had crowed: 'One wonders what the pioneers of the cotton trade would have thought of such an output of cloth from the looms of Lancashire! Not in their wildest dreams could they have foreseen such a development of the industry.'[2]

Lancashire was cotton, and cotton was Lancashire. In 1899 over 75 per cent of Britain's cotton textile workers were employed in the county.[3] With the textile industry came all manner of associated trades and industries. Manchester in 1914 was a town of warehouses, traders and shipping agents, of bleaching, dyeing and printing works, chemicals, iron works and engineering concerns, brokers, bankers and insurers. The state of the cotton market had a decisive influence over the local economy. When the cotton trade was doing well, Manchester prospered; conversely, a depression in the trade impacted on the whole area's economy. And, by 1913, Lancashire's supremacy was creaking. It was the beginning of the end for the golden age of 'Cottonopolis'.

While the 1913 headline figures were impressive, the details and analysis were unsettling. Britain's world share of exports had contracted from 82 per cent in 1884 to 58 per cent by 1913 (on a weight-of-cloth basis). The emerging consumer markets that had kept Lancashire's mills busy through the nineteenth century were now developing their own domestic textile industries. The most significant among these would be India. The market for cotton there had grown fast over the previous twenty years and Britain had been the principal beneficiary; by 1913 India was consuming 45 per cent of the total yardage of cloth that Britain exported. But it was not going to last. India's own textile industry was expanding rapidly; during the period 1900–1913 the number of factory spindles in operation in India increased by one-third and the number of power looms operating more than doubled. Thanks to the growth of the Indian consumer market, Lancashire had enjoyed a boom. But it was about to peak – and fall.[4]

In July 1914 Manchester was looking at international events with trade, not war, in mind. Sir Charles Macara, President of the Federation of Master Cotton Spinners' Associations (FMCSA), was a worried man, and his concerns were being put into print all over the local press. Lancashire's best customers were not buying. 'The state of the cotton trade throughout the world is uniformly bad,' Macara wrote.

Year	Cloth exports – millions of yards
1800	66
1810	212
1820	251
1830	442
1840	791
1850	1,385
1860	2,776
1870	3,267
1880	3,725
1890	5,125
1900	5,032
1910	6,018
1913	**7,075**

Figures relate to exports of cotton piece goods, i.e. cloth. They don't include yarn, sewing thread etc. But cloth accounted for around 75 per cent of all cotton textile exports by value. Source: Sandberg, *Lancashire in Decline*, p. 4.

All the great foreign markets are depressed. Famine and plague in India, revolution in China, and war in the Balkan States have handicapped the three countries which, in the order I have mentioned them, are England's best customers. Further drawbacks have been the war between Italy and Tripoli, the Mexican revolution, the depression throughout South America, and last, but not least, the high price of raw material. Notwithstanding this accumulation of reverses, mills for the production of cotton goods have been growing in number at a rapid rate, with the result that markets are over-supplied, and the prices have fallen to a level which leaves not only no margin of profit, but a serious loss.[5]

At the start of July the General Committee of the FMCSA recommended that all mills working American cotton should suspend operations. With the whole trade co-operating to manage down output, it was hoped that the recent fall in the prices of finished goods could be arrested.[6] On 31 July 1914 the FMCSA duly voted in favour of organised short-time. However, overseas events were suddenly pushing trade concerns out of the headlines. In the words of the *Manchester Guardian*, 'bigger things were in the air'.[7] At the end of July, as Austria presented its ultimatum to Serbia, cotton prices dropped sharply. The mood of mercantile Manchester deteriorated correspondingly. 'There are war-clouds on the horizon,' wrote the *Manchester Evening News*, 'but people hope that they may not burst. The European question never loomed bigger, but surely means will be taken to localise war if it breaks out at all.' The next day, as Austria declared war on Serbia, it seemed like those clouds were perhaps, after all, bursting. 'It is difficult to recollect days such as these,' reflected the *Evening News*.[8]

Towards the end of July the *Manchester Guardian* published a series of leader articles that argued emphatically against Britain being drawn into a European conflict. C.P. Scott, the *Guardian*'s owner and editor, took up the leader writer's pen himself.[9] Britain should maintain its neutrality, the *Manchester Guardian* insisted. She must steer well clear of all entangling alliances (secret, or otherwise) and maintain her freedom of action. Britain's only involvement in the developing European conflict should be in the role of peacemaker.[10]

'It is impossible to exaggerate the danger that now threatens Europe,' C.P. Scott wrote on 27 July.

> The European war which has been talked about for so long that no one really believed that it would ever come is nearer embodiment than any of us can

---

COTTON DEPRESSION.

Lancashire's Outlook for 1914.

A Difficult Situation for Employers and Operatives.

The effort to avoid serious losses in the cotton trade of Lancashire during the year 1914 is likely to be one of extreme difficulty.

This is generally admitted by all judges engaged in the spinning and weaving of American cotton.

In every centre during the coming months short time is likely to be the rule.

The world's requirements to-day are on a scale that make a big cotton crop an absolute necessity.

In markets like the Near East and South America credit is crippled, and merchants only purchase with extreme caution.

Manchester Evening News, 1 July 1914.

Manchester Ship Canal, *c.* 1910.

remember. The responbility is a terrible one, even for England, which has no direct interest in the quarrel between Austria and Servia, and is in no danger of being dragged into the conflict by treaties of alliance. Can England use this favoured position to save Europe from disaster?[11]

But the situation was evolving faster than the *Guardian* expected. On 31 July the *Manchester Guardian*'s leader article alleged that there were 'strong influences' at work, 'social and bureaucratic, which are anxious for war'. It was a 'conspiracy' C.P. Scott wrote, and there was a real danger now that the perpetrators of that conspiracy would drag Britain into a war. He implored:

We have a completely white sheet before us upon which we are free to write anything or nothing so far as our contracts with European Powers are concerned. But the Government is not free as regards its own people. It is the trustee of the nation and bound above all else to consider its interests and the interests of the mass of the community on whom the burden of all war really falls . . . Honour is not involved abroad. It is irretrievably involved at home.[12]

A series of readers' letters was published by the *Manchester Guardian* on 31 July, all essentially in accord with the paper's own non-interventionist stance. Names of manufacturers and traders are prominent among the correspondents. Any diplomatic event that was likely to disrupt trade – finished goods going out, or raw materials coming in – was not in Manchester's interest, it was argued. Liberal, mercantile Manchester had no taste for sabre-rattling. And war? In the de rigueur phrase of the day, 'Not bloody likely!' One such typical reader's letter ran thus:

> THE DANGER
> OF
> A EUROPEAN WAR.
> ——
> SHOULD GREAT BRITAIN BE INVOLVED?

Manchester Guardian, 31 July 1914.

Everyone connected with the cotton trade knows the whole trade depends entirely on its overseas trade, and we should all be only too willing to face and bear a burden, however heavy, if we were defending India, China, or any of our colonies, but in this case we have no interest of any sort in the war, with nothing to gain and an enormous trade to lose, and to enter into the fight would, therefore, be madness.[13]

On 31 July, as Russia ordered general mobilisation, there were extraordinary fluctuations in cotton prices. In response, both London and Manchester Stock Exchanges took the decision to close. 'These events are not mere spectacle,' the *Manchester Guardian* wrote, 'but may, in their development, involve the ruin of those who witness them . . . Of the unpopularity of war in Manchester there is no question, and the prevailing note seems to be an indignant incredulity.'[14] 'Everything conspires to confine business to its smallest dimensions,' reflected the *Manchester Evening News*. 'The uncertainties

Market Street, Manchester, *c.* 1910.

Deansgate, Manchester, c. 1910.

Manchester Royal Exchange, c. 1900.

14

regarding the European troubles render it advisable to watch and wait. It would be intolerable for Great Britain to be mixed up with Continental quarrels.'[15] But Britain – and Manchester – was about to get very much mixed up.

On 1 August the German government ordered general mobilisation and declared war on Russia. France, in turn, mobilised. The following day the German government sent an ultimatum to Belgium demanding that its armies be granted free passage across the country into France. Albert, King of the Belgians, telegraphed George V, appealing for diplomatic intervention.

> **THE CLOUDS DARKEN.**
>
> GERMANY'S ULTIMATUM TO RUSSIA.
>
> Demobilisation or Retaliation !
>
> A "NOTE" TO FRANCE.
>
> OMINOUS SPEECH BY THE KAISER.
>
> "Sword Forced Into Germany's Hands."

Manchester Evening News, 1 August 1914.

It wasn't just Manchester's businessmen who were alarmed by the direction of international developments. On 2 August an open-air meeting was held in Tib Street, Manchester. Convened by the Manchester and Salford Independent Labour Party, it drew a large attendance. The meeting adopted a resolution appealing to the government to 'do their utmost to limit the area of the war, and demanding that this country should observe strict neutrality'. A speaker warned the audience that they 'were face to face with the greatest holocaust the world had ever seen'.[16]

> **EUROPE IN FERMENT.**
>
> SKIRMISHES ON THE FRANCO-GERMAN FRONTIER.
>
> NAVAL ACTION.
>
> GERMAN CRUISER BOMBARDS RUSSIAN PORT.
>
> GERMANY'S OFFER TO BELGIUM.
>
> A PROPOSED ENTENTE DECLINED.

Manchester Evening News, 3 August 1914.

On 3 August a *Manchester Evening News* editorial – headlined 'War!'– warned:

If ever there was a time for caution it is now. A priceless possession to-day is a cool head. Many influential people and many influential newspapers are clamouring for war – war with a nation who are of the same stock as ourselves, and our best customers . . . For years it has been dinned into our ears with deafening force that the way to avoid war is to be prepared for war. Acting on that advice Great Britain, along with other nations, has piled armaments upon armaments, has spent millions upon millions. The totals are appalling. Now the bubble has burst. Now we know that elaborate preparations for war do not prevent war. To-day Europe is literally an armed camp, with three of the biggest Powers and one small country already in the field and others conscious that, however much they may desire to hold back, they may at any moment be dragged in.[17]

With the majority of bank holiday excursions cancelled, Mancunians had flocked to the city's parks on 3 August. It was a fiercely hot day. Between the shade-seeking and the ice-cream wafers, one topic dominated conversations. As each new edition of the papers came out, they were eagerly purchased. Impatience to learn of the latest developments increased as the day went on. By the afternoon there were crowds around the newspaper offices. The *Manchester Guardian* recorded:

There was always a congregation of two or three thousand men and women inquiring anxiously for news and asking, 'What is the Cabinet decision?' Small straws show which way the wind blows, and it may not be out of place to show that the Manchester folk did not at all appreciate joining in a war which might tend to strengthen Russia against Germany. On all hands one heard grumblings against what appeared to be a possible development. Mingled with the loud conversation or argument of the people who gathered in groups was the cry of the newsboys, who did a rare trade.[18]

A meeting of Manchester business leaders was convened, with the *Manchester Guardian*'s editor, C.P. Scott, presiding. The meeting unanimously passed a resolution urging that terms be made with Germany, 'on the basis that this country shall remain neutral, provided the German government undertakes not to attack the northern and western coasts of France, or to operate by sea through the ports of Holland and Belgium'.[19] But while Manchester was drafting resolutions, German troops were gathering on the Belgian border. The situation was slithering over the brink.

ENGLAND'S ULTIMATUM TO GERMANY.

A QUESTION OF LIFE OR DEATH TO GERMANY.

GERMANY DECLARES WAR ON BELGIUM.

Manchester Evening News, 4 August 1914.

On 4 August Britain issued Germany with an ultimatum demanding assurance that Belgian neutrality would be respected. The German government had until 11.00 p.m. to respond.

An image from the *Manchester Courier* captioned 'Manchester anxious to hear the latest war news'. It shows crowds outside the newspaper's offices waiting for the latest bulletins. *Manchester Courier and Lancashire General Advertiser*, 4 August 1914.

That evening a public meeting was convened at Milton Hall, Deansgate, Manchester. The speakers included members of Manchester and Salford councils, prominent citizens and representative of various religious denominations. A newspaper report conveys the tone of the night's speeches:

> When people clamoured for war they thought only of the glamour of it. They forgot the silent mills, the blackened forges, the desolate workmen's homes, the starving women and children, the horrible loss of life, and the suffering it involved. (Hear, hear.) They forgot that it meant the cessation of all social reform. We were being forced into a war at the beck of the autocrat and the armament makers – (cheers and interruption) – a war for no object that was not worth the life of a single Englishman. (Cheers.)'

But when a speaker asked, 'Was it worth while to pour out England's blood and treasure even to preserve the neutrality of Belgium?' the audience responded with cries of both 'No' and 'Yes'. A resolution was passed stating that the government ought to have maintained 'absolute neutrality'; copies were to be telegraphed to the Prime Minister and Sir Edward Grey. The meeting was broken up, around 9.00 pm, as a group of youths invaded the building and made 'a patriotic demonstration', with cheers and choruses of the National Anthem.[20]

Elsewhere in Manchester, an estimated three-thousand people were packed into Stevenson Square. Both the Patriotic League and the Neutrality League had convened rallies in the square and 'oratory was at full flood':

The Chairman asserted that the welfare, happiness, and prosperity of the citizens of Manchester were all threatened by what was to be one of the most awful wars history had known. He could see no reason why we should be dragged into such a calamity precipitated by Russia. (Voices: 'We don't want German rule.') 'If you want Russian rule,' Mr Burditt rejoined, 'you will get it not only at Constantinople, but in India some day.' (Hear, hear.) We were in the war now, and must stand shoulder to shoulder, but nothing should prevent men from stating emphatically that they disagreed with such a war, and he trusted that whenever the hour came in which they could speak a word for peace they would do it with all their hearts. (Cheers.)

A resolution was passed, protesting 'against the manner in which the Government is forcing us into war'. But, again, the speakers had to shout over opposing voices and the gathering was ultimately broken up by noisy choruses of the National Anthem.[21]

At 11.00 pm Britain's ultimatum to Germany expired.

The Manchester papers carried reports of London's reaction to events: of the cheering throng marching down Fleet Street; of Union Jacks flying and straw hats being waved frantically; of the choruses of the 'Marseillaise', 'Rule Britannia' and the National Anthem being sung; of the crowds at Buckingham Palace and the demonstrations outside the German embassy.[22]

What, then, was Manchester's reaction to Britain now being at war? Long after midnight people were still on the streets, debating what would happen next. Though Mancunians might not have demonstrated their feelings in such striking or loud numbers, there was evidently still a certain amount of that exuberant hat-waving that had been reported in London. A crowd of youths gathered in Albert Square, mounting the steps of the Town Hall. There were vigorous rounds of cheering and hearty renditions of the National Anthem and the 'Marseillaise' ('or at least the tune of it', as the *Manchester Guardian* noted).[23]

Attempting to sum up the mood of the city on 5 August, the *Manchester Courier* concluded:

The opening of this deadly struggle has been heralded by no 'mafficking', by none of those incoherent ebullitions of the less-reasoning type of patriotism which sapped our morale and tempted us to court disaster in the campaign of South Africa. Throughout the course of the grim preparations for war which have marked the past few days there has been an utter absence of any spirit of reckless boastfulness. The British nation has realised that it has before it the greatest struggle for life in which it has ever been engaged. We are not disposed to underestimate our difficulties.[24]

Smithfield Market, Manchester, *c.* 1910.

There seems to have been an immediate disposition to suppose that those forthcoming difficulties might include food shortages; those grim preparations for war included a lot of shopping. The first day of the war saw a run on food shops in Manchester. Rumour was rife that, with imports likely to be disrupted shortly, prices would now start to rise. 'Sellers did not know what to ask, and as the demand increased and became insistent, sellers had no option but to advance prices very considerably,' a provision dealer (Mr R. Graham of Messrs Wall & Co., Greenwood Street, Manchester) told the *Manchester Guardian*. The next few weeks would see talk of hoarding, of profiteering and speculating. Robert Roberts, whose family ran a corner shop in Salford, would recall:

> The fourth of August 1914 caused no great burst of patriotic fervour amongst us. Little groups, men and women together (unusual, this), stood talking earnestly in the shop or at the street corner, stunned a little by the enormity of events. But soon public concern yielded to private self-interest. A rush of customers to the shop gave us the first alarm – sugar, flour, bread, butter, margarine, cheese, people began frantically to buy all the food they could find the money for. 'Serve no strangers!' my mother ordered after the first hour. 'Only "regulars" from now on.'[25]

'Ow'd'st thee like a smack at th' — Germans, Alf?'

On 4 August the War Office issued an order for the mobilisation of the Territorials. The orders reached Manchester in the evening and placards were promptly posted throughout the city. All members were ordered to report to their headquarters and, by 8.00 pm, several of the drill halls in Manchester were 'besieged by eager crowds'. It was the first time, since it had been established in 1908 that the Territorial Force had been called to arms and conjecture was widespread as to what use it would be put. 'At present, of course, the possibility of the Force being required for active service appears extremely remote,' wrote the *Manchester Courier*, 'and there is every hope that it will never be so required.'[26]

Among the Territorials the mood seems predominantly to have been one of boisterous humour. Observing the 6th Battalion of Manchester Territorials ('the 6th Battalion consists of young men of comparatively good social position, not a few of them public school men') reporting to their drill hall, a journalist recorded:

> Little of anxiety or apprehension was written on their faces. They pushed their way through the throng which gathered outside the building, and crowded down the corridors with the air of undergraduates leaving a lecture room. Those who were not engaged in chaffing their friends on the subject of possible death and mutilation were singing or whistling rag-time tunes.[27]

A more martial mood was noted among the 7th Battalion ('of the artisan class, many of them big and burly fellows'). The *Courier* related:

> As they read the notices ordering them to parade to-day they made strongly-worded comments on the situation generally.
> 'As every bloomin' blighter gotter turn up?' was the inquiry of a large and lusty navvy.
> 'Every —— of us,' he was cheerfully assured by his comrade.
> 'Ow'd'st thee like a smack at th' — Germans, Alf?'
> Alfred's reply was hardly printable, but it boded ill for any German conscript he might chance to meet at close quarters.[28]

Seemingly the Territorials were not the only ones who wanted 'a smack at th' — Germans'. The Manchester papers also remarked, with some surprise, on the apparent eagerness of young men to enlist. Army recruiting offices were suddenly 'in a state of siege' and it was necessary to bring in policemen to marshal the candidates for the King's shilling.[29]

Robert Roberts recalled a neighbour, a Mr Bickham, a veteran of the Boer War, venting his frustrations after having just had the offer of his services declined:

> He stopped by my mother as she hung washing across the street. 'Turned down!' he said disgustedly – 'Bad teeth! They must want blokes to bite the damned Germans!'
> She laughed, sympathizing.
> Mr Bickham went on his way. 'They'll be pulling me in, though,' he called over his shoulder, 'before this lot's done!'
> By 5 August 1915 he had been lying dead three months in France.[30]

While young men (and not-so-young men) queued, eager to play their part, other Manchester men were continuing to take up their pens, adamant still that Britain ought not to be involved in the war. Liberal and commercial Manchester was expressing its alarm on the correspondence pages of the *Manchester Guardian*. These letters convey a seemingly widespread conviction that war was going to be economically ruinous for Manchester. 'Lancashire has probably more to lose by a war than any county in the kingdom,' protests one letter. 'Apart from moral obligations', insists another, 'commercial interests demand a cessation of this ruthless butchery and destruction of Lancashire's customers and commerce.' A third warns: 'Events have already shaken the foundations of business and credit. Were we to fight the consequences would be too awful to contemplate.'[31]

The declaration of war suddenly compounded the difficulties that were already being faced by Manchester's traders and manufacturers. With banks expected to tighten credit, and raw cotton imports from the USA and Egypt likely to be impacted, the outlook seemed stark. The *Manchester Guardian* wrote:

> To-day's news shows that, owing to the war, the cotton trade in all its branches is fast becoming paralysed . . . There is, in fact, a very decided danger of a cotton famine, for all the usual organisation in the buying and selling of the raw material has temporarily collapsed. All foreign trade, of course, requires the creation of credits, and credits necessitate the discounting of bills of exchange. For the moment this has almost ceased, and business cannot be done.[32]

On 3 August the directors of Liverpool's Cotton Association had decided to cease trading until further notice. With Liverpool notifying the New York and New Orleans exchanges of this decision, it effectively stopped the movement of raw cotton into Liverpool. It was estimated that, under normal conditions, there were sufficient stocks in Liverpool to keep the trade going for about twelve weeks. But, as the *Manchester Guardian* explained, while the supply of raw cotton might be an immediate worry, the long-term paralysis of demand was a greater concern. 'The mills might presently have to close for want of cotton,' the paper conjectured, 'but they will soon be closing right and left because there is nobody to take the goods they produce.'[33]

On 4 August the FMCSA had advised that all manufacturers should move onto short time immediately. On 7 August a statement was issued by the Operative Cotton Spinners, Card and Blowing Room Operatives, and Weavers' Amalgamation advising all cotton workers to start saving their money and not to take their annual holidays, on account of the unemployment and distress that the war was shortly likely to cause. 'There can be no immediate hope of a return to steady trade and sure employment', the announcement starkly warned.[34] That same day a meeting was convened at Manchester Town Hall. Attended by representatives of trade and industry, it set out to debate what the war would mean for Manchester's

> **BLACK PROSPECT**
> FOR THE
> **COTTON TRADE.**
> —
> **MANY MILLS SOON TO BE CLOSED.**
> —
> **FOREIGN TRADE PARALYSED.**

Manchester Guardian, 4 August 1914.

economy, how it might impact on workers and how any resultant hardship might be addressed. 'There will be need, distress, and misery among those at home,' commented the *Manchester Courier* as it reported the meeting's proceedings.

> It will be widespread and intense, perhaps of long duration . . . everybody is in for sacrifice. The lowest and the highest are united in this catastrophe of war. It is really a magnificent testimony to our national character to feel how this has already been realised. Go where one will, the expression is, 'Let us bear our share.' There never was such spirit in the nation or such backbone shown.[35]

By the end of the first week of the war a 'being in, we must win' attitude starts to emerge on the pages of the Manchester newspapers. A feeling of resigned necessity begins to dominate. By mid-August the readerships of all of Manchester's newspapers were being urged to support the nation's efforts. 'Some time the responsibility for one of the greatest errors in our history will have to be fixed but that time is not now,' C.P. Scott wrote in a piece for the *Manchester Guardian*. 'Now there is nothing for Englishmen to do but stand together and help by every means in their power to the attainment of our common object – an early and decisive victory over Germany'.[36]

In September 1914 a *Manchester Courier* editorial took a moment to look back at the events of the past few weeks and pondered how posterity might view Manchester's response to the outbreak of war. It is an interesting reflection of the city's mood in that instant, and, as such, is worth quoting at length:

> The outward calm with which Manchester accepts the present situation must not be taken as meaning that citizens are not deeply moved by the crisis of the Empire. The demeanour of the people is a sign of their unanimity and their determination. There have been no bands and banners waving, no hysterics, and no mafficking. The mind of the people is made up. They feel that they have to go through with this war and that that means a tremendous struggle, with terrible losses and much sorrow, with perhaps scarcity, want, and hardship here at home. But the feeling is, it has got to be done. Therefore everywhere the demeanour of the people is silently eloquent of determination – 'it is dogged as does it'. . . . One can imagine posterity wondering how we felt who lived in such stirring, clashing, martial times. But if they are only supplied with pictures of the daily appearance of the city they will be amazed. They will see the old routine of business and traffic proceeding apparently in the usual way, no excited citizens, no anxious crowds. We in these times are hardly able to realise how mighty are the events, of which we are a part, yet which we are accepting as almost inevitable commonplace occurrences. Our attitude is due to our confidence, and our confidence is due to trust in our leaders and belief in the justice of our cause.[37]

'A set of ogres, every man of them'
That sense of justice was reinforced through September 1914 as the Manchester press

began to carry accounts of 'atrocities', 'outrages', 'barbarism' and 'Hunnish horrors' in Belgium. There was an unequivocal – and unsubtle – moral appeal in the reporting of these stories.

At the end of the war the *Manchester Guardian* journalist C.E. Montague would reflect, 'If you cannot hit or kick during a fight, at any rate you can spit. But, to be happy in this arm of the service, you have to feel sure that the adversary is signally fit to be spat upon. Hence, on each side in every war, the civilian will-to-believe that the other side are a set of ogres, every man of them.'[38] The Germans were certainly now turning into ogres on the pages of the popular press. On 26 August the *Guardian* printed Official Press Bureau releases containing statements by the Belgian government's recently convened Committee of Inquiry. These alleged 'fearful and atrocious crimes committed wilfully and deliberately by the invading hosts against helpless non-combatants, old men, women, and children'.[39]

By September parties of Belgian refugees were starting to arrive in Manchester. Their reception demonstrates the strength of popular feeling:

> The length of the street between the station and the Town Hall was thronged with many thousands of people waiting to give a sympathetic and encouraging cheer to the first representatives they had seen of the nation which bore the brunt of the Germans first rush and has suffered most horribly from its barbarities. There has been no crowd like it in Manchester since the King was here.[40]

'They told of their treatment at the hands of the Germans,' recorded the *Guardian*, 'and their stories add to the record of the cruelty of which the German troops have been guilty.' Testimonies were printed in the local papers describing how children had been thrown from upper windows and caught on the bayonets of soldiers below. Local voices too would soon be telling stories of the enemy's frightfulness. A Private William Burns, of the 2nd Manchester Battalion, injured at Mons, was interviewed by the *Manchester Courier*. He told the paper:

> On the roadside everywhere in Belgium they saw the slaughtered country people – women, girls, children, as well as men and boys. He said he had thought of the sight ever since, and it took away his appetite. The women and girls were awfully slashed about the body, ears and noses and arms cut off, and the little children also partly dismembered in this way . . . He has the supreme disdain for the German ranker as a soldier. 'They're no good at all,' he said. In his own blunt way, he added that it made one 'almost disbelieve there was a God' that such things should have been permitted.[41]

Letters to the local papers called for the Germans to be punished for these outrages. One correspondent demanded:

> The blood of thousands of innocent men, women and children, the blood of our brave soldiers and sailors call out hot for vengeance, as no retribution could equal

the crimes committed, but for punishment. The German people called for the arbitrament of war, they have planned it, they have struck a treacherous blow at the liberty, humanity, and civilisation of the world; and not to make them realise this and punish their ruthless action would be a sentimental crime.[42]

This enemy was unambiguously bad – and advancing towards England. The cause, as presented in the papers, was just and pressing. Right was unequivocally on the Allies' side. The emotional appeal still sounds loudly.

Through the autumn of 1914 the local papers report collections for Belgian orphans and recitals of Belgian music. Manchester was clearly taking 'poor little Belgium' to its heart. Though there seems to have been little noisy jingoism, a serious determination is in evidence and also a powerful civic pride; Manchester now wanted to play its part. The reporting of atrocities in Belgium seems to have reversed the Manchester clergy's initial disapproval of Britain's involvement in the war, and, seemingly, they too now meant to play their part. By the start of September Bishop Welldon, the Dean of Manchester, had given his house to the military authorities to use as a hospital, had become Honorary Chaplain of the 1st City Battalion and was speaking forcefully at 'call to arms' meetings. At one such, at the Salford Hippodrome, he appealed to all eligible men to enlist at once:

> **A MASSACRE.**
> **Terrible Acts in Belgium.**
> **More Evidence of German Atrocities.**
> **Hundreds of Civilians Shot.**
> **Women and Children Burnt.**
>
> *Manchester Evening News*, 20 November 1914.

Discussing the German atrocities, he said the smoking ashes of Louvain cried to Heaven for vengeance. There was a time when those who wantonly destroyed works of art and treasures of learning were called 'vandals'. 'Blot the word "vandal" out of your dictionary,' he exclaimed, 'and call them Germans.' (A voice: 'We'll blot them out, too.') 'We must see this war through,' Bishop Welldon is recorded as concluding. 'We will never accept the terms of peace except as victors.' (Cheers).[43]

Similar sentiments were now issuing from pulpits all over the city.

'Alien enemies'
Manchester had a sizeable and long-established German population. The census of 1911 showed there were some 1,318 people of German origin living in Manchester and another 201 in Salford.[44] Companies with identifiably German names – traders, bankers, textile and chemical manufacturers – are numerous in the trade directories of the time. Several grocers and butchers shops in Manchester had German names over the door, there were German bars and restaurants and large numbers of the waiters working in the city were of German origin. Manchester's German population was highly visible.

People of German origin were reported to be leaving Manchester in large numbers in the first weeks of August. On 4 August, according to the *Manchester Courier*, the German bar of the Midland Hotel closed, owing to its staff having for the most part decided to return to Germany.[45] At this early stage attitudes to local people of German origin were not yet necessarily hostile. While Robert Roberts would recall that suspicion of Germans was prevalent in the area long before the commencement of hostilities ('Spy stories abounded. Germans who came here to "work", we were assured, could be spotted by a special button worn in the lapel. Each man had, we believed, sworn to serve Germany as a secret agent'), other sources reflect a more positive relationship between Manchester and its German community.[46] The *Manchester Courier* reported that, as one German restaurant in the city closed on 4 August, the proprietor ('he sells excellent lager and provides good snacks') was cheered up by his English customers 'who assured him that whatever might happen he was a "jolly good sort," and that they wished him well.'[47]

One day after the declaration of war, the Aliens Restriction Act passed, virtually unopposed, through the House of Commons. All Germans resident in Britain had to now register themselves at the nearest police station. The *Manchester Guardian* protested:

Many of the Germans who registered yesterday have lived in Manchester for a generation or more on the happiest terms with their neighbours, and, save for the formal act of naturalisation, they have become British citizens. Nearly all their connections are with England; some of them have found wives here, and their families have been brought up on English lines. Many of them, too, it may be added, have worked heart and soul for friendship between the two countries. War between the land of their birth and the land of their adoption comes as a heartrending disillusion.[48]

By 13 August over 2,000 Germans had registered their presence in Manchester. All aliens now had to carry a certificate of registration and they were be permitted to travel no further afield than 5 miles from their registered home address. Furthermore, they must not possess firearms, flammable liquids, any signalling apparatus, homing pigeons, photographic equipment, military maps or motor vehicles.[49]

Throughout August there seems to have been a quiet obeisance on the part of Manchester's German population. However, at the start of September, with the German army advancing towards Paris, some shift in attitudes occurred – both on the part of the German immigrant population and the Manchester authorities. On 3 September some thirty or so German men were arrested in Manchester, having 'boasted objectionably in cafes and other public spaces'. 'They have freely expressed their satisfaction at the success of the German Army,' Chief Superintendent Vaughan of the Manchester Constabulary told the *Manchester Courier*, 'and have made boasts of what they would do as soon as their soldiers land in England, which, they said, would be before many days were out.' More seriously, some of them were accused of discharging firearms. Declared prisoners of war by the Manchester police, they were brought into custody and transferred to the military authorities.[50]

GERMANS ARRESTED IN MANCHESTER.

THIRTY PRISONERS OF WAR.

SCENES IN THE STREETS

TEUTONIC BRAGGARTS ABUSE OUR TOLERANCE.

Manchester Courier, 4 September 1914.

Manchester Evening News, 5 September 1914.

On 4 September a second round of arrests was made. Again the individuals in question were accused of endangering the public peace 'by their open exultation in the temporary success of their countrymen in the field'. The total number of 'alien enemies' arrested in Manchester was now 107. The men were photographed manacled and chained together as they were transferred to military detention camps. [51]

Over September the arrests multiplied. By the middle of the month over 400 'alien enemies' had been taken into custody. 'It is stated unofficially,' the *Manchester Guardian* reported, 'that the recent arrests have been made on general instructions received from the Government and that sooner or later every alien enemy in the city capable of military service is to be arrested'.[52]

Further restrictions on aliens were brought in at the end of the month. Germans residing in Manchester were required to sign a declaration to the effect that they would not communicate (directly or indirectly) with any persons in Germany. They were also banned from publicly expressing any opinions about the war. Moreover, men were now forbidden to leave their homes in the evenings and would be required to report to the police four days per week.[53]

Through the autumn of 1914 England succumbed to a 'virulent epidemic' of spy mania. By October 1914 Manchester was clearly thus afflicted. On 20 October the *Manchester Evening News* reported that the city was being used 'as a relay or transmitting station for some form of wireless telegraphy'; it was believed that, by some means, enemy spies were communicating information from within the Manchester area. During the previous fortnight, the article went on to record, every pigeon loft in the district had been visited by the police.

Anti-German feeling would intensify over the next few months and, in May 1915, in the wake of the sinking of the *Lusitania*, it would break out into significant riots. Starting in Gorton, Openshaw and Salford, disturbances spread across the Manchester area over the course of the next three days, mostly taking the form of attacks on shops with German-sounding names. In the case of the Openshaw disturbance, the attacking crowd was estimated to contain some 10,000 people. Scores of businesses (pork butchers, clothes shops, public houses and hotels) were mobbed, looted and set alight. 'Thousands of people gave themselves up to the lust for damage,' the *Manchester Courier* reported. An account detailed that the rioters sang 'It's A Long Way To Tipperary' as they ransacked a house in West Gorton, throwing furniture out of the windows and setting fire to it in the street. Subsequent damage claims totalled £4,375. Many of those involved were mill girls. The *Courier* described the riots as 'without parallel in the history of the city'.[54]

'Join together; train together, and go forward together'[55]

It was between the newspaper columns that documented atrocities in Belgium and 'alien enemy' aggressions at home, that the city was appealing to its populace to play their part. Reading these entreaties in this context, it becomes easier to understand why young men were now queuing outside Manchester's recruiting stations.

In August 1914 the Regular British army numbered just some 235,000 men. Even with the Territorials and the Reservists, the army was only 733,514 strong. By contrast Germany had an army of almost 4 million men. Something urgently needed to be done to bring up the numbers.

On 5 August Asquith asked Parliament (on behalf of Lord Kitchener, the newly appointed Minister for War) to sanction an increase in army numbers of half a million men. Volunteers were to be asked to sign up for 'General service,' for 'a period of three years or until the war is concluded'. Kitchener's 'Call to Arms' was first published in the Manchester press on 7 August.

Manchester Courier, 10 August 1914.

Your King and Country Need You.

A Call to Arms.

An addition of 100,000 men to His Majesty's Regular Army is immediately necessary in the present grave national emergency.

Lord Kitchener is confident that this appeal will be at once responded to by all those who have the safety of our Empire at heart.

Terms of Service.

General Service for a period of Three years or until the war is concluded.

Age of enlistment between 19 and 30.

How to Join.

Full information can be obtained at any Post Office in the Kingdom, or at any Military Depot.

GOD SAVE THE KING.

Normal recruiting machinery in peacetime was equipped to process an annual national quota of around 30,000 men; now recruiting stations had had to cope with a rush of 40,000 volunteers in a week.[56] In Manchester new recruiting stations had to be opened in order to cope with the numbers coming forward and, by 25 August the 11th Battalion of the Manchester Regiment, the first to be raised in accordance with the New Army scheme, was already nearly at full strength. The pressure on the recruiting stations was reported by the *Manchester Guardian*.

> There are ten recruiting stations in Manchester and for the last three weeks the staff has been working almost night and day. At the central offices at Hunt's Bank the crowd is great enough to need the regulation of the police, and with swarms of men from the district stations who come to complete the process of attestation, the number of recruits seems limited only by the capacity of the staff to deal with them.[57]

Many of the first men to come forward were unemployed and of 'the poorer, unskilled classes', as the *Manchester Evening News* put it. With 'subsistence allowance', recruits received about £1 a week (the equivalent of just over £100 in 2014 terms) until the army was in a position to provide them with food and accommodation. Thereafter they were promised a minimum of 1*s* a day, with a separation allowance being forwarded to their wives.[58] The prospect of being paid £1 per week to stay at home had an obvious and

Manchester Courier, 25 August 1914. The caption reads: 'A crowd of would-be soldiers outside the recruiting office'.

immediate appeal – as did the promise of a full stomach. Robert Roberts recalled recruiting sergeants in Manchester shouting the rallying cry, 'Meat every day!' And, a few months on, as local recruits returned home on their first leave 'pounds – sometimes stones – heavier' this transformation convinced other men of the army's attractions.[59] With the war generally expected to aggravate hardships in Manchester, military service had a clear financial allure. Winnie Parker would recall:

> As soon as we heard about the Germans, my Dad said, 'This'll be bad on the docks. I'd best go and see.'... He came back in a while to tell us that the Manchester Ship Canal was completely at a standstill and there'd be no more work for who-knows how long. My oldest brother Tom was seventeen, and he told Mam not to worry, as he'd join the army and give her his pay. 'I'll be a general in no time,' he said.[60]

By the end of August the Manchester newspapers were observing that the 'class of recruits' was beginning to improve. 'Alert young men from the counter, the office desk, and the warehouse have responded with alacrity,' reported the *Manchester Evening News*.[61] That such men felt able to volunteer was down to the promise of support from their employers. From the Manchester papers it is possible to observe an accelerating growth in civic – and workplace – pride. By the third week of August employers were starting to offer inducements to their employees in order to encourage them to enlist and, at a meeting of the Home Trade Association on 24 August, a scheme of incentives for workers was agreed. Manchester's major employers collectively decided to pledge workers a minimum of four weeks of full wages from the day of leaving, a guarantee of re-engagement on their return and financial support for their dependents. 'Already the effect is seen at the recruiting offices,' wrote the *Manchester Guardian* on 27 August, 'where the type of recruit has improved distinctly during the last few days.'[62]

On 28 August Kitchener issued a second appeal for volunteers – another 100,000 men were needed. That day the *Manchester Evening News* remarked on the 'extra-ordinary fervour and enthusiasm' being shown by the young men of the city. 'If every other recruiting centre in the kingdom is responding as well as Manchester to the call to arms, the second army of 100,000 men under Lord Kitchener's great scheme will be raised even more rapidly that the first.' From 9.00 am until well into the evening there was 'a constant stream' of men outside the city's six recruiting stations.[63]

'The men appear mostly drawn from the warehouses, workshops, and factories,' the *Manchester Courier* noted, 'and a large number presented themselves in attire worn when at their trades. Obviously many of them had come straight from the desk and bench, the assurances of their employers that those at home would be cared for having finally led them to take the step.'[64]

> # "PALS' BATTALION."

Manchester Courier, 29 August 1914.

Lord Derby had recently made a targeted recruiting appeal, through the Liverpool press, to 'clerks and others engaged in commercial business'. Lord Derby's scheme offered white-collar workers the chance to 'serve with their friends and not to be put in a Battalion with unknown men as their companions'. This was the start of the 'Pals' battalions – the term itself seemingly coined by Lord Derby. The idea had clear and instant appeal and, consequently, within days, a similar recruiting scheme was being advanced in Manchester.[65]

On 28 August the Lord Mayor of Manchester, Alderman Daniel McCabe, convened a meeting with the city's largest employers to discuss the possibility of forming a battalion of 'Clerks and Warehousemen'. The meeting resolved to 'raise, clothe, and equip (excepting arms) one battalion formed from the employees of the offices and warehouses of Manchester.' It was estimated that the cost of clothing and equipment would amount to around £7,000, but by the time that the meeting was finished £15,000 had already been pledged by the members present, with the Gas Committee alone offering £7,000. The organisers of the movement sent a circular letter to 200 of the city's largest employers asking if they would participate in the recruiting scheme. Those willing to take part were then asked to call their staff together (that is, all men between the ages of 19 and 35) 'and explain to them the necessity, for all those who are able, to respond to the call of Lord Kitchener'. Tickets were issued to the participating companies (bearing the name of the firm) which the volunteers were asked to present to the recruiting officer. Those employees enlisting in the ranks within the following two weeks were to be offered:

Lord Derby Frontispiece, *Manchester City Battalions' Book of Honour* (1916). (All images from the 'Book of Honour' are reproduced with the kind permission of the Manchester & Lancashire Family History Society)

- Four weeks' of full wages from the day of leaving.
- A guarantee of re-engagement on discharge from service.
- For married man: Half-pay during absence on duty from the date that full pay ceases, to be paid to the wife.
- And 'special arrangements' were offered for single men with relatives dependent on them.

The Mayor sent a telegram to Lord Kitchener requesting his sanction for the formation of this new battalion. Consent was received by return telegram.

'It is believed by the promoters of the new battalions,' the *Manchester Guardian* explained, 'that the spirit of comradeship will rise high among men who have in ordinary affairs so much in common – similar employment and similar prospects and outlook upon life – and who are already in association with one another in their benevolent institutions.'[66]

Seemingly the idea did have appeal. Even before the recruiting office had opened, early applicants were making enquiries at the Town Hall. Friends came together. The *Manchester Evening News* remarked: 'It was noticeable that they seldom came singly. They were in twos and threes – many of them well developed. Young fellows in sporting jackets, flannel trousers, and carrying stout sticks.'[67]

Recruitment for the 'Clerks and Warehousemen's' battalion officially opened on the afternoon of 31 August. There were 2,000 enlistment tickets issued to employers participating in the scheme. Men, holding those tickets, now queued throughout the day. 'Within twenty-four hours the ordinary channels of recruiting were blocked,' the *Manchester City Battalions' Book of Honour* would record, 'and Albert Square was crowded by a band of keen young men all asking to be taken on, and all dissatisfied at the necessarily slow process.' By the time that the recruiting office closed on 1 September, the 1st City Battalion (being called 'Lord Derby's Battalion' in the local press) was full. It was decided to proceed forthwith with the formation of a second battalion - and to secure the use of a larger recruiting station.[68]

Volunteers were already queuing outside the Free Trade Hall on the morning of 2 September. When the doors opened, at 9.00 am, a thousand men quickly filled the hall. A total of 3,500 enlistment tickets had been issued and 6 medical men and a large team of clerks were now waiting to examine and enrol them. As the volunteers waited in line, a pianist entertained them and soon the corridors of the Free Trade Hall were ringing with popular choruses and patriotic airs. Later a cinema film was played, showing images of the Territorials in camp. It was reported to have aroused a good deal of enthusiasm. 'Again a steady stream of Manchester's youngest and best blood flowed on with only one idea, namely, to do their little bit,' the *Manchester City Battalions' Book of Honour* would record.[69]

MANCHESTER'S GIFT TO THE ARMY.

SPECIAL BATTALION.

LORD KITCHENER'S CORDIAL APPROVAL.

From the War Office, London,
28th August, 1914, 5 6 p.m.
The Lord Mayor, Manchester.
Your telegram just received. Hope you will be able to raise a battalion in Manchester, and thus give your signal help to the armed forces of the Crown. Any men joining the battalion will be doing a patriotic deed, and I shall hope to welcome them in the Army, where their comrades await them. Will give you every assistance. Let me know how you succeed.
KITCHENER.

Manchester Courier, 29 August 1914.

THE "PALS" REGIMENT.

The 1st City Battalion waiting to be formed into companies at the Artillery Barracks, Ardwick, on Saturday.

Manchester Courier, 7 September 1914.

The 'high-water mark' in terms of recruiting was achieved on 3 September, with 2,151 men being enlisted in Manchester alone. Only London (3,521) recorded a higher number of recruits. Nationally 33,204 men enlisted that day. By the end of the day Manchester's second City battalion was complete, and the local papers were already talking about a fourth and a fifth. Civic pride radiates from the local papers. It is clear that the 'Pals' were of – and belonged to – the city. There was also a strong sense of collective workplace identity and employers measured themselves against their peers in terms of their contribution to recruitment. When the *Manchester City Battalions' Book of Honour* was published in 1916, men were listed by workplace, beneath the insignia and good wishes of their employers.[70]

On 8 September the *Manchester Courier* expressed sympathy for the 'perspiring medical officers and clerks in their shirt sleeves' working all-out to cope with the numbers of recruits. The strain was starting to show. With the great influx of recruits over the past fortnight, it was now, in the words of the *Manchester Guardian*, coming 'to an extraordinary pass'. While posters were still announcing the urgency of recruiting, the machinery for dealing with the new recruits was struggling.[71]

With recruiting offices and regimental depots throughout the country similarly taxed, the War Office realised that it needed to intervene. It decided to raise the bar – quite literally. From 11 September the minimum height requirement for the infantry (other than for ex-servicemen) was adjusted upwards, from 5ft 3in to 5ft 6in. The impact was immediate. The new standards brought recruitment in Manchester almost to a standstill. 'The number of men now being passed daily can be little greater than the number of officials employed to examine them and register their enlistment,' the *Manchester Guardian* wrote.[72]

With the congestion somewhat relieved, the minimum height was reduced to 5ft 4in in late October. And, on 5 November, it came down again – back to 5ft 3in. In the first week of November 800 men signed up and it was expected that the pace would pick up. But it did not. By mid-November it was apparent that the rally was losing steam; the numbers of recruits coming forward was tailing off. 'Perhaps as a result of the depressing weather,' queried the *Manchester Courier*, 'which at its worst is sufficient to damp the most martial of spirits'.[73]

Recruitment for the 5th City Battalion began in mid-November, and with it new initiatives were being launched. The Manchester newspapers described the huge 'barometer' that had been installed on the wall of the Town Hall. 'It will be over fifty feet in height,' detailed the *Manchester Evening News*, 'and it will register the daily growth in the strength of the new battalion. As tickets for enlistment are issued by the committee the "mercury" in the "barometer" will rise, and interest in the movement will undoubtedly be stimulated by this means.'[74] From 17 November the *Manchester Guardian*

Manchester Courier, 1 October 1914.

CITY BATTALION DRILLING AT HULME BARRACKS.

The photos show: (1) The 4th Battalion of the City "Pals" Regiment going through exercises at Hulme Barracks. (2) A company marching to the barracks.

would publish a regular graphic illustrating the upward movement (or otherwise) of that 'mercury'.⁷⁵

But this new recruiting drive did not stop at barometers. The *Manchester Evening News* went on:

> At the picture-houses and the music-halls silent appeals will be made through the medium of the cinematograph. Pictures showing the 'Pals' in camp, at drill, and at play, will probably be shown, and there can be no doubt that the many who might otherwise hold back will be persuaded to throw in their lot with their friends who are already serving their King and country. The tramcars, too, will in all likelihood be pressed into the service, and upon them will be exhibited appeals in which the seriousness of the position and the duty that lies before young men of eligible age will be made clear . . . It is confidently anticipated that the campaign will lead the way for a general rally to the colours such as that in which Manchester took so prominent a part in a couple of months ago.⁷⁶

Posters appeared all over Manchester and the men already enlisted into the new battalions were paraded through the city streets. Speaking at the Free Trade Hall that week, the Lord Mayor stated: 'No young man can satisfy his conscience by leaving this duty to others; just as he benefits by the good laws and social order of this country, so he is bound by every tie of honour to give himself in their defence.'⁷⁷

By 23 November 1914 the *Manchester Courier* could brag, 'Proportionately to its population, Manchester has already done better in the matter of recruiting than any other town or city in the country'. By this point the city had already completed four New Army battalions, the 5th and 6th were expected to be full imminently and the War Office had just given permission for a 7th to be raised. The paper estimated that Manchester had by now supplied 50,000 men to the forces in total. But, the *Courier* asked, could the city go further? 'Can Manchester supply Lord Kitchener with a complete infantry brigade, comprising eight battalions [sic]?'⁷⁸

The recruitment machinery was cranking up a gear – and, with a view to achieving that eighth battalion, it was about to expand its targets.

Manchester Guardian, 17 November 1914.

TO HELP RECRUITING.

A Manchester Corporation goods tramcar is touring the city, bearing a message to every man eligible for military service. The photograph shows the car in Albert Square, surrounded by intending recruits, who are being urged to join by a Scottish piper.

It is YOU we want. YOU who have lived in your English home with its comforts and pleasures—secure from outside attack, safe behind the walls of England.

YOU are the man your country needs; to strike with a strong right arm against the darkest danger that has ever confronted our Empire—the German Military Tyranny which has forced the world to War. Enlist TO-DAY at the Manchester Town Hall.

Manchester Evening News, 12 January 1915.

A recruiting march of the 4th City Battalion through Manchester, *Manchester Courier,* 25 November 1914.

A group of young Manchester Pals, arranged in declining size.

COME AND JOIN US.

A recruiting campaign in Manchester Piccadilly, *Manchester Evening News*, 29 May 1915.

Chapter 2

'Bobs' Own'

A correspondent to the *Manchester Courier*:

'Wherever we go we behold the King's call, "To arms," "Your King and country need you," etc. But what a terrible disappointment when a man tries to answer the call, but is rejected because he is only 5ft. 0½in., although he is possessed of all his faculties and yearns to do his share.'

The editor's reply: 'We advise our correspondent to put on a pair of big boots and try the "Bantams".'[1]

In August 1914 a *Manchester Evening News* reporter spent a day at a city recruiting station. He recorded his observations under the heading 'Manchester Men's Physique'. The journalist concluded:

In view of all that has been said in recent years about the dwindling stature and poor physique of the men of Lancashire, the experience of the doctors at the Dickinson Street recruiting station in this city is reassuring.

The examination each applicant has to pass through before being accepted for either the regular army or the special reserves is of a searching character, lasting from four to six minutes, yet the rejects only number from 25 to 27 per cent.

It is true that all the applicants do not get as far as the doctors owing to their being too obviously short in weight, height, or chest measurement; but, on the other hand, it must be remembered that the bulk of the applicants are of the poorer, unskilled classes who only too often fail to get even the minimum of nourishment necessary for proper development.[2]

It's difficult to quantify how many men were being turned down as 'too obviously short', but it seems likely to have been a significant percentage. An article from the same newspaper, a couple of weeks later, makes it clear, though, that whatever the rejected men may have lacked in inches they could make up for it in enthusiasm:

The anxiety of the youth of Manchester to respond to the country's call was strikingly shown in the lining up with the others of young men who must have known that they were below the minimum height of 5ft. 3in. One, a mere boy, was

MANCHESTER RECRUITING.

Recruits being examined by doctors this morning at the Manchester Town Hall.

REJECTED!

Sound in wind and sound in limb,
Muscles hard and nerves in trim,
Eyesight splendid, hearing keen,
Age last Christmas Day—nineteen.
What could stop him "getting through"?
Goodness knows! I don't; do you?
True, he is not built for show,
Yet he's game from top to toe;
Five feet nothing in his socks,
Just five feet, but hard as rocks.
If he's short an inch or two,
None the worse, I say—don't you?
Call him undersized who will,
He's a grand young Briton still;
Answering to his country's call
Like the bravest of them all.
Sure a better fate were due
Than "rejected"!—what say you?
Courage knows no standard height:
Pluck, not inches, wins the fight.
Regulations most were made
For an army—on parade!
When there's serious work to do
Hang red tape, I say—don't you?
Sound in wind and sound in limb,
Muscles hard and nerves in trim,
Five feet nothing in his socks,
But five feet, yet hard as rocks;
British bulldog breed all through,
Yet "rejected"!—what think you?

W. GLEAVES.

Poem published in the *Manchester Evening News*, 27 November 1914.

Manchester Evening News, 13 January 1915.

picked out from the crowd by a police officer engaged in marshalling the men. He was taken to an improvised measurement board roughly drawn on the jamb of a doorway, and it was then found that he failed to 'pull' the standard height by about two inches. The youth looked very disconsolate when informed that it was no use for him to trouble the doctor.³

The *Manchester Evening News* disclosed that the doctors were permitted to use 'a little elasticity' in passing men who only just missed the required physical standards, if it was deemed likely that they would develop under training. However, some eager volunteers required more elastic than the doctors could supply and frustration was increasingly being vented on the correspondence pages of the Manchester papers. 'It is all very well being strict in time of peace,' ran one such letter to the editor, 'but in time of stress like this country is in at present I think the height and chest measurements might be reduced a little. What is an inch in a crisis like this?'⁴

By November 1914 this matter had been brought to the attention of the War Office. An article from the *Manchester Courier* revealed:

A feature that has occasioned no little comment has been the fact that many of the men presenting themselves have been slightly under the minimum height standard. In other respects they have been all that could be wished – eyesight good, teeth good, and physical proportions of the best. It has been considered that the War Office, considering the urgent need there is for soldiers, might accept these men and train them for the service of their country. Speaking in Manchester last night, Sir Frederick Smith expressed the opinion that the Government should accept men five feet tall for the Army, as many of the hardiest men were small and thick-set. He himself knew many colliers, for instance, who would make excellent soldiers. A step further was taken by Sir Alfred Hopkinson, who, speaking at a recruiting meeting in Beswick last night, said that every man who was physically fit, no matter what his age, should be allowed to go to the front if he so wished. The Germans were sending every man, and we could surely do as well.[5]

It is generally acknowledged that the story of the Bantam battalions began in Birkenhead. Lieutenant Colonel H.M. Davson's *The History of the 35th Division in the Great War* recounts a recruiting office scene. Very similar scenarios were playing out in Manchester's recruiting offices:

A fine, sturdy little man walked into Birkenhead Recruiting Office towards the end of September, 1914. He was very angry when rejected, because he was an inch too short. He had tried four of five other recruiting offices, but always with the same result. Mr Alfred Mansfield talked to the man and came to the conclusion that we were losing some of the best manhood of our race. Splendid little men, who were keen and anxious to do their bit, were being rejected daily. He (Mr Mansfield) went to Mr Alfred Bigland, M.P., who was chairman of the Birkenhead Recruiting Committee, and asked him if something could not be done to get these men into the Army. Mr Bigland promptly took the matter up with the War Office next day. He asked permission to form a 'Bantam Battalion' at Birkenhead – and got it.

Apparently the 'sturdy little man' offered to fight any man in the room and was only removed from the recruiting office with some difficulty.[6]

On 20 November a letter from Alfred Bigland was published in the *Manchester Guardian*, appealing for recruits for the Birkenhead Bantam Battalion. He wrote:

We are now ready to receive the names of men who are willing to join what it has been decided to call the 'Bantam Battalion', believing that a man is as good a soldier and as plucky a fighter at 5ft. 2in. as 5ft. 6in. In proof of this I would point out that if Britain had fixed its standard for officers the same as for privates the Empire would have lost the priceless services of the Field Marshal who was lovingly dubbed by his men 'Bobs' and whose death the nation now mourns.[7]

Field Marshal Lord Roberts – a popular figure, affectionately nicknamed 'Bobs' by the newspapers – had died just days earlier. Bigland now asked Manchester men willing to join the new battalion to send him their names and addresses. Just three days after recruiting opened, Birkenhead had over 2,000 Bantams attested and had to form a second battalion. 'So began', Davson wrote, 'the formation of the "Bantam Division."'

Just below Bigland's letter, on the correspondence page of the *Manchester Guardian*, was a letter from D.E. Anderson, Chairman of the National Service League, North Western Area. It was not just Birkenhead that had a mind to raise a Bantam Battalion. Anderson wrote that, in recruiting for the New Army battalions over the past few weeks, it had troubled him to have to reject so many men from Manchester who were excellent soldierly specimens in every respect except their want of height. 'Personally I am firmly convinced that a "little good one" is far preferable to a "poor big one",' he reflected. His letter went on:

> To-day, in London, the greatest soldier of modern times has been laid to rest in St. Paul's. He was small in size, but what a glorious record he had left. Knowing the high estimation Lord Roberts had for little men, I feel convinced that the present is a most opportune time for ending the injustice of refusing men short in stature the opportunity to fight for King and country. Surely that long-established slight to small men can be removed seeing how greatly changed are the present war conditions from the past.[8]

With that in mind, Anderson proposed to begin compiling a list of the names of volunteers between 5ft and 5ft 3in. Men were invited to register their particulars at the National Service League Offices and, if a sufficient number of names could be collected within the next week, Anderson proposed to submit his list to the War Office. If Manchester could follow Birkenhead in setting up a Bantam battalion, Anderson proposed that it should be called 'Bobs' Own'.

The *Manchester Guardian*'s editorial of that day was sympathetic to Anderson's cause. 'In most modern fighting lack of inches is an actual advantage,' the paper considered. It went on:

> It is ridiculous nowadays to make the test of able-bodiedness one of inches. The sole test should be whether a man is in fit physical condition to stand the heat of a battle and the more exhausting fatigue of waiting and preparing for battle, and that is not a question of length or breadth, though it may be of proportion.

On 24 November Anderson wrote to the War Office, drawing attention to the 'useful material that was being wasted'. That night the Lord Mayor of Manchester received a telegram giving the go-ahead for the city to raise a battalion of below-standard height men. By the time that the battalion was sanctioned, the National Service League had collected the names of 1,208 would-be Bantams.[9]

The first recruit for the 8th City Battalion was attested on 25 November. As the recruiting office was being set up in the Town Hall, word was sent out to the city's newspapers that enrolment would begin in earnest the next day. With the simultaneous enlistment of the 7th and 8th City Battalions – in the same building, at the same time –

RECRUITING THE MANCHESTER "BOBS' OWN" BATTALION.

Manchester Guardian, 26 November 1914.

Husbands and sons and brothers too — they want to go. Will Manchester's womenfolk hold them back at this critical hour? — the hour when the fighting man is the vital need.

Let Manchester's 7th and 8th City Battalions supply the answer.

Bid the menfolk enlist **NOW**. Send them along to the Manchester Town Hall **to=day.**

The War Office have sanctioned recruiting for a 7th and 8th City Battalion. Manchester can quickly raise them if her young men come forward now. In memory of the late Lord Roberts the 8th will be known as the "Bobs" City Battalion, and the height standard is from 5 ft. up to 5 ft. 3 in. Other conditions as usual. Minimum chest measurement, 34½ in. Age 19 to 38.

For the 7th City Battalion the previous height standard still holds good, 5 ft. 3 in.

E. TOOTAL BROADHURST.
A. HERBERT DIXON.   Special
E. M. PHILIPS.
ARTHUR TAYLOR.   Sub-
KENNETH LEE.
VERNON BELLHOUSE.   Committee

RIVAL BATTALIONS

7th and 8th Race for Recruits.

Little Men Turn up in Force

"Fighting Cocks" or "Bobs' Own."

Manchester Evening News, 26 November 1914.

RECRUITING SCENES FOR CITY "BOBS" BATTALIONS.

Manchester Courier, 25 November 1914.

the recruiting committee decided to encourage a 'race' between the two battalions. 'This recruiting race should provide an added stimulus to those who are engaged in persuading men to join,' proposed the *Manchester Courier*.[10]

When the doors of the Town Hall opened on 26 November over a hundred men were there waiting to enlist. As they queued, the Lord Mayor delivered an address. 'It is not bigness that makes a soldier,' he told them, 'It is pluck and endurance.' He also touched on the seemingly contentious issue of what the battalion was going to be called:

> 'I understand you object to being called "Bantams". [Some laughter.] A magistrate suggested to me "Fighting Cocks" was a more fitting name. [More laughter.] It has also been suggested that "Bobs' Own" is the best name. Lord Roberts was a little man, but he was a very great Field Marshal. [Hear, hear.] I am sure you, too, will do good work. You know, little men can get round corners where big fellows can't. [Laughter.]'

Photographers from the Manchester newspapers were there as the men made their attestations. The Lord Mayor himself swore in the first batch. With the flare of a photographer's flash the Mayor is reported to have quipped, 'That's the first time you have faced fire'.[11]

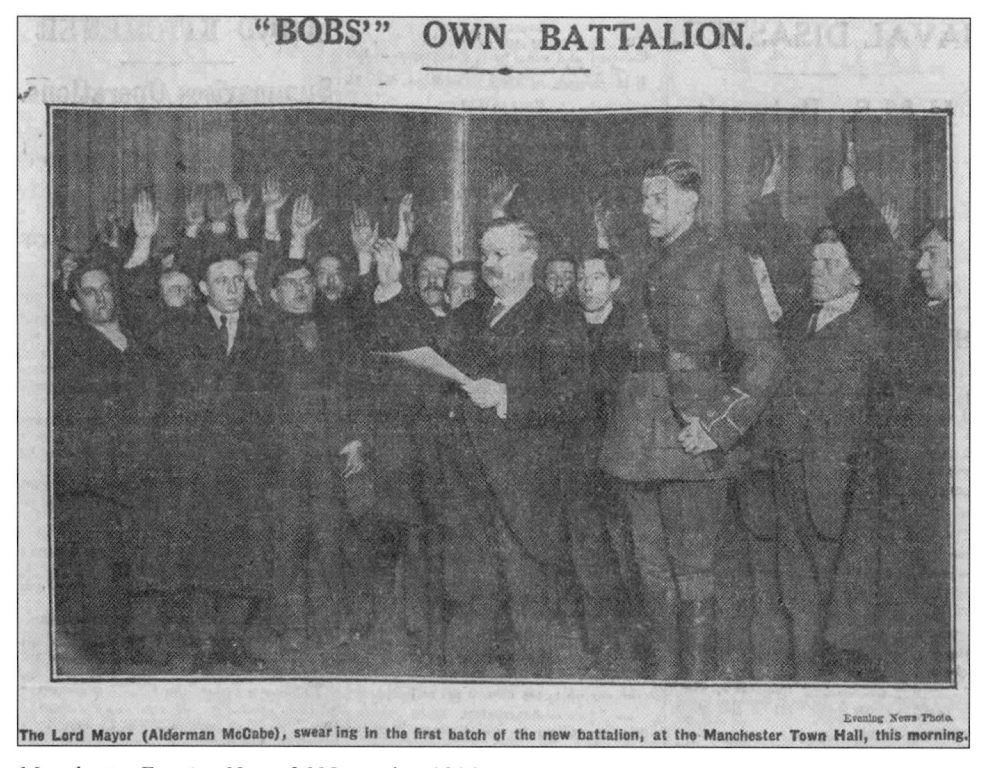

Manchester Evening News, 26 November 1914.

"BOBS'" OWN BATTALION.

A busy time in the Manchester Town Hall. Recruits having their attestation papers filled in by clerks, who are seated on the left of the photograph.

Manchester Evening News, 27 November 1914.

On 27 November Manchester Town Hall was crowded with 'sturdy little deep-chested stalwarts'. Prominent citizens addressed speeches to the men as they waited to be sworn in. In the afternoon Sir Henry Mackinnon, the General Officer Commanding Western Command, attended. 'During the General's visit an example of the fine physique of the little men was forthcoming,' the *Manchester Courier* recorded, 'which created no little amusement among those who saw it.' The report continued:

> Major Allen, the Assistant Inspector of Recruiting in the Western Division, called out one of the men to see whether the 'standard chest measurement of 34½' was being adhered to. On the tape being put round the recruit's chest, it was found to register 39 inches. This fine physical development has been a feature of those joining the 8th Battalion. Yesterday a large number of colliers from the Pendleton Pits offered themselves. They delighted the hearts of the officials, and though they were but short in height they were almost as broad as they were long, and had chests and arms that many a professional 'strong man' might envy.[12]

Over the course of the day 325 men enlisted. While some of the men joining the battalion evidently were miners, volunteers seem to have come from a wide variety of occupations. The *Manchester City Battalions' Book of Honour* gives some clues as to the occupational profile of the battalion; the majority of individuals identified as members of the 23rd Battalion therein worked in cotton mills or engineering, but they were also employed in chemical works, iron works and warehouses, for assurance companies and shipping agents, in clothing manufacturing and for Manchester Education Committee. One man worked for Richard Johnson & Nephew's barbed wire works. As such they really are a cross section of Manchester trades.

While some volunteers might have been able to boast a 'strong man' physique, a significant percentage of men were being turned away because they could not attain the minimum chest measurement. This caused 'a certain amount of murmuring', the *Manchester Guardian* recorded. Some scrupulousness was evidently being exercised in the selection of this battalion, its promoters already being well aware that its performance would be subject to particular scrutiny. 'The 8th Battalion is not designed as a refuge for patriots of a poor physique,' the *Guardian* insisted:

> Its fighting quality will not be one whit less than that of the best of the other city battalions, and the chest measurement, although exacting, is being rigidly enforced in order that at the finish Manchester may have particular pride in the last battalion to complete the second City Brigade . . . Lieutenant Bartrum, who has the supervision of recruiting at the Town Hall, is taking particular care with this battalion, aiming at a first-rate standard in each individual. He was completely satisfied with yesterday's recruits, describing them altogether and severally as 'topping good chaps'.[13]

On 28 November another 265 men signed up, bringing the total to 590. The Manchester papers remarked that some candidates had travelled considerable distances for a chance of joining the unit, as men under the standard height were not yet being accepted in many other localities. Letters of application were received from as far away as Ramsgate, and the recruiting office of the Isle of Man requested permission to enlist men on behalf of the battalion. Some of the volunteers arriving in Manchester, it was reported, had walked long distances and slept rough en route. There were examples of men arriving in front of the recruiting officers wet through.

Not every man came forward with absolute confidence and certainty, though. There was evidently some last-minute dithering to be witnessed in Albert Square – but there were parties always ready to usher the men through the door. The *Manchester Evening News* observed:

> The 'five-foot recruits' visit the Town Hall in batches. They seldom come singly. Frequently one sees a score or more march in to be examined. Some of them are diffident about taking the final plunge, and gather in small knots in Albert Square. They are frequently approached by men who have already joined or by public men who have taken an interest in recruiting, and do not then take long to make up their minds. Mr J. R. Lancashire has done a good deal of work in this direction. He

A recruiting officer at work in Albert Square, *Manchester Evening News*, 26 January 1915.

Manchester Guardian, 28 November 1914.

Manchester mothers let your sons go. Hold them not back, but urge them on, on to duty. All who can must enlist NOW—if England's homes are to be guarded and the women folk held safe.

Send your sons to-day. They want to go—their pals have joined already.

The War Office have sanctioned recruiting for a 7th and 8th City Battalion. Manchester can quickly raise them if her young men come forward now. In memory of the late Lord Roberts the 8th will be known as the "Bobs" City Battalion, and the height standard is from 5ft up to 5ft. 3in. Other conditions as usual. Minimum chest measurement 34½in. Age 19 to 38.

For the 7th City Battalion the previous height standard still holds good, 5ft. 3in.

made a haul of no fewer than thirty recruits in this way to-day. He saw the men talking together outside and joined in the conversation. A minute or two later he was escorting the batch upstairs to receive their tickets preliminary to examination.[14]

Also on 28 November an article – 'Small Bodies and Big Souls' – was published in the *British Medical Journal,* and it gave authority to the arguments of those who had proposed the Bantam battalion. Though the language and logic might seems slightly odd to modern ears, this expert justification boosted the confidence of those involved in the raising of the battalion. It was reproduced in the Manchester papers. 'We are glad to see,' the *Journal* began, 'that the War Office has set aside the absurd standard of height so far as regards an East Lancashire battalion, and had given permission for a "midget" battalion to be raised.' The article went on:

Not a little is to be said in favour of short infantry. Short men occupy less room in transport; they find cover more easily, and offer a smaller mark to bullets and shrapnel; they are better sheltered in trenches and require to dig less deep trenches to protect themselves. It takes less khaki to clothe them, and less leather to boot them. The army blanket covers them more amply, and they need less food than tall thin men to keep up their body heat and maintain their marching energy; a smaller service transport, therefore, suffices for their needs. Many short men are tough and wiry, and when sturdily built, like the north country miner, are strong and capable of the greatest endurance. The managers of factories where skilled work is done know that the small man is often a better workman than the big one, who is apt to be clumsy . . . The cavalry and artilleryman requires to be big and powerful, but as to those who burrow in the trenches, how can it matter whether they are 4ft. 9in. or 5ft. 6in.? We are not out for a show and a parade, but to win – a war of sieges and attrition. To hang on with tenacity, and use the rifle with skill, to keep warm and healthy in body, and courageous in spirit – these are the qualities, and the short men have them. The brave soul of the little man in the face of the giant is proverbial. The Japanese soldier has earned the highest reputation for endurance, courage, and fighting capacity, and his average height is between 5ft. and 5ft. 3in. There is waiting the call to enlist an army corps of bantam weights – the sturdy, short-limbed men of the North and the short men of the South and of Wales. The difference is in part due to difference of race, but valour and worth must not be valued by the length of a femur.[15]

By 30 November the total number of recruits in Manchester – those 'sturdy, short-limbed men of the North' – had increased to 730. One volunteer, who had just completed his attestation, told the authorities that he had previously been rejected by thirty-four recruiting depots. The volunteer proudly proclaimed that he 'felt a man again and no longer a boy, now that he had been accepted as a soldier of the King'.[16]

The 7th Battalion won the 'race' to completion on 1 December. The 8th Battalion's 'mercury' inched up slowly over the next two days, with many men again being turned away on account of insufficient chest inches. After beginning at a rapid pace, recruitment slowed down to a crawl at the finish.[17]

On 4 December, nine days after recruiting had officially opened, the battalion was complete. With 39 men required at the start of the day, the recruiting officers actually had 100 to choose from. By 2.00 pm the recruiting offices were being dismantled. The *Manchester Courier* hurrahed:

Manchester Guardian,
27 November 1914.

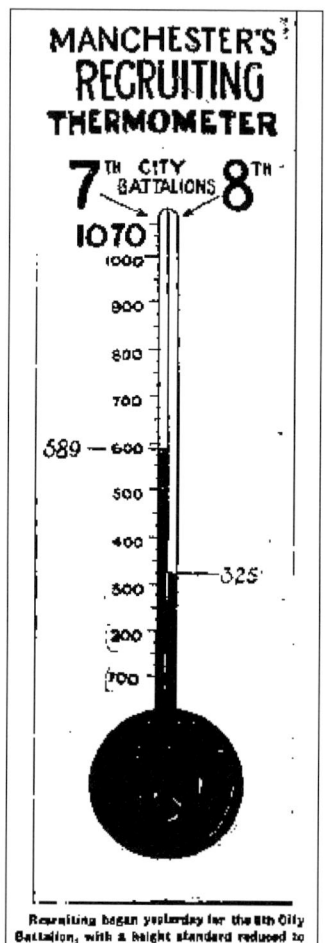

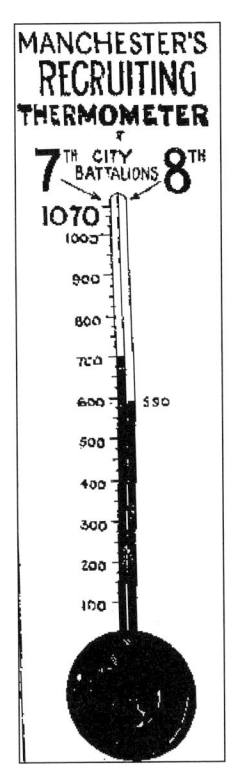

Manchester Guardian, 28 November 1914.

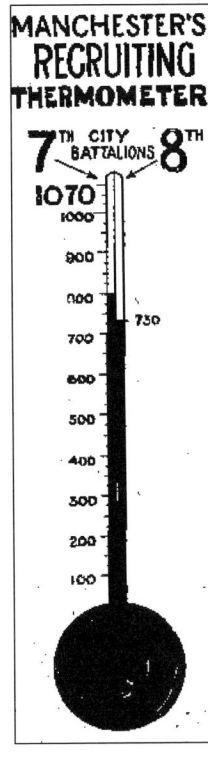

Manchester Guardian, 30 November 1914.

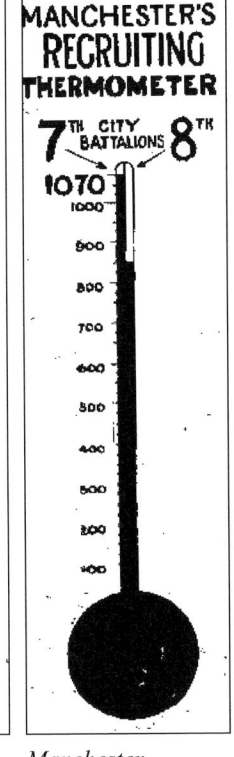

Manchester Guardian, 1 December 1914.

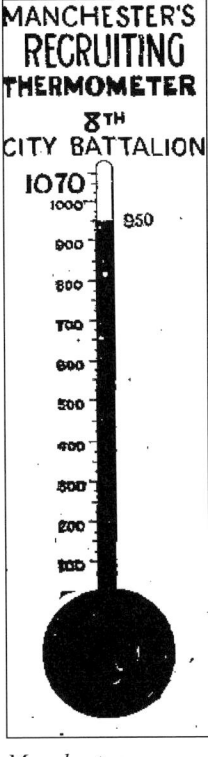

Manchester Guardian, 2 December 1914.

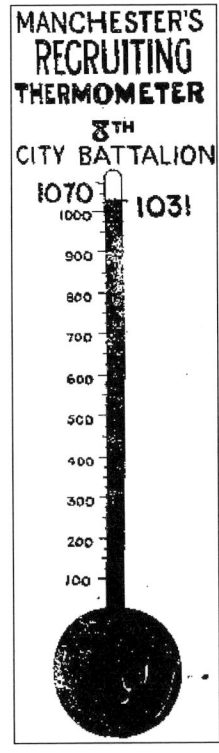

Manchester Guardian, 3 December 1914.

There is only one thing that is objectionable. He should not be described as a 'Bantam'. We appreciate the alliterative allurement of the title 'Bigland's Birkenhead Bantams', but do not like it. We dread the infection. Fancy 'Manchester's Military Mannikins', or 'Leeds Little "Loiners"'. They are not Football League teams; but if we do object to the gallinaceous title we know that they are 'game'.[18]

This was the start of a newspaper fascination with the gallinaceous-titled battalion. On 4 December the 8th City Battalion – now designated by the War Office to be the 23rd Manchester Battalion – paraded for the first time at the artillery headquarters in Hyde Road. Journalists were there to watch. 'The men presented a very smart appearance,' observed the *Manchester Courier*.[19]

The training and accommodating of eight battalions now presented Manchester with a significant logistical challenge. In September the Parks Committee of Manchester Corporation had given the go-ahead for Heaton Park to be used as a camp for the City

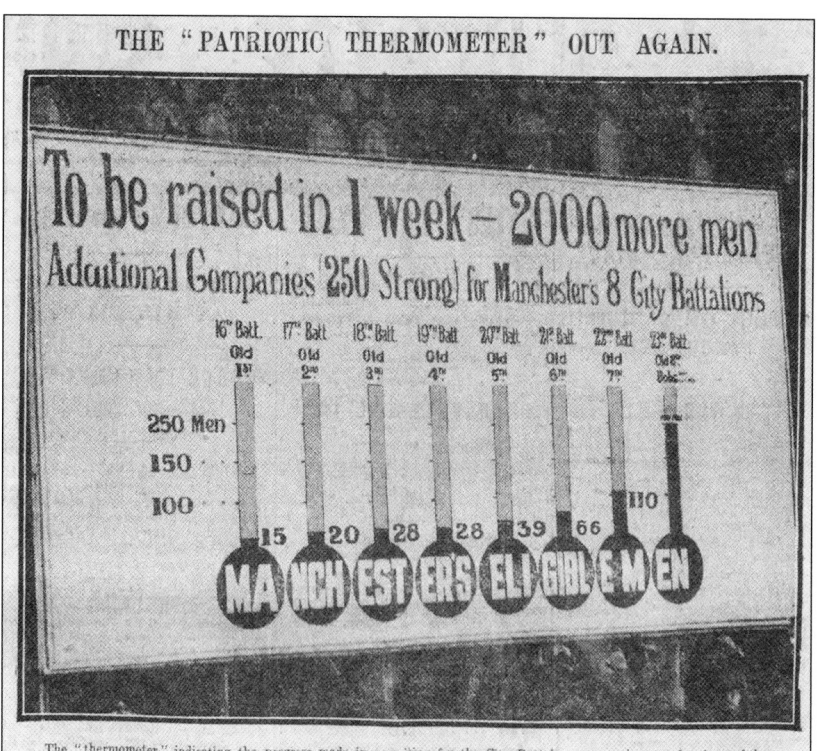

Manchester Courier, 12 January 1915.

Manchester Guardian, 30 November 1914.

battalions. A frantic building programme had commenced but, by the end of the year, it had become apparent that it was just going to be impossible for all eight battalions to be accommodated at Heaton Park.

In mid-December it was announced that the City battalions were to be organised into two brigades; the first brigade that had been formed; the 90th (comprising the 16th, 17th, 18th and 19th battalions) was to train at Heaton Park, while the second, the 91st (20th, 21st, 22nd and 23rd battalions), would undergo its initial training in the Lancashire seaside resort of Morecambe.

By the autumn of 1914 Morecambe's economy had been started to feel the pinch. The summer season had been prematurely terminated in August and, while the war went on, the prospects for the holiday trade picking up were not promising. By the start of November, then, discussions were going on as to what alternative sources of income could be found for the resort. There were suggestions that lodging houses could take in Belgian refugees – or, alternatively, like nearby Southport had done, perhaps Morecambe could accommodate troops? The Mayor and Council began actively to promote the town as a prospective centre for the billeting of training soldiers. Deputations travelled to London to make Morecambe's case. By early December the town was in discussions with the Manchester authorities. This was seen as a 'golden opportunity' by the resort. As they waited for confirmation that they would indeed host the Manchesters, Morecambe's population was reported to be 'on the tip-toe of expectation'.[20]

On 30 December, then, the Manchester battalions began departing for Morecambe. The *Manchester Evening News* observed that, as the battalions entrained for the 'Naples of the North', slogans had been chalked on the train carriages, such as 'Berlin via Morecambe' and 'First Stop Berlin'. Others expressed hostility to the Kaiser 'in terms more forcible than polite'.[21]

On 2 January 1915 the 23rd Battalion (now generally being called 'Bobs' Own' by the Manchester papers) marched towards Exchange Station. Headed by a bugle band, 'Bobs' Own' were applauded as they trooped through packed streets. '"Tipperary" was taken up with enthusiasm by the men,' it was reported, 'who volleyed a resounding response to the inquiry "Are we downhearted?"' The *Manchester Guardian* observed:

> The men have not yet received their uniform, but, all the same, they created a good impression, and they were jubilant at getting away so early in their military career. That the men are not averse from the description of the 'Bantams' was proved by the fact that a pair of bantam fowl which a recruit had brought with him, enclosed in a

An advertisement placed in the *Manchester Guardian*, 30 November 1914.

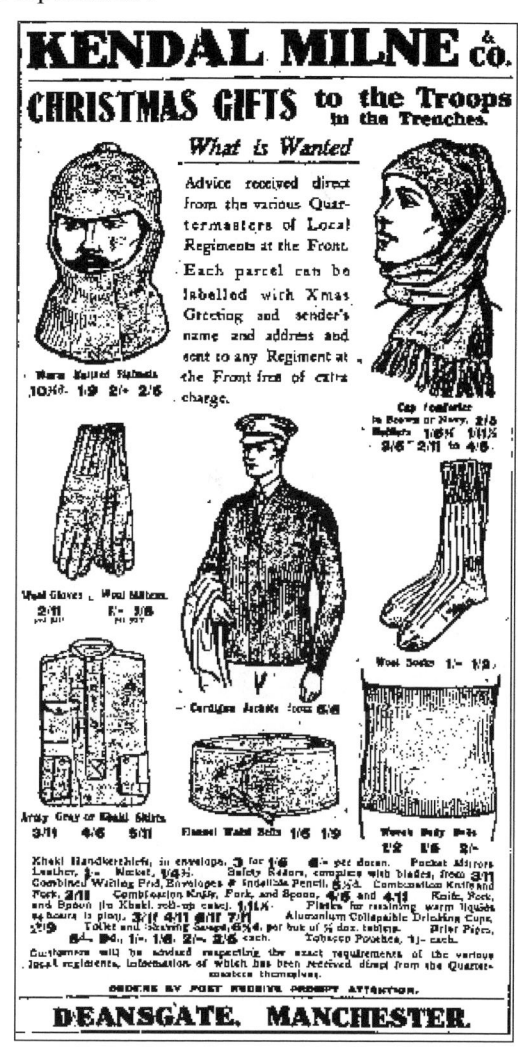

CITY BATTALIONS LEAVE HOME FOR MORECAMBE.

The 5th and 6th "Pals'" Battalions, known in the Army now as the 20th and 21st Battalions Manchester Regiment, left Manchester yesterday for Morecambe, where they will be billeted in the town and undergo strict training for the front. Our picture shows some of the 21st Battalion awaiting entrainment at Exchange Station.

Manchester Courier, 31 December 1914.

    wicker cage surmounted by miniature Union Jacks, aroused great enthusiasm all round. The fowls were proudly carried with the battalion to Morecambe, and will eventually, one supposes, be adopted as the mascots of 'Bobs' Own'.[22]

The *Manchester Evening News* noted: 'The greeting and farewell extended to the Bantams seemed particularly hearty, for the corps caught the popular fancy from the moment of its inception, and it has retained its own special corner in the affections of Manchester.'[23] Platform Five was reserved for their departure. Civilians were not admitted, but friends and relatives crowded onto the next platform and cheered as the trains moved off. The *Manchester Evening News* recorded: 'The men, though evidently not yet the finished, polished military article, were in high spirits, and when they had got into the long trains they crowded to the windows, laughing, singing and cheering and shouting to the civilians and soldiers left behind.'[24]

FROM CITY TO SEA-SIDE.

Manchester Battalions' Departure.

HEARTY SEND OFF THIS MORNING.

Manchester Evening News, 2 January 1915.

Chapter 3

'From City to Sea-side'

Though the Bantams had now left Manchester, the city's fascination with the battalion was not about to diminish. As they trained in Morecambe, through the spring of 1915, the Manchester papers regularly despatched journalists to the coastal resort in order to satisfy the public enthusiasm for stories about the Bantams. Every item of their training, accommodation, diet and extra-curricular amusements was scrutinised in the pages of the Manchester press. There is a cheery tone to that reporting; it conveys something of the fortune that the men themselves must have felt. Though they had been told that they were going to be worked hard, they were beside the seaside and that clearly had its compensations.

In August 1914 Morecambe effectively 'shut up shop and threw up its hands aghast'.[1] The start of the war put a sudden end to the summer season. The billeting of the Manchesters was now going to give Morecambe the chance to take down the shutters – and it was very glad of it. With each householder being paid 2s 6d per day per man, the town was set to make £4,000 per week in billeting money alone (around £412,000 in 2014 terms). In addition, the *Manchester Evening News* calculated, 'If every man spends 5s. a week in drink, tobacco, presents, etc., it will mean at least £5,000 brought to Morecambe every week'. The people of Morecambe had been told that the battalions that they were about to receive were 'composed of better class men, many of whom are well to do, and have private means apart from their army pay'.[2] Little wonder, then, that the resort offered a friendly welcome to its soldier guests. 'Landladies seemed to be looking forward to the coming of the soldiers as if it was another season coming along,' the *Morecambe Visitor* reported, 'and it will be a God-send to many.'[3]

Public notice printed in the *Morecambe Visitor*, 9 December 1914.

The arrival of the Manchesters in Morecambe, on 30 December 1914, excited great interest. Crowds gathered to welcome them at the station. Ladies exclaimed at their smartness. As the Manchester men marched from the station towards their seaside

The manifold attractions of Morecambe, *c.* 1915.

lodgings, they were greeted with smiles along the streets and waving handkerchiefs from upper windows. Landladies, meanwhile, were airing beds with hot-water bottles and preparing cooked dinners to greet their soldier guests. There were *some* worries, though. One householder wrote an account of the day for the local paper and told how he and his wife had spent an anxious few hours considering what the men that they were about to host might be like. 'What sort would we get? Would they turn the place into a "bear garden" because they had been accustomed to drilling in Belle Vue menagerie grounds? We wondered.' They were generally, though, pleased with their lot: 'They are just average fellows as regards birth, but they are perfect gentlemen as regards behaviour. They seem to think – and perhaps they are right, that we have inconvenienced ourselves to take them in, and they are evidently determined to give us as little trouble as possible.'[4]

This poem was published in the *Morecambe Visitor* on 30 December 1914:

>Welcome!
>
>Welcome, brave boys, to our town and shore:
>May we billet you well and fare;
>Our thanks for your coming we've said before –
>That you'll prove true is our prayer.

We've much to face in the fight to come,
That much my lads we'll do;
The German shall go to 'Kingdom Come',
His big gun and sausages too!

We're not downhearted and never can be,
As we see you march on parade,
Though Berlin they say is a town on a spree,
But no spree ever made us afraid.

'They will have a strict but invigorating and doubtless a happy time,' the *Manchester Guardian* predicted, 'during a stay which Morecambe hopes will last at least three months.' In the end, the Bantams would keep the West End's boarding houses filled for the next six months.[5]

West End of Morecambe from the Alhambra, *c.* 1915.

THE BANTAMS AT THE SEASIDE.

Manchester Guardian, 5 January 1915.

C Company, Platoon No. 12, Morecambe, 21 April 1915. (Image reproduced with the kind permission of Sidney Allinson)

"Send me good lads and I'll treat them right"
As the 23rd Manchester Battalion marched through Morecambe on the afternoon of 2 January 1915, they seem to have caused some amusement – not least because they were still proudly brandishing those mascot bantam cocks. They might well have had cause to feel rather pleased with themselves as they paraded towards the seafront; specific districts of the resort had been allocated for the billeting of the various battalions, and the Bantams had the luck to be allotted the up-market West End, with their headquarters at the Alhambra Theatre. 'Away at the west end, where there are higher social pretensions than in the older portions of the town, the 8th City Battalion is quartered,' the *Manchester Guardian* recorded. 'It enjoys its privileged location and rather looks down upon the super 5ft. 3in. men billeted higher up.'[6]

Billeting officers had toured the town the week previously and had provisionally fixed the number of men that each boarding house could accommodate. Particular companies had been allocated particular streets and chalk numbers on the doorposts indicated how many men each household was taking. 'Four chums!', and similar, shouted out the billeting officers, as they progressed from doorstep to doorstep. While those who bagged billets with a sea view might consider themselves fortunately accommodated, 'exceptionally favourable' conditions were, it seems, to be provided for all. Every man was to have his home comforts. The *Manchester Evening News* recorded: 'The men are to be provided with beds – actual beds. Billeting usually means sleeping accommodation, which does not necessarily mean beds, but Morecambe has declared for beds, and the principle officially prescribed is one man one bed.'[7]

The Manchester authorities had gone into every detail in their negotiations with Morecambe council. Strict rules were to be applied as to the ventilation of bedrooms ('the landladies have a further obligation, which is to see that the bedrooms are thoroughly

A photograph taken outside a Morecambe boarding house. Chalk marks are just visible on the right-hand side of the door surround.

ventilated. They are required to have all bedroom windows wide open for at least an hour after the men leave in the morning, and the men themselves are required to keep the windows slightly open top and bottom during the night') and every house must also have a bath ('where a house has not a fixed bath, a good-sized hip bath to be provided'). Householders were required to manage bed-making and cleaning of bedrooms, but the washing of clothes ('a personal matter') was to be arranged between each soldier and his landlady. 'For hygiene and economical reasons' it had been advised that bedroom carpets could be taken up and that 'superfluous furnishings' be removed, but reports from the Morecambe paper suggest that few hosts went to these lengths.[8]

Whatever the authorities concerns as to hygiene, it seems that the battalion's 'pets' were also now enjoying accommodation in the West End. That pair of bantam cocks, which had been paraded through Manchester and Morecambe ('this battalion's sole pride at present'), were now also enjoying the hospitality of a guest house ('caged, lest they should stray').[9]

This song was published in the *Morecambe Visitor* on 20 January 1915:

> The Bantam Soldiers' Ditty
>
> We are – The Bantams!
> The Cock-o-doodle Bantams:
> Morecambe breezes suit us grand.
> Firm as Heysham rocks we stand,
> Grenadiers at heart tho' small,
> Proud to answer country's call.
>
> 'Roll on' – The Bantams!
> The Cock-o-doodle Bantams;
> See our squads along the front,
> Hearts aflame to bear the brunt;
> Smart we'll be, then next you'll see,
> Bantam ranks in Germany.
>
> 'Eyes front' – The Bantams!
> The Cock-o-doodle Bantams;
> Not the men to make retreat,
> Never! Never! Take defeat;
> Quick respond to duty's call,
> Comrades all we stand or fall.
>
> 'By the right' – The Bantams!
> The Cock-o-doodle Bantams;
> Gain our spurs in battle, so
> Our fighting cocks shall loudly crow;
> Bantam broods may yet combine
> Honours post – on right of line.
>
> 'Quick march' – The Bantams!
> The Cock-o-doodle Bantams;
> Off to Kaiser-land we go,
> Heads erect to meet the foe;
> Kultur's roosts we'll soon intrude,
> Bayonets for his Landsturm brood.
>
> 'Shoulder arms' – The Bantams!
> The Cock-o-doodle Bantams;
> When we meet the foe to press,
> Scores of Kultur's wrongs redress;

Growl the thunder of the guns,
You shall see us shock the Huns.

'Present arms' – The Bantams!
The Cock-o-doodle Bantams;
We're the men who count to-day,
Some of those who answered 'Yea'.
Stumps of good old England, true
To the old red, white, and blue.

'Cheer ho' – The Bantams!
The Cock-o-doodle Bantams;
Speed the ship across the deep.
Let the lonesome lasses weep;
Soon forget that hearts were sore,
Fighting where the cannon roar.

'The men will have no need to fear that they will not be properly looked after,' the *Morecambe Visitor* reported on 30 December 1914, 'for as one landlady put it, "They will be all right, sir, here. Send me good lads and I'll treat them right."' The lads seemed to agree. In early February a *Manchester Evening News* reporter asked one of the Manchesters how he was enjoying his time in Morecambe. '"It's ripping," was the prompt reply.'[10]

'The Front', in this case, being the sea front. A cutting from the *Morecambe Visitor*, 20 January 1915.

OVERHEARD ON THE FRONT.
1st Bantam: This is a grand game, isn't it?
2nd Bantam: It were a good job t' war broke out, weren't it?
1st Bantam: Aye, I wish it 'ud last a lifetime!
Evidently the men have found comfortable quarters at Morecambe.

A postcard of the Sands, Morecambe, sent in 1915.

'How to Feed the Troops'
If accommodation was strictly regulated, diet was even more so. Morecambe's landladies were required to supply the Manchesters with 'a full and varied dietary'. The *Manchester Courier* detailed the schedule of meals that had been agreed between Morecambe and Manchester:

> For Breakfast.- Six ozs. of bread, butter, jam, one pint of tea with milk and sugar, and four ozs. of bacon or fish.
> For Hot Dinner.- One pound of meat previous to being dressed or equivalent in soup, fish, and pudding. Eight ozs. of bread, eight ozs. of potatoes or other vegetables, one pint of beer or mineral water of equal value.
> For Supper.- Six ozs. of bread with butter, one pint of tea with milk and sugar, potted meat or two ozs. of cheese.[11]

In December 1914 the *Morecambe Visitor* estimated that the troops would consume an average weekly total of 24,000 loaves of bread (nearly 20 tons), 16 tons of meat and 4 tons of bacon. An article ('How to Feed the Troops') stipulated that they must be given 'good, plain, substantial food'. Clearly there had been some questions circulating as to whether landladies would be obliged to weigh out the men's rations, but the paper advised that this was not strictly necessary. The paper clarified the situation:

> All that is required is that the men shall have good, plain food and sufficient to satisfy them, and if Morecambe boarding-house keepers cater in their usual excellent fashion the men will be able to write to relatives and friends of the splendid manner in which Morecambe people attend to their visitors. This will prove an excellent advertisement for the boarding-house keepers which will be repaid a hundredfold.

There's a clear appeal to the enterprise of the canny Morecambe landlady – and evidently boarding-house keepers were not the only ones who were considering the financial opportunities that the billeting of the troops might provide: the *Morecambe Visitor*, at this time, is full of grocers' and wholesalers' advertisements, obviously keen to obtain the business of provisioning the hungry troops.[12]

In February 1915 the *Manchester Evening News* sent a reporter over to Morecambe to assess the progress of the city's troops-in-the-making. He observed a seaside town thronging with soldiery: 'You meet them everywhere, officers and some non-coms. in khaki, the rank and file in blue. They dominate the place, giving it a military atmosphere that is as novel as it must be acceptable to the regular inhabitants.' The journalist's interview with an unnamed 'Pal' gives an interesting insight into how the Manchesters were spending their time in Morecambe. Clearly the day was structured around those meals:

> 'Give me an outline of the day's work,' I requested.
> 'It won't be as good as Kipling's,' he answered, smiling. 'And there's nothing

BRITISH SOLDIERS INVADE MORECAMBE.

JAMES BAXTER,
Fish, Poultry, and Game Dealer, etc.

1, THE CRESCENT, Top of Queen St.

HAS MADE GREAT PREPARATIONS FOR

BILLETING ORDERS

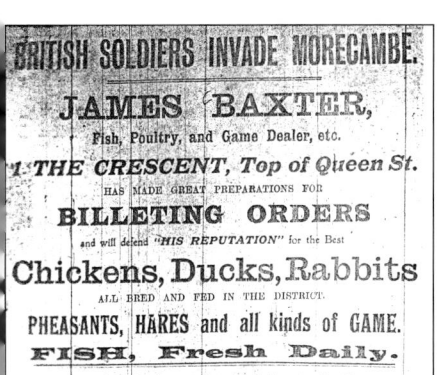

and will defend "HIS REPUTATION" for the Best

Chickens, Ducks, Rabbits

ALL BRED AND FED IN THE DISTRICT.

PHEASANTS, HARES and all kinds of GAME.

FISH, Fresh Daily.

Agent for Palethorpe's Celebrated Sausage.
All the Very Best English Local Fed Stock obtainable at Rock-bottom Prices.
Prompt Delivery to all Orders, Large or Small. Hotels, Cafes, Caterers, &c., supplied.

THE ADDRESS IS IMPORTANT:

1, The Crescent, Top of Queen Street,
TELEPHONE 133. OPPOSITE CLOCK TOWER.

An advertisement from the *Morecambe Visitor*, 6 January 1915.

Billeting of Troops

Mild Breakfast Bacon,
By the Side, about 14 to 16 lbs., **9d.** per lb.
By the Half-side, about 8 lbs., **9½d.** per lb.
Any weight sliced **10d.** per lb.

Loose Cocoa — **1/4 per lb.**
Perfectly Pure. Any weight sold.

Gallon Jars **MIXED PICKLES, 2/9** each
Best selected Vegetables in pure vinegar.

F. H. SIMPSON,
THE MODERN GROCER,
20, Regent Road, and 4, Euston Road,
Tel. 136. Tel. 84.

An advertisement from the *Morecambe Visitor*, 3 February 1915.

---

exciting about it. Each morning a bugler comes round to your street and sounds the reveille. The men offer up prayers for him. Shortly after, an orderly corporal enters your digs and shouts upstairs: "All out, there?" "Yes," we shout back. "Any sick?" "No." "Right," and off he goes, while we snuggle down for another ten minutes snooze. But we're not late for breakfast. Bread and butter, bacon and tea or coffee. After that each man goes to his company's parade ground and falls in by nine o'clock. Then we march to a field and drill till 12.30, or have a turn at Swedish exercises. It gets us ready for dinner, which consists of Yorkshire pudding, two vegetables, and a pound of meat for each man, milk pudding, and a pint of beer – if you want it. At two o'clock we parade again and drill till about five.'

'In all weathers?' I interjected.

'No. If the weather's bad we attend lectures on military matters, or watch picked squads drill. At five, except those on picket duty or headquarters guard, we are dismissed for the day and make a bee line for tea. Bread and butter and stewed fruit with tinned salmon now and then for a change. That's the last meal for those who claim their pint of beer at dinner. If you don't, you get a light supper.'[13]

It comes across that the Pals are rather enjoying their comforts 'in digs'.

'Is the food right?'
'I'm too hungry to be critical at meal times,' he said. 'But it's good enough for anyone. You see, this isn't an ordinary camp. We're billeted with people who are

used to catering, and we're not crowded. At my place each man has a bedroom to himself. Personally I'm just as comfortable as I was at home.'

His voice and manner told me that his home surroundings were good, and I nodded appreciation.'

That the training troops had hearty appetites isn't perhaps surprising. 'You should see the platefuls of bread and butter disappear!' one boarding house keeper exclaimed on the correspondence page of the *Morecambe Visitor*. 'If you want a fine photo for a future '*Visitor*', Mr Editor, send a photographer round to No. — Terrace, about 1.15 p.m., when our fifteen are about half-way through their dinner!'[14]

> At early morn the bugle calls,
> And, if on sleepy ear it falls,
> Such dilatory souls appals.
>
> Then orders sharp to "Double up";
> They run, as if for challenge cup;
> After this—home; to eat and sup.
>
> Next, "Kit Inspection" 'tis, I wean,
> The men look spruce, and fit, and clean,
> No smarter set can e'er be seen.

Extract from a poem published in the *Morecambe Visitor*, 5 May 1915.

'The call of the bugle, the roll of the drum'

'The townspeople of Morecambe are taking the keenest interest in the army in the making that is in our midst,' the *Visitor* reported in the first week of January 1915. It went on:

> By now the novel experience of the call of the bugle, the roll of the drum, and the constant tramp of the marching of men has become quite familiar, and the drilling of the various units in the streets of the town a sight that no longer seems strange. The presence of 5,000 troops in our midst has made a vast difference in the appearance of the town. Everywhere animation prevails, where a week ago everything was quiet. Whichever way one turns there are soldiers.[15]

The *Manchester Evening News*' interview with the anonymous 'Pal' continued:

'You ought to be feeling fit, you youngsters,' I commented. 'Good food, regular hours, steady exercise, and sea air are a healthy combination.'

'Undoubtedly,' he agreed. 'When I came here I was pale-faced and weedy looking. Too much indoor work, and not enough exercise. Now I can feel my muscles moving, and nothing tires me. It's making men of chaps like me. It will make soldiers of us in time. Good ones, I think.'[16]

In between the busy schedule of meals, they were indeed being made into soldiers. Their training began with a great deal of drill and physical exercises. In January 1915 a *Manchester Guardian* journalist observed a typical day of training in Morecambe.

> Their principal parade grounds are the piers and the promenade, a three-mile stretch of broad road on the shore of the bay. There they go for squad drill and various instructional exercises comprised in a soldier's early training. A walk from end to end of the Promenade gives the civilian a rudimentary knowledge of the method of turning an almost raw recruit into a first-class fighting man.

At one end of the Promenade the journalist observed the men of the 5th City Battalion receiving instruction on handling rifles. In the West End, meanwhile, the Bantams were drilling:

> The Bantams were going through the elementary routine of forming fours and inclining this way and that, never getting fairly going in any direction before being pulled up on the confines of another squad's patch of road, and doing the same things over and over again in pursuit of that mechanical accuracy which is the requisite second nature of the military man.[17]

Drilling grounds were established in the suburbs of Bare and Torrisholme, on the Golf Links, Promenade, piers (until 7.00 pm), sands and foreshore. The many photographs taken of the Manchesters going through their exercises on the seafront show that this was quite a crowd-drawing spectacle. In January 1915 the *Morecambe Visitor* observed that

This image was reproduced in the *Morecambe Visitor*, 10 February 1915, and the caption reads: 'The Manchester Battalions now busy training at Morecambe find the Promenade a capital drilling "ground". The picture shows various companies on the "Prom" opposite the Golf Links.'

the squads of drilling Manchesters were stretched right across the town and 'but a yard or two apart'. To one side men were turning, inclining and forming squad, while elsewhere sections were marching at the double. 'There was spirit in the work,' the local paper approvingly observed, 'and many were the comments passed on the excellent material there is in these battalions for moulding into first class soldiers.'[18]

Theatres, churches, schoolrooms, the Central Pier Pavilion and skating rink and the

Squad drill in Thornton Road, from the *Morecambe Visitor*, 21 April 1915.

C Company of the 23rd Manchester Battalion practise Swedish Drill. (Image reproduced with the kind permission of Sidney Allinson)

"E" Company. Platoon No 17.
Competing Section. March 20th 1915.
Winners of Swedish Drill Competition.

E Company of the 23rd Manchester Battalion, winners of the Swedish Drill Competition. (Image reproduced with the kind permission of Stephen McGreal)

Winter Gardens were now serving as lecture theatres and inclement-weather training venues for Manchester's civilian soldiers.[19]

Through the second half of February night marches and extended route marches were added to the men's routine and, with the four battalions competing to outstrip one another, the *Morecambe Visitor* observed that there had been a marked improvement in fitness and discipline all round.[20]

> Now, orders clear, and sharp as steel—
> "Form sections!" "Fours!" "Mark
>   time!" "Right wheel!"
> "Attention!" "Halt!!"—right off the
>   reel.
>
> One wonders sometimes how they know
> Which way to march, or where to go,
> The voices ordering mingle so,
>
> And some the neighbouring fields invade,
> And break the sod with pick and spade,
> Until big trenches they have made.

Extract from a poem published in the *Morecambe Visitor*, 5 May 1915.

At the end of February spades, picks and 'other implements incidental to the work of making trenches' were handed out and it was reported that the Manchesters were being trained in their use.[21] A dugout was built on Bare Lane ('so constructed as to command an uninterrupted view of Lancaster and the surrounding countryside') and later there are accounts of exercises in which positions are attacked and defended.[22]

IN THE TRENCHES AT MORECAMBE.

MEN OF THE 20th SERVICE BATT. MANCHESTER REGT.

Morecambe Visitor, 21 April 1915.

Happy Manchester Boys at Morecambe

Are we Downhearted? "NO!" "B" Company, 7th and 8th Platoons.

Morecambe Visitor, 24 February 1915.

RIFLE DRILL, IN WHICH GREAT PROGRESS HAS BEEN MADE

Morecambe Visitor, 21 April 1915.

In January the *Manchester Guardian* had described the men receiving instruction in handling arms. NCOs were tutoring classes of around thirty men, 'explaining the mechanism of the piece and telling of its ways under fire', '"Don't pull the trigger," was a sergeant's warning; "press it. Press it so gently that you can't tell to a second when it will go off. If you pull it you will spoil your aim."' Another sergeant was showing half-a-dozen men how to bring the rifle properly to the shoulder, 'Proficiency was made to appear to depend upon correctness in a multitude of small details.'[23] In photographs published by the *Morecambe Visitor* in February only the instructors appear to have rifles, but by April they were more widely issued and platoons were practising rifle drill, each man with his own weapon.

By April the *Morecambe Visitor* was printing images of the Manchesters doing bayonet training. Photographs showed the bayonet exercise area that had been set up on the Golf Links, near to the sea front. Here was erected a wooden framework from which were suspended bags of straw. 'They have become very adept at the work,' the paper reported, 'and the exercise is witnessed by hundreds of interested spectators. Those young men of Morecambe who ought to enlist, however, cannot for sheer shame watch this serious preparation for war. They go another way.'[24]

Seemingly sufficient progress was being made that the War Office was satisfied. In March the battalions in Morecambe were inspected by General Sir Henry Mackinnon, General Officer Commander Western Command, who, according to a report in the *Manchester Guardian*, complimented the men 'upon their steadiness on parade, which showed the trouble their officers had taken in training them'. Speaking particularly to the Bantams, General Mackinnon was reported to have remarked 'he was sure when they

BAYONET EXERCISE. ON THE GOLF LINKS.

Morecambe Visitor, 21 April 1915.

In training. (Image reproduced with the kind permission of Stephen McGreal)

went to the front the whole country would be watching them with the greatest interest and following their doings in the field. He hoped every man would remember that. They must not forget they were a very special and a very marked battalion of the regiment.'[25]

'Manchesters at play'
Whatever the toils and disciplines of their training, the Manchesters were also having some fun in Morecambe. The *Manchester Evening News'* interview with the 'Pal' moved on to the subject of recreation.

'And how do you spend your leisure time?' I asked.

'It depends,' he said. 'Some have to be indoors at 9.30, others later. There's no music halls or theatres here, only picture palaces and the Winter Gardens, but there are boxing competitions and football. The latter is very popular. Every platoon, company, and battalion has a team, and each wants to be top dog.'[26]

When the Manchesters arrived in Morecambe, footballs were provided for them, fields and goal posts lent and local referees offered their services. It would be a regular sight, for the next few months, to see parties of men having a kick-about on the sands.[27]

In March an inter-battalion cross-country race was organised. The men set off from the Promenade and proceeded over the Golf Links, watched by thousands of spectators. The winner, Private Bergmeier, who incidentally happened to be the world half-mile champion, finished in 32 minutes. A prize was given to the first Bantam to cross the line – Private T. Broom, who finished in 39 minutes.[28]

In April a Brigade Sports Day was held and reported in detail in both the Manchester and Morecambe newspapers. The Bantams are noted as achieving glory in the wrestling (Private Laithwaite and Corporal Young, both of the 23rd Battalion, and both 'clever exponents of the Lancashire style of wrestling', met in the final) and Privates Mellor and Prestwood triumphed in the three-legged race ('Pte. Prestwood,' the Morecambe paper noted, 'enjoys a big reputation for obstacle and sack races'). Despite the cold weather, 5,000 spectators paid 6*d* and 1*s* apiece to watch the sports, all funds raised going to the local hospital and the Red Cross.[29]

Privates Mellor and Prestwood got to demonstrate their three-legged prowess again at a Bantam Sports Day, staged at Morecambe Cricket Ground. Once more large crowds

Competitors in the cross-country race, *Morecambe Visitor*, 10 March 1915.

attended and 'capital sport was witnessed'. There were relay races, sack races and wrestling. 'Fun was well provided at intervals,' the *Morecambe Visitor* reported, 'and this reached its height during the wheelbarrow race, the officers competing with the men in this extremely humorous competition.' The men won. A collection from the officers provided 'useful and handsome prizes'.[30]

When they were not occupied with training or sports, Morecambe worked hard at keeping the troops fully – and respectfully – entertained. Soldiers' Institutes were set up, at which the men could 'spend a pleasant evening and obtain coffee and light refreshments at night'. Reading rooms were provided, free letter writing paper, newspapers, dominoes, chess sets and draughts. There were 1,096 letters recorded as having been sent from just one of the Soldiers' Institutes.[31] Every week there were programmes of soldiers' concerts, organised by Morecambe's various churches and chapels, the YMCA and the Temperance League. The town's cinemas put on programmes of swashbuckling films for the men and the theatres staged military dramas. Meanwhile French evening classes were organised by the YMCA and by Belgian refugees in the town. 'Such an agency as this could not fail to add to the value and efficiency of every man who would go to France', the local paper applauded. German classes were also offered for officers.[32]

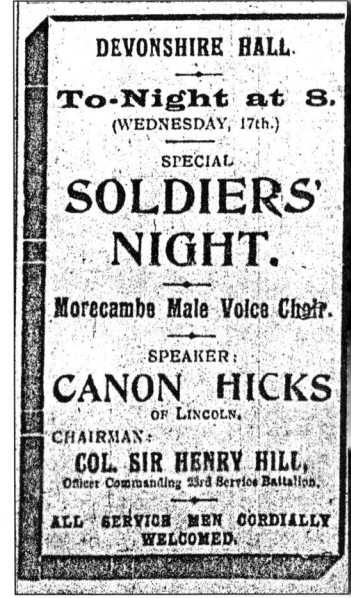

Advertisement for a typically wholesome soldiers' concert, hosted by Sir Henry Hill, commander of the 23rd Battalion, *Morecambe Visitor*, 17 March 1915.

> Many happy hours have shared,
> And concerts often have we dared
> To give . . no effort has been spared.
>
> And men, with special gifts endowed,
> Have used them freely for the crowd.
> Our "artistes" really make us proud!
>
> For one has played the flageolet,
> And one would concertina get,
> Such ready players I ne'er met.

Extract from a poem published in the *Morecambe Visitor*, 5 May 1915.

Certain men of the Manchesters enjoyed taking to the stage themselves – indeed the Bantams seem to have been something of a hit in Morecambe, with their popular band (producing concerts of 'genuine merit', according to the local paper) and enthusiastic solo performers. In February 1915 the officers and men of B Company staged a concert at Morecambe's Devonshire Hall (a music hall, with seating for 800). Lieutenant Heath presided and Lieutenant Noble acted as stage manager. After boxing competitions ('very popular items'), there was a programme of songs, violin and cornet solos, sketches, dances and recitations. A song in unison – 'My Old Shako' – by the officers of the company was 'exceedingly well received and proved quite a novelty.' Lieutenants Noble (song) and Simpson (recitation) were noted to have gone down particularly well with the audience, while Privates Millbanks (song and dance) and Gill (song) were lauded by the local paper as 'very capable concert artistes'.[33] Indeed Private Gill seems to have acquired quite a liking for the stage during his stay in Morecambe. By April he had risen to corporal and was taking to a Morecambe stage for the thirty-sixth time. 'No wonder Corporal Gill has been popular at our local concerts!' the *Morecambe Visitor* enthused, as Gill took to the stage again to do a comic turn at a YMCA concert. 'His patter and his mannerisms would cause laughter anywhere. As per usual, he was encored, the audience enjoying another period of hearty laughter.'[34]

Miss M.H. Brown, an enthusiastic supporter of the Bantams Band, composed a song (to the tune of 'Tipperary') for the battalion. The men could frequently be heard singing it 'with heartiness and gusto', *Morecambe Visitor*, 19 May 1915.

The Song of the 8th

Into dear old Morecambe came 'Bobs' Own', the 8th, one day,
Telling tales of Kitchener to cheer them on their way.
Now that they've got settled here they say they want to stay,
But when he gives the order they'll go singing on their way.

(Chorus)
It's a long way to go to Berlin, it's a long way to go.
It's a long way to go to Berlin, but we're on our way, you know;
Good-bye to all in Morecambe, farewell, dear old land,
For when the Allies go marching into Berlin
They'll be led by Bobs' Own Band.

> We're only little fellows, but we've heard our country's cry.
> It cut us pretty deeply when first you passed us by;
> Now you're realising that we little chaps can do
> As much for dear old England as those pals of 6 foot 2.
>
> We're only little fellows, but we're every bit as keen
> As any other Briton to fight for King and Queen;
> So send us out to battle and let us prove to you,
> That mighty hearts are beating in these lads of 5 foot 2.
>
> We're only little fellows and no doubt it made you smile
> When first you saw us marching, but we keep on mile by mile;
> So give us your assistance and cheer us on our way,
> Our King and Country need us and we're ready to obey.

Other Bantams made a name for themselves on the page. Many Manchester men submitted letters and poems to the 'Soldiers' Page' of the *Morecambe Visitor*. Certain soldiers of the 23rd Battalion would turn into regular contributors – and would remain so long after they had left Morecambe. The 5th Manchester Battalion might be able to claim Wilfred Owen as its own, but the 23rd Manchesters had their own bard, in the form of one Private Percy Gidley. Gidley would go on submitting his cheery verses and letters to the *Morecambe Visitor* until July 1916.[35]

The *Manchester Evening News*' interview returned to the subject of the pint of beer that the anonymous 'Pal' had mentioned earlier. Though a pint of beer was offered to all men with their meals, it seems that only a minority took it. The Pal's account seems to confirm that, while life in Morecambe had its comforts, it also had its disciplines.

> 'At my billet the beer is seldom asked for, and I know it's much the same at lots of places. Drinking is not encouraged. A man who turned up drunk at parade would almost certainly be discharged. Quite a lot of the chaps are teetotallers. Most drink moderately. We're not milksops or saints. We're just decent chaps.'[36]

In a move to promote that 'decency', the licensees of the town had collectively come to an agreement not to serve the troops after certain hours. 'This suggestion is being carried out with remarkable results,' the *Morecambe Visitor* reported, 'for the most prohibitionist will find nothing in the conduct of the Army in Morecambe to elicit any complaint, and upon this feature the town and the men from Manchester are to be heartily congratulated.'[37] Certainly there are no accounts of drunkenness in the local paper. Indeed, there is a conspicuous lack of bad behaviour reported. One theft was committed by a Bantam, who stole a bicycle and rode it back to Manchester ('because he had got into trouble with a woman'!).[38] Otherwise, there are no reports of any crimes or misbehaviours. Rather, the *Morecambe Visitor* regularly comments on how very good the conduct of the troops is.[39] Recalling his time with the 20th Battalion in Morecambe, William Hunt gave a rather less rosy account of the Manchesters' comportment. Hunt remembered a lot of the men being 'rough individuals' who liked to go out at night and were 'fond of their drink'. Interviewed in the 1970s, he recounted a story about baskets of mussels being stolen and brought into billets, much to the wrath of the landlady. 'They weren't particular about wetting the bed and things like that,' Hunt went on. 'That was another trouble.'[40] Such anecdotes perhaps were not to the taste of the patriotic and proud local press?

Many of the Manchesters are reported to have attended Morecambe's various churches and chapels on a Sunday. And, while stories of around-the-piano hymn singing in billets might seem slightly too virtuous to be entirely convincing, the resort's practical, moderate, soldier-friendly religious institutions do seem to have made some converts. In April 1915 4,000 men of the Manchester battalions – i.e. pretty much the whole brigade – attended a Divine Service held in the Winter Gardens to celebrate Good Friday. Every seat was filled. 'Unique indeed was the occasion,' the *Morecambe Visitor* reflected, 'and at no place in England, it were true to say, were so many men gathered together in one building for Divine Service.'[41]

'And what about the officers?'
The *Manchester Evening News* interview moved on to the subject of officers:

> 'And what about the officers?' I asked.
> 'A bit mixed,' he answered. 'Our Colonel is a top notcher. Controls the battalion as easily as he manages his horse. The men know it, they're always at their best when he's about. But they're not all like him. We have one who recites the drill book word for word, like a curate intoning a psalm. It makes the men grin and get slack. They know a duffer at sight, and they've a keen sense of humour.'[42]

Non-commissioned officers of the 23rd Manchester Battalion, from the *Manchester City Battalions' Book of Honour*, p. 355.

Officers of the 23rd Manchester Battalion, with Lieutenant-Colonel Sir Henry Hill (centre), from the *Manchester City Battalions' Book of Honour*, p. 353.

Officers (and their wives) of the 23rd Manchester Battalion. (Image reproduced with the kind permission of Sidney Allinson)

The appointment of officers had been a subject of some anxiety for Captain Walkley, the staff officer in charge of the Manchester recruiting centre. Local men were encouraged to apply for commissions and, ultimately, most of the officers appointed to the 23rd Battalion, and certainly the subalterns, were from Lancashire. Many of their names appear in the *City Battalions' Book of Honour*, indicating that they were employed by Manchester firms. Several of them were old boys of Manchester Grammar School. Volunteers were initially appointed, acting provisionally, and 'liable to be called on service elsewhere'. Throughout March and April 1915 the Manchester newspapers report the appointment of new officers to the battalion.

In December 1914 Lieutenant-Colonel Walter Cook had been appointed as the first commanding officer of 'Bobs' Own'. Cook was a highly decorated veteran who had served in the Second Afghan War (he had been recommended for the Victoria Cross in 1880) and taken part in the Burmese Expeditions of 1885–7 and 1887–8. He served under Lord Roberts ('peculiarly appropriate' the *Manchester Evening News* observed) and had been an officer in India for thirty-seven years, where he commanded a battalion of Ghurkas ('another race of splendid little fighting men'). Cook had retired in 1912 and, in 1914, was aged 57.[43] He would not remain with the Bantams for long, though.

In January 1915 Cook was replaced in command of the 23rd Battalion by Major Sir Henry Blyth Hill. Like Cook, Hill was a decorated veteran who had been lured away from the comforts of retirement. Hill had retired from the army in 1908 (having taken part in the Soudan Expedition of 1898 and been present at the Battle of Khartoum), but

Bugle Band of the 23rd Manchester Battalion, from the *Manchester City Battalions' Book of Honour*, p. 257.

had volunteered his services again in 1914 and had spent the past few months as the second-in-command of the 10th Battalion (Derry) Royal Inniskilling Fusiliers. 'Sir Henry is the sixth baronet' the *Manchester Guardian* informed. 'The family is descended from Oliver Cromwell's treasurer in Ireland, and has many associations with Ulster.'[44]

In Morecambe the officers were billeted in the smarter hotels – the Grand, Midland, Clarendon and Park Hotel. The *Morecambe Visitor* detailed that officers boarded at the rate of 4s 6d per day. It went on: 'Their schedule of meals is: - Breakfast: Porridge and two dishes, tea and coffee. Lunch: Hot and cold meats; sweet, cheese. Afternoon tea: Bread and butter and cake. Dinner: Soup and fish, joint, sweet, cheese.'[45]

'We are living history'

On 20 March 1915 it was announced that Lord Kitchener would be visiting Manchester the next day in order to inspect the new City battalions. 'The inspection will take place in Albert Square, and provide a military display without parallel in the history of the city,' the *Manchester Courier* enthused.[46]

As the Bantams prepared to head back to Manchester to be inspected by 'K of K' there seems to have been some self-consciousness (and grousing) that they were not yet universally properly attired as soldiers. The heavy woollen district in Yorkshire, despite working at time-and-a-half, was unable to provide enough khaki to keep the army supplied. Over 12,000 looms were busy. Between 250 and 300 miles of khaki cloth was being woven every week. Some 50,000 tailors were speedily sewing the material into garments. Still, it was not sufficient. Seemingly, though, there was no shortage of blue serge. The temporary uniform, blue with a dark-grey overcoat, was being made by the Co-operative Wholesale Society. 'And very serviceable it looked,' the *Manchester City Battalions' Book of Honour* recorded. The men themselves were less impressed: 'We looked like tram guards,' recalled W. Hunt of the 20th Manchester Battalion.[47] By mid-February, local newspaper reports indicated that the City battalions were now progressively being issued with khaki kit, but, as late as the end of March, the 2nd Brigade in Morecambe were still largely wearing the blue service dress. As far as the Bantams went, there does seem to have been a further complication: added delays were now being experienced as many of the men had grown broader and taller during the course of their training and uniforms tailored to their measurements at enlistment now failed to fit. Articles of clothing arrived piecemeal and, on the day of Kitchener's inspection, their appearance seems to have been something of a mixed bag. The *Manchester Courier* observed: 'A large number were in khaki, and these were carrying the full marching equipment, while those wearing the blue service dress had khaki hats and putties, and not a few shouldered the rifle.'[48]

While the rest of the Manchester battalions would march directly up from Heaton Park, those presently billeted in Morecambe were to travel back to Manchester early in the morning by special train. Large crowds gathered around the station, awaiting their arrival. The *Manchester Courier* described the reception:

> As the men proceeded towards the centre of the city they were heartily cheered, and although a large number of barricades were erected, these did not prevent

The City battalions are inspected in Heaton Park. (Image reproduced with the kind permission of Stephen McGreal)

relatives and friends from handing gifts of cigarettes to the men in uniform. For some time the troops were 'at ease' in Corporation-street, and the soldiers whiled away the time by singing many patriotic songs, the choruses of which were enthusiastically joined in by the onlookers.'[49]

The *Manchester Guardian* observed the mood thus:

There was a feeling both in the men and in the spectators that is not to be found in an ordinary military parade. These were not ordinary soldiers . . . The crowd knew the men in the ranks individually. It could address the soldiers, and it did so frequently, by their Christian names. A wish of good luck was shouted with the addition of 'Jack' or 'Bill' to guide it to its proper destination, and Jack or Bill turned his head to smile an answer.[50]

As the column of men waited, in the sun, on the edge of Albert Square, the crowds gave them oranges and apples. The men who had come from Morecambe had brought their greatcoats with them, not expecting this sudden warm spring weather, and they were now suffering somewhat from the heat.

Though they might look warm, the men who had been training in Morecambe evidently also looked well: 'The countenances of the Morecambe men constituted

The 23rd Manchester Battalion en route to inspection by Lord Kitchener. (Image reproduced with the kind permission of Stephen McGreal).

convincing evidence of the superiority of seaside air,' the *Manchester Guardian* commented, 'they were tanned and reddened as though they had been on foreign service.'

The crowd had an especially enthusiastic cheer for the Bantams. The *Manchester Guardian* observed:

> The Bantams kept the same pace as the bigger men and did it without effort. It was not smallness but uniformity of stature which distinguished them. With no more than three inches between the tallest and the smallest, they all came within one physical grade – short but thick-set, and seemingly endowed with strength and endurance out of proportion to their size.[51]

'The "Bantam" clearly justifies himself as thoroughly on parade as he will in the trenches,' the paper's editorial confidently predicted. Seemingly their appearance struck Kitchener too:

> Over an impressive scene in Albert Square, where the troops marched past in a style which everybody agreed was magnificent, the sun smiled benignantly.
> So also did Lord Kitchener, the man so often described as 'without a smile'.
> An old soldier standing near the dais at the Town Hall entrance saw the War Secretary smiling as the 'Bobs' Own' from Morecambe came up to the salute.

'I've known Kitchener for thirty years,' he said, 'and I've never seen him smile before. But he's fairly smiling now – well, wouldn't anybody smile at seeing such a fine lot of little chaps!'

This particular smile was not the only one with which Kitchener greeted his new levies, but it was the longest.[52]

The march-past took an hour. Lord Kitchener watched from a raised platform in front of the main door of the Town Hall.

Though he may have smiled at the sight of the Bantams, one aspect of the battalion's appearance is reported to have concerned Kitchener. He remarked that the officers of the 23rd Battalion 'by some quirk of administrative planning' were mostly men of 6ft and more. Kitchener is said to have pointed out that the officers would be immediately singled out as an easy target for snipers. It was subsequently, therefore, ordered that all of the officers in the Brigade should be measured and shorter men re-assigned to the Bantams.[53]

Large crowds watched the Morecambe battalions filing along Oxford Road after the review. Though they had had a long day on duty, the men were reported to be showing few signs of fatigue and they sang as they marched:

Lord Kitchener, and other dignitaries, salute the march-past. (Image reproduced with the kind permission of Stephen McGreal)

As they 'marched at ease' homewards or stationwards last evening they let everybody know their views:

> We don't like drill;
> It makes us ill;
> But we do like a 'snice mincepie.

Other battalions filled the air with their declarations as to the distance from Tipperary, and denied in loud tones the possibility of their being downhearted. In other words, they were tired but happy – and wonderfully fit.[54]

The *Manchester Guardian*'s closing reflections are, with hindsight, poignant to read. 'We are living history,' the editorial considered:

But the dullest could not see the march of the twelve thousand yesterday without knowing that of this his children's children will be told. Nor could he see it without a deepening and quickening sense of his personal relation to the facts behind it. For Manchester's army is Manchester, and the new army is Britain, in a way that no soldiers ever have been before, or, it is hoped, will ever need be again.[55]

As General Mackinnon had predicted a few weeks earlier, the Bantams clearly were the focus of a particular public and press fascination. By April the '"brave little Bantams" business' was clearly starting to rankle with some. Reporting a 'mutiny' in a Morecambe guest house (frustrated with their hosts' humours, the soldiers billeted there had thrown

A Company, Platoon I, of the 23rd Manchester Battalion, from the *Manchester City Battalions' Book of Honour*, p. 359.

their bedding out of the windows), the *Manchester Guardian* observed:

> Some of the men in the 'Bantam' battalions now completing their training in the North would be glad if they could add a cubit or two to their stature, for they are tired to desperation of the subject. The 'brave little Bantams' business has been overdone, and the experience of one patronising patriot on whom a party of the 'dear little fellows' have been billeted may be a warning to others.[56]

Frustration was starting to be felt in other quarters too. By March the battalions that had been training in Heaton Park were feeling eager to make a move closer to the war. The *Manchester Evening News* repeated a joke that was being passed around the camp 'to the effect that a responsible officer had taken a house in North Manchester "for three years or the duration of the war"'.[57] But, if they were fearing that the War Office had forgotten their existence, it seemed that they had now been remembered; on 1 April 1915 the *Manchester Courier* reported that the troops in Heaton Park were shortly to leave for Belton Park, Grantham. The paper noted, though, that definite instructions had not yet been issued to the brigade in Morecambe.[58]

By May the Bantams may well have been wondering whether the War Office had forgotten *them*, as the other battalions billeted in Morecambe (the 20th, 21st and 22nd Manchesters) received their orders for Grantham. Morecambe seems to have been genuinely sorry to see them go. There were concerts and dances to send them on their way and handkerchief-waving sweethearts – and landladies – aplenty in the crowds that accompanied them to the station. 'Cheer after cheer' followed the trains as they pulled out from the platform. 'By one o'clock the last train conveying

Headline from the *Morecambe Visitor*, 5 May 1915.

A Company, Platoon II, of the 23rd Manchester Battalion, from the *Manchester City Battalions' Book of Honour*, p. 361.

troops had gone,' the local paper reported, 'and Morecambe was silent, and to some extent sad.'[59] How did the Bantams feel, then, as the cheers and the crowds and the noise of the bands faded away?

One of the reasons for the Bantam's extended seaside sojourn is that a reorganisation of infantry brigades was occurring through the spring of 1915. In May 1915 the 23rd Manchesters became part of the 104th Infantry Brigade. The brigade was commanded by Brigadier General G.M. Mackenzie and the Brigade Major was one B.L. Montgomery – later to become Field Marshal Viscount Montgomery of Alamein.

Bernard Law Montgomery had been severely wounded in October 1914 while commanding a platoon of the 1st Battalion of the Royal Warwickshire Regiment in an attack on enemy trenches at Méteren, during the Battle of the Aisne. He was promoted to captain the day after he was wounded and was awarded the DSO for his part in the action, but it left him at home and highly frustrated.[60] In the new year he would beseech three successive Army Boards to let him get back to active service again. Finally, in February 1915, a Board graded him as fit for home service. He was posted as the Brigade Major (Senior staff officer) of 112th Brigade in Manchester – shortly to be re-designated as the 104th Brigade, 35th Division – 'a Division of small men who did not want to be left out,' as Montgomery himself put it. The 104th Brigade's battalions, alongside the 23rd Manchesters, were the 17th, 18th and 20th Battalions of the Lancashire Fusiliers. Though he was still aged just 27 in 1915, Montgomery's letters convey a sense of a young man who is committed, efficient and ambitious. He clearly threw himself into his new role with some determination. Montgomery would later write: 'It would be true to say that I really ran the Brigade and they all knew it'. Montgomery would remain with the 104th Brigade until January 1917.[61]

Gerald Mackay Mackenzie was aged 55 in 1915. Having served in the Second Boer War with the Royal Inniskilling Fusiliers (he was Mentioned in Despatches), Mackenzie had been promoted to brevet colonel in 1905 and retired the next year. He was appointed a temporary brigadier-general in January 1915. Montgomery's notes describe his brigadier, as 'an old retired officer called Mackenzie– a very nice person but quite useless'.[62] Though Montgomery might have had doubts about his senior officer's suitability (primarily he doesn't seem to have the dynamism that Montgomery wanted to see in a superior), they clearly got on and Mackenzie was keen to give Montgomery's career a friendly upwards push. In January 1916 Mackenzie sent a letter to Montgomery's father complimenting the abilities of his son and predicting a bright future for him. Whatever Montgomery's doubts, Mackenzie was clearly astute. He wrote:

> With regard to your son Bernard, I have the very highest opinion of him. He is equally good at Administration as at Training of Troops. He ought to have a brilliant future in the Army, and rise to high rank. Be my stay with this Brigade long or short, I shall not fail, before I leave it, to bring his admirable services to the notice of the authorities, and to do all I can to further his advancement with them. He has taken a great deal of routine work and drudgery off my hands, doing the work in a quiet unobtrusive way. It is, of course, his job, you may say, but it is

not every Staff Officer that I have met, nor many, who have been so thorough and helpful in the work. General Pinney too knows his work and worth, and I am sure will look after his future interests.⁶³

At the end of May, with their departure assumed (*surely!*) to be imminent, a 'Bobs' Own Day' was held in Morecambe. The event was the initiative of the battalion commander, Sir Henry Blyth Hill, and was ostensibly organised in order to raise funds for the Morecambe Nursing Division and St John's Ambulance Brigade. It must also have given the now evidently restless Bantams something to focus their energies on. The *Morecambe Visitor* reported that helpful ladies spent the day touring the resort selling 'Memento Badges' of the battalion's stay there, while the men spared no exertion in selling tickets and programmes for a 'grand military concert' which they were staging that evening. The concert – 'given almost entirely by military artistes of the battalion' – was attended by General Mackenzie. Sergeants Megson and Crowther performed cornet solos, Privates Hassell and Jamieson duetted on concertina and flageolet and all participants 'contributed admirable items to an excellent programme, which was greatly enjoyed by the large audience'. After the concert, the Bobs' Own Band paraded on the Promenade, beating retreat.⁶⁴

In June 1915 the *Manchester Evening News* reported that the 23rd Battalion was finally leaving Morecambe, having been there for six months. 'During their stay in Morecambe the Bantams, or Bob's [*sic*] Own, as they prefer to be designated, have made many friends, and they leave the town amidst general regret.' The paper went on:

Bernard Law Montgomery ('Monty') and James Walter Sandilands ('Sandy'), the latter shortly to become the commanding officer of the 104th Brigade. This photograph is taken from the Private Papers of Major General Sir Reginald Pinney, IWM 66/257/1, Army Diary No 4, August 1916. (Image reproduced with the kind permission of Philip Pinney)

> Their departure yesterday afternoon was witnessed by a large crowd of people, and there was a good deal of cheering and singing as the trains steamed out of the Midland Railway Station. There was also a fusillade of fog signals to further mark the departure. The troops looked in the pink of condition, and the appearance was in striking contrast to that which they were when they arrived in Morecambe in mid-winter.⁶⁵

Percy Gidley wrote a letter to the *Morecambe Visitor* thanking the people of the town, on behalf of the battalion, for their hospitality, care and encouragement. Writing from Salisbury Plain, Gidley recalled:

When we left the busy city of Manchester on January 2nd to enter upon strenuous work amongst strangers in Morecambe, we pictured all manner of things as to how we should fare in the 'Naples of the North'. The result was a pleasant surprise for us and surpassed the wildest of our dreams. We never thought such friendship and fellowship would spring up between we strangers and the good people of Morecambe. The cheerfulness, encouragement, and care of those providing the billets, and the generosity of Morecambe in general, made new men of us.

Morecambe took to us as a duck to water, and the touching scenes witnessed when we had to leave will never be forgotten. Morecambe did a lot for us. We enjoyed and appreciated the beneficial sea and mountain air; we received every comfort and good meals in billets; everything possible in the way of entertainment and pleasure was provided for us, and we shall never forget the nobleness of the various institutions and friends.

The '"Bobs' Own" Bantams' can truthfully say that 'Morecambe made men of them'.[66]

Percy Gidley composed a poem to mark the occasion of the battalion's departure from Morecambe. Published in the *Morecambe Visitor*, 7 July 1915, it is considerably kinder to Morecambe than it is to Masham.

> 'Bobs' Own's' Departure
>
> Our leaving Morecambe caused us pain,
> Our farewell left a sting,
> As we marched onward to the train,
> For training in full swing.
> Quite bitter felt the parting,
> For each Morecambe soul – a friend,
> Helped from start, to our departing,
> Their kindnesses ne'er end.
>
> Day by day your friendship grew
> To we sma' lads, 'Bobs' Own',
> A friendship now forever true,
> No matter where our zone.
> Yea – together are we linked like chains
> (And stamped on every link),
> The stamp of friendship that ne'er wanes,
> And sticks like printer's ink.
>
> We regard you just as our own,
> You claimed us as a son;
> But alas! The little 'Bantam's' flown
> To peck the 'Eagle-hun'.

> Should we be spared when we have won,
> Back to you we will fly;
> And say, 'Now friend, now duty's done',
> Well, we know well your reply.
>
> To meet each other – oh! How grand,
> Of our victory to converse;
> To see the last of 'Vaterland',
> Their 'last' to sing in verse.
> We are more eager now to go
> Than ever we have been;
> For Masham's not like Morecambe – no,
> 'Tis not at all serene.
>
> But grumbling now will never do,
> 'Tis perhaps a great mistake;
> Still 'tis leaving Morecambe that we rue,
> Tho' our friendship shall not break.
> The scenery around here is fine
> (That's all that we can say),
> And all 'Bobs' Own' lads opine
> Morecambe beats it any day.
>
> We shall soon be up and doing now,
> Soon quite prepared to face the foe,
> To quell the Hunnish crimes somehow
> Our prowess we shall show.
> To do this one and all of you
> Have helped us in our aim.
> To you a thousand thanks are due
> For aiding us to fame.

It is evident that Morecambe saw the billeting of the Manchesters as potentially a great advertisement; the troops' health and happiness were seen as excellent testimony for the resort's hospitality and invigorating sea air. Morecambe was keen for the soldiers to return, to come back with their families and friends, and to tell all of Manchester of Morecambe Bay's charms. It was not just, though, that Morecambe was glad to have the present – and possible future – income that the Manchesters would bring; the town was proud to be hosting the soldiers-in-training and genuinely seemed to grow fond of them. One boarding-house keeper expressed it thus:

> We did try to remember that they had in many cases left comfortable homes, good food and loving friends at the call of their country. We try to remember that if this

terrible war continues long, our guests will take their places in the fighting line, and that perhaps ours is the last home which really may be called one, this side of eternity, for some of them.[67]

Masham, June–August 1915

On 5 July 1915 the 35th (Bantam) Division, comprising the 104th, 105th and 106th Brigades, was officially formed, becoming part of a new Kitchener army, K4. The 23rd Manchesters, now finally in khaki and keen to be moving on, were about to take their place within that division. But, instead of moving war-wards, they were about to find themselves heading further north.

From Morecambe, they moved to Masham, near Ripon, where the whole of the 35th Division would train together for the first time. Camp was pitched at Roomer Common, just south of the village of Masham, along the River Ure. With the Fourth Army's training centre based in Ripon, the whole of the district was congested with army camps. The *Burnley Express*, reporting on the arrival of the Accrington and Burnley Bantams (the 'Howitzers') at Roomer Common, reflected that here the men would 'reap the benefit of the fresh moorland air'. It went on, 'At Masham there is hill and dale with beautifully wooded stretches and that alone contrasts strongly with the flatness of the Fylde coast.' Whatever the charms of the surrounding landscape, it was unfortunate, given the weather of that summer, that the men were now accommodated in tents. August brought heavy rains. It poured down for days on end. The camp was washed out and the ground everywhere sodden. It must indeed have made the Manchesters sigh for the hot-water-bottle-warmed beds of Morecambe.[68]

A Company, Platoon IV, of the 23rd Manchester Battalion, from the *Manchester City Battalions' Book of Honour*, p. 365.

A Company, Platoon III, of the 23rd Manchester Battalion, from the *Manchester City Battalions' Book of Honour*, p. 363.

B Company, Platoon V, of the 23rd Manchester Battalion, from the *Manchester City Battalions' Book of Honour*, p. 367.

Few records survive detailing the training of the 35th Division at Masham, but in addition to the sort of physical training that the Bantams had been doing in Morecambe (drill, route marches, cross-country runs etc.), accounts suggest that they were digging trenches, working on their musketry skills and taking part in larger scale exercises. This was now training 'in earnest'.

It was while they were training in Masham that John Duffield joined the 23rd Battalion as its chaplain. Duffield was a curate in a parish in Leeds before the war. He was appointed to the troops in Yorkshire under the direction of the Bishop of Ripon and would remain with the 23rd Battalion until he was invalided out in July 1916. Eustace Lockhart Maxwell, later the commanding officer of the battalion, would describe Duffield as 'the best of the lot, I think – Irish, very young, rather witty, and evidently much beloved of all ranks'.[69] While the 35th Division were based in Masham, a Sunday service was taken by the Archbishop of York and the Archbishop of Ripon, who offered a blessing to the troops on their impending departure overseas.

The Bantams were being assessed as they trained. *The History of the 35th Division in the Great War* records that, whilst in camp at Masham, some 'weaklings' were withdrawn from the ranks. In addition to those deemed to be medical unfit, a draft of under-age youths were now sent home. A significant number, it seems, had at the time of enlisting 'become somewhat hazy about the actual date of their birth'.[70] John Duffield observed that there were quite a lot of Bantams who had 'sworn at the age of sixteen that they were nineteen'. While there evidently were some 'weaklings', the men were generally much stronger and more physically fit than they had been when they had left Manchester – and, probably because so many of them were young, they were starting to gain in height as well. 'They began to grow,' Duffield recalled, 'and so we had several "Bantams" who were nearly six feet high!'[71]

In June 1915 Major General Reginald John Pinney, who some weeks earlier had been commanding the 23rd Brigade, 8th Division, at Neuve Chappelle, was selected for the command of a division. 'Everyone very kind in their congratulations,' Pinney's diary noted. But, on 28 June, Pinney was summoned to the War Office and informed that not only was he going to get a New Army Division, it was also going to be a Bantam division. His reaction was not exactly one of delight. 'Have 35th Divn (bantams) in Yorkshire. 4th Army,' Pinney wrote. 'When I said "damn", Archibald Murray paid compliments about best man to train them.' Pinney officially took command on 4 July.[72]

Pinney was experienced and trusted – Douglas Haig reportedly commenting that he 'could be sure' when Pinney's divisions were in the line. Not all opinions were equally approving, though, and Pinney (a religiously

The Revd John Duffield, photographed with other officers of the 23rd Battalion, *Manchester Courier*, 1 October 1915.

B Company, Platoon VI (Percy Gidley among them), of the 23rd Manchester Battalion, from the *Manchester City Battalions' Book of Honour*, p. 369.

devout, non-smoking teetotaller) won few admirers in the ranks when he banned the rum ration in the 33rd Division in 1916. Pinney's Army Diaries, though, give the impression of a practical commander, of a man who cared to get the best out of – and the best for – the men under his command. He would regularly visit the units of the 35th Division at the front and must have been a highly visible senior officer.

Parkhouse Camp, Salisbury Plain, August 1915– January 1916

At the end of August 1915 the 35th Division was finally moving south. They now relocated to Salisbury Plain, for their Active Service Training. Salisbury Plain was very much the stepping-off place for overseas – the 'finishing school', as some called it. The 23rd Manchesters were based at No. 1 Parkhouse Camp, near Tidworth. 'This was a very pleasant spot,' wrote Bernard Montgomery, 'and some real good work was put in.'[73]

On 1 September Percy Gidley ('the most enthusiastic of all the writers amongst the "Bobs' Own" Bantams') sent a review of the facilities at Parkhouse Camp to the *Morecambe Visitor*. Seemingly Salisbury Plain compared favourably with camping in the rain in North Yorkshire. Gidley wrote:

Photograph from Army Diary No. 2, Private Papers of Major General Sir Reginald Pinney, IWM 66/257/1.

Parkhouse Camp prior to the construction of huts early in 1915.

Parkhouse Camp – with huts.

At last we have made a move, and the huts here are absolutely 'home from home' and the last word in comfort. We are well off with electric lights, baths, wash-houses, cook house, etc. We have a thousand and one things that were denied us at Masham. The Y.M.C.A. is simply marvellous, and the C. of E. Institute is the same. We are really thankful for the change.[74]

Once again Gidley was inspired to put his thoughts into rhyme:

> We've deserted dreary Masham now
> For a stay on Salisbury's Plains,
> A nearer step towards our vow
> To aid our King who reigns.
> None were sorry of our leaving.
> We left without the least regret.
> For the blend of genuine grieving
> None has equalled Morecambe yet.
>
> We are on to sturdier duty now.
> And no doubt you think 'tis time
> To show the hateful Germans how
> 'Bobs' Own' are in their prime.
> Your confidence must never waver
> For our feelings shall be the same:
> Tho' small, none others shall be braver
> Once our Empire calls our 'Game'.
>
> 'Tis 'time' no doubt the game we started.
> Time we played away from 'home'.
> Time from England we departed.
> Time we on foreign soil did roam.
> Kaiser Bill shall never 'bowl' us.
> Never shall he get his 'catch'.
> Ne'er shall we drop in his 'maulers',
> England's just above his match.
>
> Yes, the 'Mad Dog', has made a 'slip'.
> Soon his reign shall have 'long-stop'.
> We'll 'cover' him now we've the grip,
> His monarchy he soon must 'drop'.
> Our partnership with France shall flourish.
> Old England never 'breaks' her word.
> Our allied forces Bill can't nourish.
> We'll 'bowl' him 'over', mark my word.

'K. of K.' conducts the team
Of 'bhoys' from far and 'wide',
And the Bantams' eyes doth brightly gleam,
'Cause they are on his side.
They'll help to 'bail' the Kaiser 'out',
Be found wanting – 'Bobs Own' – never!
Then they'll raise their 'battle shout',
'We're for England's glory ever'.[75]

B Company, Platoon VII, of the 23rd Manchester Battalion, from the *Manchester City Battalions' Book of Honour*, p. 371.

Despite Percy Gidley's positive review, it is evident that some of the Bantams were grousing about conditions – and that those complaints had reached ears back up in Manchester. In December 1915 a letter to the *Manchester Courier* appealed for '"Comforts" for the Bantams at Park House Camp'. The writer, one Edith Hampson, stated: 'The plain [Salisbury] is very bleak, cold, and desolate and the men are consequently suffering much discomfort. Many of them are urgently in need of "Comforts" – mittens, scarves, socks, mufflers, woollen gloves and the like. Any contributions would be gratefully received by the little men.'[76]

They were spending a lot of time out on that 'bleak, cold, and desolate' plain. While

B Company, Platoon VIII, of the 23rd Manchester Battalion, from the *Manchester City Battalions' Book of Honour*, p. 373.

they were at Parkhouse Camp the men finessed their musketry skills on rifle ranges, practised field firing, did 20-mile route marches, took part in mock attacks, constructed trench systems and spent nights in those trenches. When they did not have night manoeuvres to grumble about, there were buttons, buckles and boots to be buffed to a shine. There was a lot of Brasso and dubbin being worked at Parkhouse Camp. This was a time of 'spit and polish' parades.

Obligatory church parades, with their requirements for gleaming buttons and boots, seemed to have provoked some quantity of swearing and blasphemy. The *Manchester Guardian*'s C.E. Montague wrote:

> Like the infinite cleaning of brass-work, the hearing of many well-meaning divines in the Tidworth garrison church had been one of the tribulations through which the defender of Britain must work out his passage to France. With the final order to tarnish his buttons with fire and oil there came also a longed-for release from regular Sunday adjurations to keep sober and think of his end.[77]

Not all, though, were averse to the ministrations of those 'well-meaning divines'. The Bantams' chaplain, John Duffield, prepared several men for confirmation while they were based at Parkhouse Camp. A joint confirmation service, for around thirty men, was held in Salisbury Cathedral. 'It was a great moment,' Duffield would recall.[78]

There were some earthly pleasures at Parkhouse too. There was a cinema on the site and market women from Tidworth came over to the camp to sell baskets of oranges. In Tidworth itself – a town of purely military character at this time, and at a walkable distance from the camp – there were places where refreshments could be had and a garrison theatre to entertain the troops.

In June 1915 Lieutenant Colonel H.B. Hill, who had been commanding the 23rd Battalion, transferred to the 19th Manchesters. In September 1915 Lieutenant Colonel R.P. Smith took command. Having retired from the Devonshire Regiment some years earlier, Smith had been recalled in November 1914.

Percy Gidley had the following verses published. The first appeared in the *Morecambe Visitor* on 13 October 1915:

> At Park House Camp
>
> Am doing my 'bit' at Park House Camp,
> Preparing – and soon shall be fit:
> Afar off from home, yet out of the damp,
> (Our huts – 'Home from Home' – are just 'it').
> Whilst training down here, we're willing – depend
> ('Bobs' Own' never were known to shirk).
> There's a pleasure that's great – a word from a Friend –
> So send one to read after work.
>
> Yea, now from his home nest the Bantam has flown –
> Away from the friends he loved best;
> You must 'drop a line' to your little 'Bobs' Own',
> To enjoy and peruse in his next.
> You'll be doing your share in this strife, rest assured,
> For thoughts of you give him good cheer;
> Then, when the Kaiser's complaint we have cured,
> He'll return to his friends, never fear.
>
> 'No news is glad news,' some people will say,
> But then they perhaps are not here.
> At all events – 'Bobs' Own' won't take it that way,
> Whilst so far from the home they love dear.
> So just get paper, a pencil or ink,
> Send your thoughts on to Park House Camp,
> And say whether or not you are 'in the pink',
> We'll bless writer, writing-paper and stamp.

This second poem by Gidley was featured in the *Morecambe Visitor* on 22 December 1915:

Greetings from 'Bobs' Own' – Christmas 1915

We cannot stroll along the prom,
Or gaze upon your briny bay,
We're bound to follow 'roll of drum',
To draw closer to The Day.
Still, we'll ne'er forget the days gone past
And our 'joys' upon your pier.
We wish you a Merry Christmas,
And a Happy New Year.

What's in store for us, it matters not,
In the year 1916.
To King and Queen we've thrown our lot,
And to help them we are keen.
Whate'er we do, where'er we be,
Forget old Morecambe, never,
We'll come to you when we are free,
Our friendship shall not sever.

Whate'er we do, you are sure to know,
Whilst there's paper, pen and ink,
The Bobs' Own Bantams mean to show
Of Morecambe we still think.
Whilst fitting now for foreign foe,
Of which we have no fear,
On you our blessings we bestow
This Christmas and New Year.

Stonehenge, *c.* 1916.

C Company, Platoon IX, of the 23rd Manchester Battalion, from the *Manchester City Battalions' Book of Honour*, p. 372.

Manchester Courier, 1 October 1915.

93

C Company, Platoon X, of the 23rd Manchester Battalion, from the *Manchester City Battalions' Book of Honour*, p. 377.

As early as the start of October rumours were circulating at Parkhouse Camp that the 35th Division was going to be moving overseas imminently. Finally, in December 1915, the 104th Brigade was notified that they were under orders for Mesopotamia. It is said that the men cheered as they received the news.

However, within a month, those orders would be changed. In late January the 35th Division were told that they were heading to the Western Front instead. The button polishing and church parades were over. The Bantams were finally heading for France.[79]

'I suppose you are hoping to get to the front before it's over?' the *Manchester Evening News* journalist had asked the anonymous 'Pal' at the end of that interview back in Morecambe.

> 'No,' he answered, thoughtfully. 'I'm not. Life's in front of me, and I don't want it spoiling. I'm here because I think Prussia has got to be taught that military arrogance is out of date. But if I have to fight,' he added, straightening up, 'I'll do my best.'
>
> I believed him. As we walked back together I saw the 'Pals' striding past. I felt that he was right. They are intelligent, healthy, well behaved, and self-respecting. Fine material, from the diminutive 'Bobs' to the six footers. As good as the Army contains, and 'they will do their best'.[80]

C Company, Platoon XI, of the 23rd Manchester Battalion, from the *Manchester City Battalions' Book of Honour*, p. 379.

C Company, Platoon XII, of the 23rd Manchester Battalion, from the *Manchester City Battalions' Book of Honour*, p. 381.

D Company, Platoon XIII, of the 23rd Manchester Battalion, from the *Manchester City Battalions' Book of Honour*, p. 383.

D Company, Platoon XIV, of the 23rd Manchester Battalion, from the *Manchester City Battalions' Book of Honour*, p. 385.

D Company, Platoon XV, of the 23rd Manchester Battalion, from the *Manchester City Battalions' Book of Honour*, p. 387.

D Company, Platoon XVI, of the 23rd Manchester Battalion, from the *Manchester City Battalions' Book of Honour*, p. 389.

E Company, Platoon XVII, of the 23rd Manchester Battalion, from the *Manchester City Battalions' Book of Honour*, p. 391.

E Company, Platoon XVIII, of the 23rd Manchester Battalion, from the *Manchester City Battalions' Book of Honour*, p. 393.

E Company, Platoon XIX, of the 23rd Manchester Battalion, from the *Manchester City Battalions' Book of Honour*, p. 395.

E Company, Platoon XX, of the 23rd Manchester Battalion, from the *Manchester City Battalions' Book of Honour*, p. 397.

Chapter 4

'The Latest Methods of Making War'

On 23 January 1916 the 23rd Manchester Battalion finally received its orders for embarkation. It was now almost fourteen months since the battalion had been established. As 'Bobs' Own' made final preparations for their overseas move, the *Manchester Evening News* was musing about what form the spring campaigns would take. The newspaper was putting its confidence in an 'all-important change in the general conduct of operations', with the Allies now pledging to co-operate more closely and co-ordinate combined future attacks. The paper predicted: 'As Nature awakens from her winter sleep and reveals the first faint traces of coming plenty, the guns, opening fire, will spread death and destruction on a scale previously unknown.'[1]

On 28 January 'Bobs' Own' entrained for Folkestone. In the harbour the men were ordered aboard a paddle steamer – a former Isle of Man ferry boat, one of several that had been chartered by the Admiralty to carry troops.[2] As their ship waited to depart one of the Bantams' number clambered on top of the paddles and gave a rousing cry to his comrades. 'Are we downhearted?' he shouted. Instead of triggering the habitual sing-along, however, the question got a more sobering response. Moored alongside the Bantams' steamer was a ship that was returning troops who had been home on leave. Replying to the enquiry as to their downheartedness, one of the returning men barked loudly in response: 'You bloody well *soon* will be!' The Revd John Duffield, recalling this incident, observed, 'It cast quite a gloom'.[3]

That 'soon' was yet to be suspended, though. Once again, the Bantams' departure for France was about to be delayed. As John Duffield put it, they were now going to sample 'a little war experience'.[4]

The sea was calm. The weather was fair. Visibility was clear. The flotilla was on a steady course. But, then, at 11.15 am, two hours after setting off from Folkestone, HMS *Viking*, the destroyer that was accompanying the convoy, hit a submerged, moored mine. A series of smaller blasts followed the initial detonation, probably caused by shells on the upper deck firing. The oil in the ship's tanks caught fire and then there was a huge explosion from the after-magazine and the guncotton store. Smoke and flames poured from the stricken destroyer; ten of her crew were dead. The convoy had strayed into a German minefield. 'We turned gallantly back and went hell-for-leather back to Folkestone', John Duffield recounted. 'We were more downhearted than ever.'[5]

Landing back in Folkestone, the 23rd Manchesters bedded down on a cement floor

Steamers arriving in Boulogne.

for the night. They must have experienced some complicated mixture of emotions as they did so. The next day they re-embarked. 'Nobody said "Are we downhearted?"', John Duffield recalled, 'But we were very thankful to get to France.'[6]

Docking in Boulogne-sur-Mer, on 30 January 1916, the weather was cold, dull and misty. But, though the scenery might have disappointed, there was clearly much relief that the crossing was complete. Some accounts of troops arriving in Boulogne around this time express surprise at the seeming apathy of the local inhabitants; instead of flags and cheers, like they had seen in the film reels, troops were taken aback to find that the natives did not bother to look at them twice. However, one of Percy Gidley's letters to the *Morecambe Visitor* indicates that the Manchester Bantams – ever keen to display their smiles and smartness – received a friendly reception. The only pressing concern that their arrival on foreign shores seemed to be presenting to the Bantams was the scarce supply of Woodbines thereabouts. Gidley wrote:

We Bobs' Own arrived in France on January 30th and received a grand welcome. We at once found French folk very 'chummy' indeed, and we get on very well with them. One thing here to be regretted is that the name of Woodbine is almost defunct, the sight of one a nightmare and the taste of one a curio – so scarce are they.[7]

As usual, Gidley saw fit to compose a patriotic verse to commemorate the occasion – this time 'apropos of the Bantams commencing active service'. It was published in the *Morecambe Visitor* on 16 February 1916.

> Now that from their home nest the Bantams hath flown,
> 'Gainst 'Vulture of Kultur' to take up their chance,
> To do as were hatched for – to face danger zone,
> Their nest for a while will be 'somewhere in France'.
>
> They'll be help to their comrades who have been here a while,
> To lessen their work, which had always been hard;
> But in spite of the hardship – true British – they smile,
> And in spite of war's sorrows, such sorrows discard.
>
> Friends at home and at Morecambe we never forget,
> E'en in sternest of struggles with minds so hard set,
> We hope that Dame Fortune (we wish you to know)
> Will upon you forever her blessing bestow.

British troops arriving in Boulogne-sur-Mer.

Boulogne-sur-Mer, as it was selling itself in 1915. Not quite the sight that met the Manchesters.

After a night in a transit camp, the Manchesters were marched to the Gare Centrale on 31 January. There they got onto trains which took them inland, as far as Blendecques, to the south of St Omer. It was a bitterly cold and slow journey. Bernard Montgomery wrote to his mother: 'The men don't get 3rd Class carriages in France but have to use cattle trucks. A cattle truck holds 8 horses or 25 men. They are very cold things to travel in as they don't give them straw.'[8]

From Blendecques the 23rd Battalion marched on to the village of Quiestède, some 5 miles or so to the south-east. 'In marching over the Bantam's load has hitherto been reckoned at sixty pounds,' Eustace Lockhart Maxwell, who was shortly to assume command of the 23rd Manchesters, wrote home in February, 'or very little less than half his own weight.' No weight allowance was made for the Bantams, Maxwell disclosed, 'who naturally have to carry the same load as others'.[9]

The Manchesters would be billeted in Quiestède for the next eighteen days. Well behind the lines, here the battalion would continue their training, with particular focus being placed on bombing and automatic gun fire. Throughout February the weather remained damp and cold, alternating between rain and snow, but *The History of the 35th Division* asserts that this climatic incivility 'did not damp the ardour of the troops'.[10]

It was on such a typically cold, wet day – 11 February 1916 – that the 35th Division as a whole was assembled to be inspected by Lord Kitchener and Lieutenant General Richard Haking, GOC of XI Corps. Bernard Montgomery detailed the day's events in a letter to his mother:

> We were inspected this morning by Lord Kitchener. He is out here for a few days and we had a sudden message yesterday afternoon at 4 p.m. that he would inspect us at 10 a.m. this morning. This of course meant a lot of work for me, but we were all ready for him. It has been horribly wet all day, and the conditions could not have been worse. All the country round here is very highly cultivated and there is not a meadow or grass field anywhere. So we had to form up in a ploughed field. The mud was awful and it was raining hard. But K. got out of his motor and went all round the ranks in the mud, and afterwards stood on the road while we filed past him. He was very pleased indeed with the parade and told us so.[11]

'All stood very steady,' Major General Pinney's diary recorded; and the men seemed cheered by the words that Kitchener had addressed to them.[12]

On 13 February the 23rd Manchester Battalion were finally designated General Reserve. After a final round of lectures ('Miscellaneous subjects'), the 35th Division

The extreme wet weather was reported in the French press. New rubber boots were issued to *poilus* in Artois, as seen in these images from *Le Miroir*, 23 January 1916.

DANS LES TRANCHÉES ENVAHIES PAR L'EAU

A map from *The western front at a glance: a large-scale atlas of the Allies fighting line in the west* (George Philip & Son, Ltd, London, 1917).

began their move closer to the front line. For the next two days they marched eastwards, skirting around the north of Béthune, billeting overnight first in Boëseghem (a day's march of around 8 miles), Calonne-sur-la-Lys (around 11 miles) and then Le Touret (another 8 miles or so). This was a district of orchards and beet fields and roadside shrines. But however interestingly foreign the scenery might have been, and however momentous this front-wards journey, many of the men were finding it difficult to focus on anything other than their feet; by the time that they reached Le Touret, the men's boots were in very bad condition. With the wet weather, and the long days of marching, they were coming apart at the seams.

Also passing through the village of Le Touret in the spring of 1916, Edmund Blunden recorded some impressions of the locale in which the Bantams now attended to their suffering feet. Blunden observed that Le Touret, though it was only about 3 miles behind the front line, was 'making no such heavy weather of the war'. He went on, 'In the afternoon, looking eastward from le Touret, I had seen nothing but green fields and plumy grey-green trees and intervening tall roofs; it was as though in this part the line could only be a trifling interruption of a happy landscape. I thought, the Vicarage must lie among those sheltering boughs. There are farmhouses, chickens and staring children – but also the nearby crash of heavy shells.'[13]

The Bantams' trench education was about to commence. Arrangements had been made for the 35th Division to be attached 'for instruction' to the 38th (Welsh) Division, 'so that all might learn the latest methods of making war before the Division was given a sector of the line to hold on its own'.[14] The idea was that fresh-out-of-Blighty New Army men could be put in with more practised troops (the Welsh had been in France since November 1915) and be initiated in the realities of trench warfare while on the job. The 38th Division was occupying trenches to the south of Neuve Chapelle.

The front line ran just ahead of the ruined village of Richebourg-l'Avoué. Heavy fighting had taken place in the vicinity in 1915, but, since that time, the line had been fairly static in this sector. Behind, the twin village of Richebourg St Vaast was much knocked about.

Edmund Blunden recorded detailed descriptions of the localities that the Manchesters were now passing through on their way to the front. Seemingly the Richebourgs ('two tattered villages south-west of Neuve Chapelle') attracted many a soldier sightseer:

Richebourg St Vaast was a prosperous-looking (but deserted) village, with aspiring poplar colonnades; nailed to the most satisfactory trees for the purpose were the tall ladders of artillery observers. The windows of the houses were mostly heavily sand-bagged, and the walls loopholed, as though there had been or was to have been street fighting in the old days. The large church, and the almost rococo churchyard, astonish everybody; they had been bombarded into that state of demi-ruin which discovers the strongest fascination. At the foot of the monolith-like steeple stood a fine and great bell, and against that, a rusty shell of almost the same size; the body and blood of Christ, in effigy of ochred wood, remained on the wall of the church. Men went to contemplate that group, but more to stare into the very popular tombs all round, whose vaults gaped unroofed, nor could protect their charges any longer from the eye of life. Greenish water stood in some of these pits; bones and skulls and decayed cerements there attracted frequent soldiers past the 'No Loitering' notice-board. Why should these mortalities lure those who ought to be trying to forget mortality, ever threatening them? Nearly corpses ourselves, by the mere fact of standing near Richebourg Church, how should we find the strange and the remote in these corpses? I remember these remarks: 'How long till dinner, Alf?' 'Half an hour, chum.' 'Well, I'll go and 'ave a squint at the churchyard.'[15]

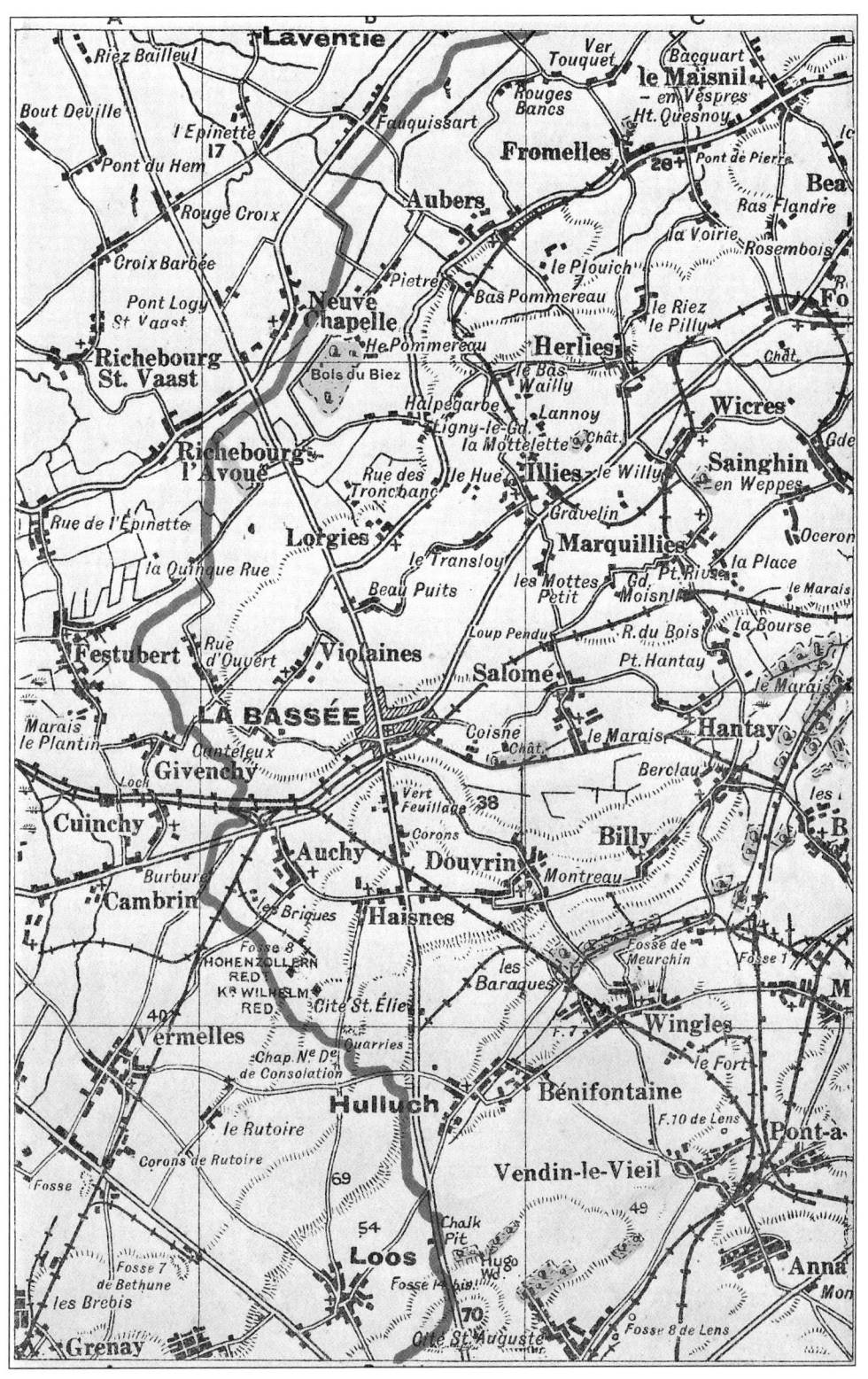

A map showing the British front from Laventie to Loos at the time of the opening of the Somme, to the south.

A stereoscope image – 'Inspecting the ruins of the once beautiful Richebourg Cathedral [sic]'.

The 'cajoling ghostliness' of Richebourg St. Vaast clearly made an impact on Blunden. It is to be imagined that it made an impact on the Manchesters too. Having waited so long to play their part in the war, they must have been well aware, as they passed through such scenery, that they had now arrived.

When the companies of Bantams moved forwards a note in their orders stipulated: 'Two sandbags per man for filling and placing on the fire-step will be provided . . . Parapets are not to be lowered.' Thus it was about to become a common sight to see a Welshman standing on the firestep with a Bantam perched on a pile of sandbags beside him. Identifying that a Bantam battalion had assumed the line opposite, there were some reports that enemy troops were heard to make 'crowing' noises.[16]

The Manchesters were in the line with the Welsh in front of Richebourg-l'Avoué between 20 and 27 February, companies circulating in and out of the front line until all had been initiated. What is most commented upon in the records of this week is not the aggression of the enemy, but rather that of the weather. It snowed heavily in the first days that the Manchesters were in the trenches. And, when it was not snowing, it rained and an icy wind blew. The trenches became waterlogged. Again there were complaints as to the adequacy of the Bantams' boots. Perhaps the enemy too were preoccupied coping with the discomforts of the cold. Whatever the source of their preoccupations, they were certainly quiet. Indeed so quiet that it was a matter of remark in the War Diaries of the Welch battalions.[17]

As Edmund Blunden put it, this was a '1915 sector' and some 1915 rules still applied, such as 'the conventional performance of rifle fire swelling up and dying out at dawn and dusk'. Thus far it conformed to the textbook. There were to be some all-too-1916 incidents, though. On 23 February several trench mortar bombs were fired into a section of trench occupied by the Bantams. 'They made a considerable noise,' the battalion's War Diary noted, but damage was slight and only one man (of the 14th Welsh) was slightly wounded. And then, on 25 February, the 23rd Manchesters would suffer their first casualties.[18] While in the line with the 10th Welsh, Second Lieutenant W.M. Reid went out on a patrol. Along with five of the men out with him, he was wounded. Private Martin Cunningham died that day. William Reid died the next day of his wounds.[19]

> Private Martin Cunningham died of wounds on 25 February 1916. He was aged 20, from Miles Platting, Manchester. He is buried in Merville Communal Cemetery.
>
> Second Lieutenant William Reid died of wounds on 26 February 1916. He had been appointed a temporary second lieutenant in the 22nd Manchester Regiment in March 1915. He was aged 19 and from Edinburgh. He is also buried in Merville Communal Cemetery.

At 4.00 am on 27 February the Manchesters came out of the trenches and marched back to billets at La Pannerie, 8 miles or so to the rear, north of Béthune. From there, after a couple of days of cleaning up, stock-taking and housekeeping ('Internal Economy'), they marched north, back to billets in Calonne-sur-la-Lys.

After the extreme weather conditions that they had just experienced in the trenches, and in preparation for their return, the men were now fitted out with long waterproof

Merville Communal Cemetery, c. 1918. From October 1914 to April 1918 Merville was in Allied hands. On 11 April 1918, though, the Germans took the town and it was not recaptured until August. The cemetery was not used again until the concentration of battlefield burials after the Armistice. Merville Communal Cemetery contains the graves of 1,268 Commonwealth troops.

Troops by the calvary at Calonne-sur-la-Lys.

capes and goatskin coats. Though these garments were noted to provide much-needed warmth effectively, they did have the disadvantage of being attractive to fleas and lice and, when wet, did not tend to smell particularly attractive – hence their nickname as 'stinkers'. The men were also issued with whale oil for their feet, to prevent trench foot.

A further new item of kit was the 'tin hat'. Helmets had first been issued to British troops in October 1915, but they were kept in Trench Stores, to be used only in the line and passed from unit to unit as they took over the sector. In December 1915 a question was raised in Parliament regarding the wider use of helmets: why should they not be issued generally to the troops and become a standard piece of equipment? It's estimated that, by the spring of 1916, 250,000 helmets had arrived on the Western Front. They were now starting to appear in the 35th Division, but only in limited numbers – and not

LES TENUES FANTAISISTES DE LA TRANCHÉE

LA LUXUEUSE PEAU DE BIQUE | LE BERGER DE LA TRANCHÉE | LA CHAUDE PEAU DE MOUTON

The French newspaper *Le Miroir* features winter fashions on the Western Front, 9 May 1915.

everyone was *entirely* impressed. Eustace Lockhart Maxwell, who would shortly assume command of the 23rd Manchester Battalion, wrote to his family:

> Equally useful but vastly less convenient are the steel helmets. Of these latter we have but fifty, intended for the use of sentries and look-out men in the trenches, but I suppose we shall each have one in time. To that time I look forward without enthusiasm, for a most abominable form of hat (for any purpose but the warding off of splinters and glancing bullets) it is impossible to imagine. It is a steel basin, in shape between oval and round, furnished with a rim beaten out from itself; the bottom of the basin is padded and rests on the crown of one's head; it is painted green, and weighs apparently about two pounds. It is no doubt efficacious in the purpose for which it is designed, but it will give the hardest-headed man a pretty bad headache![20]

It was not just the discomfort. The exchange of the soft cap for the tin hat seemed to underline some change in the character of the war – transitioning from a conflict in which a soldier still might nobly aim a rifle at his foe into an industrial war.

NOS SOLDATS SAUVÉS PAR LE CASQUE D'ACIER

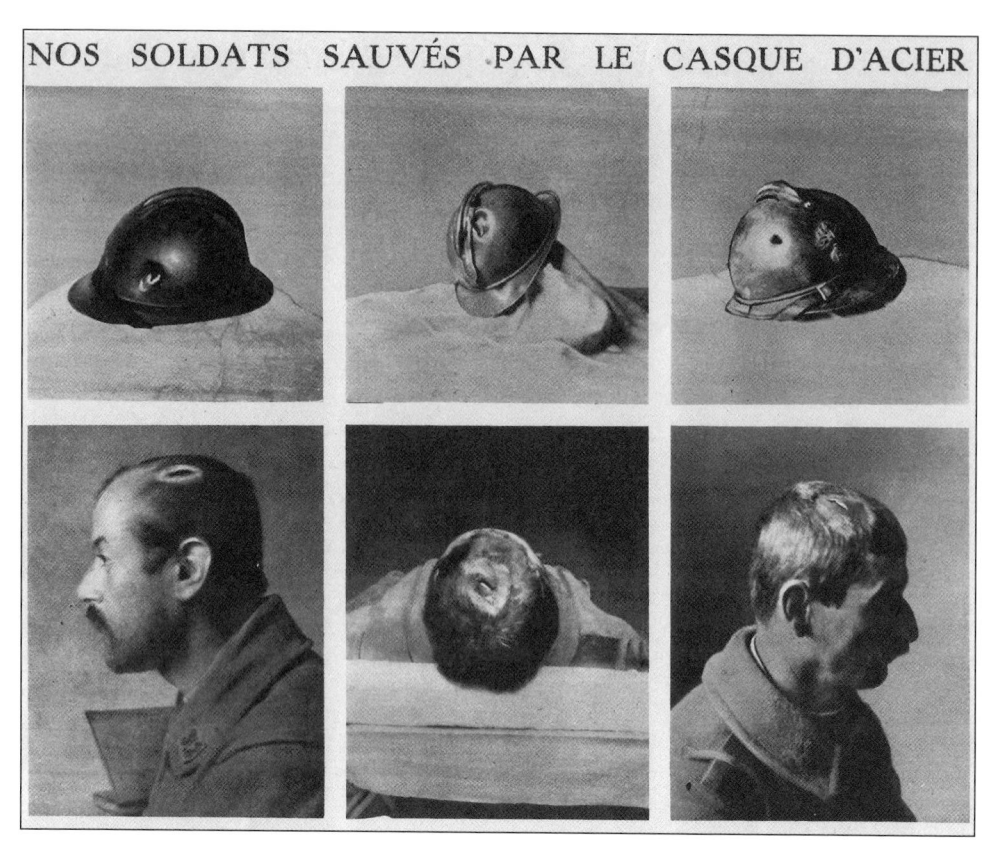

An article in *Le Miroir*, 30 January 1916, shows images of men whose lives have been saved by their '*casque d'acier*'. The article estimated that the steel helmet would reduce the incidence of head wounds by around 40 per cent.

And so, suitably kitted out, the Manchesters returned to training – albeit this too turned out not to be without its dangers. On 2 March a defective bomb went off during a practice session. Captain Doidge, the bombing officer of the 104th Brigade, was killed. Reports indicate that a bomb went off in his hand. Reginald Chamberly Doidge, formerly a solicitor in Ashton under Lyne, whose parents kept a pub in the town, was with the 17th Lancashire Fusiliers. He had enlisted as a private with the Nottingham Hussars, a territorial cavalry regiment, at the start of the war and risen through the ranks. Captain Doidge was buried in Calonne-sur-la-Lys Communal Cemetery. He was aged 26 and left a young widow.[21]

Second Lieutenant Durandeau, of the 23rd Manchesters ('one of the most popular officers'), was also injured by a piece of shrapnel and three other men were wounded. Being a subaltern in the 23rd Manchesters was starting to look like a dangerous occupation.

An article, issued by the Press Association in March, and reprinted in the *Manchester Evening News*, remarked on the arrival of the Bantam battalions in France. Of a cheerily complimentary tone, it began, 'While the soldiers of more liberal inches have plenty of good-humoured badinage for their little brethren, they do not attempt to conceal their admiration for them.' The journalist went on to quote a 'distinguished General' (unnamed) who commented on the 'sturdy appearance' of the Bantams when marching and their 'very distinct advantage over tall men' for trench warfare ('more particularly of that reckless type so familiar to platoon officers, who grow weary of reiterating the injunction "Keep down!"') But the advantages afforded by their small stature might not last forever. The article concluded: 'One of its lieutenants told me, with a note of real concern in his voice, that many of the men have grown appreciably since they first went into khaki, and that he has had to admonish some of them that if they are not very careful they will soon exceed the bantam standard.'[22]

"Bantams'" Officer Killed in France.

Local Names in To-day's Lists of Losses.

Captain R. C. Doidge, of the 17th (1st South-East Lancashire Bantams) Battalion, has been accidentally killed in France. His death is announced by the War Office to-day in a list of casualties among officers in the Expeditionary Force (reported under date March 4), which also includes other local names. Captain Doidge, who was a man of fine physique and about six feet in height, was gazetted as second lieutenant in April, 1915, and received his first promotion in September last. Previously he had served in a cavalry regiment.

He joined the Bantams battalion while it was stationed at Chadderton, and was very popular among his brother officers. When the battalion moved to Salisbury Plain he was appointed brigade bombing officer.

Manchester Evening News, 11 March 1916.

POPULAR "BANTAMS" OFFICER WOUNDED.

News has been received in Manchester to the effect that Second Lieutenant R. F. Durandeau, one of the most popular officers of the 23 Service Battalion Manchester Regiment, has been rather badly wounded by shrapnel. He received his wounds on March 2, and has undergone an operation, but as yet it has not been possible to remove him from the clearing station, although he is reported to be progressing favourably. Second Lieutenant Durandeau is 25 years of age and his home is in Chorlton Road, Manchester.

Manchester Evening News, 13 March 1916.

Chapter 5

'The Time Had Now Come'

'The time had now come', Davson's *The History of the 35th Division* recorded, 'when the division was to take its place in the line as a complete unit'. The Division would spend the next four months (from March until the end of June 1916) variously in and out of the line between Laventie and La Bassée.[1]

On 6 March the Bantams left Calonne. Waggons were supplied to transport the men's packs, but they were obliged to carry their own fur coats, waterproofs, great coats and equipment. The day was bad for travelling, with snow and wind, and the weight of their winter wardrobe proved too much for some of the Bantams. Bernard Montgomery wrote to his mother:

Map showing the front between Le Bassée and Laventie on 1 July. From *The western front at a glance: a large-scale atlas of the Allies fighting line in the west* (1917).

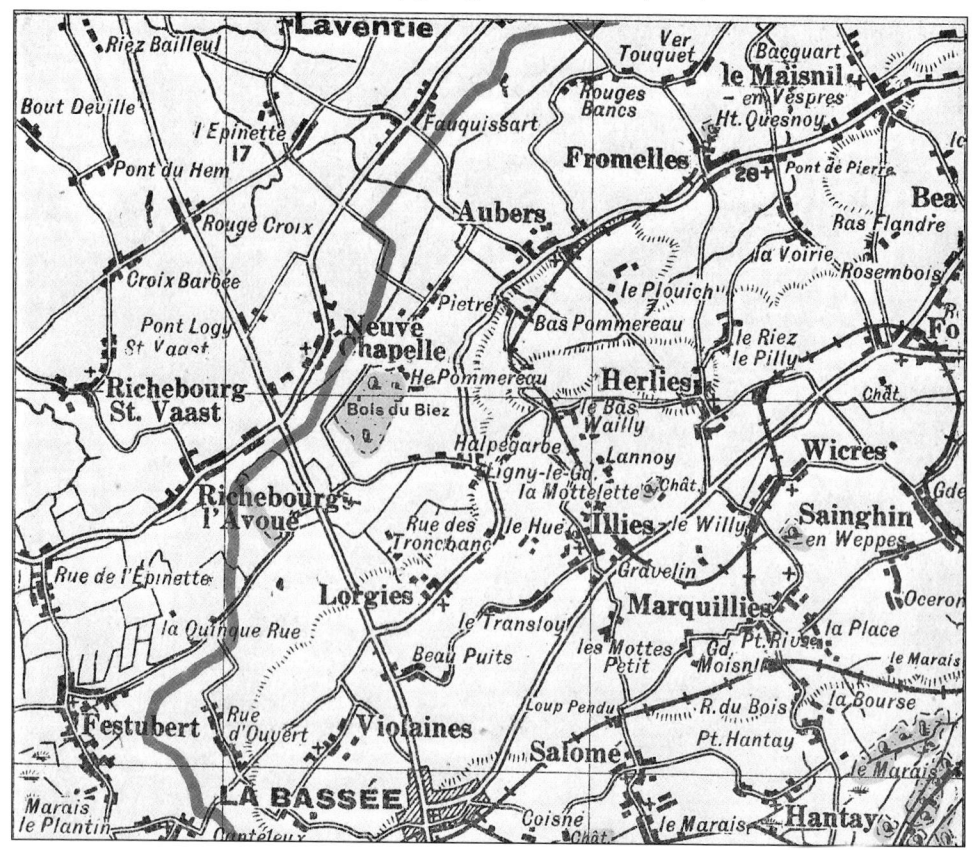

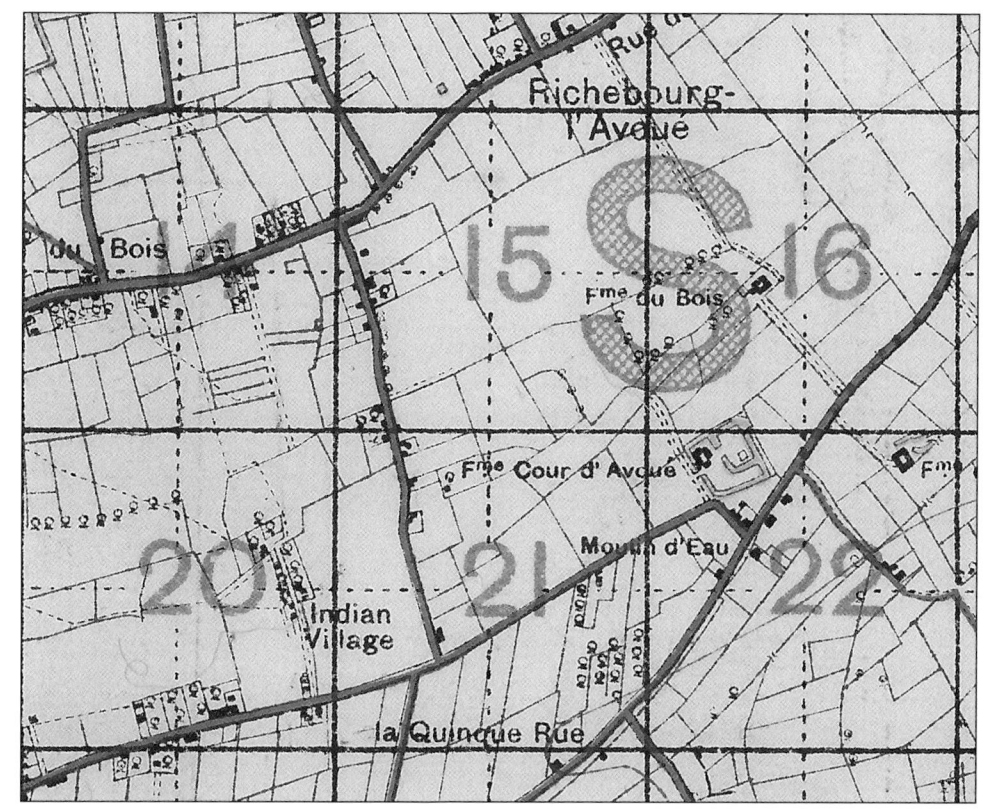

Detail from a trench map showing the Ferme du Bois Sector (Béthune Combined Sheet 36A S.E., 36 S.W., 36B N.E., 36C N.W.).

> We are moving today to take over a new part of the line further south. It is at present snowing hard and the roads are very slippery for riding. I wonder when this cold weather will stop; of course as long as it lasts all the muddy ground round the trenches is quite nice as it is all frozen hard, but when a thaw comes the mud will be awful.[2]

On 7 March the 35th Division took over a sector of trenches from the 19th (Western) Division. That night the 23rd Manchesters moved into the Ferme du Bois stretch of trenches, between Quinque Rue ('Kinky Roo') and Richebourg-l'Avoué. Notwithstanding the ungenerous weather, the relief was completed in two hours.

Straightaway it was apparent, though, that this was not going to be quite such a cushy number as their previous stint in the trenches. The next day saw a stretch of the line heavily shelled. For three hours communication between the front line and battalion headquarters went down. It continued the next day. The front line parapet was blown in in several places, while snipers in the ruins (Cour d'Avoué) in no-man's-land 'were very troublesome'. In addition to the new discomfort of enemy hostility, the men were suffering badly from the cold and the ground was becoming very muddy.

Trench life – its primitive, but so prized, small elements of domestication, the sharing of discomforts, the sudden fears and the long boredom – bound men together. C.E. Montague wrote:

> Trench life is very domestic, highly atomic. Its atom, or unit, like that of slum life, is the jealously close, exclusive, contriving life of a family housed in an urban cellar . . . a man's world was that of his section – at most, his platoon; all that mattered much to him was the one little boatload of castaways with whom he was marooned.[3]

In the mud of Richebourg-l'Avoué, sharing the cold and their discomforts, the Bantams probably did feel very much like castaways.

During this stint in the line, the battalion was occupied working on the construction of a communication trench (Rope Trench) to the front line. When they moved into this sector reliefs had to take place at night across the open. As work was carried out now, those enemy snipers continued to be troublesome. There might well have been some cheering, then, as on 10 March the troops watched twenty-six Allied aeroplanes pass overhead en route to raid enemy territory.

'The weather is horrible,' Bernard Montgomery wrote to his father on 11 March. 'It has been very cold with several inches of snow. Now the snow has practically gone and it has begun to rain. Altogether the conditions for the men living in the trenches are very bad.'[4]

> Private Joseph Wood was killed in action on 13 March 1916. He was from Hulme. He is buried in Le Touret Military Cemetery.

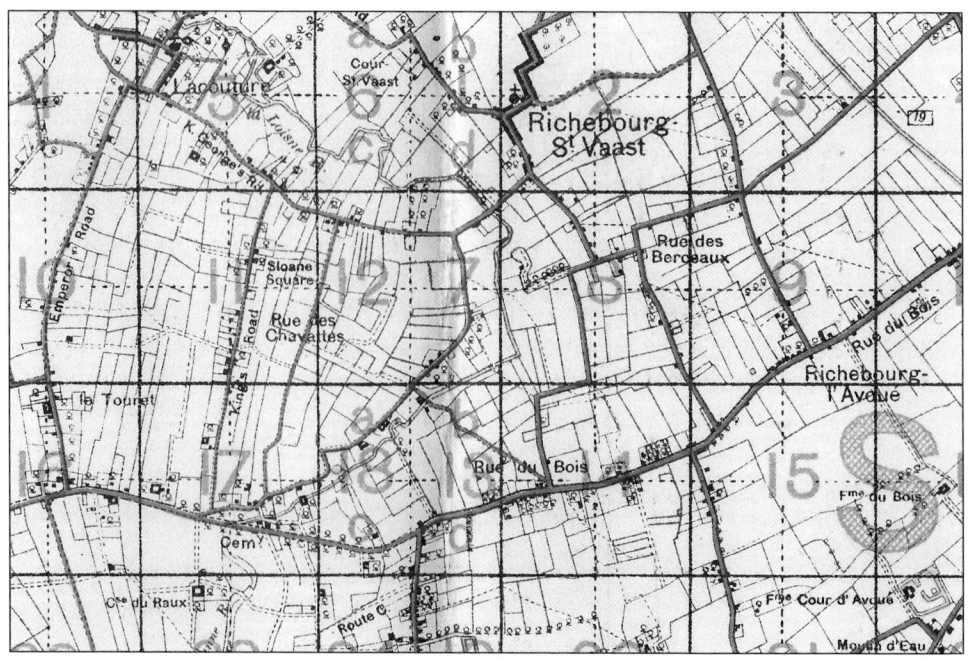

Detail from a trench map (Béthune Combined Sheet 36A S.E., 36 S. W., 36B N.E., 36C N.W.). The Kings Road area is in squares 11 and 17 above.

On the evening of 15 March the Bantams filed out of the trenches, down the communication trench that they had just completed, handing their steel helmets over to the relieving 18th Lancashire Fusiliers. Lieutenant Frank Watson was wounded by a stray bullet during the relief. They marched back to reserve billets in what was called the King's Road area, about 3 miles back from the front line.

> Having received a bullet wound to the chest, Lieutenant Frank Watson was invalided back to England and would spend the next two months in the ex-Empress Eugenie's Hospital in Farnborough. Apparently he considered that he owed his life to the silver hip flask that he had been carrying in his breast pocket when he was shot. The bullet had hit the flask and been deflected. According to his daughter, Captain Watson dined with the former Empress Eugenie (the 90-year-old widow of Emperor Napoleon III, who lived in exile in England after the Franco-Prussian War) while he was convalescing. She was so intrigued by the story of the hip flask that had saved his life that she presented him with a new one bearing her crest. Returning to service for a second time (despite the fact that the wound to his chest was still weeping), and promoted to captain, Frank Watson was with the 22nd Manchester Battalion when he died, aged 27, in April 1917. Accounts indicate that he was injured while leading his men in an attack. Though seriously wounded, he tried to go on, only to be hit a second time. His loyal orderly then made an attempt to dress Captain Watson's wounds, and was himself killed in the process. Frank Watson was from Walton, Liverpool. A former Liverpool Institute Boy, in 1914 he was working for the Treasurer's Department of the Mersey Docks & Harbour Board. At the start of the war he volunteered as a private with the 17th Liverpool Pals. He was gazetted to the Manchester Regiment in January 1915 and posted to the 23rd Battalion. Captain Watson is buried in St Leger Cemetery, south of Arras.

If the Manchesters were looking forward to some peace during their time in reserve, it was not quite to be. On 18 March their billets were shelled. Six men were wounded. There was neither peace – nor rest – in reserve it seemed, because the Manchesters were regularly employed on working party duties during this week. The Bantams were now learning the rhythms of trench warfare. John Duffield reflected:

> Trench warfare was humdrum to a degree. You went up for so many days and you went out and another lot took your place. In that period out, theoretically, you were resting, but very often half of them were up on working parties, repairing broken barbed wire and repairing trenches, ready for them to take over when they came back again.[5]

Captain Frank Watson. *Liverpool Echo*, 11 April 1917.

On 21 March two men on one of those working parties were severely wounded.

> Private Thomas Herbert Wilkinson died of wounds on 22 March 1916. He was from Rusholme, Manchester, and aged 26. He is buried at St Venant Communal Cemetery, the site of a Casualty Clearing Station, some 12 miles to the rear of Richebourg-l'Avoué.
>
> Private Cecil Leech died of wounds on 26 March 1916. He was from Rusholme, Manchester, and aged 23. He is buried in Abbeville Communal Cemetery. The dead from the three hospitals in the vicinity were buried at Abbeville. A notice placed in the *Manchester Evening News*, 26 March 1917, by Cecil Leech's family read:
>
>> One of the first to answer the call,
>> For those he loved he gave his all;
>> Somewhere in France in a soldier's grave
>> Lies dear Cecil amongst the brave.

On 25 March the Manchesters moved on to a place called Paradis. Given the weather on that day, the name can hardly have seemed apt. 'The weather was execrable!' *The History of the 35th Division* recorded. 'A cold wind accompanied by sleet, snow, and much mud made the change of position very disagreeable.'[6] Major General Pinney's diary was also noting the heavy snow. 'Please God we won't be here in winter again!' he would write at the start of April.[7] But, whatever the slog of the journey, Paradis was to the north-west, back up towards Calonne, and the move away from the front must have had some appeal.

On 26 March the officers of the 104th Brigade were summoned to 'the school' in Paradis to receive an address from Major General Pinney. Once again, Edmund Blunden had passed through this locality and left a descriptive record of it. A couple of months after the Manchesters moved on, Blunden was sent to take charge of the equipment of a bombing school in 'a little place called Paradis'. The bombing school operated from the outbuildings of a chateau – it seems likely that this was the same 'school' in which the Bantams' officers were now receiving their lecture. Blunden wrote of 'a tender and charming life' in Paradis; he takes walks down tree-lined lanes and spends his evenings being sung to in drawing-rooms. The war is not that far away, though, and Blunden describes the night-time pyrotechnics that he witnessed from the windows of the chateau, 'the incessant phantasms of flares red and white and green ascending and descending a few kilometres off in the eastward darkness'. Bernard Montgomery, not quite the romancer, called Paradis 'a very smelly little straggling village'.[8]

Meanwhile, the men remained in rest billets in the locality. There the work was lighter, but still it was work and not *entirely* rest. C.E. Montague recalled that 'Rest' generally, 'did not wholly wind up in most of the men the spring that had run down while they were in the line. And then the division would go again into the line, and the old cycle be worked through once more.'[9] '"Rest" is an official joke,' Eustace Maxwell wrote.[10]

On 28 March the Battalion was shifting northward again, this time to billets in Sailly-sur-la-Lys, a rest area for troops who were imminently to move back into the line. On 1

April Pinney inspected the 23rd Battalion and highly complimented the men's smart turn out.[11] Sailly – and the weather – were now more to Bernard Montgomery's taste. He wrote to his mother: 'Here for the last week it has been the most glorious summer weather and my glass has been higher than I have ever seen it before. Brilliant sunshine all day long and quite hot. I have discarded my woolly waistcoat, as it has been so hot!'[12]

On 4 April the Bantams marched back towards the front, this time to a section of the line due north of Fromelles (square 10 on the map below). As they moved into these trenches, relieving the 19th Durham Light Infantry, it was remarked that the enemy was quiet. But it would not remain so for long. This might be regarded as a 'nursery sector' but it was about to become amply apparent that it was not without dangers. At 'Stand To' the following morning one man was killed and another wounded by rifle fire. The next day, 6 April, a sniper wounded four men and another man was injured by a trench mortar.

Private John Clegg was killed in action on 5 April 1916. He was from Ashton-on-Mersey, Cheshire, aged 22. He is buried in Rue-Petillon Military Cemetery, Fleurbaix, south-west of Armentières. Many of the men buried in Fleurbaix died of wounds in the dressing station that was located in the buildings adjoining the cemetery. The cemetery was enlarged after the Armistice and graves were concentrated here from the surrounding area.

Private William Greenlees died of wounds on 8 April 1916. He was aged 21 and from Midlothian. He is buried in Merville Communal Cemetery.

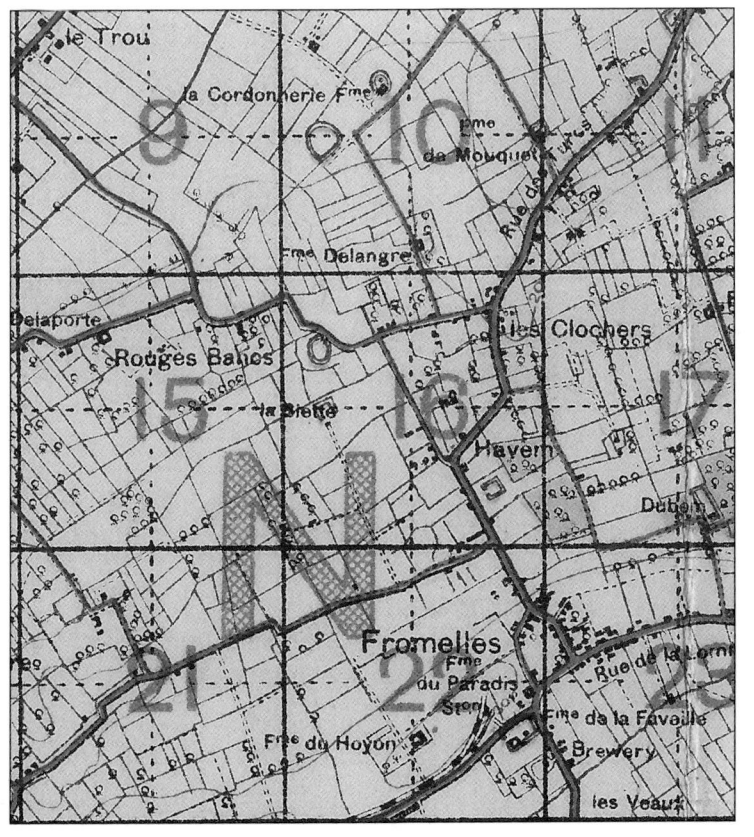

Detail from a trench map (Béthune Combined Sheet 36A S.E., 36 S.W., 36B N.E., 36C N.W.) showing square N 10.

On the night of 6/7 April patrols were sent out 'for instructional purposes'. There were twelve patrols of one officer plus two or three men and they went over the top in turn, each remaining out for around an hour. The battalion War Diary records that one man suffered shell shock during the night and two officers (Lieutenant Rose and Second Lieutenant Fitzgerald) and one man were 'wounded by smashed periscopes' (presumably they were injured by broken glass?).

On the 8th the battalion was relieved by the 18th Lancashire Fusiliers and moved back into support billets. They were not far behind the line, but at least the weather was being kind. Bernard Montgomery was studying the movements of his barometer and writing home on 10 April:

We have had delightfully fine weather here for the last week with my glass standing very high. But today it is very wet and the glass is going down. Sunday was a lovely day; it has been the same nearly every Sunday we have had. When up in the line you never know which day is Sunday, except that it is generally fine.[13]

On 11 April the Manchesters watched as six Zeppelins passed over their billets, flying in a southerly direction. April had seen an increase in artillery activity by both sides; this fact was brought home (literally) to the Manchesters as, once again, their billets were shelled. The Divisional History records that during April 1916 the artillery of the 35th Division fired around 5,500 rounds and the enemy about 1,000 less. There was considerable damage to wire and parapets and working parties were active on both sides over the course of the month.[14]

There was growing concern around this period as to how much information the Germans seemed to be able to get hold of regarding the movements in the Allied lines. It was a subject of considerable speculation within the headquarters of 104th Brigade and spies were suspected to be active in the locality. Bernard Montgomery had his own theories – and solutions. He wrote:

There are a lot of French people living quite close up behind the line, and a considerable number of Belgian refugees. I am sure a lot of these latter are spies; they probably get their information back by means of pigeons. No-one is allowed to use homing pigeons except ourselves. In our last billet we found the owner of the house kept pigeons; so we trapped them at night and made a pigeon pie![15]

On 12 April the 23rd Battalion moved back into the line. Now regarded as having accumulated some experience, it was the Bantams' turn to act as instructors. Australian units were starting to arrive on the Western Front by April 1916 and some now found themselves attached to the 35th Division to 'receive instruction in trench warfare as carried out in France'.[16]

Six officers and twenty-four NCOs of the 1st Battalion of the 1st Brigade of the Australian army were now attached to the 23rd Manchesters. On their first day in the trenches two men were injured when a dugout collapsed. On the 15th, then, there was a change over and a company of the 2nd Battalion of the 1st Brigade of the Australian Expeditionary Force (AEF) came in for instruction. Certainly there seems to have been no lack of instructive activity going on at this time. As the second party of Australians arrived, two men were injured by shrapnel. The following day, four men (including Captain T.H. Dixon of the Manchesters) were wounded by rifle grenades and one sentry was killed 'by chance shot'. On the 16th the battalion was relieved and moved back to support billets.

> Private Frederick Wigg was killed in action on 15 April 1916. He was from Moston, Manchester, aged 23. He is buried in Rue-Petillon Military Cemetery, Fleurbaix.
> Private Fred Howard died of wounds on 18 April 1916. He was from Littleborough and aged 23. He is buried in Merville Communal Cemetery.
> Private Arthur Booth died of wounds on 22 April 1916. He was from Manchester. He is buried in Calais Southern Cemetery.

On 16 April the Battalion War Diary had noted that Captain Dixon was 'slightly wounded' by a rifle grenade. His injuries were sufficiently serious, though, that he would be shipped back to London for treatment. Captain Dixon would return to France; he was killed in August 1918, still aged only 25, while serving with the 12th Manchester Battalion. He is buried in Delville Wood Cemetery, Longueval.

MANCHESTER OFFICER'S WOUND.

Captain T. H. Dixon, of the Manchesters, whose name appeared in Tuesday's official casualty list among the wounded, is at Lady Northcliffe's hospital in London. It is stated that his injury is not serious. The eldest son of Mr. and Mrs. H. C. Dixon, of Berne Cottage, Heaton Moor, he is twenty-two years of age. He was educated at Hulme Grammar School, Whalley Range, Mill Hill School, and Caius College, Cambridge. He held the rank of sergeant in the O.T.C. at Mill Hill, and joined the Manchester Regiment as second lieutenant in December, 1914.

His younger brother, Second Lieutenant Alfred C. Dixon, of the Lancashire Fusiliers and brigade bombing officer, was reported "missing and wounded" in February, and his fate is uncertain.

Manchester Evening News, 27 April 1916.

Some reshuffling of command was taking place around this time. On 14 April Brigadier General Mackenzie left the 104th Brigade and returned to England; it seems that he was making way for a younger man. Montgomery wrote home:

> I am sorry to say that General Mackenzie is being sent back to England. They say he is too old to command a brigade out here; I think myself they are right. He is 56 and is old fashioned and out of date in most things he does; a younger, more modern, man is really wanted. He is a very nice man, quite charming, but that of course has nothing to do with it![17]

Mackenzie had just recommended Montgomery for a promotion. Montgomery noted: 'But as he was himself given the sack and sent back to England the following week – nothing came of it!!!'[18] Mackenzie was replaced by the 42-year-old and newly promoted Brigadier General James Walter Sandilands (formerly Commanding Officer of the 7th Cameron Highlanders). Montgomery described Sandilands as 'a first-class officer from whom I learned a great deal'.[19] It seems that Sandilands took Montgomery under his wing and made a protégé of him. In 1945 Montgomery would write a private letter to Sandilands, telling him that he was 'the best general I ever served under'. Sandilands would remain with the 35th Division until the end of the war and would go on to write a history of the 104th Brigade.[20]

Portrait of Sandilands taken from his own book, *A Lancashire Brigade in France* (1919).

On 19 April the 23rd Manchesters handed over to the 1st Battalion of the 1st Australian Brigade and moved back to Neuf-Berquin, north-east of Calonne. The next day they marched south, 6 miles or so, to the hamlet of Bois de la Fosse (just north of Vieille Chapelle) where they were inspected by their new Brigade Commander, Brigadier General Sandilands, and would remain in rest billets for the next week. Here they were about 4 miles behind the line and Bernard Montgomery was discarding his winter layers. 'We are having the most beautiful weather now,' he wrote home. 'It is really quite hot and I have discarded the heavy top boots I have worn all the winter.'[21]

On 28 April the Manchesters moved back into the line, taking over a stretch of trenches between Neuve Chapelle and Richebourg-l'Avoué (squares 5 and 10 on the map overleaf). In March 1915 the British had launched a major attack and broke through at Neuve

Ruins of the church, Neuf-Berquin.

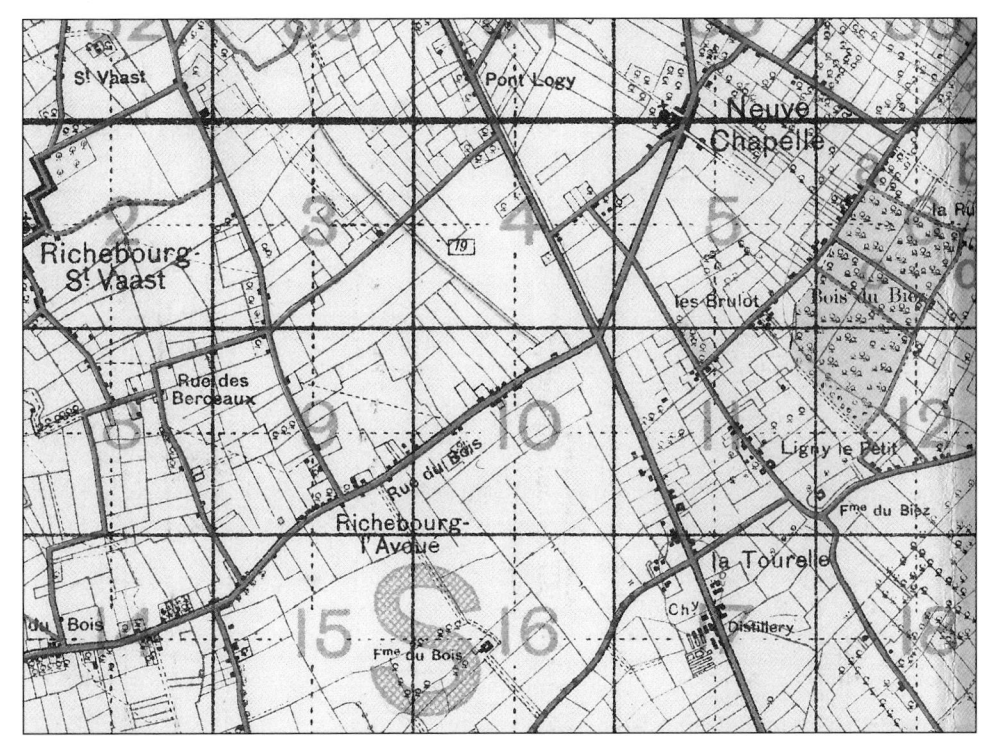

Detail from a trench map (Béthune Combined Sheet 36A S.E., 36 S.W., 36B N.E., 36C N.W.) showing square S5 and S10.

Chapelle. It was in this action that Major General Pinney had distinguished himself. The ruined village seems now to have been the source of some fascination for the Bantams. The derelict 1915 trenches had a gloomy allure. Montgomery recorded:

> Neuve Chapelle is really a most extraordinary sight. At one time it must have been a quite pretty little village; now there is nothing to be seen there at all. The whole village has been razed to the ground and is nothing but a heap of rubble; not even the walls of the houses are left standing. Our line goes about 200 yards in front of what was the village.[22]

On 30 April Pinney went up to the trenches near Neuve Chapelle, and, with Sandilands, toured around and spoke to the Manchesters in the line.[23]

On 2 May a party of three officers and eighteen other ranks advanced as far as the enemy wire at Les Brulot and bombed a machine gun on the parapet. Having achieved its aims, the party returned to the Allied lines with just two men having suffered slight injuries.[24]

This was the first raid that the 23rd Manchesters had carried out. Between December 1915 and the end of May 1916 the British army carried out sixty-three raids, the parties involved ranging from groups of just ten men to 200. A magazine of the era conveyed the excitement of raiding:

Ruins of Neuve Chapelle.

362. NEUVE-CHAPELLE. — Le Christ des Tranchées

The iconic 'Christ of the Trenches'. Portuguese troops arrived in Neuve Chapelle in April 1917. They took the figure of Christ, which had fallen from the crucifix on the Armentières–Aubers crossroads, into their trenches. The figure was eventually taken back to Portugal and incorporated into a memorial to the Portuguese Expeditionary Force.

> This form of nocturnal activity was initiated by a few daring spirits, lightly armed and clad, and with blackened faces, stealing across No Man's Land, creeping through hostile wire, and falling like a bolt from the blue upon the enemy as he moved peacefully about his trenches.
>
> Then, after causing general alarm and disturbance, distributing bombs among all the dug-outs with easy reach, and killing any foe who attempted to resist, the raiders would vanish into the night, taking prisoners and booty with them.[25]

Wrist watches would be synchronised. Faces would be camouflaged and close-fighting kit pushed into pockets. There was a real possibility of coming face-to-face with the enemy and an element of daring involved. Over the course of 1916 raids became more organised and on a larger scale. These were not off-the-cuff, loose attacks; they generally had specific objectives and were precisely planned. The logistics, tactics and timings would be well worked out and rehearsed in advance, with the intention that a minimum amount of time would be spent in the enemy trenches. Every member of the party would understand his specific role in the raid and how long it ought to take to complete.

Brigadier General Sandilands congratulated the men of the 23rd Manchesters who had taken part in the raid. It was deemed a 'complete success'. Enterprises of this sort were generally looked on favourably by commanders. Raids were a valuable means of obtaining information about the enemy; raiding parties were always on the lookout for documents, parts of uniforms that might identify the enemy unit and, if possible, they would take a prisoner. These endeavours also had an important psychological function as well; they were regarded as being likely to maintain the offensive spirit among the troops – as well as keeping the enemy tense and on his nerves.

'This is a pretty lively place,' Bernard Montgomery wrote home. He was feeling that his luck might be 'in', though:

> There is always a fair amount of shelling going on by day; at night it is very lively indeed, rifle and machine-gun fire going on most of the night. Our casualties have been wonderfully small considering the place we are in. I have been very lucky myself in escaping the places most shelled. There are 2 ways up to the trenches and they nearly always shell the particular one which I am not using at that time.[26]

On 3 May the 23rd Manchesters might have thought themselves lucky too, as they were relieved and moved back to support billets at Croix-Barbée (La Croix Barbet on modern maps), some 3 miles or so behind the lines. The weather was on their side too. Montgomery was shedding more layers of clothing and wrote to his mother on 7 May:

> We have been having the most perfect weather up to today. Real summer weather and I have got into thin underclothes in spite of the motto 'Cast ne'er a clout'. It would not have been possible to have worn winter things, it was so hot. Today it is raining hard; it is rather a good thing as it was getting rather oppressive and the dust wanted laying.[27]

Detail from a trench map (Béthune Combined Sheet 36A S.E., 36 S.W., 36B N.E., 36C N.W.) showing the location of Croix-Barbeé.

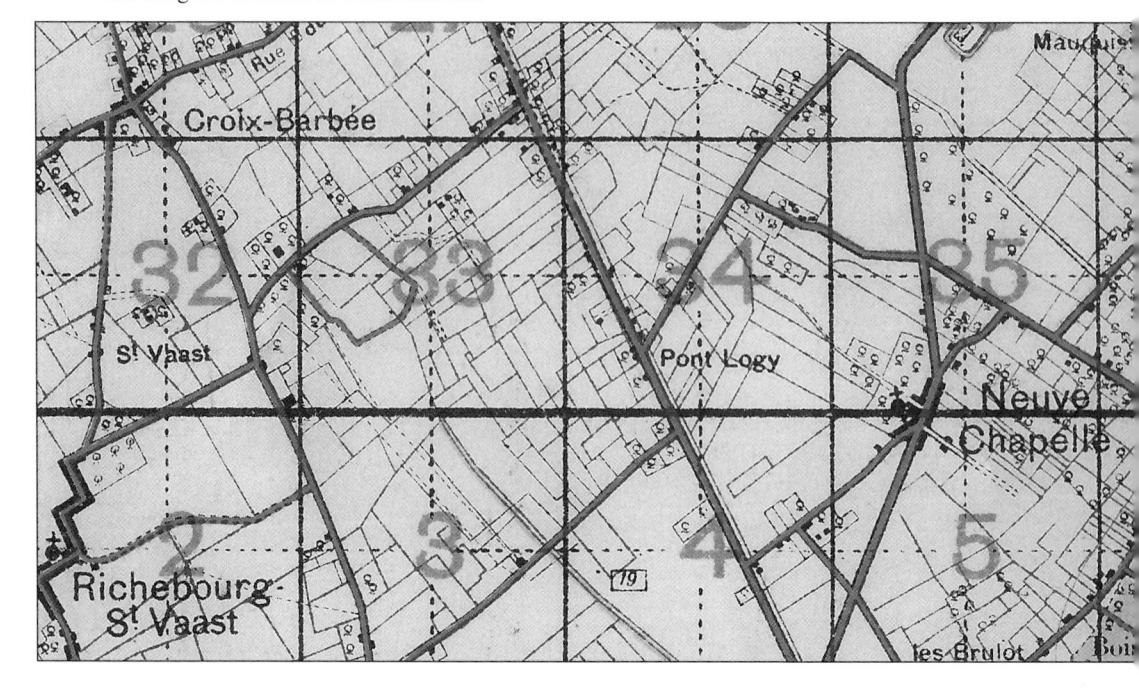

Croix-Barbée.

On 6 May the battalion returned to the trenches that they had vacated four days earlier. The next day, Pinney and Sandilands did another tour of inspection and saw the Manchesters in the line. Another raid was in the planning.[28]

On the night of 8 May, then, a party of one officer and sixteen men crawled out across no-man's-land. This time, though, the Manchesters' raiding efforts came to be less successful. As the party was approaching the enemy wire, suddenly shells were tearing down. In the noisy and chaotic minutes that followed it became apparent that two men of the raiding party had been killed and nine were wounded. Although the Divisional History states that the raiding party came under '*hostile* artillery fire' (the emphasis is mine), a note in Pinney's diary suggests a different course of events. On 9 May Pinney wrote: 'Sandilands reported last night's operation almost successful – our Raiding Patrol of Lt Rose and 12 Manchesters got a mat on bosh wire when one of *our* shells knocked out 9 of the 12.'[29] (Again, the emphasis is mine.) In the confusion that ensued, the Manchesters struggled to bring in their casualties. As the wounded men were being dragged back to the line, so shells were falling here too. The Allied trenches were now subjected to severe retaliatory shelling. In the chaos of noise and erupting earth, another seven men were killed and fifteen wounded. The casualties included Major Bannatyne, who had been temporarily in command of the battalion. It had been a costly night. In addition to the physical casualties, five men had to be withdrawn from the line suffering from shell shock. 'The night of the "Strafe" will never be forgotten,' Percy Gidley would write home. 'No one who has not been in or seen a heavy "Strafe" could realise, even in their worst imagination of Hades at loggerheads, the grim, grave, and death-dealing reality of one.'[30]

The next day Pinney went up to the line and met with Sandilands and Montgomery. He spoke with Lieutenant Rose and the surviving men who had gone out with him on the patrol. Pinney congratulated all of those who had been involved in bringing in the casualties and told them that he would do everything that he could to see that they were recognised and rewarded for their actions. Lieutenant Rose, clearly becoming conspicuous for bravery and patrolling stealth, would not this time be rewarded with a medal, but the courage of two other ranks (Private Andrew Lee and Private William Townley) and two NCOs (Sergeant Arthur Hare and Corporal James O'Connor) would be formally acknowledged. Sergeant Hare, despite being wounded himself, determinedly carried other wounded men to safety, going back out into no-man's-land four times. In the words of Percy Gidley, Hare 'did a great and noble work'.[31] Private Lee, though wounded by shrapnel in both knees, also helped other wounded men to safety. At one point, during the bombardment, the telephone wires were cut. Corporal James O'Connor, a signaller, took charge of a party of linesmen, and, 'at great personal risk', worked to restore communications. Private Townley, a fellow signaller, kept up his post and maintained connections, despite the signallers' dugout being hit by a shell. All four men would be awarded the Military Medal. In June the Manchester papers reported that General Sir Charles Monro (GOC First Army) held a parade of units from various Bantam battalions and presented decorations. The 'great gallantry and devotion to duty' of the men was recognised.[32]

> Private James Blagg was killed in action on 8 May 1916. He was from Beswick. He is buried in St Vaast Post Military Cemetery, in Richebourg-l'Avoué.
>
> Private Harry Clarke was killed in action on 8 May 1916. He was aged 36 and from Rusholme He is buried in St Vaast Post Military Cemetery, in Richebourg-l'Avoué.
>
> Lance Corporal Alexander Lynch was killed in action on 8 May 1916. He was from Harpurhey. He is buried in St Vaast Post Military Cemetery, in Richebourg-l'Avoué.
>
> Private Joseph Millward was killed in action on 8 May 1916. He was from Salford. He is buried in St Vaast Post Military Cemetery, in Richebourg-l'Avoué.
>
> Private Patrick Joseph O'Brien was killed in action on 8 May 1916. He was from Hulme. He is buried in St Vaast Post Military Cemetery, in Richebourg-l'Avoué.
>
> Private James Spellman was killed in action on 8 May 1916. He was from Ancoats. He is buried in St Vaast Post Military Cemetery, in Richebourg-l'Avoué.
>
> Private Samuel Worrall was killed in action on 8 May 1916. He was from Blackburn. He is buried in St Vaast Post Military Cemetery, in Richebourg-l'Avoué.
>
> Lance Corporal John Frederick Smith died of wounds on 8 May 1916. He was from Rusholme. He is buried in Merville Communal Cemetery.
>
> Private Abram Howarth was killed in action on 10 May 1916. He was from Royton. He is buried in Merville Communal Cemetery
>
> Private Edward Drew was killed in action on 12 May 1916. He was from Hulme. He is buried in St Vaast Post Military Cemetery, in Richebourg-l'Avoué.
>
> Major James Fitzgerald Bannatyne died of his wounds on 14 May 1916. He is buried in Merville Communal Cemetery.

On 13 May Pinney rode over to Merville to visit Major Bannatyne, who was in hospital there. Pinney's diary records: 'Found Bannatyne dying but did not know it – reading letters out from his mother – he talked of coming back soon.' He died the next day.³³

In the days following these events Percy Gidley wrote a letter to the *Morecambe Visitor*, published on 19 July 1916, to tell friends there how 'Bobs' Own' were progressing in France.

> Another well-known young Devonshire officer has died as the result of wounds. We refer to Captain J. F. G. Bannatyne, of the 11th Hussars, who up to recently had been temporarily acting as major in the Manchester Regiment. Deceased was the only son of the late Mr. J. F. G. Bannatyne and Mrs. Bannatyne, of Haldon House. At one time he was attached to the Royal 1st Devon Imperial Yeomanry. During his military career he showed great promise, which is proved by the fact that, although only 32 years of age, he was appointed to one of the senior positions in the Manchester Regiment. Captain Bannatyne was exceedingly popular among a wide circle of friends in the neighbourhood of Exeter, and they will extend to the family the greatest sympathy in their bereavement. Perhaps deceased will be best remembered locally for his splendid riding at the point-to-point races in connexion with the East Devon Hunt. He also played cricket, and often represented Haldon House where his much-beloved father so hospitably entertained all who took part in matches there.

We have made progress on our 'foreign tour,' and to quote the words of one of our officers, the Manchester Bantams have 'done all that was expected of them and proved that they are worthy to hold any line'.

Nobody can get over the smiles and good humour that made us famed at Morecambe. In spite of all trials we still have that patent smile with us. We have gone through and had many severe hardships to undergo, but we are through with flying colours. We did all we were asked to do and gave Fritz something to remember us by. In doing that, unfortunately, many of our chums have forfeited their all, and many have been wounded.

Major Bannatyne had been a captain in the 11th (Prince Albert's Own) Hussars prior to his appointment to the 23rd Manchesters. He was aged 32 and from Devon. Reporting his death, the *Exeter and Plymouth Gazette* (19 May 1915) said that he had been an 'exceedingly popular' young man and had a military career of 'great promise'.

Of course we could not expect to get off scot free, and we who are left are fully prepared to 'keep on keeping on', as a Morecambe friend advised us.

The night of the 'Strafe' will never be forgotten. Our bombers, who had already been complimented for successful raids, went 'over the top', dodged the Hun sentries, or whatever patrol they may have had out, reached the German wire and prepared for all. The 'Strafe' soon commenced, and no one who has not been in or seen a heavy 'Strafe' could realise, even in their worst imagination of Hades at loggerheads, the grim, grave, and death-dealing reality of one.

It was in this great scrap that the first Bantam honours were gained. Sergt Major Hare, Corpl. Signaller Connor, Signr. Pte. Townley and Pte. A. Lee won the Military Medal and I will venture to explain how they deservedly won the laurels.

When the German shells burst amongst our bombers on the German parapets Sergt. Hare promptly essayed to carry wounded to safety and did a great and noble work. He was wounded whilst displaying this bravery. Pte. Lee, although wounded in each knee, did likewise and in addition refused the aid of stretcher bearers, as he was aware they were fully taxed. Corpl. Connor and Pte. Townley at this stage were in their dug-out (used as Signallers' Headquarters) when a big shell came through and killed one man, yet they kept to their 'phone and duty all the while.

We are proud of them. All who took part on that memorable night did grand and are worthy of every praise.

On 8 May 1916, during the bombardment, the telephone wires were cut. Corporal James O'Connor took charge of a party of linesmen, and, 'at great personal risk', worked to restore communications.

James O'Connor was the son of a music-hall performer and grew up in Hulme, Manchester. In 1914 he was working as a packer in a city warehouse. He joined the 23rd Manchester Battalion in November 1914, at the age of 19 (height 5ft 2in, chest expansion 34½in). O'Connor joined the Signal Section and was quickly promoted – to lance corporal in June 1915 and to corporal in November. He would be promoted to sergeant in August 1916.

O'Connor was demobilised in 1919 (by that time serving with the 18th Divisional Signals Company RE). However, prior to returning to Manchester, he met and married a French woman, Prudence Laure Griselle. In 1920 O'Connor returned to France, taking a job as a caretaker and gardener for the Imperial War Graves Commission at the war cemetery in Warloy-Baillon (Somme). He would be promoted to Head Gardener in 1931, and, in 1935, take charge of a group of cemeteries around Cormicy in the Marne area. In 1936, with his wife in poor health, O'Connor returned to the England. A letter from the IWGC, at the time of James O'Connor's resignation, attests that he was a man of 'excellent character', 'an experienced gardener, a useful propagator and a good planter who has always carried out his duties in an entirely satisfactory manner'. Back in Manchester, he was employed by the Corporation Parks Department. In 1964 O'Connor attended a dinner at Manchester Town Hall held to celebrate the fiftieth anniversary of the formation of the Manchester City battalions. He died in 1966.[34]

Passing through Richebourg St Vaast just a couple of months later, Francis Charles Lewis of the 2/5th Battalion Gloucestershire Regiment would write:

Many famous regiments had done duty there, from the Guards to the Bantams. The numerous graves in and about the line gave testimony to this. Although the defences were very fragile and scanty, there was a feeling of permanence here which we were not to meet with again and one had the feeling that everything was very old, presumably this was because life itself was short.[35]

On 10 May the 23rd Battalion Manchester Regiment again returned to support billets at Croix-Barbée; and then on the 14th moved back to Fosse, where they spent a week in rest billets. There Pinney was amused to observe the Corps Commander, Lieutenant General Richard Haking, inspecting the Manchesters. 'He tap-tapped his boot with cane in his right hand, leaning heavily with his left on the bayonet of the man he was questioning.' It seems that when presented with an enquiry as to their well-being, the Lancashire men did not hold back in giving their opinions.[36]

On 22 May the battalion moved back into the line, once again taking over a sector near the Ferme du Bois. One man was killed by rifle fire and three men were slightly wounded (including Second Lieutenant Fitzgerald who was 'accidentally wounded by a very light pistol'). Otherwise this seems to have been a fairly quiet stint. On the 26th, relieved by the 20th Lancashire Fusiliers, they moved back to the support billets at Le Touret and King's Road.

> Corporal John Albert Sykes died of wounds on 27 May 1916. He was from Rochdale and aged 29. He is buried in Merville Communal Cemetery.

On 28 May Major Eustace Lockhart Maxwell assumed command of the 23rd Manchesters. Major Bannatyne had been in temporary command, standing in for Lieutenant Colonel Smith on the grounds of the latter being in ill-health. Maxwell, aged 38, had formerly been a captain in the Indian Cavalry (11th King Edward's Own Lancers – Probyn's Horse). In November 1915 he had transferred and been appointed a major within the 19th Durham Light Infantry (106th Brigade, 35th Division). There Maxwell had developed a respect and liking for the Bantam soldiers.

Maxwell wrote to his family that Lieutenant-Colonel Smith had been '"winnowed out" on the score of being "sick"'. He went on:

> 'Sick' however is a euphemism for inefficiency plus old age, so my transfer is presumably permanent until such time as I am found wanting. Whatever the C.O.'s failings may be, want of generosity is not amongst them; it must have been very hard on him to hand over to an unknown stranger – a cavalry soldier at that, which is generally a little resented by the true foot-slogger – but from his behaviour one might almost have thought that I was doing him a favour.[37]

Then Lieutenant Maxwell, with a group of officers from the Bengal Lancers. Photograph from an album created as a 'Souvenir of the Jubilee of the King Edward's Own Lancers (Probyn's Horse) Rawalpindi 1907'.

Given the outcome of Bannatyne's brief tenure, Smith may well have been happy to hand over the reins. Whatever his impression of his predecessor, Maxwell seems initially to have been somewhat alarmed by the men that he must now command. What first struck Maxwell about the 23rd Manchesters was their cockiness. He told his family:

> Of my new battalion I can of course tell you nothing after being with them only 48 hours. Its brigade staff told me, however, that its men are about the best in the division – I mentally reserved the Durhams – and that it only wants pulling together to be a first-rate battalion. I hope this is so. Meanwhile the outstanding characteristic of those who belong to it seems to be their extraordinary self-complacency! Esprit de corps is a fine thing, but the satisfaction with which they regard themselves, their battalion, its internal economy, its gallantry, its discipline, its everything else, is almost indecent! If at the end of a month my opinion of them is half as good as their own, I shall think myself uncommonly lucky.[38]

On 29 May the battalion, with its new commander, moved back to the Ferme du Bois sector. They were in for a rather more eventful stint this time – and that gallantry and discipline was about to be tested. In Maxwell's words they were about to experience 'a hot little German attack'.

'Send reinforcements, the Germans have broken through'
The 18th Lancashire Fusiliers held the line of trenches to the Manchesters' immediate left, and, to their left, were the 15th Sherwood Foresters. A report from the latter details that at around 7.20 pm an intense enemy bombardment began on the front line trenches, 'with T.Ms. Rifle Grenades, and guns of all calibres'.

Maxwell was in the Manchesters' front line at the time and remained there observing the action ('until I remembered that I was a C.O. and had better get back to headquarters and the telephone'). He wrote:

> At 7.30 on Tuesday evening there suddenly burst the heaviest bombardment that I have seen. I don't know how many heavy guns the Germans had concentrated upon them, but there was one continuous shattering roar of bursting shells, and in five minutes that part was hidden from us by a dense veil of smoke, black, yellow, white, red – this smoke blew towards the front line and veiled that too, and it was quite impossible to see whether that too was being bombarded.[39]

At 8.00 pm the range of the enemy artillery was lengthened and focused on the support posts. Around 8.15 pm it lengthened again to fire on the reserve line. 'Our own line was much battered but still manned,' the War Diary of the 18th Lancashire Fusiliers notes. 'The men very happy and cheerful but the whole of the line on the left for about four hundred yards was deserted.' Subject to such heavy bombardment, the Sherwood Foresters had withdrawn from a length of trenches. A stretch had been 'completely obliterated'. Trenches were 'smashed down and levelled'. Parapets were breached, and one of the communication trenches took at least four direct hits. Many men were missing. 'Many were blown to pieces,' the report of the 15th Sherwood Foresters went on, 'and it is feared that several lie under the ruins.' Maxwell's account continues:

> Our guns then began to reply – having been slow in getting to work, and they plastered the German trenches over against us and to the left of us – especially my old friend the Boar's Head – with great vehemence. The German counter-batteries at once began to look for our guns, our heavy batteries took it up in reply, and the resulting noise was something worth hearing. The roar of guns, the screaming of shells passing overhead, and the peculiar shattering crack of shells bursting near at hand, would have made a deaf man hear. It was not until a machine gun added its comparatively feeble, but very penetrating voice to the others that I bethought me that I ought to be at headquarters – for the machine gun is usually silent by day, and the fact of it now firing might mean an infantry attack.[40]

At 8.15 pm the enemy barrage had lifted and then intensified on the flanks either side of the evacuated section of trenches. An enemy party now made its move. At 8.30 pm a runner reached the 14th Sherwood Foresters, in the reserve area, with the message from the front line: 'Send Reinforcements, the Germans have broken through'.

Accounts convey a sense of confusion. With the thick shell smoke it was almost impossible to see what was going on in the Sherwood Foresters' trenches. Realising, though, that the enemy had entered the line, a party of the 18th Lancashire Fusiliers, to the south, and a party of Sherwood Foresters, to the north, began to work along the vacated section of trenches. At around 9.30 pm these companies connected and the line was restored. The wounded, who had remained in the trenches when they were evacuated, had been carried away by the Germans. Unexploded bombs and entrenching tools were found in the line.

The enemy bombardment continued until around 11.30 pm. When it finally finished, working parties began repairing breaches and making good the parapets. The 18th Lancashire Fusiliers finally withdrew from the Sherwood Foresters' trenches around 2.30 am. 'Casualties, I regret will be very heavy,' concluded the report of the 15th Sherwood Foresters. 'But the total amount has not yet been ascertained as many men are missing.' Four men of the Manchesters had been injured (two seriously and two slightly) and two men had to be taken out of the line suffering from shell shock.

At 'Stand To' the next morning all was quiet. Parties of enemy were sighted, taking advantage of the misty morning, to examine their wire. They were dispersed with machine-gun fire. All now set to work to repair the damaged portions of the line and to dig out the dead.

'The Divisional Staff thinks that a serious German attack, tho' on a small scale, was nipped in the bud,' Maxwell wrote.[41] There seems to have been a sense that this had been a 'near miss'. Their actions in repelling the attack did the reputation of the Bantams some good. Launcelot Kiggell, Haig's Chief of Staff, sent a message of congratulations to the Corps: 'The Commander-in-Chief is of the opinion that the behaviour of the troops of the 35th Division on the occasion of the action of 30th May was most creditable.'[42]

Maxwell did not like the Ferme du Bois trenches much, he told his family, or at least not the communication trenches. 'The Germans have them both marked off very accurately,' he wrote, 'and amuse themselves by shelling them at unexpected intervals.' Maxwell was finding his own amusement in observing the men of his new battalion. He quickly formed the opinion that the snipers of the 23rd Manchesters were a ruthless and bloodthirsty lot. One of their number had informed him that he had slain five Germans during a particular day, the sniper's cubby-hole having a good view into the German trenches. In response the Germans set to work and deepened the stretch of trench where they had been losing men. The Manchester snipers, it seems, were most disgruntled at this sport-spoiling course of action and complained to Maxwell to that effect. 'The snipers regard their having done so as a grievance and as a piece of characteristically Hunnish conduct.'[43]

The battalion was relieved on the night of the first of June. It was a prolonged and dreary relief. 'That last afternoon in the trenches is really quite a bug bear to the army at large,' Maxwell complained in a letter. 'There is generally a feeling of unsettlement and impatience.' His letter sketches a scene of a typical relief:

> Soon after dark the leading men of the leading company of the relieving regiment come plodding along and sighs of relief accompany predictions as to the time it will take for the last man of the last company to reach his place in the line . . . the newcomers are usually rather bored at the prospect of another four days grind; the outgoers are generally pretty tired; and the earnest efforts at conversation made by both sides are not always successful. This is the worst hour, or hour and a half, of the whole four days, for each minute is as long as two.

It was 'with glad hearts', then, that the Manchesters finally made their way out along the communication trenches, away from the Rue du Bois. The sky, as they departed, was lit by gun flashes in the south 'and our ears filled with the thunders of distant artillery'.[44]

Once again they moved back to the support billets at Le Touret and King's Road. Though they might have withdrawn from the line with some sense of relief, they were still being used on working parties (and sustaining casualties).

Private William Barnett was reported killed in action on 4 June 1916. He was from Oakham, Rutland. He is buried in Le Touret Military Cemetery, Richebourg-l'Avoué.

Sergeant John William Corfield Fowler died of wounds on 4 June 1916. He was aged 21 and from Stockport. He is buried in Béthune Town Cemetery.

Now out of the front line, Eustace Maxwell had time to reflect on the character of his new battalion. His assessment, in a letter home, began with an appraisal of the headquarters staff:

> The Adjutant is a very spry youth from a line battalion, good at his work, and I am told the only man in the regiment who was born a gentleman. The present 2nd in command only returned from leave today, and I know nothing of him except that some years ago he left the regular army with the honourable rank of Colour Sergeant! He is now a Major! . . . The Chaplain is the best of the lot, I think – Irish, very young, rather witty, and evidently much beloved of all ranks. Of the Company officers I have seen too little to know whether I like them or not as men; as officers some of them seem distinctly good, and I hope will prove to be really so on better acquaintance. But, taking things by and large, I think so far I can see that I might have gone to many a worse battalion than this.[45]

On 6 June the Manchesters moved back to the Ferme du Bois sector, taking a company of the 2/7th Worcesters, attached for initiation, forward with them. On the 8th a company of the 2/6th Gloucesters came in for instruction, relieving the Worcesters.

On the night of 10/11 June the Manchesters supported a raid by the 18th Lancashire Fusiliers, who were occupying the trenches to their left. Preparations had been made during the day, with a telephone line being laid out into no-man's-land. The Fusiliers' bombing party went forward at 12.45 am, with the Manchesters ready to provide covering rifle and to make diversionary efforts. Maxwell wrote:

> We 'diverted' like mad, with machine-gun fire, rifle grenades, and musketry, which alarmed the enemy so much that he put down a double barrage on us, one curtain of shells just in rear and another just in front of our trenches. With what else he had to spare from these curtains, him looking for our guns, and from what was happening next door on the left, he pounded our parapet. He breached this in four or five places, but wounded only 1 officer and two men – I dare say we hurt him no more than he hurt us, but anyway we got a rise out of him.[46]

The Fusiliers' raiding party came under shell fire and was forced to withdraw. The raid failed to achieve its aims, but the Manchesters were complimented for their part in it by Major General Pinney as he inspected the men in the reserve line the next day.[47] Maxwell wrote:

> Raids are all the fashion and we ourselves are at present poking about at night looking for a weak place in the enemy wire through which to push a party of stout bombers and their attendant bayonets – bomb and bayonet being as Castor and Pollux in these matters, or as bread and its accompanying butter. We have not found a likely spot yet, but we may do so tonight, when, however, it will be too late to be of use to us during this present tour.[48]

For the last two nights of their tour the weather was bad. They tried to light wood fires in the trenches and then commiserated the men who were relieving them. 'There was such a gale of wind and rain smiting on us,' Maxwell wrote, 'that we felt very sorry for the relieving regiment. The taking over of trenches deep in greasy mud, with torrents of rain falling, is not a very cheerful business.'[49] The Manchesters had done a six-day stint in the line and were not sorry to be coming out.

On the 12th they returned to support billets, again in the Le Touret and King's Road area. Maxwell concluded:

> Our own time has been fairly quiet during this tour – quiet, I mean, as regards everything but noise; of that there is of course plenty, which varies, however, with spells of silence, almost as tho' there were no war. Personally, I like the enemy, that part of him which is in his first trenches, much better when he is noisy than when he is quiet; it is the nervous Hun who makes most noise and does least harm. But when the beast is very quiet one never knows what he is up to.[50]

During this stint in the line Maxwell had taken his 'first offensive act in the Manchesters': he had sacked the Bombing Officer. He explained his actions to his family thus:

> The Bombing Officer is a most important man these days, and only the stoutest hearted sort of youth is required. Our youth was so visibly disconcerted when

invited to make a plan for a business (not exactly a raid, neither) that we thought was to come off about now, but which is after all postponed, that he seemed to be quite the wrong man in the wrong place. Later, after he had reconnoitred the ground over which he was to work with his bombers, and earn glory in himself and his battalion while doing great damage to the king's enemies, he was so palpably frightened at the prospect that he was relieved of his explosive but honourable functions in favour of a better youth, who of course jumped at the job.[51]

There was another youth who was 'jumpy', Maxwell wrote – and who accordingly was receiving some rather austere aversion therapy; he 'is therefore at present being sent out nightly into No Man's Land till his nerves improve'. With these two exceptions, though, Maxwell was pleased with – and amused by – his new battalion. 'I begin to like the Manchesters,' he wrote:

I don't think this is half a bad battalion, and the men are certainly good, and of a good stamp. Pitmen and factory hands mostly, I believe, and of an average age of about 26. They are amusing in their friendly attitude towards their officers; many of them actually dare to wish one 'Good morning,' and I have not yet found any of them who was not ready to enter into conversation.

Maxwell was particularly impressed by the bloodlust of the Battalion's snipers – 'murderous little beasts', as he put it:

The chief sniper here, a corporal, keeps two barbers shops in Manchester, is a perfectly wonderful shot, and cuts the battalion hair when it, and he, are out of the trenches. In fact he is as mild a man as ever (not cut a throat) that sniped a Hun. The murderous little beasts just love their work; I was in a cubby hole the other day with a sniper, and when I spoke of the deal of patience that they need, he merely said, 'It's worth it' and glued his eye once more to his telescope.

Maxwell was also impressed by General Sandilands. 'If I can satisfy him in my new job,' he wrote, 'I'll pat myself on the back.'

We have a most excellent brigadier, who is just the sort that one wants, for he has worked his way up during the war from the command of a company to that of a brigade. He therefore knows exactly the point of view and the difficulties of the battalions in the trenches and understands that the men are sometimes tired . . . one knows that <u>he</u> knows, and that he is thinking for the men. [52]

On 16 June, the Manchesters moved back to reserve billets at Long Cornet (to the north of Béthune) and then to rest billets at Annezin (west of Béthune), where they would remain until the end of the month. The division had now been in the line for four and a half months, 'and so it has earned a rest,' Maxwell wrote, 'all the more so since the

Bantams, in spite of their very serious physical disabilities – those few inches make a great difference in many ways – have made quite a good name for themselves.'[53]

The Bantams' stint in the Richebourg sector was now complete. On leaving the command of XI Corps, the GOC (Lieutenant General Richard Haking) sent a letter to Pinney. It reads:

> On the departure of 35th Division from the XIth Corps, I would be glad if you will convey to all ranks my appreciation of the fine fighting qualities they have displayed since they have been in France. The Division has carried out four successful raids into the enemy's trenches and has developed a fine fighting spirit. . . . I hope in your new surroundings that you will be given the opportunity of defeating the enemy, an opportunity which I know will be welcomed by you all.[54]

> Private William Wilde died of wounds on 19 June 1916, in No. 1 Canadian Hospital in Étaples. The most recent case of a man being wounded, as recorded in the battalion's War Diary, was on 10 June, so presumably Private Wilde was being treated for over a week. He was aged 32. Born at Hollingworth, Cheshire, he worked as a spinner in Harrison's Mill, Stalybridge, and lived in Dukinfield. He left a widow and a child and is buried in Étaples Military Cemetery.

On 19 June Major General Pinney pasted an article – headlined 'Gallant Bantams' – from the *Daily Chronicle* into his Army Diary. The writer, Philip Gibbs, had visited the division the week previously. Gibbs reported that, when the Bantams first came into the trenches, the Germans facing them had called out 'Cock-a-doodle-doo!' 'Well, they don't crow now over the Bantams,' he wrote. 'It is the Bantams who crow over them in No Man's Land.' His article goes on:

> Well, the Bantams have not been long in proving that you can't measure a man's soul with a foot rule. In the trenches at Neuve Chapelle, where the fire steps were raised for them, they endured the ordeal of heavy bombardment with a stoic courage worthy of the most hardened troops, and have shown a fine spirit of initiative and gallantry in attack as well as defence . . .
>
> There are great hearts among these little men, and no giant of six foot three could have shown finer courage, for example, than Private Lee, who was wounded in both legs by shrapnel near Neuve Chapelle, when several of his comrades fell in a night patrol to the enemy's barbed wire. Upon hearing the cry of a wounded friend, he turned back at once, and carried the other Bantam for 80 yards in No Man's Land, until he himself collapsed.
>
> In the same adventure Sergeant Hare, who was also wounded, went back four times into No Man's Land, helping to carry back his comrades.
>
> During an intense bombardment of May 8, when the telephone wires were cut by shell fire, Corporal O'Connor took charge of a party of linesmen, and, at great personal risk, restored all communications at the end of an hour.

On the same night Private W. Townley and Sapper H. E. Holmes were in the signallers' dug out, when a shell blew in the roof and side. Both men were partially buried, but remained at their posts and kept up communication as far as possible until they were rescued and relieved.

It was a night when many of the Bantams shared a real heroism, not losing their nerve, though many of their friends were killed and wounded, and helping each other with great devotion and self-sacrifice . . . It is a pleasure to go among them, as I did yesterday with a General of their division, who has trained them since they were first assembled. They are smart, merry little men, and they came up to the salute as though it were a personal greeting between them and their chief, as it really is and should be.[55]

Annezin, where the battalion was now 'Resting'.

With the division billeted in and about Béthune, a period of sports and parades began. Though Béthune, a headquarters town, had been shelled on and off since 1915, it still roughly looked like and functioned as a town. Edmund Blunden wrote that Béthune was 'a marvellous little town to be found so near the trenches. It was old, it was young; its streets were not of 1916, but its pretty faces were immediate, and the heartiness of ordinary life prevailed.'[56] As Maxwell put it, Béthune was 'considered to be positively metropolitan in its pleasures and excitements'.[57]

Images of Béthune at the end of the war.

During the first two days that they were billeted in the vicinity, large numbers of the men requested passes, keen to sample the pleasures and the pretty faces of Béthune. In order to discourage them from partaking of too many of those delights, though, an effort was made to keep them wholesomely and healthily diverted. Maxwell detailed:

> The men are kept at work all the morning; and the afternoons have been filled so far with football, boxing, and (yesterday) a sort of mild and very amateur mixture of military tournament and sports. More boxing and more football in the coming week, evening concerts, and possibly aquatic sports in the canal, are the grim pleasures imminently in store in the future.[58]

On 23 June General Sir Charles Monro (GOC First Army) presented the Military Medal to those men who had been recommended for it after the raid of 8 May. A telegram to Pinney conveyed his compliments on the appearance of the troops that he had inspected that day: 'The Infantry looked steady in the ranks' Monro observed, 'and showed a good soldier-like spirit.'[59] Maxwell told his family that the men of his battalion had done 'well and bravely' in the May raid. 'They did a very gallant thing,' he wrote.[60]

'We are having most glorious weather out here,' Bernard Montgomery told his mother on 22 June. 'My thin summer coat which I ordered when at home has just arrived and I am very glad to have it. I am sending my thick winter coat home; it is very thick and I won't want it until next winter.' He went on:

> It is very nice being in Rest and right out of the shell area even. We are about 15 miles behind the line. I expect next week they will make us start training again, but for this week we are having a complete rest. The men don't only want a rest from physical fatigues, they want mental rest as well. There is no doubt that they get mentally fatigued and they want to be left alone and allowed to laze about and sleep under the trees etc. They will sleep the whole 24 hours round if they are allowed to.

He added: 'We have got a Horse Show for the Brigade on Saturday afternoon next, and are giving prizes for the best turned out wagons, horses etc. The Massed Bands of the Brigade will play, and if it is fine it ought to be rather amusing.'[61]

The 'Bobs' Own' band was kept busy while they were in the vicinity of Béthune. It must have briefly felt like being back in Morecambe. 'I don't know whether pride at this, or fatigue from so much work, is at present most dominant among the bandsmen,' Maxwell observed.

> Pride, because my predecessor hated them and fed them on curses and neglect; fatigue, because they work morning, noon and night. Their first act of the day begins at Reveille, which the bugles sound off all together (under my window, too); then the drums and bugles march around the billets, blowing great blasts and thumping great thumps, just to get the men out of bed and to show everyone

that we start the day feeling cheery. When the morning parade begins, the band retires to practice. After breakfast it practices again for 3 hours, unless it is wanted for something else, which is usually the case; in the afternoon, it is again wanted, always. At 6 p.m. the band parades with the drums and bugles for guard-mounting, which ceremony I have revived here with all the pomps, vanities, frills, and thrills that are remembered by the ex-colour sergeant-but-present 2nd in command. Frills are not such folly – on the contrary, I think they are of very great value, and never more so than now when men are apt to get slovenly after months in the trenches . . . on the whole I am glad that I am not a bandsman; C.O.'s work is easier.[62]

Maxwell did not enjoy his CO's work so much, though, when it required him politely to applaud endless football matches. He complained of having spent a 'none too amusing afternoon' thus occupied. He wrote to his family:

Association football is never to my mind very interesting to watch, but duty drives one to it pretty frequently these days. Today the battalion team was playing another bantam battalion, and after that the latter's officers played our officers. Both matches ended in a draw, and the proceedings ended with their officers coming to tea with us, and with our team acting as hosts to the opposing team at an imposing feast in which large quantities of tinned salmon were a prominent feature.[63]

While the 23rd Manchesters might not have won the day's football matches, they were presently feeling rather pleased with themselves, Maxwell noted, having won more prizes than any other battalion in the previous day's 'military tournament'. They were also 'simply thirsting for more glory in the boxing line'. Maxwell went on:

We have put up two champions, and have challenged the brigade to find opponents to fight each of them six rounds. You'll really understand what a Bantam is when I tell you that our two heroes weigh respectively 8 stone and 8 stone 10lbs, and are not extraordinary small as Bantams. But it is a lady-like weight, isn't it, for a full-grown British soldier?

After the planned fights, Maxwell had offered to host a meal for the boxers and their seconds ('about eighteen hungry bantams all told'). He informed his sisters:

In discussing this meal with the Sergeant Cook, and while dwelling upon the interesting subject of potatoes, the chef insisted on serving these mashed, on the grounds 'that the lads fair ravish 'em'. I shall not tell you of what other items the meal is to consist, for your mouths would water even more than they do already over the ravished potatoes. But pork will be there, for the British soldier likes it, and tinned lobster, and fruit and custard, and cheese and French bread and butter, and – but there! Now I've told you.

Maxwell did have a point to make with all his tales of band practice, potato ravishing and tinned salmon teas. 'The order of all things is reversed nowadays', he considered. His letter goes on:

> It is the great things that have become ordinary, and the small ones that have become unusual and therefore absorbing. After all, it is really quite a big thing, if judged by ordinary standards, to go to the trenches and stay there for some days; but I fancy that T. Atkins, unless he definitely stops to think, associates the trenches more with the discomfort that he knows he will find there, than with the fact that he may be shot or blown up before the next relief is due. Likewise, if John Bantam is ordered to go and smash Germans in an offensive he will do so with a good heart, meanwhile, he wisely contents himself with speculations as to whether he can last out 3 rounds against the next man, or whether his platoon will win the next football tie.[64]

The brigade horse show was held on 24 June. Maxwell had his brother, Laurence, send over some riders from one of his Indian cavalry battalions. 'The B's were enormously interested,' Maxwell wrote, 'and their little eyes fairly goggled out of their heads.'[65] There were brigade sports too ('here the Batt. won two 1sts & three 2nds out of six events') and a speech from Major General Pinney. John Bantam, it transpired, was about to receive that order. A note in Pinney's diary, on 24 June, states simply: 'Let all men know, the big battle begins.'[66]

It is clear that since at least the middle of June rumour had been rife among the troops that a large-scale British attack was imminent. And, as they relaxed after their brigade sports day, they must have heard the bombardment starting and speculated as to what their part in the 'big battle' would be. 'Your eyes are no doubt fixed firmly upon the newspapers these days,' Maxwell wrote to his family on 25 June, 'for you probably know as well as we that things are about to happen – have, in fact, probably begun to happen . . . We spent much time in wondering what part, if any, the Bantam division will be given.'[67]

Pinney's diary entry for 28 June reads: 'Infantry to stand by to go in tactical trains . . . orders for move after dark issued . . . very heavy rain keeps falling.' On 30 June all leave was stopped.[68]

Poem sent to *Morecambe Visitor*, 28 June 1916, by Private W. Robinson of the 23rd Manchesters:

You will read in your daily papers
Grim stories of shot and shells,
Of the gallant sons of Britain
Out in France and the Dardanelles.
Each paper is full of the Anzacs,
Yet still there is never a word
Of the brave little Manchester Bantams,
The Fighting Twenty-third.

There's many a deed of bravery
Of which you many never hear.
And we only hope that 'groupers'
Will fight like these volunteers.
We were training so hard at Morecambe,
And now in the thick of the fray,
And some will not answer the roll call
Until the Judgement Day.

So just let your praise be divided,
Give honour where it is due,
To the lads who are out in the trenches
Fighting for England and you.
They have sweethearts, and wives, and mothers,
Who anxiously wait their return;
The brave avengers of Belgium,
The Huns a good lesson will learn.

Here's good luck to the people of Morecambe,
Who have also done their bit,
By looking well after the Bantams
And keeping them strong and fit.
So now you conscientious objectors,
Who would rather die than fight,
Just copy the Manchester Bantams,
And join in defending the right.

Chapter 6

Somme: 'The Best Type of Bantams Done In'

On 1 July 1916 Manchester newspapers carried exultant headlines. The *Manchester Evening News* reported that the British had broken into the enemy forward line over a distance of 20 miles, capturing many prisoners. 'The public had for some days been led to believe that we were on the eve of a great advance,' the paper went on, 'and the fact that the British report was so cheering has caused the greatest joy.' British casualties, it was stated, were not heavy. There were 'exuberant demonstrations of delight' in Manchester.[1]

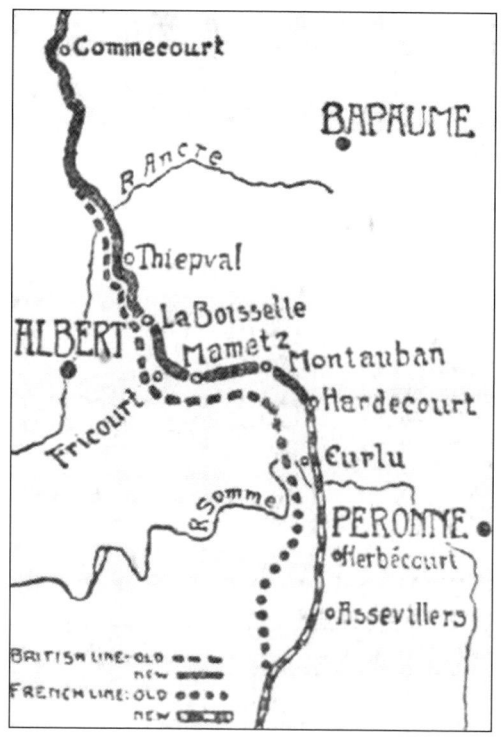

Manchester Evening News, 3 July 1916.

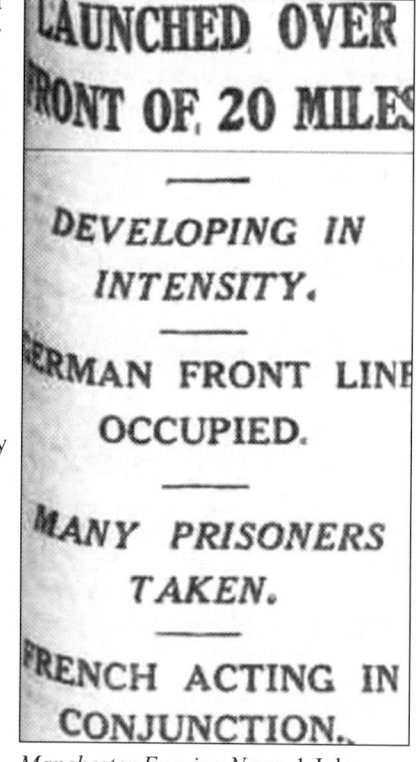

Manchester Evening News, 1 July 1916.

Over the course of the next few days, reports specific to the Manchester battalions began to come in. They had 'done excellent work and covered themselves with glory', Lord Derby told the papers.[2]

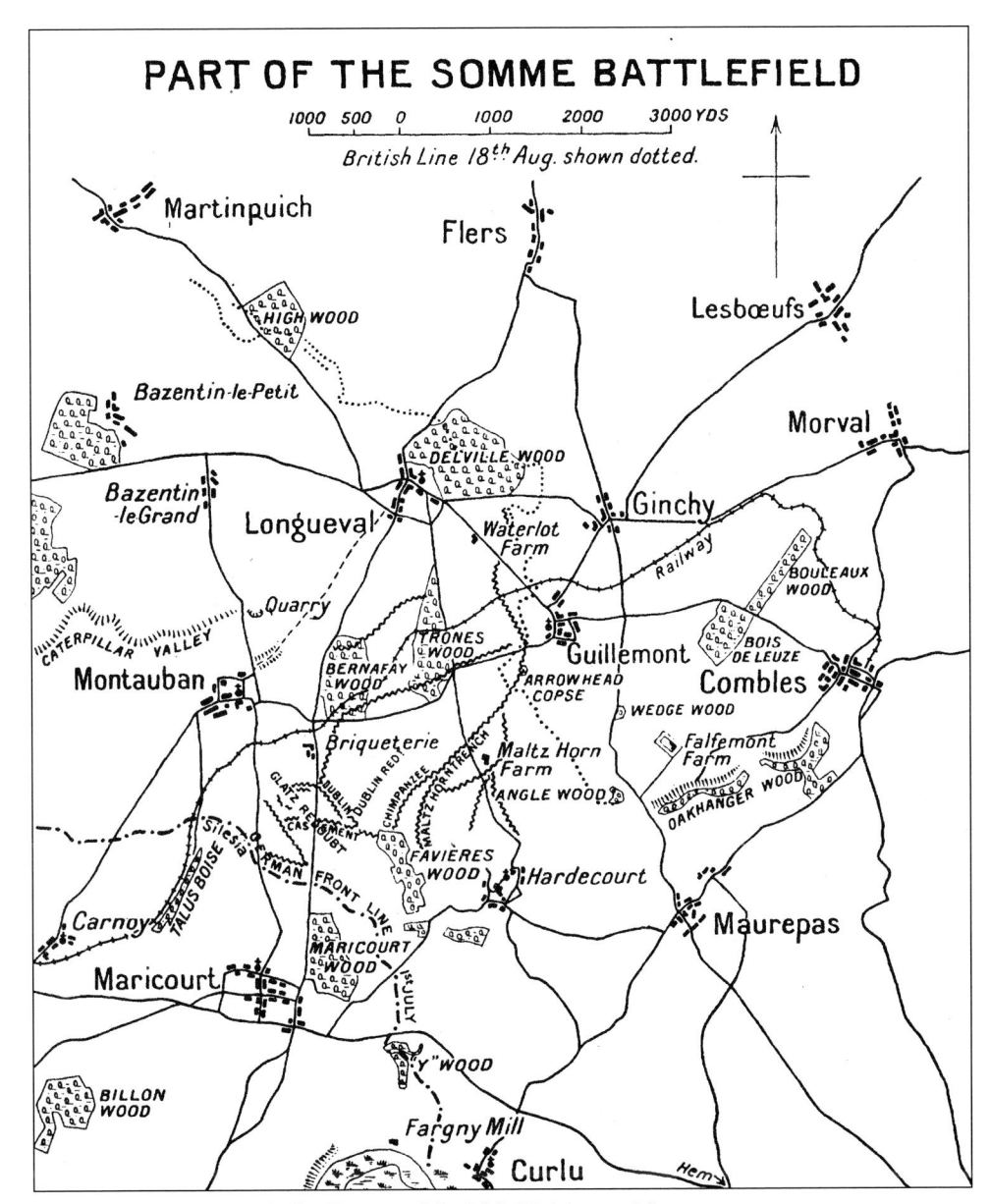

Map taken from Davson, *The History of the 35th Division*, p. 29.

'Lancashire will indeed be proud of them'

The 30th Division, which included four of the Liverpool Pals battalions and the 16th, 17th, 18th and 19th Manchester Battalions, had been on the extreme right flank of the British attack on 1 July. With the Liverpool Pals making the initial assault on the German front lines facing Maricourt, the Manchesters were then tasked with securing the well fortified village of Montauban. The English and French lines met at Maricourt, and the support of the French heavy artillery had a significant impact on the outcome of the British attack here. The bombardment of Montauban had been substantial and effective. It was pulverised. The Manchesters entered a village of smoking ruins and dying Germans. Many more came forward with their hands in the air.³

The attack on Montauban was one of the few success stories of 1 July. By 11.00 am the 30th Division had succeeded in taking all of its objectives. It achieved the most substantial penetration into enemy lines of any of the New Army formations. Lord Derby conveyed his congratulations by telegram: 'Convey to the 30th Division my best congratulations on their splendid work. Lancashire will indeed be proud of them.'⁴ The *Manchester Evening News* asserted:

> Manchester has every right to be proud of the men she breeds. Happily nowhere on the front had our artillery fire been more utterly destructive than in Montauban itself. The Manchesters would have got it, whatever the resistance had been. As it was, they romped into it almost without a check … they held on, beat off the counter-attacks, and since Monday last the place has been solidly ours.⁵

Though the 30th Division's experience compared favourably with what had been happening further to the north, it was still a gruelling and a costly day. The division did not exactly romp forwards without a check. It suffered 3,011 casualties on 1 July.

'It is utterly impossible to locate the site of a street or house,' the Michelin *Guide* to the Somme battlefields would write of Montauban in 1919. 'The only remaining

Montauban – all that remained of the church at the end of the war.

2. - MONTAUBAN (Somme). — L emplacement de l'ancienne Eglise et le Cimetière.

landmarks are the pond and the cemetery – the latter considerably enlarged by the addition of numerous German graves. Everywhere else nothing is to be seen, except heaps of stones and rubbish, beams, scrap-iron, and debris of all kinds.'[6]

With the southern end of the British front suddenly looking like it had more potential than the line further north, priorities and plans were reshuffled. Now the country north and east of Montauban, with its horseshoe of woodlands, would become the focus of a series of attacks.

The 23rd Manchester Battalion, meanwhile, were en route to the Somme. On 2 July, at short notice, the 104th Brigade entrained from Béthune and headed towards Arras. The weather was oppressively hot as the battalion transports then took them south. The brigade was now based around Bouquemaison, with the 23rd Manchesters camped around the hamlet of Neuvillette. 'A more delightful little bit of country is not to be found elsewhere in France,' Eustace Maxwell told his family.[7] They would remain here for the next four days, their time occupied with cleaning, inspections and training. The 35th Division was now allotted to VIII Corps, Reserve Army. 'We are now in Reserve,' Bernard Montgomery wrote home, 'behind the big offensive, waiting to be used if required.'[8]

The weather broke on 4 July. There was a thunderstorm and then heavy rain in the afternoon; roads and trenches quickly began turning to mud. Bernard Montgomery wrote to his mother:

It is pouring hard now and must be very unpleasant for the troops actually attacking. The beginning of the offensive was put off two days on account of the rain, and it will be very bad luck if it goes on. We have had big casualties, motor ambulances with wounded go through our present village all day and night. I don't know our total losses but they must of course be very large.'[9]

On 6 July the 23rd Manchesters travelled south-east to Bus-les-Artois (north of Albert), where they were accommodated in a wood. They were now in the Département of the Somme. 'In the wood were huts and much mud,' Eustace Maxwell wrote. 'That day it rained harder than I think I have ever seen previously in Europe; it really was like monsoon rain, with the result that the wood was not the driest place in the world, while our huts moreover were flooded.'[10]

Also on 6 July, the Germans counter-attacked at Bois Favières, south-east of Montauban, and managed to take back the northern edge of the wood. With this unexpected action, the next British attack, which had been scheduled for 7 July, was postponed until the 8th. The 23rd Manchesters, though, seem to have known little of what was happening further south. Maxwell wrote home: 'It's queer that tho' within a dozen miles of this great fight we should know less of what is going on than you do; we really depend on the home papers for what we hear, and as these have failed today we have to go hungry.'[11] Had the Bantams been able to access the Manchester papers, they would have seen Lord Derby was saying that 'Losses are not excessive'. But, over the course of the next week, it started to become apparent that losses were increasing and of a significantly larger scale than had first been reported.[12]

'Talk about the City of Dreadful Night'
On 8 July the 30th Division would be tasked with the capture of Trônes Wood.[13] It had become apparent that this woodland, to the east of Montauban, was strongly held, and, if an attack on the German second position was to succeed, Trônes Wood would first need to be taken out of the equation. The *History of the King's Regiment (Liverpool)* provides a description of the locale that they were now preparing to attack:

> The remembrance of Trônes Wood in July 1916, to those who passed through it is of a noisome, horrible place, of a tangled mass of trees and undergrowth which had been tossed and flung about in frightful confusion by the shells of both sides; of the ghastly dead who lay about in all directions, and of death lurking in every hole and corner with greedy hands ready to snatch the lives of the unwary.
>
> In shape the wood resembled a pear; it was situated between Bernafay Wood on the west, and Guillemont on the east. South of Trônes Wood was Favières Wood, the northern point of which at this period was still held by the Germans. The country around about the Briqueterie (south of Bernafay Wood and south-west of Trônes Wood) was absolutely open save only for a deep trough in which lay Maltz Horn Farm Trench and, lower down, Favières Wood. Maltz Horn Farm, only a few bricks of which remained, stood on the crest of a plateau rising from the eastern bank of the trough. The whole of the open ground was under observation from a German 'sausage' balloon north of Longueval, and as a consequence the enemy's guns (in an endeavour to make the space impassable) never ceased shelling this area, which resembled a seething furnace, the smoke from bursting shells rising like steam from the troubled earth. A sunken road, affording cover from view, ran from the Briqueterie into the trough in which lay the Maltz Horn Trench. The southern end of the latter was on high ground and abutted on Trônes Wood where the Guillemont road entered the wood. Both Bernafay and Trônes Wood were absolute thickets; only a few clearings, through which railways ran, and a few communication trenches, dug by the enemy, formed the only fairly easy means of progress. For the rest it was all that an unequipped man could do to make his way through, and unless he had a compass bearing it was odds on his losing direction.'[14]

The Allied attack on Trônes Wood began at 8.00 am on 8 July. The initial assault, from the direction of Bernafay Wood, was a disaster, as Trônes Wood's defenders directed their machine guns towards the advancing 2nd Green Howards. To the right, a French attack was about to have more success; the French took their objective, Maltz Horn Trench

---

HEAVY LOSSES IN THE GREAT ADVANCE.

MANY LOCAL CASUALTIES.

With the news of further progress by our troops now breaking through the German lines comes further evidence of the great sacrifices that are being made. Since the British offensive began the daily lists of casualties have been growing longer. To-day the War Office report 210 casualties among officers, and there are numerous local names in this list. Many other local losses are also reported from other sources to-day.

Manchester Evening News, 8 July 1916.

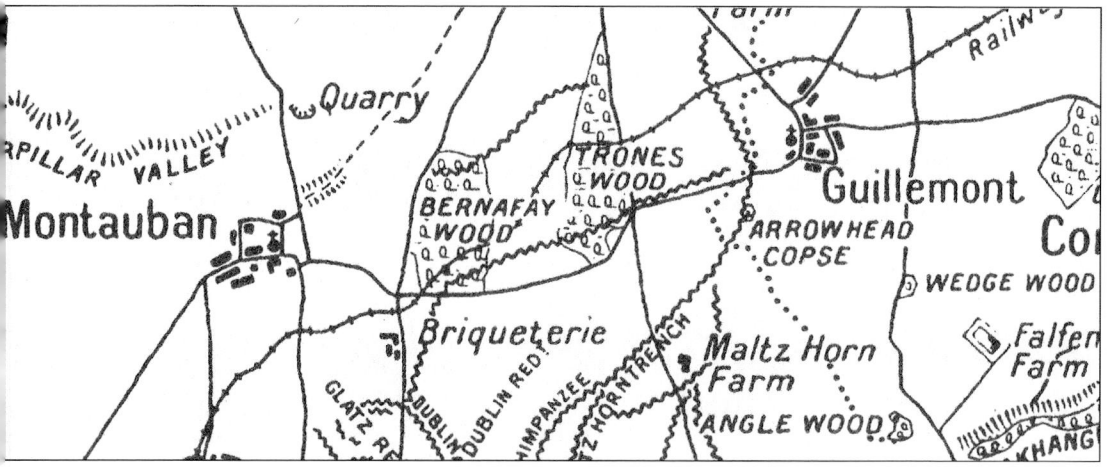

Detail of map taken from Davson, *The History of the 35th Division*, p. 29.

but, with the British advance having failed, their left flank was now exposed. 30th Division were ordered forward. By the early hours of the morning of 9 July Trônes Wood was full of dead men but it was in British hands. It would not remain so for long. Having been severely shelled and expecting a German counter-attack, the 17th and 18th Manchesters pulled back in the afternoon. By the evening the German infantry reoccupied the wood. It was the start of a pattern that was to be bloodily repeated over the next few days. In their attempts to take Trônes Wood, the 30th Division lost over 2,300 men; the 16th, 17th, 18th and 19th Manchester Battalions lost 721 men and 33 officers.

Geoffrey Malins, 'Official Kinematographer to the War Office' (chiefly remembered for the film *The Battle of the Somme*), wanted to make a film of Trônes Wood at this time.

Trônes Wood.

Asking a man who had been there to describe the place, Malins was told: '"There baint anything like it on earth, and if hell is at all like it then I have been there. It's dead; just dead – dead – dead! And the smell – awful."' 'From the description the place seemed rather satisfactory from a scenic point of view,' Malins' memoir records, 'so I made up my mind to try and film it.'

Proceeding down a trench from Bernafay Wood towards Trônes Wood, Malins was struck by the amount of flies:

> The heat in the trenches was terrific, and to add to the horrors of the stench and heat there were millions of flies. Filthy brutes! They seemed to cling to one like leeches, and, my arms being full, I could not keep them off my face . . . Thinking that more smoke might help to keep off the flies I lighted two cigarettes and puffed away at them, one in each corner of my mouth. I'm sure I must have looked a most extraordinary specimen of humanity at this moment.

But Malins' efforts to film were frustrated as the trench was shelled. An officer that he encountered there, though, described the scene:

> 'I've just come from the Wood, and, by gad, it's fair hell there! The place is a charnel house. It's literally choked with corpses; heaps of them; and we dare not bring them in. We've even tried at night, but the shelling prevents us. The place reeks. And the flies! They're awful. It's more than flesh and blood can stand!'

The officer advised Malins: '"If you respect your life don't go any further. The shell-fire is impossible, and the sight over there is too ghastly for words."'

Malins tried to film Trônes Wood on two further occasions, but the shelling was always too lively in the vicinity. 'But those attempts will always remain in my memory as a ghastly nightmare,' he recorded. 'The essence of death and destruction, and all that it means, was horribly visible everywhere.'[15]

The 23rd Manchesters, meanwhile, were still travelling south. On 9 July they had moved into billets at Lealvillers. 'We were told that we should be here for about a week,' Brigadier-General Sandilands recalled, 'but we had no sooner settled down in billets than we were ordered out again.' Orders came through at 10.30 pm that the 104th Brigade had to prepare to move at once. Eustace Maxwell wrote: 'Last night, being in a very comely bed and there eke a most deep sleep, I was suddenly hauled forth at 2 a.m.; before 3 a.m. the whole brigade had been wafted forward and away in an enormous fleet of motor buses.'[16]

The fleet of motor buses travelled as far as Bouzincourt (just to the north of Albert) and from there the Bantams marched on to Aveluy Wood (Bois d'Aveluy), occupying assembly trenches at the south-east corner of wood. 'We all got in just before daylight,' Montgomery wrote, 'and were pretty tired.' They would remain there for the next three days, the wood being heavily bombarded. Maxwell wrote to his family on 10 July:

Looking towards Bouzincourt from Albert.

Bouzincourt.

BOUZINCOURT (Somme). — Maisons en ruines. — Houses in ruins

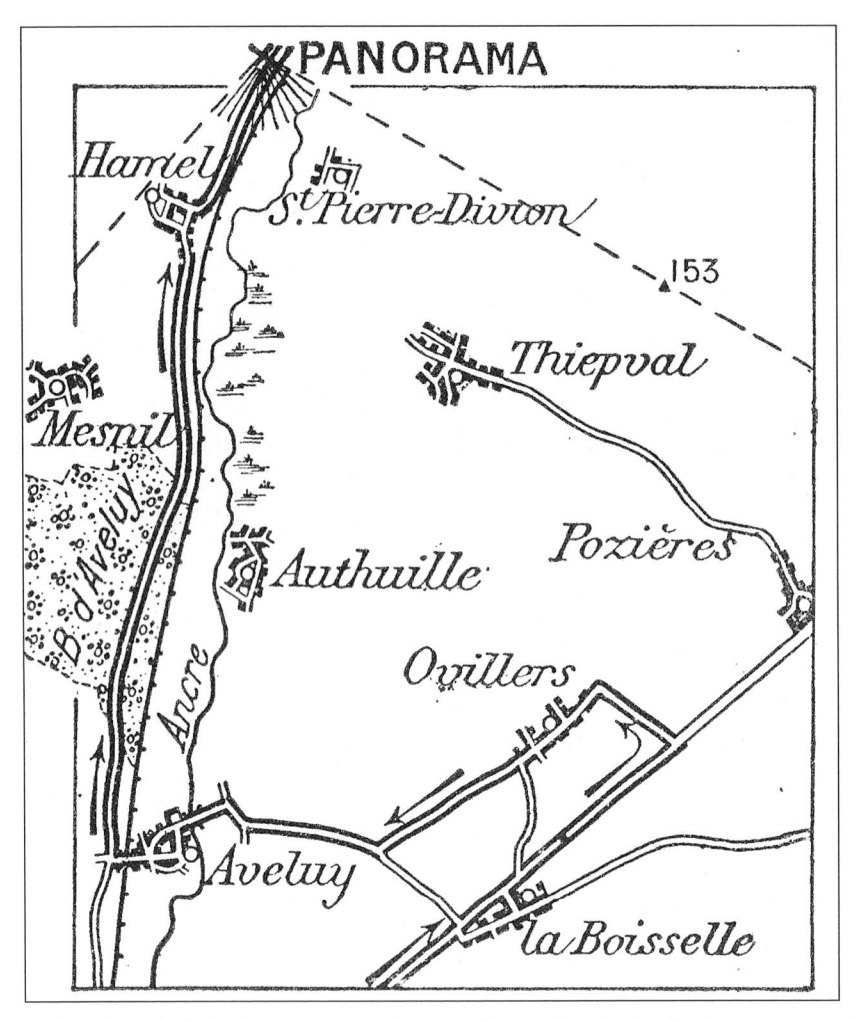

Map showing the Bois d'Aveluy and proximity to Ovillers and La Boisselle. 'Panorama' indicated relates to the angle at which photographs were taken on the following page. Taken from *Illustrated Michelin Guides to the Battle-Fields (1914–1918): The Somme, Volume 1*, p. 38.

At the moment we are all sitting in another great wood, rather cold, very hungry (we, not the wood), and deafened by the roar of guns, big, small, and very many, which are firing from behind us. At times they are so busy that it is impossible for us to hear ourselves speak.'[17]

During this time Montgomery rode out and looked over the area of recent fighting. 'I have been over the whole ground,' he wrote, 'and seen all the recent battlefield'. His letter goes on:

Of course the whole place is a perfect shambles; villages 8 [Ovillers] and 9 [La Boisselle] exist no longer. When I first saw them I was on a hill just behind them

Former site of the chateau at Aveluy (just to the south of the wood).

Panorama of the valley of the Ancre. The Bois d'Aveluy is marked 'G'. Taken from *Illustrated Michelin Guides to the Battle-Fields (1914–1918): The Somme, Volume 1*, pp. 38–9.

& they were pointed out to me. But I could see nothing except about a dozen tree stumps; there is nothing else to see as the whole of them has been reduced to dust. I now realise what it means for a place to be razed to the ground; but you have to see it to believe it. It will be a long time before we get all the British and German dead cleared away. They are lying about as they fell. All the wounded have I think been got back. German prisoners come in every day and all day. One dead German I saw this morning must have been at least 65.[18]

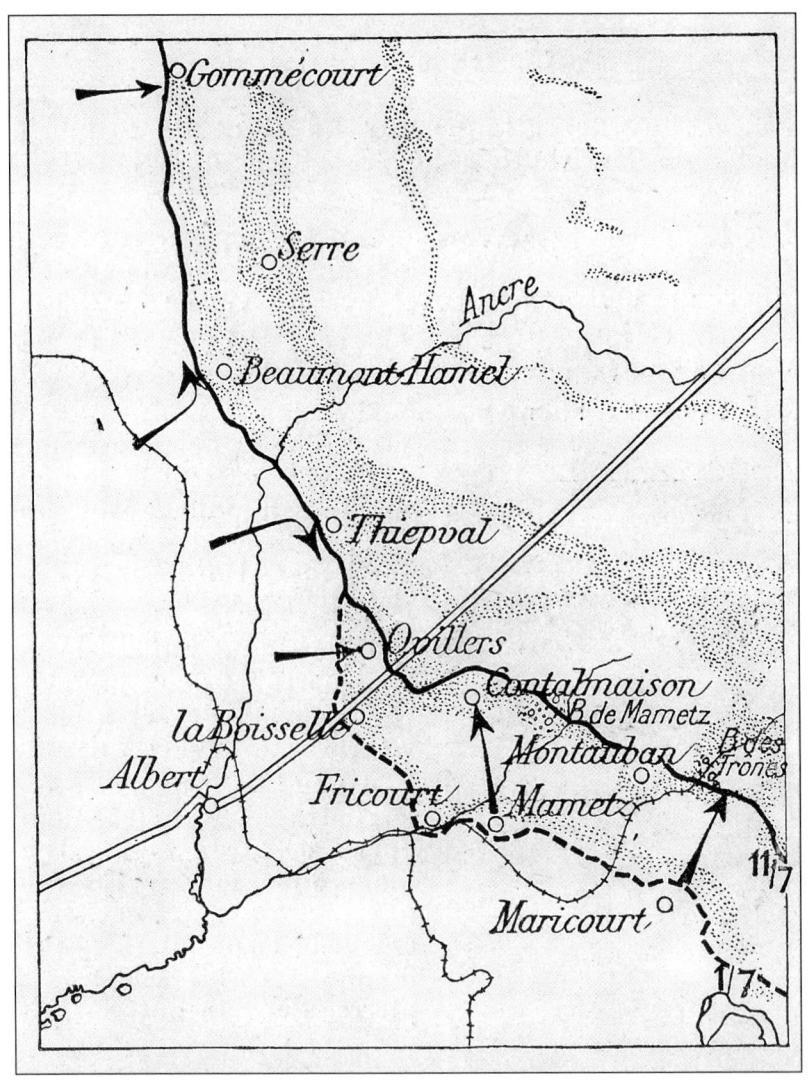

Illustration showing the Allied advances up to 11 July 1916. Map from *Illustrated Michelin Guides to the Battle-Fields (1914 – 1918): The Somme, Volume 1*, p. 15. The grey shading represents 'the German lines of resistance'.

Major General Pinney's diary notes that he went to see Sandilands and his brigade in Aveluy Wood on 10 July; 'very noisy spot,' Pinney wrote. 'About 60 guns just behind.' On the 12th Montgomery told his mother: 'We are now being heavily shelled and expecting to be ordered to advance at any moment.' He went on:

> We are living in a dug-out, and a very damp one too. However everyone is very cheerful; the men wonderfully so. We have the upper hand of the Bosche as regards artillery and our guns must be very annoying to him. The shelling goes on all day and all night and at times is intense; the noise is perfectly deafening and at times one has to put your hands to your mouth and shout, even across the table during meals.[19]

The plan as understood was that the 35th Division would soon be put in to attack towards Ovillers but when Pinney returned from his trip up to the wood he was told that the division was now being allocated to the Fourth Army and would therefore need to shift south.[20]

It had been agreed that the Allied attack on the German second position, north of Montauban, would go ahead on 14 July. In order to facilitate this, it was imperative that the entirety of Trônes Wood be captured and held. On the 13th an attack was made on the northern end of the wood by the 18th Division. It failed. But orders were issued again – Trônes Wood *had* to be taken. In the early hours of the morning of 14 July the 12th Middlesex Battalion were informed that it was now their turn to have a crack at Trônes Wood. Under the command of Francis Aylmer Maxwell VC (the elder brother of Eustace Maxwell), the 12th Middlesex began to pick their way into the splintered, shattered, corpse-filled wood. Rounding up all the men that he could find (by this stage there was some state of chaos in Trônes Wood and it was full of wandering, dazed men from different units), Maxwell formed them up into a line and thus, giving the men leave to fire at will at any object that might potentially conceal an enemy sniper, they advanced. It was a feet of extraordinarily cool-headed command and co-ordination. Maxwell's long crocodile of men – stumbling, swearing, consulting their compasses – succeeded in making their way through the wood. On 14 July Trônes Wood was finally taken.

Francis Aylmer Maxwell wrote to his sisters the next day:

> Don't like war! And shan't play any more if present conditions continue much longer . . . To talk of a 'wood' is to talk rot – it was the most dreadful tangle of dense trees and undergrowth imaginable, with deep yawning broken trenches criss-crossing about it; every tree broken off at top and bottom and trenches cut away so that the floor of the wood was almost an impenetrable tangle of timber, branches, undergrowth etc . . . Never was anything so perfectly dreadful to look at – at best I couldn't dream of anything worse – particularly with its dreadful additions of corpses and wounded men – many lying there for days and days . . . Talk about the City of Dreadful Night.[21]

British graves in Trônes Wood, 1919. Photograph from *Illustrated Michelin Guides to the Battle-Fields (1914 – 1918): The Somme, Volume 1*, p. 19.

A memorial to the 18th Division on the edge of Trônes Wood (erected immediately after the war), with the re-growing wood in the rear.

The permanent monument to the 18th Division, with Trônes Wood in the background (1919). Photograph from *Illustrated Michelin Guides to the Battle-Fields (1914–1918): The Somme, Volume 1*, p. 85.

The 23rd Manchesters, meanwhile, had been moved on to Morlancourt on 13 July, to the south of Albert, and then on to Happy Valley (the valley which runs between Fricourt and Bray-sur-Somme), where they bivouacked. 'The title was euphemistic,' a footnote in the Divisional History cautions.[22] It had not been an easy journey; the roads were blocked everywhere and the Battalion did not arrive at their destination until after midnight. They knew that the 'great Fourth Army attack' was being launched on 14 July. Eustace Maxwell wrote:

> As we had now been transferred to that army we expected to be on the move at any time from 3.30 a.m. onwards. But here we still sit, bivouacking on the sides of a valley and heartily cursing our luck . . . We spend our time listening to the guns, looking out for communiqués which rarely arrive, and keeping an eye on the weather, which today is vile and very hard on the men, who are shelterless. We are very dirty.[23]

Happy Valley was an infantry rear area. Amidst the units bivouacking and waiting to move forwards, the valley was full of artillery guns. Enemy bombardment here was continuous and heavy. While they were in Happy Valley the Manchesters took part in a practice attack. They were under orders to be ready to move at short notice. It would be four days, though, before those orders arrived. On 14 July Pinney rode up to the area to inspect the 104th Brigade. His diary records: 'Manchesters "mobbed" me for news – I thought some would get under the horse'.[24]

On 14 July four Fourth Army divisions attacked the German second position along the ridge from south of Pozières to Longueval. There were more celebratory headlines in the Manchester papers by the end of the day. Business was suspended on Manchester Exchange as members discussed the latest developments in France. 'The most optimistic feelings prevailed,' reported the *Manchester Evening News*, 'encouraged by the glad tidings of this further success.'[25]

Maxwell wrote to his family on 16 July. He was feeling impatient.

> ATTACK AT DAWN TO-DAY
> ON FRONT OF FOUR MILES.
> STRONGLY DEFENDED LOCALITIES CAPTURED.
> HEAVY FIGHTING CONTINUES.

Manchester Evening News, 14 July 1916.

> Your anxieties, so far as my worthy self is concerned, have hitherto been quite misplaced, for we have as yet taken no share in the action. It is almost humiliating to have to say this over again . . . The other two brigades of this Bantam division have been lent to other divisions, and will be fighting tomorrow; we have been left out of it because our brigade was supposed to have had rather a rotten time in the wood from which I last wrote. It is very tiresome. But our turn will come if only we can be patient.[26]

Maxwell's patience was straining, but he was about to get his turn. This would be the last letter that he would send.

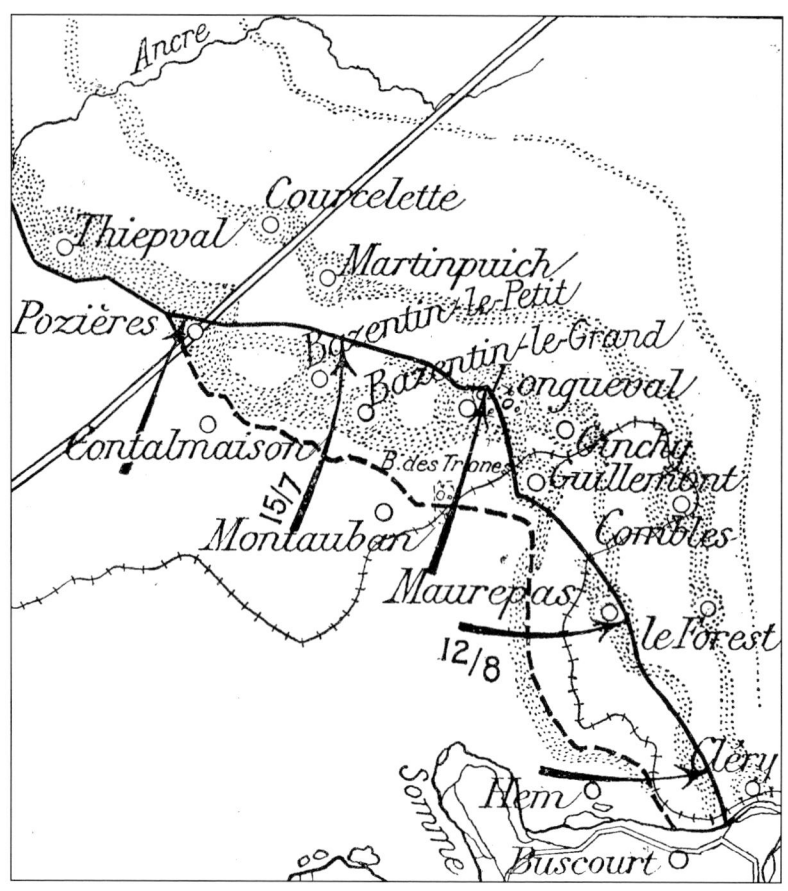

Map showing the Allied advances as far as 15 July 1916. From *Illustrated Michelin Guides to the Battle-Fields (1914–1918): The Somme, Volume 1*, p. 18.

On 18 July the Bantams moved up to Talus Boisé. The weather had been wet and the roads were not good. They arrived at their destination in the early hours of the morning and bivouacked in a field next to the wood. The 35th Division were now relieving the 18th Division, which had been engaged in the Trônes Wood area for the past three weeks.

'This operation did not work according to plan': Maltz Horn Farm
For 20 July the War Diary of the 15th Sherwood Foresters records simply: 'W & Z Coys attacked enemy's position in conjunction with French attack on our Right at 5 a.m. Unsuccessful, casualties heavy. 23rd. Manchester Regt. assisted.'

Major General Pinney arrived at Brigade HQ ('Stanley's Hole, an evil-smelling dugout about 400 yards south-west of Maricourt') on the evening of 19 July. He had just come from a Corps' conference. He gave the order now that units of the 105th Brigade were to go forward the next day and to capture 1,000 yards of enemy trench between Arrow Head Copse and Maltz Horn Farm. The operation was intended to secure a more advantageous position from which the forthcoming attack on Guillemont could go ahead.

Maltz Horn Farm, an important defensive position for the enemy, faced the junction of the British and the French armies. The Bantams were about to become very familiar with it. A lot of them would never leave it.

The orders for the attack were issued to the 15th Sherwood Foresters, who had been occupying the trenches opposite the objective since 16 July. Through the 18th and 19th the position had been subjected to heavy bombardment include tear and gas shells. The Sherwood Foresters were exhausted, hungry and having their nerve and stamina severely tested.

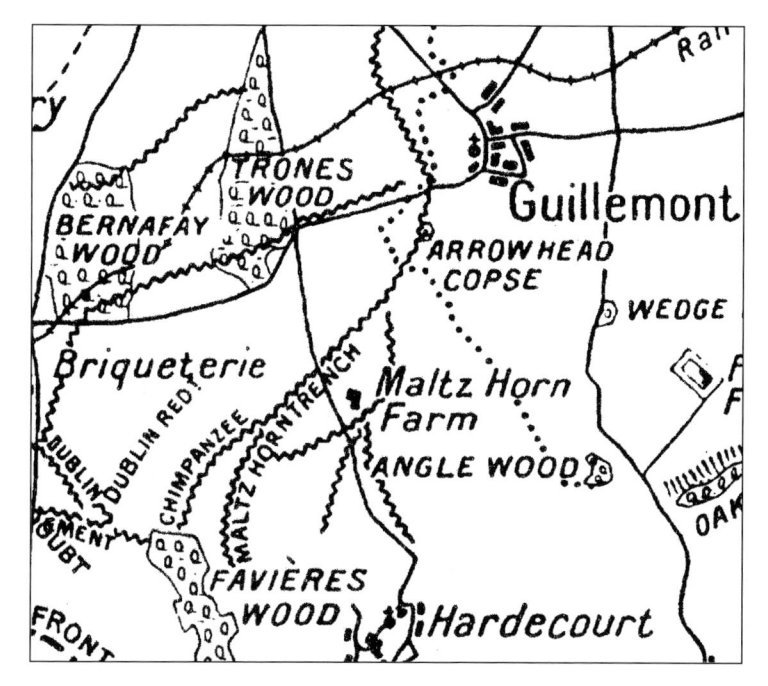

Detail of map taken from Davson, *The History of the 35th Division*, p. 29.

The 15th Sherwood Foresters received their orders at 9.50 pm on 19 July. The length of front was too long to be attacked directly by one battalion; therefore, instead, the plan was to focus the attack on two points – Maltz Horn Farm and Arrow Head Copse. The orders stated that the enemy was to be shelled that night and then heavily bombarded from 4.25 am to 5.00 am, at which hour the artillery would lift and form a barrage. One Company of the Sherwood Foresters was then to attack, in four waves at fifty yard intervals, from the south-west of Arrow Head Copse. Meanwhile four waves of a second company were to attack from just south of Maltz Horn Farm. Bombing squads were then to work their way along the enemy trench until the two attacking parties met up. From midnight Pioneers were to begin to dig a trench out towards Arrow Head Copse which could be joined up to the enemy's trench once captured. There was a sap running in a westerly direction ahead of the enemy front line ('supposed to be occupied as sniping has been observed from it') and wire along the front line trench ('but it is not considered strong').

The histories emphasise that the plans for the attack were made hurriedly. 'It was an arrangement that left much to be desired, but time was short', Davson's *The History of the 35th Division* concluded.[27] Circumstances were, however, to deteriorate further. Shortly before midnight Lieutenant-Colonel R.H.S. Gordon, commanding the 15th Sherwood Foresters, sent an urgent message to Brigade HQ: having been subjected to three days of shellfire and gas attacks, his battalion was badly shaken. The men had been in gas masks for the past four hours and it was going to be a challenge to find two companies' worth of men in a fit state to attack. 'Disconcerting news,' wrote Pinney in his diary. Gordon asked that reinforcements be sent up and, his request having been agreed to, new orders were issued to the Sherwood Foresters at midnight. Two companies of the 23rd Manchesters had been ordered forwards, and would support the attack from the right (i.e. from the Maltz Horn Farm end), occupying the trenches vacated by the attacking companies of Sherwood Foresters and providing carrying parties. 'At very short notice on July 20th the 105th Brigade attacked Maltz Horn Farm,' Brigadier General Sandilands would recall. 'At still shorter notice, without even being given time to digest or issue orders, the 23rd Manchesters were sent up to help them.' W and X Companies of the 23rd Manchesters, having struggled up the line in darkness, arrived ahead of Maltz Horn Farm at 4.55 am. The attack was due to commence in five minutes. In response to the Allied bombardment, the Sherwood Foresters' position was experiencing severe retaliatory shelling.

As the artillery were not able to secure positions from which they could observe the trenches near Maltz Horn Farm, there was evidently some best guesswork in their aiming. Moreover, as there was less than 500 yards distance between the Allied and enemy positions, it seems that it was difficult to target the enemy front line without some danger to the Sherwood Foresters. The register of messages over the course of the day indicates that the artillery was falling short. At some time before 4.25 am the Allied frontline trench was evacuated for the sake of the safety of its defenders.

At 5.00 am the first two lines of Sherwood Foresters advanced towards the enemy. They would not make it very far. A Report of Operations, written afterwards by Lieutenant Colonel Gordon, recorded:

> On the signal for the advance being given, four waves moved forward and on topping the rise came in full view of the enemy, where they were met by a devastating fire from Machine Guns as far as can be ascertained from concealed positions to the East of MALTZ HORN FARM. From reports received from survivors it appears that the Coy. had suffered severely from the enemy's barrage fire, and owing to the lateness of the time for the attack and the light shining directly on them, they afforded an easy mark for the enemy's fire.[28]

Somehow, though, a few men did succeed in reaching the enemy's front line trenches. French observers, also advancing towards Maltz Horn Farm, recorded that they had seen some of the Sherwood Foresters reaching the enemy line, but they were driven out.[29]

The company attacking from the Arrow Head Copse end also faced devastating enemy fire as soon as they topped the ridge. The scattered survivors dug themselves into shell holes. The next two waves, again facing hostile fire, made it less far and were compelled to retire back to their trenches.

At 6.50 am a message was sent back to 105th Brigade HQ, notifying them that the attack had failed. An immediate reply ordered that the attack must be continued. 'As the right of the attack near Maltz Horn Farm was at the junction with the French, who were attacking simultaneously and had made progress, it was important that headway should be made,' *The History of the 35th Division* explained. At 7.30 am a telephone call was made back to Brigade HQ, warning that, if the attack was to be recommenced, further support was imperative. Brigade replied that another two companies of the 23rd Manchesters (Y and Z) were being sent up. The attack was to be repeated at 11.35 am. In the meantime the troops in the front line trenches were experiencing heavy shelling.

At 10.45 am, in advance of the planned bombardment of the enemy's position, the companies of Manchesters who had been occupying the frontline trenches were ordered to evacuate and to take up assembly positions to the rear. The bombardment started at 11.05 am. At 11.08 am a phone call was made back to the brigade informing them that the reinforcing companies of Manchesters (Y and Z) had not yet arrived. Guides were sent out. Eventually arriving some time shortly after 11.35 am, the attack had already started by the time that the Manchesters reached the position. One of the companies was immediately ordered to follow the attack 'over the top' and the second to hold the trench.

The attack advanced in eight waves. 'Officers & men went over with no clear idea of their direction or objective,' records the Manchesters' War Diary. A sense of confusion is clear. Major Maxwell was the first man over the top. Once over, they faced machine-gun and rifle fire. Those that could retired back to their trenches, which were now subject to intense bombardment by enemy artillery.

Shortly after 12.00 pm a message was received from the French indicating that they had observed signs of the enemy concentrating troops to the east of Guillemont with a view to counter-attacking. 'I considered the situation at this period to be extremely critical,' wrote Gordon. He went on:

> The men of the Sherwood Foresters who had already occupied the Trenches for four days and had been incessantly subjected to intense bombardment during the whole period, and the remaining men of the Manchesters who had come up into a new part of the line without any knowledge of their whereabouts or the local condition after a trying forced march, were practically in a state of collapse, especially as the enemy had in addition been sending over considerable quantities of Tear and Chlorine Gas Shells.

Gordon directed six special runners to Advanced Brigade HQ and sent up the 'SOS' signal by rocket. In the meantime, the remaining officers attempted to rally the men to be ready for a counter-attack. At 12.05 pm a phone call from brigade ordered Gordon and the remaining Sherwoods and Manchesters to hold the line 'at all costs'. Fortunately no counter-attack took place.

In the afternoon reports were sent to 105th Brigade HQ 'strongly recommending'

(Gordon) that the Sherwoods and Manchesters should be relieved. The Manchesters were left without any senior officers and the Sherwoods with only one effective officer per company. The relief was sanctioned and, finally, at 9.00 pm, they began the handover to the 18th Lancashire Fusiliers. It must have been with some weariness that the Manchesters began the journey back to Talus Boisé. John Duffield recalled the mental state of some of the men that evening: 'We had such a lot of casualties, and, that night, I was in charge of about 50 or 60 men, all badly shell-shocked, lying on the ground, waiting for ambulances . . . I went about amongst them and tried to talk to them and they really were broken men. There was no cowardice about it.'[30]

On 20 July the 15th Sherwood Foresters had lost ten officers killed and nine wounded; thirty-nine other ranks had been killed, 146 wounded and thirty-six were missing.[31] The day's entry in the Manchesters' War Diary concludes: 'Major Maxwell fell in the attack. He was the first over and was later reported missing, believed killed. Capts. Rothband & Gosling were killed, Maj. Grimshaw shell-shocked & Capt. Cooper, Lt. Wilson & 2nd Lts. Hamer, Simpson & Lye wounded (2nd Lt. Lye died on the 21st). 28 other ranks were killed, 98 wounded, 9 shell-shocked & 13 missing.'

There were forty-six men of the battalion ultimately listed as 'killed in action' or 'died of wounds' on 20/21 July 1916. Of these, thirty-six, with no known grave, are commemorated on the Thiepval Memorial.

Private Harry Barnes was killed in action on 20 July 1916. He was from Pendlebury. He is commemorated on the Thiepval Memorial.

Private John Thomas Beaumont was killed in action on 20 July 1916. He was from Manchester. He is commemorated on the Thiepval Memorial.

Private Albert Booth died of wounds on 20 July 1916. He was aged 20 and from Hulme, Manchester. He is buried in Corbie Communal Cemetery Extension.

Private Andrew Cassell was killed in action on 20 July 1916. He was aged 31 and from Manchester. He is commemorated on the Thiepval Memorial.

Private George Henry Conley was killed in action on 20 July 1916. He was from Manchester. He is buried in Flatiron Copse Cemetery, Mametz.

Sergeant William Cox was killed in action on 20 July 1916. He was from Bolton. He is buried in Flatiron Copse Cemetery, Mametz.

Private William Crawshaw was killed in action on 20 July 1916. He was aged 22 and from Newton Heath. He is commemorated on the Thiepval Memorial.

Private James Cropper was killed in action on 20 July 1916. He was aged 23 and from Bolton. He is commemorated on the Thiepval Memorial.

Private Thomas Cummins was killed in action on 20 July 1916. He was from Salford. He is commemorated on the Thiepval Memorial.

Private Charles Lawrence Darlow was killed in action on 20 July 1916. He was aged 21 and from Salford. He is commemorated on the Thiepval Memorial.

Private Fred Dodd was killed in action on 20 July 1916. He was from Harpurhey. He is commemorated on the Thiepval Memorial.

Private William Dossantos was killed in action on 20 July 1916. He was from Hulme. He is commemorated on the Thiepval Memorial.

Sergeant Thomas Henry Faraghan was killed in action on 20 July 1916. He was aged 24 and from Chadderton, Oldham. He is commemorated on the Thiepval Memorial.

Private James Forrest was killed in action on 20 July 1916. He was from Middleton. He is commemorated on the Thiepval Memorial.

Private Walter Gorin was killed in action on 20 July 1916. He was aged 37 and from Redditch, Worcestershire. He is commemorated on the Thiepval Memorial.

Private Walter Heaney was killed in action on 20 July 1916. He was aged 21 and from Manchester. He is commemorated on the Thiepval Memorial.

Private Joseph Heaps was killed in action on 20 July 1916. He was from West Gorton. He is commemorated on the Thiepval Memorial.

Acting Quartermaster Sergeant Rowland Herrick was killed in action on 20 July 1916. He was from Salford. He is buried in Flatiron Copse Cemetery, Mametz.

Private Frank Holden was killed in action on 20 July 1916. He was from Hulme. He is commemorated on the Thiepval Memorial.

Private William Horridge was killed in action on 20 July 1916. He was aged 38 and from Gorton. He is commemorated on the Thiepval Memorial.

Private Robert Simeon Hulme was killed in action on 20 July 1916. He was from Newton Heath. He is commemorated on the Thiepval Memorial.

Corporal William Edward Hulston was killed in action on 20 July 1916. He was from Ardwick. He is commemorated on the Thiepval Memorial.

Sergeant William James was killed in action on 20 July 1916. He was from Oldham. He is commemorated on the Thiepval Memorial.

Private Joseph Johnson was killed in action on 20 July 1916. He was aged 25 and from Middleton, Manchester. He is buried in Flatiron Copse Cemetery, Mametz. He was originally reported missing, but subsequently was identified.

Private William Johnson was killed in action on 20 July 1916. He was from Ardwick. He is commemorated on the Thiepval Memorial.

Private Peter Laithwaite was killed in action on 20 July 1916. He was from Orrell, Lancashire. He is commemorated on the Thiepval Memorial.

Private Richard Lambert was killed in action on 20 July 1916. He was from Chorlton-on-Medlock. He is commemorated on the Thiepval Memorial.

Private James Leigh was killed in action on 20 July 1916. He was from Collyhurst, Manchester. He is commemorated on the Thiepval Memorial.

Lance Corporal Michael Levy was killed in action on 20 July 1916. He was aged 29 and from Leicester. He is commemorated on the Thiepval Memorial.

Corporal William Christopher Lowry was killed in action on 20 July 1916. He was aged 21 and from Ancoats. He is commemorated on the Thiepval Memorial.

Private Walter Matthews was killed in action on 20 July 1916. He was from Collyhurst. He is commemorated on the Thiepval Memorial.

Private Charles Millward was killed in action on 20 July 1916. He was aged 19 and from Todmorden. He is commemorated on the Thiepval Memorial.

Private Arthur Edwin North was killed in action on 20 July 1916. He was 21 and from Coppice, Oldham. He is commemorated on the Thiepval Memorial.

Private Ernest Owen was killed in action on 20 July 1916. He was from Manchester. He is commemorated on the Thiepval Memorial.

Private Harry Cromwell Pilling was killed in action on 20 July 1916. He was aged 29 and from Ashton under Lyne. He is commemorated on the Thiepval Memorial.

Private George Robinson was killed in action on 20 July 1916. He was from Collyhurst. He is commemorated on the Thiepval Memorial.

Private Bertram Taylor was killed in action on 20 July 1916. He was from Manchester. He is commemorated on the Thiepval Memorial.

Private Joseph Ward was killed in action on 20 July 1916. He was from Manchester. He is commemorated on the Thiepval Memorial.

Private Philip Wilkinson was killed in action on 20 July 1916. He was aged 24 and from Pendleton. He is commemorated on the Thiepval Memorial.

Company Sergeant Major William Henry Wolstenholme died on 20 July 1916. He was from Salford. He is commemorated on the Thiepval Memorial.

Private John Yates was killed in action on 20 July 1916. He was aged 19 and from Accrington. He is commemorated on the Thiepval Memorial.

Private Herbert Blacklock was killed in action on 21 July 1916. He was aged 32 and from Lower Broughton, Manchester. He is buried in Péronne Road Cemetery, Maricourt.

Private William Doyle died of wounds on 21 July 1916. He was from Newton, Manchester. He is buried in La Neuville British Cemetery, Corbie.

Private Richard Pontefract died of wounds on 21 July 1916. He was aged 38 and from Pendleton. He is buried in La Neuville British Cemetery, Corbie.

Private George Frederick Wall died of wounds on 21 July 1916. He was aged 42 and from Blackley. He is buried in La Neuville British Cemetery, Corbie.

Lieutenant Gilbert Lye died on 21 July 1916. He was aged 23 and from Rochdale. He is buried in Corbie Communal Cemetery Extension.

Pinney wrote in his diary: '400 Manchesters went for MALTZE HILL FARM [sic] and all got in, but it is on forward slope of hill and they got blown to pieces by Bosh [sic] guns, even before they had finished off the Bosh garrison. The best type of Bantams done in.'[32]

It was a hastily – and badly – planned attack. As *The History of the 35th Division* conceded, arrangements did indeed leave much to be desired. The battalions of the 35th Division would later face criticism for their performance on the Somme, but evidence suggests that the 23rd Manchesters played their part on 20 July to the best of their ability. Lieutenant Colonel Gordon's report on the day's events concluded:

> I also wish to bring to notice the conduct of the Officers and men of the 23rd. Manchester Regt. who, arriving at very short notice, carried out the second attack

BOOTH.—In loving memory of my dear brother, ALBERT BOOTH, died of wounds received in France July 20th, 1916.
   Merciful Lord Jesus, grant him eternal rest.
   Sadly missed by his loving Sister (LIZZIE) and JOHN (in Egypt).

BOOTH.—In loving memory of Private ALBERT BOOTH (22972), 23rd Manchester Regiment, died of wounds received in action July 20, 1916, age 21.
   I cannot forget him, I loved him too dearly
     For his memory to fade from my mind like a dream,
   My lips need not speak for my heart mourns sincerely,
     And thoughts often dwell where they seldom are seen.
MOTHER, SISTERS, Brother-in-law WALTER, also his Brother JOHN (in Egypt).—54, Owen-street, Hulme.

BOOTH.—In sad but proud memory of my dear pal, Private ALBERT BOOTH, age 20, of the 23rd Batt. Manchester Regiment (Bantams), who died of wounds received in action in France, on July 20, 1916.
   Some may think the wound has healed,
     When they see me smile,
   But they little know the sorrow
     That the smile hides all the time.
                 From his pal JIM.
64, Great Jackson-street, Hulme, Manchester.

BOOTH.—In ever-loving memory of our dear friend, Private ALBERT BOOTH, age 20, of the 23rd Batt. Manchester Regiment (Bantams), who died of wounds received in action in France, on July 20, 1916.
   We think of him in silence,
     His name we oft recall,
   But there's nothing left to comfort us
     But his photo on the wall.
        From Mr. and Mrs. DRINKWATER and FAMILY.

DODD.—Private FRED DODD, 21787, Manchester Bantams, killed in action July 20, 1916.
   Sleep on, dear Fred, in a far-off grave,
     A grave we may never see;
   But as long as life and memory last
     We will fondly think of thee.
Deeply mourned by his sorrowing Father, Brothers (one in France), Sisters and Sister-in-law.

HULME.—In loving memory of Lance-Corporal R. S. HULME, 22991, who fell in action July 20, 1916, Manchester Regiment.
   Could I have raised his dying head,
     Or heard his last farewell,
   The grief would not have been so hard
     For one who loved him well.
   But sleep on, my husband dear, in a soldier's grave,
     A grave I may never see,
   But as long as life and memory last
     I will always think of thee.
        From his sorrowing wife, NELLIE.
20, Buckley-street, Newton Heath.

HULME.—Lance-Corp. R. S. HULME, killed in action, July 20th, 1916.
   Somewhere in France in a nameless grave,
     Lies our dear brother amongst the brave.
From his Sister and Brother, EDITH, HARRY, and Nieces, FLORRIE and EVELYN.

HULME.—Lance-Corp. R. S. HULME, 22991, killed in action, July 20th, 1916, Manchester Regiment.
   Sleep on, dear brother, in a soldier's grave,
     A grave we shall never see,
   But as long as life and memory lasts,
     We shall always think of thee.
Deeply regretted by his Sisters-in-law, Alice, Harriet.

MISSING.

The relatives of the following soldiers, who are reported missing, would be glad to receive news concerning them:

H. Hughes.   J. Johnson.   E. Sills.

Private JOE JOHNSON (21806), Manchester Regiment, missing since July 20. His brother Samuel was reported missing after an engagement on September 25 last year. Mother: 18a, Fielding-street, Middleton.

A selection of the 'in memoriam' and 'missing' notices for men of the 23rd Battalion posted in the *Manchester Evening News* (31 July, 5 August, 14 September 1916, 20 and 25 July 1917).

---

with great fortitude and dash and although driven back cheerfully set to work to repair the line and place it in a state of defence in expectation of a counter-attack. I consider the conduct of the Officers and men deserving of high praise especially in view of the fact that they had lost their Commanding Officer and all their senior Officers.[33]

That evening General Magnan, of the French *153rd Division*, sent a message to Pinney. The advance of the 23rd Manchesters had been witnessed by several of his observing posts. He recorded: 'It was splendid, as on parade, but they had no chance on the front face of the hill.'

Among the officers of the 23rd Manchester Battalion killed on 20 July was Captain Jacob ('Jack') Eustace Rothband. According to family papers, Jack Rothband walked along the parapet just prior to his Company's attack. Trying to rally his men, he shouted, 'Come on boys, don't be afraid of their guns'. He was shot through the head almost immediately.[34]

Jack Rothband was from Cheetham Hill. An old boy of Manchester Grammar School, he had been an officer with the Jewish Lads' Brigade in Manchester. He worked for the family firm of W.S. Rothband & Co., rubber manufacturers, in Cheetham. When war broke out he was in San Francisco, but he returned immediately to Britain and enlisted in the Public Schools Battalion of the Middlesex Regiment. He became a temporary lieutenant in April 1915 and was subsequently granted a commission with the Manchester Regiment. On his death the *Manchester Evening News* published a letter from Lieutenant George Simpson. He wrote of Rothband: 'His humour and cheery disposition often kept us going when everything else seemed against us. I have lost a beloved company commander and true friend.' Jack Rothband was aged 34. He is buried in Flat Iron Copse Cemetery, Mametz.

> ROTHBAND.—In proud memory of Captain J. E. ROTH-BAND, who sacrificed his noble life July 19, 1916. Never forgotten by the staff of W. S. Rothband and Co.
>
> ROTHBAND.—In proud and loving memory of JACK EUSTACE ROTHBAND, Captain Manchester Regiment, who fell whilst leading his company in the attack on Malts Horn Farm on July 19th, 1916.

Manchester Evening News, 27 July 1916 and 19 July 1917.

Among those killed on 20 July was Captain Frederick William Gosling. A former Liverpool Institute boy, he was working for Liverpool Corporation in 1914. Gosling volunteered as a private at the start of the war, but received a commission in November 1914 and was attached to the Manchesters. His rise was rapid and he was promoted to captain in November 1915. He is commemorated on the Thiepval Memorial.

Manchester Courier, 1 October 1915.

Eustace Lockhart Maxwell's elder brothers (Laurence Lockhart Maxwell and Francis Aylmer Maxwell) were both commanding battalions on the Western Front at the time of his death. They investigated his disappearance in the weeks that followed, keen to piece together the course of events, to discover whether he truly had been killed and, if that was the case, to locate his body. They spoke to his fellow officers, his men and repeatedly went over the ground.

Francis Aylmer Maxwell wrote in his journal:

> The 2nd in command of Eustace's battalion, I gathered, had failed – it was he who should have taken the final company into action. Eustace therefore, against orders, took his place and seeing how bad things were, took a rifle and bayonet and went forward to certain death.[35]

Major Grimshaw – 'the ex-colour sergeant-but-present 2nd in command' – was recorded in the battalion War Diary as suffering from shell shock. Francis Maxwell's journal goes on:

> Eustace was last seen to hand his waterproof to his orderly and to take the orderly's bayonet. With that he went forward and was seen to fall at the German trench which was being attacked. That was all I could learn of the matter for certain, after several visits to the spot and from letters and interviews with his Brigadier, the officers of his battalion and wounded men of his battalion in hospital and from officers (of other units) who later took over the trenches whence this attack had been made.[36]

A note adds:

> The dead and wounded of 23rd Manchesters after the unsuccessful attack were left in No Man's Land – "but all were eventually brought in, or accounted for by night patrols – with the exception of Eustace". The chaplain who later buried the dead stated that there was no trace of Eustace…

> Conclusions –
> He may have been hit directly by a shell in which case there would have been no trace of him.
> He may have fallen – yet not been picked up by our people later – he may in that case have been buried undefined since.
> He may have reached the German trenches – been killed or captured there.[37]

His body was never recovered. The anxiousness of the Maxwell family to know the truth about Eustace's fate reflects what so many families must have been feeling at this time. Eustace Lockhart Maxwell is commemorated on a family grave in the Municipal Cemetery, Guildford, Surrey, and on the Thiepval Memorial.

James Walter Sandilands wrote: 'He was last seen leading his men in the gallant manner to be expected of one of such a distinguished group of soldier brothers.'[38]

> Lieutenant Colonel Leighton Marlow Stevens, formerly of the Worcestershire Regiment, now took over command of the 23rd Manchesters.
>
> Leighton Marlow Stevens, the son of a Weston-super-Mare vicar and a former Somerset rugby player, had served with the 1st Battalion Worcestershire Regiment in the South African War. In 1914 the then Captain Stevens was Adjutant to the 5th (Reserve) Battalion of the Worcestershire Regiment. In May 1916, now a major, he was given temporary command of the 2nd Battalion of the Worcesters and, in July 1916, he was transferred to 23rd Manchester Battalion and became a temporary Lieutenant Colonel. In 1918 he would be promoted to the command of the 24th Infantry Brigade, where Bernard Montgomery would act as his brigade major. Leighton Marlow Stevens was awarded the DSO and was three times Mentioned in Despatches during the war.
>
> Photograph from Sandilands, *A Lancashire Brigade in France*, p. 47.

The next morning, 21 July, there was a heavy bombardment and gas shells were aimed at Talus Boisé, where the 23rd Manchesters were in bivouac camp. The War Diary records that Lieutenant Beard was shellshocked, one man killed and four wounded by shrapnel. John Duffield was on the receiving end of a gas shell. 'I got one all to myself and my wartime experiences finished at that point,' he recalled. The position was heavily shelled again the next day; there were more casualties and another officer, Lieutenant Willey, was diagnosed with shell shock.

> Private John Firth was killed in action on 22 July 1916. He was aged 24 and from Collyhurst. His obituary in the *Manchester Evening News* (23 July 1917) included: 'Let those who made the quarrel be the only men who fight.' He is commemorated on the Thiepval Memorial.
>
> Private George Garner died of wounds on 22 July 1916. He was aged 23 and from Salford. He is buried in Dive Copse British Cemetery, Sailly-le-Sec.
>
> Private John Thomas Whittall was killed in action on 22 July 1916. He was aged 25 and from Ancoats. He is commemorated on the Thiepval Memorial.

On the morning of 23 July units of the 30th Division attacked Guillemont. Wyrall's *History of the King's Regiment* records Guillemont as 'a pleasant-sounding name, but of dreadful memories'.[39]

The attack began at 3.40 am, preceded by a massive artillery bombardment. The 35th Division provided the artillery support, with their 18-pounder batteries directed to break through the enemy wire. The 19th Manchesters attacked from the eastern side of Trônes Wood and, on reaching the enemy wire, found that much of it was all too intact. Some men did make it into the village, where fighting was fierce. No support succeeded in following up, though, and the 19th Manchesters eventually found themselves isolated and exhausted and forced to withdraw. They would lose 571 men that day; of those, 496 were recorded as missing. 'In spite of very gallant fighting the attack was a failure,' the *History of the King's Regiment* records. The troops fell back 'baffled and broken.'[40]

But, needing Guillemont to be captured before an Anglo-French attack could push further north, Rawlinson issued instructions for the continuance of operations. 'Again and again our troops entered the village, but were forced out of it by fierce counter-attacks or failure on the flanks,' the *History of the King's Regiment* would record. It would become 'a fierce and sanguinary struggle, which continued for many days and weeks'.[41]

'One More Will Finish Us'
The 23rd Manchesters had meanwhile been ordered back up to the front line, returning to the Trônes Wood-Maltz Horn section of trenches. On 23 July they relieved the 17th Lancashire Fusiliers, who had suffered heavy shelling to their position throughout the day. It continued into the evening. During the course of the relief three of the Manchesters were killed, ten wounded and seven shell-shocked.

Private William Boardman was killed in action on 23 July 1916. He was from Middleton. He is commemorated on the Thiepval Memorial.

Sergeant Arthur Hare was killed in action on 23 July. Sergeant Hare had received the Military Medal for his actions during the failed raid of 8 May 1916. He was from Doncaster. He is commemorated on the Thiepval Memorial.

Private George Jones was killed in action on 23 July. He was aged 19 and from Bolton. He is buried in Dive Copse British Cemetery, Sailly-le-Sec.

Private David Moran was killed in action on 23 July. He was aged 27 and from Pendleton, Manchester. He is buried in Serre Road Cemetery No. 2.

Montgomery wrote to his mother that day:

23 [Trônes Wood] is a regular charnel house, full of dead men. So are 24 [Bernafay Wood] and 25 [Delville Wood]. The fighting here has been very fierce; we have lost heavily in the brigade, particularly in officers. However you can't take part in a show of this sort without losing. We have been unlucky in losing rather a lot of officers in proportion to men. We have up to date taken part in 3 big attacks and I expect one more will finish us for the time being. They will take us out to refit and to collect ourselves, and will fill us up with fresh drafts.

The whole country round here is a perfect shambles; everything absolutely shelled to bits. We have an enormous amount of artillery here & we shell the Germans all day & all night. His artillery fire is also very intense as he too has amassed a lot of guns against us.[42]

The enemy shelling continued through the next day – and intensified in the evening.

At 9.20 pm an SOS was sent up from the Manchesters' trenches. The enemy bombardment was causing considerable casualties and it was feared that an attack was imminent. In response, the Allied artillery put down a barrage. All communications were cut. Reinforcements were sent up from the 18th Lancashire Fusiliers, but the shell fire gradually subsided and no attack developed. The War Diary for the day records two men killed, thirty-eight wounded and seven shell-shocked.

> Private Percy F. Forth was killed in action on 24 July 1916. He was aged 17 and from Urmston. He is commemorated on the Thiepval Memorial.
>
> Private Joseph Kirkpatrick died of wounds on 24 July 1916. He was aged 19 and from West Gorton. He is buried in La Neuville British Cemetery, Corbie.
>
> Private Harry Taylor was killed in action on 24 July 1916. He was aged 23 and from Ashton under Lyne. He is commemorated on the Thiepval Memorial.

On 25 July the Manchesters were relieved by the 18th Lancashire Fusiliers and returned to Talus Boisé. During the course of the day the battalion lost another officer, Second Lieutenant Cook, to shell shock. In total, seven men were killed, twenty-five wounded, three shell-shocked and one reported missing that day.

> Private George William Allonby was killed in action on 25 July 1916. He was aged 22 and from Gorton. He is commemorated on the Thiepval Memorial.
>
> Private Frank Crowther was killed in action on 25 July 1916. He was from Hulme. He is commemorated on the Thiepval Memorial.

A selection of the 'in memoriam' notices for men of the 23rd Battalion posted in the *Manchester Evening News* (10 and 12 August 1916, 25 July 1917).

> Private John Finn was killed in action on 25 July 1916. He was aged 20 and from Openshaw. He is commemorated on the Thiepval Memorial.
>
> Lance Corporal Charles Frederic Harvey was killed in action on 25 July 1916. He was aged 47 and from Manchester. He is buried in Longueval Road Cemetery.
>
> Private John Hilton died on 25 July 1916. He was aged 21 and from Middleton. He is buried in Flatiron Copse Cemetery, Mametz.
>
> Lance Corporal George Lovett was killed in action on 25 July 1916. He was aged 23 and from Macclesfield. He is commemorated on the Thiepval Memorial.

Private Herbert Mitchell was killed in action on 25 July 1916. He was from Ancoats. He is buried in Tincourt New British Cemetery.

Private Peter Spratt was killed in action on 25 July 1916. He was from Hulme. He is commemorated on the Thiepval Memorial.

> SPRATT.—Killed in action July 25, 1916, Private PETER SPRATT, 28597, Manchester Regt.
> Duty called; he nobly answered.
> Ever remembered by his FELLOW-WORKMATES.

Private Joseph Stretch died of wounds on 25 July 1916. He was aged 34 and from Pendleton. He is buried in Corbie Communal Cemetery Extension.

Private Harold Thorniley was killed in action on 25 July 1916. He was aged 26 and from Hulme. He is commemorated on the Thiepval Memorial.

> Pte. HAROLD THORNILEY, 32, Park-street Hulme, and formerly employed by Messrs Chadwicks, Little Peter-street, Manchester was killed by a shell near Trônes Wood on July 24. He would have been 27 to-morrow.
> THORNILEY.—Private HAROLD THORNILEY, killed in action, July 24, Pals, Manchester Regt., Bob's Own. He gave his life for those he loved.
> PARENTS and BROTHERS.—32, Park-st, Hulme.

H. Thorniley.

On the 26th the battalion moved back to the bivouac camp at Talus Boisé again. The next day Brigadier General Sandilands sent a message of congratulations to the men of the 104th Brigade. It read:

> The General Officer Commanding wishes to thank all ranks of the 104th Infantry Brigade, 104th M.G. Coy., 104 Trench Mortar Battery for the way in which they held the right of the British Line for six days and seven nights, under the most trying conditions. The General Officer Commanding considers that the Brigade had upheld the traditions of the Lancashire Regiments, which have always played such a conspicuous part in the history of the British Army.[43]

A letter written by Bernard Montgomery that day, illustrates something of what those 'trying conditions' comprised:

> We had an absolutely hellish time the last few days and yesterday morning I went up to Trônes Wood to help extricate one of our Battalions which had had a particularly bad time. They were scattered about all over the place and very much shaken up. To collect them, I had to run all about the place in the open between Trônes Wood and Guillemont; the latter place is strongly held by the Germans & we have so far failed to take it. Heavy shelling was going on and I was sniped at incessantly by the Bosches. However I escaped with the exception of a bit of high explosive shell which grazed the palm of my hand.[44]

> Private Fred Lowe died of wounds on 26 July 1916. He was from Oldham. He is buried in Étaples Military Cemetery.
>
> Private Albert Shelmerdine died of wounds on 26 July 1916. He was aged 29 and from Longsight. He is buried in Corbie Communal Cemetery Extension. 'Duty nobly done', said his obituary in the *Manchester Evening News* (5 August 1916).
>
> Private Enoch Owen died of wounds on 27 July 1916. He was aged 32 and from Llandudno. He is buried in Abbeville Communal Cemetery.
>
> Private William Shepherd died of wounds on 27 July 1916. He was aged 19 and from Warrington. He is buried in La Neuville British Cemetery, Corbie.

After the failure of the first attack on Guillemont, the following few days would see a sequence of orders and counter-orders, as the next move was repeatedly announced and then postponed. This was a tense period of waiting, with all of the Manchester battalions conscious of the high number of casualties that the 19th Battalion had just suffered. Finally, the next attempt to take Guillemont was ordered for 30 July. Pinney rode around the 104th Brigade on the afternoon of 29 July and wished luck to the 23rd Manchesters who were to play a role in the attack.[45]

On the night of 29/30 July the 18th Manchesters picked their way through Trônes Wood, heading for assembly trenches on the far side. The wood was being heavily bombarded by the enemy that night, with both gas and explosive shells. Having stumbled through the wood in gas helmets, through a nightmare of tangling undergrowth and splintering trees, they finally made it to the assembly trenches at 4.30 am. Zero hour was 4.45 am. As dawn broke a dense fog obscured the view ahead – in places it was not possible to see more than 10 yards. The 18th Manchesters were to approach Guillemont from the north-west, while the 2nd Royal Scots Fusiliers were to attack from the south-west, with the support of the 17th Manchesters. The 16th Manchesters were in reserve and the 23rd Manchesters were assigned to provide carrying parties.

With the assistance of the thick mist the leading parties of the 2nd Royal Scots and 18th Manchesters succeeded in making it into the village and they connected up around 5.45 am. Soon they would find themselves engaged in fierce hand-to-hand fighting – and it would quickly become apparent that this was an isolated fight. German machine guns were now firing from the quarry and the station, sweeping the flat expanse in between Guillemont and Trônes Wood. It was going to prove difficult to keep in contact or to get reinforcements and ammunition to them. The latter task had been assigned to the 23rd Manchesters. At 5.00 am a party of Bantams (carrying twenty boxes of SAA and fifty-six boxes of bombs for the 18th Manchesters) did make it into the village. A group got through to the 2nd Royal Scots at 8.00 am, bringing up water and bombs, and another party made it in at 10.00 am, carrying Very lights and rockets. That would be the last contact with the Scots. Eventually, with German counter-attacks coming from the south and the east of the village, the British (those that could) were ordered to pull back. Most of the men in the village, though, could not get out. Surrounded and isolated, they were either killed or taken prisoner.

Together with the 17th Manchesters, the Bantams held the trenches running north and south from Arrow Head Copse for the remainder of the day. The area was intensely shelled in the evening. The War Diary of the 2nd Royal Scots Fusiliers reported 633 casualties on 30 July, of whom 546 were missing in Guillemont. The 18th Manchesters' casualties totalled 484 and the 17th Manchesters' 279. The War Diary of the 23rd Manchesters recorded five men killed, thirty wounded, four gassed and eleven missing.[46]

Major General Pinney received a telegram from Major General Shea, his opposite number at 30th Division. It read:

> In the name of my Division, I wish to thank you and yours, most sincerely for all you did for us. You gave us all help you possibly could, and it is our earnest hope that some day we may be able to repay you. We much deplore your losses, but will always remember the gallantry of your men.

Pinney wrote in his diary: 'I was proud that not only had we done what we were called on to do, but army & corps commanders had praised our efforts in doing it well.'[47]

Private Edward Entwistle was killed in action on 30 July 1916. He was from Bury. He is commemorated on the Thiepval Memorial.

Private Albert Hill was killed in action on 30 July 1916. He was aged 21 and from Royton. He is commemorated on the Thiepval Memorial.

Private Arthur Lawrence Mitchell was killed in action on 30 July 1916. He was from Ardwick. He is commemorated on the Thiepval Memorial.

Private Charles Parker was killed in action on 30 July 1916. He was from Manchester. He is commemorated on the Thiepval Memorial.

Private William Taylor was killed in action on 30 July 1916. He was from Rochdale. He is commemorated on the Thiepval Memorial.

Private Joseph Travis was killed in action on 30 July 1916. He was from Oldham. He is commemorated on the Thiepval Memorial.

Corporal John William Valentine was killed in action on 30 July 1916. He was from Shaw. He is commemorated on the Thiepval Memorial.

Second Lieutenant Frank Norcross died on the 30 July 1916. He was aged 19 and from Stockport. He is commemorated on the Thiepval Memorial.

Private Thomas Kelly died of wounds on 31 July 1916. He was aged 40 and from Manchester. He is buried in St Sever Cemetery, Rouen.

Private Ernest Emile Roberts died of wounds on 31 July 1916. He was aged 20 and from Manchester. He is buried in Salford (Weaste) Cemetery.

Private Harry Bulger died of wounds on 3 August 1916. He was aged 22 and from Bury. He is buried in St Sever Cemetery, Rouen.

Private David Carson died of wounds on 3 August 1916. He was aged 33 and from Chorlton-on-Medlock. He is buried in St Sever Cemetery, Rouen.

Private Joseph Russell died of wounds on 12 August 1916. He was aged 37 and from Seedley, Manchester. He is buried in Netley Military Cemetery in Hampshire. The cemetery was used by the Royal Victoria Military Hospital.

> Second Lieutenant Frank Norcross was killed in action on 30 July 1916. Aged 19 and from Stockport, he had been gazetted to the Manchesters just earlier in July. Only seven months earlier the local paper had been reporting Frank Norcross's achievements at Manchester Grammar School, winning a scholarship in classics to New College Oxford and his school's poetry prize. He was a sergeant in the Grammar School contingent of the Officers Training Corps. (*Manchester Evening News*, 16 December 1915). He is commemorated on the Thiepval Memorial.

In the days that followed Bernard Montgomery wrote home: 'I don't suppose anyone can realise the awfulness of the show generally in this Somme push unless they've been in it. The French, who are on our immediate right, say that Verdun at its worst was as nothing compared to this.'[48]

Guillemont – all that remained of the village at the end of the war.

Looking from Trônes Wood towards Ginchy, September 1916. From the magazine *Twenty Years After – The Battlefields of 1914–1918: Then and Now* (1928).

In the evening of 30 July a corps conference was held. 'Big attack has failed', Pinney noted in his diary.[49] The XIII Corps commander, Lieutenant General Congreve, ordered the relief of all the forward troops of the 30th and 35th Divisions. They would be replaced by the 55th Division who, over the next fortnight, would suffer 4,100 casualties. The 23rd Manchesters were withdrawn on 31 July and moved back to Happy Valley.

The next day a Minden Day Parade was held by the Lancashire battalions in Happy Valley. Minden Day celebrations date back to 1759, when the Lancashire Fusiliers marched across Minden Heath to Hanover, facing the French. Legend has it that the advancing troops picked wild briar roses and stuck them in their hats. Somehow red and white roses also appeared on steel helmets on 1 August 1916. The sun shone on Happy Valley. General Sandilands inspected the 104th Brigade and made a speech during which he read out the messages of thanks from the commander of 30th Division.

On 2 August the 23rd Manchesters marched to Sailly-le-Sec, south-west of Albert, on

> **WHY THE ROSES WERE WORN.**
>
> Members of the Lancashire Fusiliers in Manchester to-day were wearing red and white roses in their caps. It was their traditional way of recalling the anniversary of the battle of Minden (August 1, 1759), in which the XXth Regiment, the Lancashire Fusiliers of to-day, fought with gallantry. The fact that the famous regiment was then engaged with the Germans against the French in no way dims their glory.
>
> There are several hundreds of men at the Heaton Park camp, and these all received this morning, at the hands of Captain Leach and other officers, roses of red and white to remind them that their regiment fought as valiantly in Westphalia a century and a half ago as they are fighting in France to-day.

Minden Day was being observed in Manchester too, *Manchester Evening News*, 1 August 1916.

By 1919, when this photograph was taken, there was little left of the church in Sailly-le-Sec. Photograph from *Illustrated Michelin Guides to the Battle-Fields (1914–1918): The Somme, Volume 1*, p. 67.

the banks of the River Somme. The men rested here. The weather was hot and they swam in the river. The officers sat in the sun in a garden in the village, quietly looking out across the rooftops towards the church.

On 5 August the battalion was in railway carriages again. They marched, then, to Camps-en-Amiénois, to the west of Amiens. Bernard Montgomery wrote to his mother the next day:

> I am glad to say we are now back resting and refitting. We are about 40 miles behind the line in a place where they send all Divisions to rest and refit and get made up to strength again. It is very pretty countryside indeed . . . It is really very nice getting right away from it all and being in civilization again.[50]

While the men enjoyed the calm of the rest area, the officers found themselves much occupied with the subject of the new drafts of reinforcements who were arriving. They were being examined, tested, shuffled and worried about. The battalion War Diary notes that many of them were men 'of bad physique'. With a narrow recruitment criteria, it was clearly difficult to replace the original Bantams with men of equal physical standards. Divisional medical officers endorsed the concerns about the new drafts and recommended those men who were not up to the mark should be sent back to depots. GHQ agreed that sub-standard men should be weeded out, but it should wait until after the division had left the Fourth Army and moved to their new sector.

Having travelled a good distance to the rest area, the Bantams expected to be there for at least a week, but just four days after arriving they received orders to go back for their second dose of the Somme. 'We were of course very annoyed at only being given 4 days rest,' Bernard Montgomery wrote. 'It certainly does seem rather absurd taking us all the way back there for four days.'[51]

In fierce heat they marched wearily north to Airaines and from there entrained to Corbie, returning then to their billets in Sailly-le-Sec. They had another five days here, by the banks of the River Somme, but their enjoyment must have been coloured by the knowledge that they were about to go back in to the line. 'The heat the last week has been very trying,' Montgomery told his mother, 'and I have had bad headaches.'[52]

On 15 August they marched back to Happy Valley. The weather changed as they did so, and can have done little to improve the mood. The roads were wet and slippery. In Happy Valley, as it rained for the next three days, the 104th Brigade slept in tents and practised an attack. The valley's name must have felt deeply euphemistic. Even with the rain, Pinney's diary noted that there were great plagues of flies everywhere. 'It is of course very uncomfortable for the troops,' Montgomery wrote.[53]

On 18 August the 104th Brigade marched to Talus Boisé and the next evening went back into trenches. With the relief completed at 3.00 am, the men found themselves in pretty much the same stretch of the line that they had held previously, just with the front line advanced a thousand yards or so. 'This time we had our back depots etc in a part which was our front line trench last time we were in,' Montgomery wrote.[54] Some of the length of trench that the Manchesters were now taking over Lonely Trench had only just been captured that same afternoon and a grisly prospect greeted them – the trenches were in a very knocked-about condition, the parapets were badly damaged and the relieved battalion had not been able to evacuate or to bury their dead. 'Lonely Trench, Gordon Alley and Cockran [sic] Alley will always be remembered by the 104th Brigade', recalled Sandilands. 'It was almost impossible to walk down any of these without treading on the dead bodies of our men or on those of the enemy.' The place was beginning to smell rather badly. The men had plenty to do. But they set to and during the night of 20/21 they dug a new trench (Bantam Trench) in advance of the front line (Gordon Trench) that they had just inherited.[55]

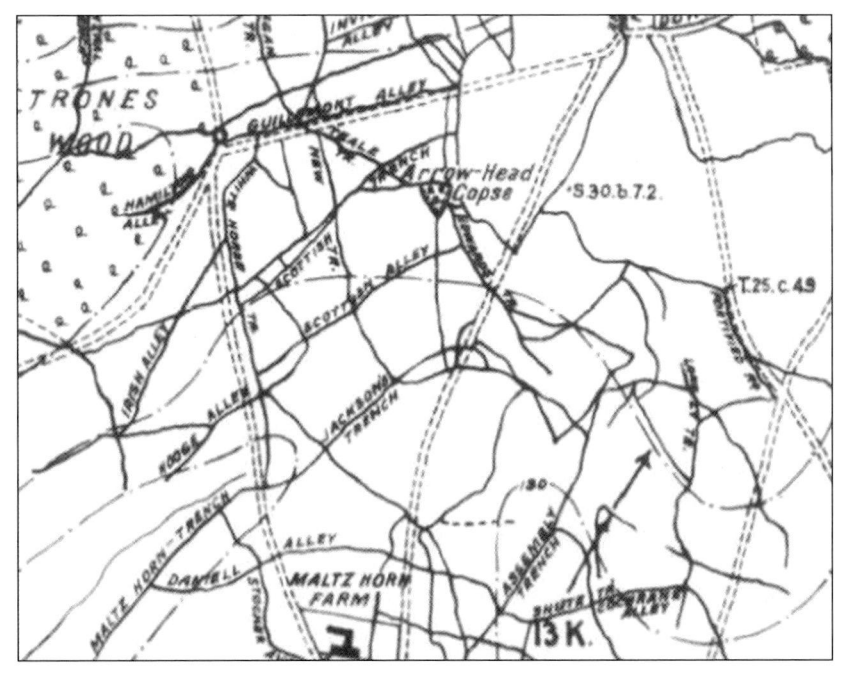

Map showing the location of Lonely Trench and Cochrane Alley. From Everard Wyrall, *The History of the King's Regiment (Liverpool), 1914–1919* (1930), Vol. II, p. 317.

Acting Sergeant Daniel Ball was killed in action on 20 August 1916. He was aged 23 and from Sale. He is commemorated on the Thiepval Memorial.

Private Henry Bradbury was killed in action on 20 August 1916. He was 29 and from Ashton under Lyne. He is commemorated on the Thiepval Memorial.

Private Fred Carpenter was killed in action on 20 August 1916. He was from Manchester. He is commemorated on the Thiepval Memorial.

Private Arthur Greaves was killed in action on 20 August 1916. He was killed by shrapnel while resting in a trench. He was from Salford. He is commemorated on the Thiepval Memorial.

> Private George Harrison was killed in action on 20 August 1916. He was from Hulme. He is commemorated on the Thiepval Memorial.
>
> Private Benjamin Heath was killed in action on 20 August 1916. He was aged 30 and from Stafford. He is commemorated on the Thiepval Memorial.
>
> Private Richard Henry Kay was killed in action on 20 August 1916. He was aged 28 and from Hulme. He is commemorated on the Thiepval Memorial.
>
> Private Nelson Mellor was killed in action on 20 August 1916. He was aged 23 and from Stalybridge. He is commemorated on the Thiepval Memorial.
>
> Private George Woodward was killed in action on 20 August 1916. He was from Manchester. He is commemorated on the Thiepval Memorial.
>
> Private Harold Mellor died of wounds on 21 August 1916. He was aged 19 and from Oldham. He is buried in Corbie Communal Cemetery Extension.

The next day Lieutenant M.H. Rose was sent to reconnoitre the facing enemy position. Rose stealthily picked his way out across no-man's-land and, seemingly unspotted, clambered down into the enemy line. He found himself at the entrance to a dugout. A German, his back to Rose, was speaking on a telephone. Sensing Rose's presence, he turned. They stared at one another. The German began to speak. Being unarmed and alone, Rose decided that it was time to make his exit.

Back in the Manchesters' trenches a raid was now planned. As darkness fell, Rose was repeating his creeping route out across no-man's-land, only this time with forty men following him. Making it once again into the enemy line, the party advanced along, bombing dugouts as they went. With all objectives successfully reached, the party made its way back, bringing a trophy machine gun with them. No casualties were sustained. In September 1916 Lieutenant Rose would be awarded the Military Cross for his actions during this raid. The citation reads:

> For conspicuous gallantry and determination on reconnaissance. Having discovered some of the enemy in a dug-out at the bottom of a steep bank, and being accompanied only by one man, he returned to our lines, and the same night organised a successful bombing party against the dug-out, capturing a machine gun. The success of this raid was entirely due to the coolness and ability displayed by Lieutenant Rose.[56]

In October the Manchester papers reported that the 23rd Battalion had offered the captured machine gun as a gift to the city. A letter from Lieutenant Colonel L.M. Stevens to the Lord Mayor read:

> 'In view of the general interest which you have always taken in the welfare of the battalion, it is the unanimous wish of the officers and all ranks that this gun should be a present to the city, and we trust that you will see fit to accept the same in the spirit in which it is sent. If you are agreeable I shall ask Lieutenant Rose to take the gun to England with him when next he proceeds on leave.'[57]

Matthew Howard Rose was born in Islington in 1882, but lived in Preston during his school days, where his father, Henry Rose, was editor of the *Lancashire Daily Post*. Before the war Rose was an actor, part of Miss Horniman's company in Manchester. He was appointed to the 22nd Manchesters as a temporary second lieutenant in April 1915 and then promoted to lieutenant in February 1916 (*London Gazette*, 5 July 1915 and 5 February 1916). After the war he returned to acting and then, in the 1920s, became a drama producer for BBC radio. He would be awarded the OBE. His obituary in *The Times* stated:

> Among actors, Howard Rose was something of a legend in his own day. He knew the exact effect he wanted from every line of a play and was single-minded in his determination to get it. Tall and distinguished, always well dressed, with a rose in his button-hole, he could be an awe-inspiring figure when the dramatic temperature in the studio began to rise. To some he remained a martinet; but to others he was an inspiration. He had a remarkable ear for the nuances of speech and a profound understanding of true depths and intricacies of character. In his own person he was the least theatrical of beings; he never looked for personal acclaim, the work was everything. He enjoyed a supremely happy marriage, the affection of numerous friends, and the beautiful garden which he had made was very near to his heart.[58]

The 23rd Manchesters were relieved on the night of 22/23 August. They moved back to the Citadel, a camp on a hillside towards the northern end of Happy Valley (today the site of Citadel New Military Cemetery). They would not be out of the line for long, though.

Private Cecil Dodd was killed in action on 22 August 1916. He was aged 35 and from Sale. He is buried in Quarry Cemetery, Montauban.

Private Charles Stonehouse was killed in action on 22 August 1916. He was from Walsall, Staffordshire. He is commemorated on the Thiepval Memorial.

The road between Combles and Guillemont.

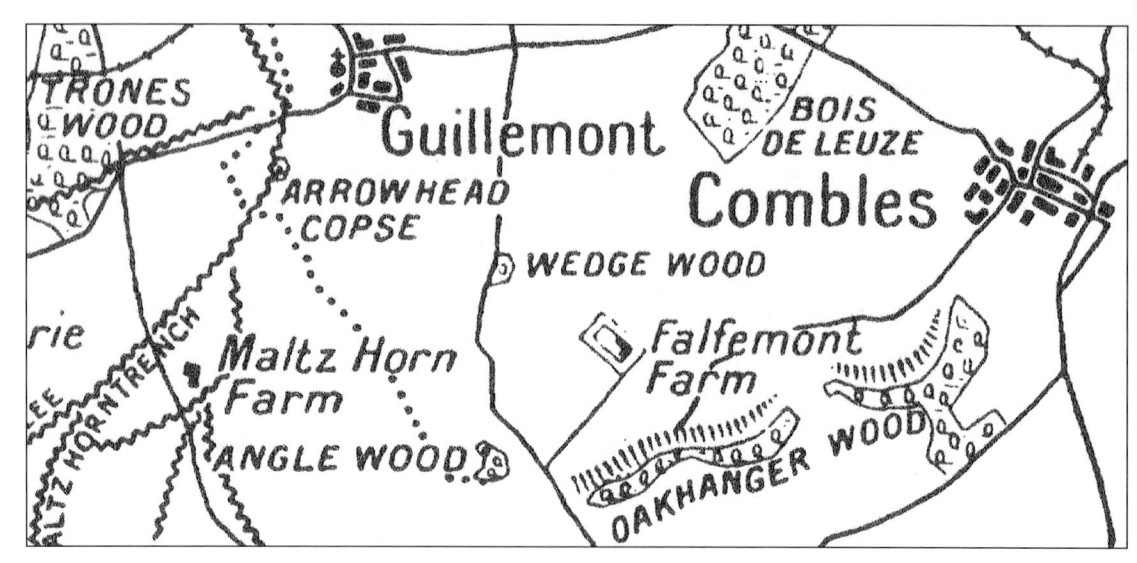

Detail of map taken from Davson, *The History of the 35th Division*, p. 29.

The following morning the 104th Brigade received orders that it was to take part in an attack the next day, in conjunction with the French, on the ridge on which sat Falfemont Farm, the high ground south-east of Guillemont. The brigade was to advance to the left of the French, from Angle Wood, and to capture and hold the enemy trenches to the south of Falfemont Farm. A representation was made to divisional HQ pointing out that this plan of attack – towards a complex of buildings on high ground, with no troops advancing to the battalion's left – had little prospect of success. 'But,' the Divisional History records, 'the situation made it necessary that it should be proceeded with'. 'We have 24 hours' notice for an operation that wants 4 days preparation,' Pinney wrote on 23 August. 'None of us had time even to see the front on which we were to attack,' recorded Sandilands. The 17th Lancashire Fusiliers, who had just taken over trenches from the French south of Angle Wood, were ordered to undertake the attack.[59]

Orders had been given to dig assault trenches from which to launch the attack, but when Pinney went up to inspect the position on the morning of the 24th he found that little preparatory work had been done. With the position subject to heavy shelling through the night, and the guides bringing the men up getting hopelessly lost, it had proved impossible to dig the advance trench and only one company of the 17th Lancashire Fusiliers had been able to make it up to the forward position, where they now lay concealed in shell holes. 'I went down and found the situation hopeless,' Pinney wrote. The plan had 'gone to blazes'. Pinney quickly reported back to the Corps Commander and asked that the Lancashire Fusiliers' part in the attack be scaled back. The attack was launched at 5.45 pm. As the French advanced, and reached their objectives, the Lancashire Fusiliers moved forward 300 yards and, on this new alignment, dug in.[60]

The 23rd Manchesters had moved back up on 24 August and supported the Fusiliers' attack, carrying up rations, ammunition and water to Angle Wood. The next day they started to dig a trench to connect up with the Fusiliers' new position.

The last-minute scaling back of 104th Brigade's role in the attack on Falfemont Farm seems to have raised questions about the effectiveness of the Bantams. Pinney's diary records that General Sir Henry Rawlinson turned up at divisional HQ on the afternoon of 24 August. Pinney noted that Rawlinson 'asked many critical questions about Bantams'. In reply he told Rawlinson that he was extremely disappointed with the quality of the reinforcements that he was getting sent. 'The new material were hopeless,' he complained. 'The degenerates I had sent away had come back and worse with them.' The next day Pinney lamented on the pages of his diary: 'Our new drafts have put the whole Divn out of their depth.'[61]

Private James Mellor was killed in action on 24 August 1916. He was aged 25 and from Middleton. He is commemorated on the Thiepval Memorial.

Private Samuel Smith was killed in action on 24 August 1916. He was aged 28 and from Morecambe. He is commemorated on the Thiepval Memorial.

Private Arthur Cunningham was killed in action on 25 August 1916. He was from Manchester. He is commemorated on the Thiepval Memorial.

Lance Corporal Michael Gavaghan was killed in action on 25 August 1916. He was aged 23 and from Rochdale. He is commemorated on the Thiepval Memorial.

Private Joseph Green was killed in action on 25 August 1916. He was aged 28 and from Miles Platting. He is commemorated on the Thiepval Memorial.

Private John William Howell was killed in action on 25 August 1916. He was from Oldham. He is commemorated on the Thiepval Memorial.

Private Enoch Falshaw Lupton was killed in action on 25 August 1916. He was from Oldham. He is commemorated on the Thiepval Memorial.

Private Robert Rodgers was killed in action on 25 August 1916. He was from Manchester. He is commemorated on the Thiepval Memorial.

Lieutenant Lewis Harold Barnard died on 25 August 1916. He was attached to the 104 Trench Mortar Battery. He was aged 23 and from Manitoba, Canada, and had enlisted in September 1914 as part of the first Canadian contingent. He is buried in Guillemont Road Cemetery.

Private John Barlow was killed in action on 26 August 1916. He was aged 22 and from Royton. He is commemorated on the Thiepval Memorial.

Private William Waite was killed in action on 26 August 1916. He was aged 20 and from Shaw. He is commemorated on the Thiepval Memorial.

The 23rd Manchesters came out of the trenches on the night of 26 August. The relief was not completed until about 6.00 am the following morning, though, as the relieving companies (the 1st Royal West Kents) lost their way and missed the guides. The Bantams now returned to the Citadel Camp, where they would remain for three wet days. 'We shall probably be going right away behind somewhere to rest and refit,' Montgomery conjectured in a letter. 'I don't think we shall be brought up into it again; the men could hardly stand three helpings of that sort of thing.'[62]

> Sergeant James Renshaw was killed in action on 27 August 1916. He is commemorated on the Thiepval Memorial.
>
> Private Alfred King died of wounds on 28 August 1916. He was from Oldham. He is buried in La Neuville British Cemetery, Corbie.
>
> Private Walter Chester died of wounds on 31 August 1916. He was from Skipton, Yorkshire. He is buried in Oldham (Hollinwood) Cemetery.
>
> Private George Radcliffe died of wounds on 31 August 1916. He was aged 31 and from Middleton. He is buried in Abbeville Communal Cemetery.

Geoffrey Malins' film *The Battle of the Somme* opened in cinemas in Manchester on 28 August 1916. 'The public displayed great eagerness to see the film,' the *Manchester Guardian* recorded, 'and the Oxford Street house was besieged from before the time of opening in the afternoon until late evening.' Judging by the *Guardian*'s report, the mood of the cinema-goers seems to have changed over the course of the film. The Manchester audience cheered as the troops went over the top, but the cheers 'died down to silence before the vision of the still, lifeless figure slipping back into the trench and the bodies just beyond the parapet. There was tense silence, too, as well there might be, when the slowly moving panorama of trench debris brought to view the huddled heaps of the fallen.'[63] The *Manchester Guardian* commented that the film 'leaves out many terrors that we know to exist; but, on the whole, it reveals war in its true aspect – as a grimly destructive and infernal thing.' The newspaper considered, 'In the future one can imagine the film being used by some who desire to revive monitory memories then beginning to fade.'[64]

Meanwhile, back in France, Pinney was inspecting reinforcements that day. He examined all of the men who had been drafted into the 104th Brigade since 15 July. His verdict was: 'Lancs Fus about half passable. Manchesters bad.' He reflected: 'It is no good putting large numbers of such men straight into a battle. Some degenerates quickly demoralize the lot. They have to be broken in to be brave and it takes time.' Pinney complained that it was 'rather hard on me personally to have to command poor material' and clearly he meant to do something to change that situation. His diary notes that he had arranged a meeting with GHQ to discuss the future of the Bantam Division.[65]

On 30 August the 104th Brigade moved as a whole, marching to Heilly (between Albert and Amiens) in the pouring rain. Here they boarded trains and headed back north. The Manchesters found themselves back in Neuvillette (Bouquemaison), where they had been billeted at the start of July. It was here that they had first trained for the Somme. How odd, then, it must have seemed to be back here.

The 35th Division was now transferred to VI Corp, Third Army. The Divisional History concludes this chapter:

> The period of the Battle of the Somme cannot be considered to have been either a happy or successful time for the infantry of the division. The serious losses suffered at the commencement, whilst battalions were either engaged in digging trenches or

The ruins of Guillemont.

serving under other commands, had an undesirable effect upon all ranks, and, when the opportunity finally came to act as a division and carry out attacks, which a month previously would no doubt have been crowned with success, the men who would have executed the orders were no longer there, and those who had taken their places were in many cases unfitted for the work which they were called upon to perform.[66]

It was now time to address the issue of those 'unfits'. On 31 August Pinney issued a memorandum to all captains and medical officers in the division. It suggests that the men now coming in as reinforcements had not had enough training or experience before being sent to the front. It, politely but clearly, communicates frustration on Pinney's part. It reads:

Memorandum ref. Reinforcements
Men found medically unfit or men who are obviously deficient in physique or mind are to be returned to the Base forthwith under instructions issued separately.

Officers are not to reject men who were merely nervous under their first experience of fire and are otherwise fit. Such men are to be carefully brought up to the standard of the Bantam Division by being gradually trained in Trench Warfare, as the Division was originally trained.

Similarly, men temporarily unable to march from sore feet etc are to be taught how to get their feet into good condition and are not to be taken as permanently inefficient.

We have to use every means in our power to overcome the enemy. We must therefore get the best out of all men who can possibly become soldiers.

A note in Pinney's diary, written the same day, has a rather less diplomatic tone. He had met with GHQ doctors that day and they had together reviewed the results of an inspection of the reinforcements. Pinney wrote: 'Careful inspection of 2000 reinforcements bore out my report. These are 20% to 30% of degenerates. Some of them miserable objects of humanity. We are to send away these useless ones.'[67]

There were wider changes afoot as well. Looking at the length of the casualty lists in the Manchester papers gives a real sense of the enormous concentrated impact of the Somme campaign on communities – and a sense of the tragic twist in the logic of the 'Pals' concept. This was realised at the time and, after the Somme, an effort was made to mix men more (wounded men, once recovered, could be sent to any battalion requiring numbers). The 'Pals' battalions would now start to lose their local identity.

Guillemont was finally taken on 3 September 1916. The *History of the King's Regiment* recorded, 'Guillemont had fallen! At last that rubble heap, of which scarce one stone or yard of ground was unstained by the blood of gallant men, was in our hands.' When the British line was consolidated, and there was opportunity to explore the ruins of Guillemont, there were found to be networks of subterranean passages under the remains of the village and enormous cellars in which large numbers of the enemy had evidently sheltered.[68]

AROUND GUILLEMONT
Then and Now

In 1928 a magazine called *Twenty Years After – The Battlefields of 1914–1918: Then and Now* published images of Guillemont. The twin photographs show the same road, between Guillemont and Montauban, in September 1916 (top) and 1928 (bottom). Guillemont Road Cemetery is to the left rear of the car.

At the end of the month the film maker Geoffrey Malins visited the vicinity. His memoires record:

> The village of Guillemont literally does not exist, in fact, it is an absolute impossibility to tell where the fields ended and the village began. It is one of the most awful specimens of the devastating track of war that exists on the Western Front. The village had been turned by the Bosche into a veritable fortress; trenches and strong points, bristling with machineguns, commanded every point which gave vantage to the enemy. But, after much bloody fighting, our troops stormed and captured the place and the German losses must have been appalling. Many have been buried, but the work of consolidating the ground won and pressing on the attack does not permit our men thoroughly to cleanse the square miles of ground and bury the bodies and fragments that cover it.[69]

In 1919 the Michelin *Guide* summarised Guillemont for battlefield tourists thus:

> Guillemont (razed to the ground) was entirely captured by the British on September 3, 1916. No trace whatever remains of the houses, the sites of which are now indistinguishable from the surrounding fields. The whole area was devastated and is now overrun with rank vegetation. After its capture it was strewn with wreckage of all kinds—stones, bricks, beams, agricultural implements, and household furniture from the shattered farms and houses. The fine modern church, Gothic in style, which stood in the centre of the village, has entirely disappeared.[70]

The Thiepval Memorial to the missing of the Somme, photographed soon after its inauguration in 1932.

Chapter 7

Arras: 'City of the Dead'

The first week of September 1916 saw the 23rd Manchesters heading north. On 3 September, as the battle for Guillemont was in its final stages, the Bantams were arriving in Arras. They would remain here, in reserve billets, for the next week. Arras seems to have been a curious mixture of comfort and ruination.

The German army had briefly occupied the town, for three days, in September 1914. Facing a French counterattack, most of the German troops withdrew on 9 September, but some positions were solidly entrenched and fighting endured around Arras for a month. With the town finally retaken by the French at the start of October, the front settled, bulging around the east of the town, only a mile or so from its centre. Trenches started to be dug in the eastern suburbs – even cutting through St Sauveur Cemetery. German heavy artillery began to bombard Arras on 6 October 1914. It is estimated that, over three days, 1,000 shells fell on Arras. The Hôtel de Ville burned down. The famous belfry fell. Over the next few weeks much of the town's historic centre was destroyed and fires spread through the suburbs.

Publishing photographs of the 'Martyrdom of Arras', the French press compared the

Iconic image of the ruins of Arras after the bombardment of October 1914. Part of a wall of the Hôtel de Ville remains standing.

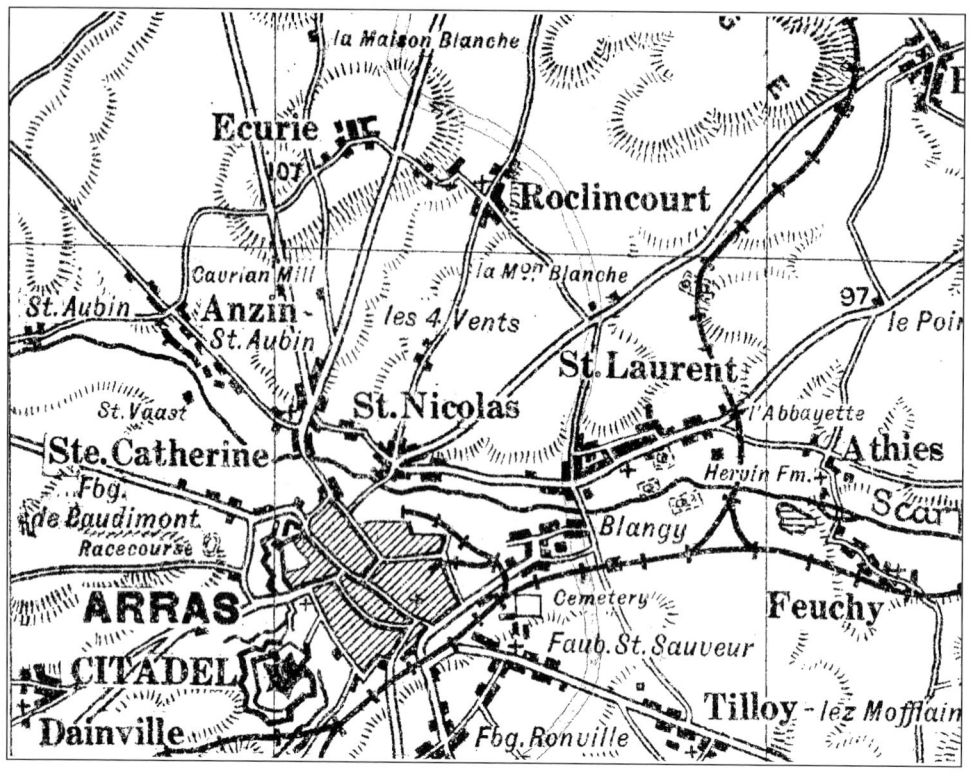

Map from *The western front at a glance: a large-scale atlas of the Allies fighting line in the west* (George Philip & Son, Ltd, London, 1917).

sight to the ruins of Pompeii. American artist, Walter Hale, in Arras in July 1915, was also reminded of antique ruins. 'Arras was like a city of the dead,' he wrote.

> It gave one something of the sensation of walking through the ghostly cairns of Pompeii or St. Pierre Martinique. It was like a giant catacomb and the lowering clouds of yellow smoke hanging like a pall overhead, the deserted streets, the empty shell of houses, the growl of artillery, and the occasional violent detonation when an explosive bomb landed, increased the uncanny feeling of death and disaster.[1]

Bombardments would continue over the next two years. When the French handed this length of the line over to British forces in the spring of 1916, Arras was already largely a town in ruins.

The journalist Philip Gibbs was in Arras in the winter of 1916. He described the atmosphere of the town:

> It was enormously quiet at times in Arras. The footsteps of my companion were startling as they clumped over the broken pavement of the square, and voices—

GUERRE 1914-15-16

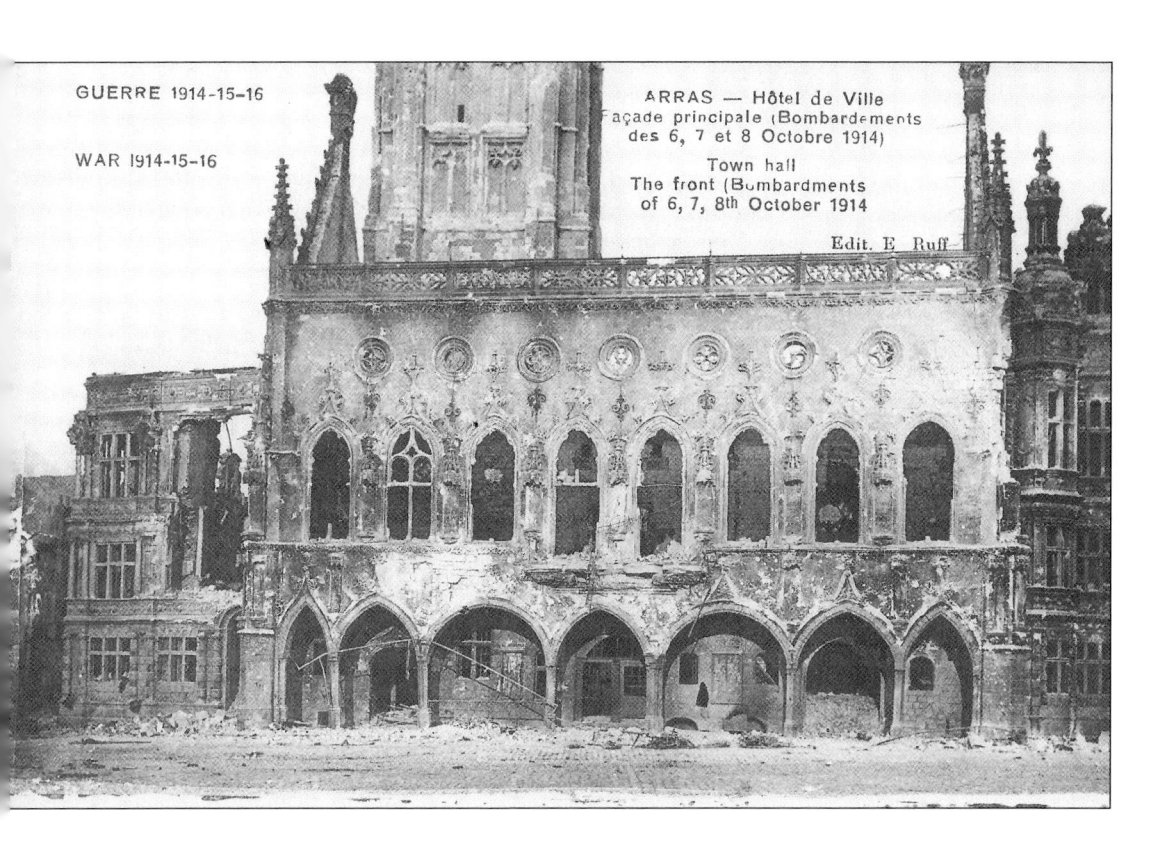

WAR 1914-15-16

ARRAS — Hôtel de Ville
Façade principale (Bombardements
des 6, 7 et 8 Octobre 1914)

Town hall
The front (Bombardments
of 6, 7, 8th October 1914

Edit. E. Ruff

The Hôtel de Ville after the bombardment of October 1914.

GUERRE 1914-15-16

WAR 1914-15-16

Edit. E. Ruff

ARRAS — Hôtel de Ville
(Bombardements des

Town hall, seen from
(Bombardments of the

vue de la rue Saint-Géry
6, 7 et 8 Octobre 1914)

Saint-Gery street
October 6, 7, 8th 1914

women's voices—coming up from some hole in the earth sounded high and clear, carrying far, in an unearthly way, in this great awful loneliness of empty houses, broken churches, ruined banks and shops and restaurants, and mansions cloistered once in flower gardens behind high white walls.[2]

Walking east, passing through the ruins of the shops and restaurants, the traveller came to the suburb of Blangy. It was through these eastern fringes of the town, in between the remains of breweries, forges and factories, that the trenches were now cut. Walter Hale made this journey:

Following the Rue Douai in the environs toward Blangy there is nothing left of the town at all. There was not a house standing intact and only a few of the chimneys. Trees, freshly hewn off as if by an axe, were flung across the streets – everywhere great holes in the cobble stones where the shells had torn up the pavement. One house was gutted, but its green tiled fireplaces, one on top of the other, were as carefully polished as though their owners had just left them. Further out was a little cottage that brought us to a stop with a catch in our throats. Its walls were blown out and in the rear the ceiling of the second floors had fallen over the kitchen range. The front bedroom remained, with its outside wall swiped off; in it were a little white bed, a table with a reading lamp, a pair of slippers, a wardrobe hung with women's clothes, and some hat boxes above. The door jamb underneath was supported by the only part of the front wall still standing. Set in bricks at the side was a neat brass plate with the sign 'Madame Houdain, Modes'. The story of Madame Houdain would seem to need no further telling.[3]

Shelled houses on the Rue de Douai, Arras.

French troops in the front line trenches in the suburbs of Arras.

Directed down a communication trench, dug among the broken suburban streets, the shot-up factories and the tumbledown shops, Hale found himself in the front line trenches. It surprised him how quickly he arrived there.

On 10 September 1916 the Manchester Bantams were making that same journey. They had orders to move into the 'I Left sub-sector' of the Arras trenches, relieving the 20th Lancashire Fusiliers. I Sector extended from a point south of the Cambrai Road to the banks of the Scarpe at Blangy. It was their turn to sample this curious suburban troglodyte existence.

According to Brigadier General Sandilands, I Sector had 'been very lightly held' by the French. By the time that 104th Brigade inherited the sector, there were a series of saps (from 100 yards to 200 yards long), which had previously been communication trenches between the support line and front line. The old front line had been wired up to prevent passage through it and the sap heads were held by posts. This was clearly deemed to be an unsatisfactory arrangement and the first task that the Bantams faced on their arrival in Arras would be to put the trench system into 'good order'. The Manchesters now set to. The Divisional History details:

> In a short time they were not only cleaned, revetted, and fully duck-boarded but, by making use of the waterpower of the Scarpe, battalion headquarters etc., were eventually lit by electric light. It must be acknowledged that the soil of Arras lent itself to good trench-making, and similar results might not have been obtained in certain other portions of the line without a prodigious amount of labour.[4]

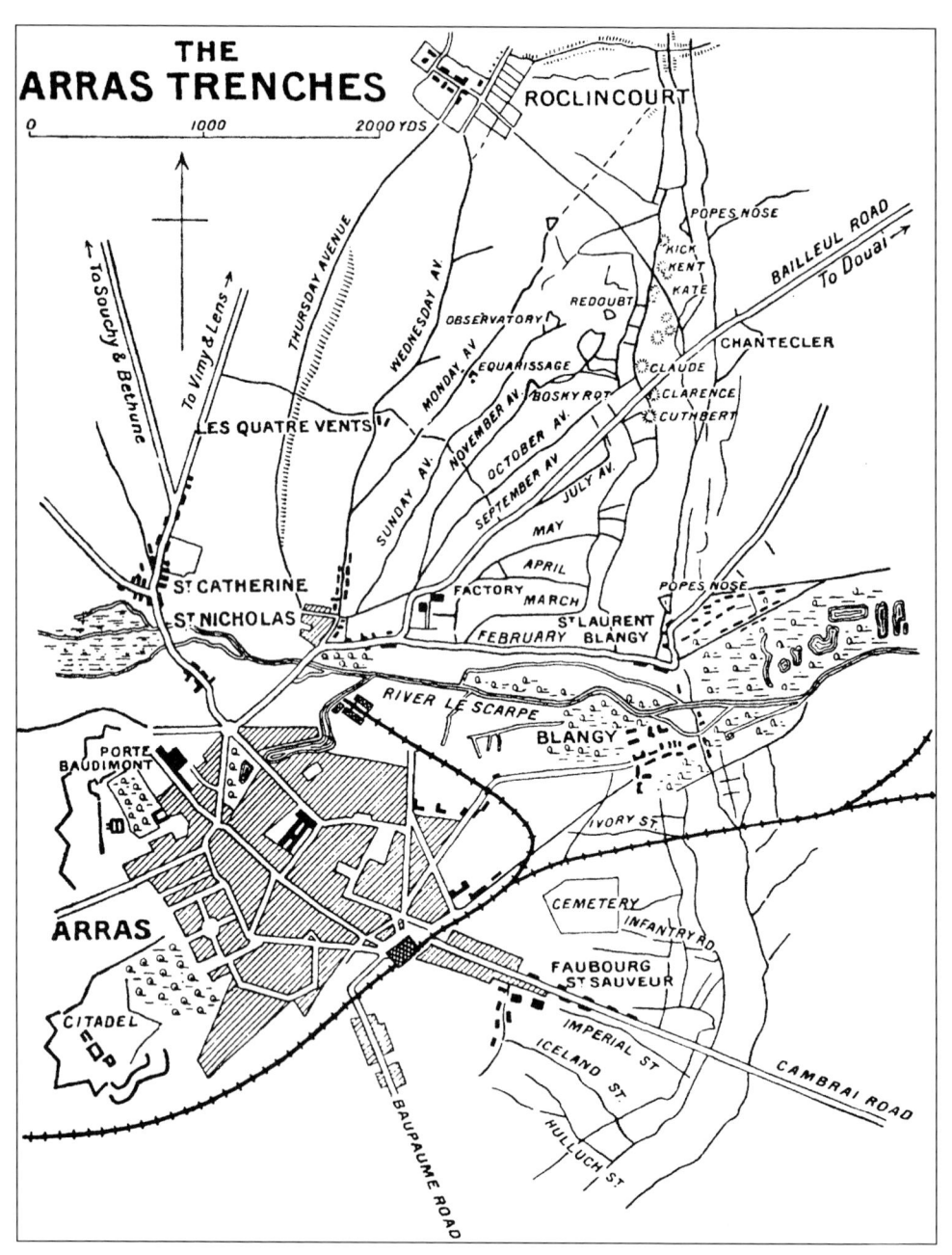

The I Sector trenches (all of their names beginning with 'I'), are to the south of Blangy on the plan above. Taken from Davson's *The History of the 35th Division*, p. 59.

Over the next few weeks the Bantams would turn the Blangy line into 'a model of what trenches should be'. Though this housekeeping work was occasionally interrupted by shelling, how calm and quiet days must have seemed after the Somme. It was assumed

Blangy. The sender of this postcard has added the note: 'This used to be a village of 1800 inhabitants??'.

that the men occupying the enemy trenches were also, effectively, recuperating after having been in action further south.

There were to be some excitements, though. On the night of 15/16 September the Manchesters launched a raid with the aim of securing an identification of the enemy unit facing it. The target was the saps running parallel to and immediately north and south of the railway line. This area had been bombarded the previous day, with the aim of destroying the wire. At ten minutes prior to zero two parties of twenty men, each led by an officer, and a covering party of ten men, advanced beyond the British wire. At five minutes before zero an intense artillery barrage was put down on the enemy front line. It lifted as the raiding parties advanced. The raid started at 2.30 am. Reaching the German wire, the Manchesters discovered that although it was damaged it was still significant. The party north of the railway line found it impossible to get through the wire and, after bombing the sap, they withdrew. The party south of the railway, led by Second Lieutenant Abraham, was also having issues with the wire, but they eventually managed to work their way through by using mats. When they entered the enemy sap it was deserted but, alerted to the raiding party's presence, the enemy advanced into the sap and an exchange of bombs ensued. Though items were retrieved (a steel helmet and a few stick bombs), the raiding party failed to secure an identification. The party returned without casualties, but, in retaliation for the raid, the cemetery area was shelled. One man was recorded as killed and two wounded by aerial torpedoes and a transport man was killed by a fall of earth.

> Private James William Holland was killed in action on 15 September 1916. He was from Manchester. He is buried in Faubourg d'Amiens Cemetery, Arras.
>
> Private Thomas Summers was killed in action on 15 September 1916. He was from Ancoats. He is buried in Haute-Avesnes British Cemetery, to the west of Arras – a cemetery that was used by field ambulances.

On 16 September the Manchesters were relieved by the 20th Lancashire Fusiliers. The 23rd Battalion now moved back into the reserve billets, which were situated to the rear of I Sector, around the cemetery in the Faubourg St Sauveur. 'Battalions out of the line lived in the most comfortable conditions in the town of Arras,' Sandilands recalled:

> The men of one of the reserve Companies were billeted in houses in the Douai Road – houses which actually contained pianos! Newspapers only one day old were delivered to them every morning by a little Frenchman, who, it is rumoured, was ultimately killed by a shell. Another reserve Company used to live in trenches and dug-outs in the cemetery. Here, it will be remembered, the reserve rations and water were housed in someone's family vault. The cemetery defences were very well constructed, and the surroundings did not appear to depress anyone unduly.[5]

The gates of Saint Sauveur Cemetery in Arras.

> In September 1916 Private J.H. Carmont was awarded the Military Medal. Private Carmont, 24 years old and from Ardwick, had joined the Welsh Regiment at the start of the war, but was discharged as medically unfit. He had made several attempts to join the Manchester Regiment before he was taken on by the 23rd Battalion.

Over the course of their week in reserve the Manchesters acted as working parties for the Royal Engineers.

On 22 September the Manchesters moved back into the line. The War Diary of the 17th Lancashire Fusiliers, occupying the stretch of trenches to the Manchesters' right, records: 'Enemy absolutely passive. He is distinctly nervous and appears anxious to avoid combat in any form . . . The enemy is extremely careful in expenditure of Artillery ammunition and it is the exception for his Artillery to fire. He appears to be very short of guns and ammunition opposite this front.' As the Divisional History put it, it was becoming increasingly apparent that the enemy's chief wish 'was to be left alone'.[6]

> Private Joseph Healey Bamber was killed in action on 28 September 1916. He was aged 42 and from Withington. He is buried in Faubourg d'Amiens Cemetery, Arras.

On 21 September Major General Pinney received a telegram offering him the command of the 33rd Division. Increasingly concerned by the deteriorating quality of the reinforcements being sent to the Bantam division, and how this was reflecting on his abilities, he accepted the job. He left the next day, but not before issuing a message of farewell to the Bantams. It read: 'Major General Pinney bids farewell to the 35th Division and wishes them good luck in the war and after. He carries with him a lasting memory of the goodwill and friendship shown him by all ranks.'[7] In exchange, Major General Herman Landon, formerly the GOC of the 33rd Division, now assumed command of the 35th. The decision to rotate commanders seems to have been made in order to give Landon (whose health was not entirely robust) a less active command, the 35th Division now having moved to a relatively quiet sector. Pinney, the younger man, was presumably thought to be a more effective commander for an active division. As one contemporary commented of Landon, 'He has been given light duty' – but he did not mean to give the Bantams an easy ride.[8] Having been with them since their Masham training, Pinney had a personal investment in the reputation of the 35th Division – and his army diary also communicates an affection for the men within it. Landon had no such complicating connections. Indeed, in being swapped for a younger man and now given a Bantam division to command, his pride might well have taken a knock.

Major General H.J.S. Landon. Image from Davson, *The History of the 35th Division*, p. 86.

Landon – and the enemy - were not going to let the Bantams continue to enjoy a quiet life in Arras. Sandilands recalled:

> The line was very quiet when we first took over – a most pleasing change from the Somme. But within a week or two a great craze came into fashion for seeing who could get off the greatest number of 'Stokes', 2-in mortar shells, and rifle grenades in a day, with the natural result that by the end of October there were moments when the front line could be distinctly breezy.[9]

On 4 October the Manchesters moved back into the line. During September gas cylinders had been arriving in Arras; they had been carried forward and were lined up in specially dug pits. In the course of October orders, and then last-minute counter-orders, for the discharge of the gas would arrive with some frequency. The proximity of this 'frightfulness' seems to have kept the men in a constant state of unease. Sandilands recalled:

> On two occasions we had gas cylinders put in on our front, which were the cause of a considerable amount of anxiety, as on the second occasion they were in position for weeks before the wind was favourable for the discharge. The words 'Duncan and Jack, Rubber and Gravel', which meant that the gas would be or would not be discharged, became a perfect nightmare, as they used to come through three or four times in the same night.[10]

Private Harry Ball died of wounds on 3 October 1916. He was aged 20 and from Manchester. He is buried in St Pol Communal Cemetery Extension.

Private William Leonard was killed in action on 6 October 1916. He was from Manchester. He is buried in Faubourg d'Amiens Cemetery, Arras.

But, on the night of 8 October, the gas would finally be used. The 35th Division received orders to discharge the gas at 8.45 pm. This was carried out all along the division's front. The War Diary of 17th Lancashire Fusiliers, holding the length of trench to the Manchesters' right, details: 'The flotation occasioned considerable confusion in the enemy lines; a great deal of excited shouting was heard and red & green rockets were fired apparently for barrage hostile retaliation which was however distinctly weak and apparently feeble.'[11]

At 10.45 pm three patrols were sent forward by the Manchesters, tasked with investigating the effects of the gas on the enemy. These parties, however, discovered that the enemy front line was strongly held and on alert for an attack. All of the gaps that had been cut in the wire were covered by machine guns and bombing parties, 'rendering entry into his line a matter of considerable difficulty'.[12] The patrols were bombed back. They did however get close enough to register that the gas was lingering heavy in the enemy trenches. Indeed, some of the reconnoitring party suffered its effects. Subsequent information from prisoners indicated that twenty-five of the enemy suffered the effects of the gas, and most of these died. Thirty-three men of the Manchesters would also need treatment, as the gas was slow to disperse from their trenches after the discharge.

> Private Abraham Singleton died on 8 October 1916. He was from Hyde, Cheshire. He is buried in the Faubourg d'Amiens Cemetery, Arras.
>
> Private Walter William Grahame Betts died of wounds on 10 October 1916. He was aged 20 and from Nottingham. He is buried in Avesnes-le-Comte Communal Cemetery Extension.

After a few days in reserve billets, the Manchesters were back in the line on 16 October. On the night of the 20th they were raiding again. Advancing through a gap in the enemy wire, opposite Infantry Road, a raiding party reached the parapet but there they were observed and challenged. Bombs were exchanged. Second Lieutenant Hines and his NCO were wounded and two men were killed. The raiding party, becoming confused and disorganised, was forced to retreat. It had failed in its objective to secure an identification.

> Private William Carrigan was killed in action on 20 October 1916. He was aged 26 and from Tidworth, Hants. He is commemorated on the Arras Memorial.
>
> Lance Corporal William Cox was killed in action on 20 October 1916. He was aged 23 and from Hulme. He is commemorated on the Arras Memorial.
>
> Private John Ward died of wounds on 21 October 1916. He was aged 22 and from Salford. He is buried in Salford (Weaste) Cemetery.

By mid October the weather had turned wet. Towards the end of the month heavy rain was causing trench walls to collapse (on one occasion, in I Sector, a collapse buried a store of gas cylinders which then had to be carefully dug out by hand). Clearly the rain was creating problems in the opposite lines too. The Manchesters' War Diary for 7 November notes: 'Our trenches were very badly damaged by heavy rain. Several small enemy parties were seen throwing earth from the enemy line.'

> Private Joseph Riley was killed in action on 28 October 1916. He was from Manchester. He is buried in Faubourg d'Amiens Cemetery, Arras.
>
> Lance Corporal Arthur Morrissey was killed in action on 8 November 1916. He was aged 22 and from Salford. He is buried in Faubourg d'Amiens Cemetery, Arras.
>
> Sergeant James Bowers was killed in action on 11 November 1916. He was aged 25 and from Failsworth. He is buried in Faubourg d'Amiens Cemetery, Arras.
>
> Private Richard Hall died of wounds on 13 November 1916. He was aged 26 and from Bury. He is buried in Habarcq Communal Cemetery Extension.

In early November a lot of activity is noted was the enemy lines. Digging and carrying parties are observed and there is repeated mention, in the battalion War Diary, of heads looking out over the top of the facing parapets. Numerous enemy aeroplanes are noted, flying low over the Manchesters' trenches on 5 and 8 November. There was an increasing suspicion that an attack was imminent.

After a week back in reserve billets, the Manchesters returned to the line on 17 November – and things were heating up. The number of trench mortars available to the enemy seemed to have significantly increased, and their bombs were now being copiously pitched at the British lines. In addition, hostile patrolling had become more regular, on a larger scale and more spirited. On 20 November, at dusk, a line of around fifty men was sighted behind the facing trees. The Manchesters' Lewis guns played along the trees at intervals during the night. The next day parties were observed carrying wire and stakes - and were fired on by the battalion's snipers. On the 22nd ninety-two rifle grenades were fired at the Manchesters' lines and it was noted that about twenty trees had been felled by the enemy during the night along the Blangy–Tilloy Road.

> Private Alfred Brearley was killed in action on 23 November 1916. He was aged 38 and from Ashton under Lyne. He is buried in Faubourg d'Amiens Cemetery, Arras.
>
> Private Charles Victor Clampitt died of wounds on 3 December 1916. He was from Stockport. He is buried in Habarcq Communal Cemetery Extension.

On the night of 25 November the 104th Brigade's front line trenches were vacated as gas was again to be released. Having been subjected to mortar fire for much of that afternoon, the men gladly retired, leaving only a few Lewis gun parties in the forward saps. The gas was due to be released at 11.45 pm, but at 11.35 pm the order was cancelled. At 12.35 am the discharge was rescheduled. It was finally then released in two batches – at 2.35 am and 4.05 am. The War Diary of the 23rd Manchesters notes that there was 'practically no enemy retaliation'. This perhaps gives a deceptively tranquil impression of the night's events.

There were three enemy raids that night (one against each of 104th, 105th and 106th Brigades), though, as the Divisional History puts it, the evidence concerning these events is somewhat 'confusing'. It seems that, while it was mostly vacated for the gas discharge, and subject to a heavy trench mortar barrage, a German raiding party had entered the right section of the I Sector, the length of trenches manned by the 17th Lancashire Fusiliers. The few men that remained – the Lewis and Stokes gunners – emptied their ammunition on the raiding party but thereafter retreated. 'The Germans are in!', the gunners exclaimed when they reached the reserve platoon. A party then went forward, only to find that the raiding party had already left. Damningly it was reported that 'the garrison offered little opposition' to the raid.[13]

Meanwhile, to the north, in K Sector, the 106th Brigade had experienced a similar raid. Again, the details seem to be somewhat – and significantly – confused. Around 2.25 am. Lieutenant James Mundy of the 19th Durham Light Infantry, the officer on duty, accompanied by Lance Sergeant Joseph Stones, encountered a German raiding party. King's Crater, defended by the DLI, was only thinly guarded at this time as the Durhams were about to launch a raid themselves 700 yards to the north of the crater and retaliatory enemy shelling was anticipated. The enemy raiders shot Lieutenant Mundy, whereupon

Sergeant Stones ran and raised the alarm (notably – and fatally – dropping his rifle in the process).[14] The enemy raiding party meanwhile moved to the north of the crater. On seeing them approaching, one of the sentries there is alleged to have shouted, 'Run, for the Germans are on you'.[15] Among those who accordingly retreated to the support lines were Lance Corporal Peter Goggins and Lance Corporal John McDonald, both of whom would shortly be detained by the military police. The enemy party, some eight to twelve men, then proceeded some way down the front line, bombing dugouts as they went, before returning to their own lines.

This would not be the only incident that would reflect badly on the Durhams that night. At 3.00 am their own planned raid went ahead. Though the leading group succeeded in advancing through the wire, the remainder of the party (two officers and some forty-five men), were halted in their forward progress by British shells 'dropping thickly' in no-man's-land. When someone allegedly shouted the order 'Get back', chaos ensued and men scattered back towards their own lines. The upwards reporting of the night's incidents seems to have been uncomplimentary to the 19th DLI – and to the Bantam division as a whole. The Divisional History concludes its account of the events of 26 November thus: 'Although the general result of the enemy raids was much to be deplored it may be said to have had one good effect. It brought forcibly to notice that which commanding officers had been reporting for some time, namely, that the major part of the recently received reinforcements could not be trusted to hold the line.'[16]

It clearly was indeed 'brought forcibly to notice'. It's difficult not to conclude that the knives were already out – and sharpened – for the Bantams. A series of courts martial were held between 24 December 1916 and 1 January 1917. Lance Sergeant Stones and the seven men of the sentry group were variously charged with casting away arms, quitting their posts and cowardice.[17] The sixteen men of the unsuccessful raiding party were also charged with cowardice. In total twenty-six men were tried and received the maximum penalty. Major General Landon's opinion seems to have determined the final outcome and the three NCOs (Stones, Goggins and McDonald) had their sentences confirmed. Landon commented that the NCOs, having exhibited 'mental and physical degeneracy', must be held 'as having especially failed in their soldierly duties and responsibilities'.[18] He clearly believed that an example should be made of them. All of the other accused had their sentences commuted to ten to fifteen years penal servitude.

Stones, Goggins and McDonald were executed by firing squad on 18 January 1917. An eyewitness account of their execution, written by Private Albert Rochester, then a military prisoner, was published in Ernest Thurtle's anti-death penalty pamphlet *Shootings at Dawn*:

> 'The next scene - a piercingly cold dawn; a crowd of brass hats, the medical officer, and three firing parties. Three stakes a few yards apart and a ring of sentries around the woodland to keep the curious away. A motor ambulance arrives conveying the doomed men. Manacled and blindfolded, they are helped out and tied up to the stakes. Over each man's heart is placed an envelope. At the sign of command the firing parties, twelve to each, align their rifles on the envelopes. The officer in

charge holds his stick aloft and as it falls thirty-six bullets usher the souls of three Kitchener's men to the great unknown. As a military prisoner I helped clear the traces of that triple murder. I took the posts down. I helped carry those bodies towards their last resting place; I collected all the blood-soaked straw and burnt it. Acting upon police instructions I took all their belongings from the dead men's tunics (discarded before being shot). A few letters, a pipe, some fags, a photo. I could tell you of the silence of the military police after reading one letter from a little girl to 'Dear Daddy', of the blood-stained snow that horrified the French peasants; of the chaplain's confession that braver men he had never met than those three men he prayed with just before the fatal dawn.'[19]

Landon's comments, as to the 'mental and physical degeneracy' of the troops, clearly reflect a wide and growing concern as to the Bantams' will and capability to carry out orders. On 27 November the 35th Division's Assistant Director of Medical Services inspected men of the 104th brigade, with a view to assessing their 'military efficiency' and 'physical and mental disabilities'. Patience with the Bantams was running out. The 35th Division was about to be radically overhauled.

On 1 December orders were received that the division was to be relieved in the Arras sector. The 23rd Manchesters, though, would still spend the rest of December in Arras, now providing working parties for the 9th Division. Arras's ancient subterranean vaults and passages were being deepened and lengthened. Cables and roads were being laid. Vast stores of ammunition and equipment were being brought in. Much of this work was in preparation for the spring offensive.

The journalist Philip Gibbs was in Arras at the end of December 1916. He recorded:

The queerest music I have heard in this war zone was three days ago, when I was walking down a city street. The city was dead, killed by storms of high explosives. The street was of shuttered houses, scarred by shell-fire, deserted by all their people, who had fled two years ago. I walked down this desolation, so quiet, so dead, where there was no sound of guns, that it was like walking in Pompeii when the lava was cooled. Suddenly there was the sound of a voice singing loud and clear with birdlike trills, as triumphant as a lark's song to the dawn. It was a woman's voice singing behind the shutters of a shelled city!
Some English officer was there with his gramophone.[20]

Chapter 8

'De-Bantamization'

We are the Bantam sodgers,
The short-arse companee.
We have no height, we cannot fight.
What bloody good are we?[1]

In August 1916 the 35th Division had been transferred to IV Corps, which was commanded by Lieutenant General Sir Aylmer Haldane. Haldane's autobiography indicates that he was keeping a close eye on the performance of the Bantam division right from the start. Though respectful of the performance of the original Bantams (he wrote that the division was 'heavily engaged on the Somme' and 'distinguished itself' in so doing), Haldane had serious concerns about the men who were now being brought in to fill the gaps.[2]

Haldane's autobiography notes that, when the 35th Division went back into the trenches in August 1916, the Germans facing indicated their awareness of the Bantams presence by 'imitating the crowing of the barnyard fowl'. The fact that Haldane sees fit to mention this crowing is perhaps more important than whether it actually ever occurred or not. The Bantams were starting to be seen as a weak link – and it was perceived that the enemy was of this opinion too.

It is perhaps also significant that Haldane's account of the demise of the Bantam Division incorporates an anecdote from Philip Gibbs' ('I will not vouch for the accuracy of the story,' Haldane wrote, 'but it is amusing and worth repeating'). Though Gibbs had earlier written in complimentary terms about the Bantams' conduct, he knew that the 'strange mingling of the pitiful and comic' that the Bantam battalions presented made amusing and emotive copy. 'Poor little men born of diseased civilization!' Gibbs would write. They were 'the dwarfed children of industrial England and its mid-Victorian cruelties'. Gibbs' yarn, repeated by Haldane, ran thus:

'One anecdote went the round. A Bantam died – of disease ('and he would', said General Haldane) – and a comrade came to see his corpse.

'Shut ze door ven you come out,' said the old woman of his billet. 'Fermez la porte, mon vieux.'

The living Bantam went to see the dead one, and came downstairs much moved by grief.

'I've seed poor Bill,' he said.

'As-tu fermé la porte?' said the old woman, anxiously.

The Bantam wondered at the anxious inquiry; asked the reason of it.

'C'est a cause du chat!' said the old woman. 'Ze cat, Monsieur, 'e 'ave 'ad your friend in ze passage tree time already to-day. Trois fois!'[3]

'They afforded many jokes to the army,' Gibbs wrote. Haldane was not keen on the idea of commanding a joke division.

By the end of November 1916 the future of the 35th Division was being considered; the performance of the Bantams was being examined, influential voices were saying that the experiment had failed and change now seemed to be inevitable. The raids of 26 November showed the division in a poor light. Whether the events of that night were accurately reported, and blame was appropriately apportioned, or not, the line had been breached. It looked like a near miss. Haldane wrote:

> I felt sorry for them, for they had not the stamina to make themselves battle-worthy, but the army commander was merciless and insisted on the extreme penalty being carried out. I, however, took the opportunity to report that I could not be responsible for the security of my front so long as the division continued to be constituted as it was, and suggested that a thorough combing-out was essential.[4]

There was a dual nature to the issue. First, it seems that the 'original' Bantams, those men who had volunteered back in 1914 and who had now served for a year in France, were physically and mentally exhausted. Secondly, the recruits now arriving to fill the gaps were widely deemed to be, as Haldane put it, 'indifferent material'. The reinforcements seem to have often been physically weaker than the original Bantams; these were not the short stocky men who had walked miles to volunteer their services in 1914; often recruits were now small, slight men. But the difference was not just physical. There was also evidently a noticeable physiological distinction between the 1914 men and the reinforcements. The original Bantams were men who were eager for the army to take them – they had tried hard to get in and had something to prove. By January 1916 it was mostly conscripts who were arriving to fill the gaps. They did not necessarily have the keenness and pride that seemed to have been such a pronounced feature of the original Bantam battalions. It was becoming apparent that the concept of the Bantam battalions was faulty: there just was not an inexhaustible supply of those original sturdy little warriors. The Divisional History reflected:

> Those who had knowledge of the division when first formed unite in describing the original drafts as a fine body of men, whose shortness of stature was compensated for by breadth of chest and physical condition, and, if the supply of such could have continued, the arguments of those in favour of the employment of small men would have been proved.[5]

For the officers who had served with the division for some time there was a tendency to point an emphatic finger at the second issue, identifying that it was the later drafts who were diluting the overall quality of the ranks. But the problem was not *entirely* to do with the reinforcements. The men found to be at fault on 26 November 1916 were mostly old-timers.

From as early as August 1916 the War Diary of the 23rd Manchester Battalion was recording that new drafts were generally men 'of bad physique'. This trend seems to have become even more widespread and remarkable as the year went on. The Divisional History relates:

> As it happened it was found no more possible to support a bantam division consisting of well-developed men below the average height of the nation, than it was to fill up the ranks of the Household Cavalry with men above it. The result, in the former case, was that the type of recruit deteriorated. Many who joined were immature, and, with the laudable intention of serving their country, had, when enlisting, become somewhat hazy about the actual date of their birth. Others, conscripted later, were weaklings who would never be fit for the strain of active service and who were passed to the division as the supply of men of the original bantam standard had failed. These men had not the fortitude to endure fatigue and hardship, and although possibly a long period of training might have given them the mechanical discipline which would have, to some extent, counterbalanced the failing, this was denied them. The complaints of battalion commanders became frequent, and the efforts of the divisional commander to have the weaklings removed were only partially successful. Whilst in training at Masham, a certain number were withdrawn, but the recruiting authorities refused to have them discharged, and instead sent them to the depots and kept them there. The result was that, but half-trained and as yet unsubordinated to habits of automatic obedience, they rejoined at a critical period of the war.[6]

Thus it was decided to 'change the character' of the division. On 6 December 1916 a circular letter informed all officers that this would henceforth cease to be a Bantam division. Future replacements would now be men of standard height. On 11 December the War Diary of the 23rd Manchesters records that the battalion received a new draft of 171 men – all of 'average height and over, 95 of them Yeomen'.

It was not just a matter of bringing new men in. Those men that Landon had deemed to be of 'low physical and moral standard' would have to be combed out. Sandilands related:

> In order to do this, endless parades used to take place, at which Commanders and medical officers of all ranks used to inspect the men. Everyone in turn used either to poke the man in the back, pinch his legs, or look down his mouth with a view to ascertaining whether he was fit or not to be a soldier.[7]

Between 8 and 21 December, Haldane, Landon and the ADMS undertook a series of inspections. In total 2,784 men – roughly one in four – were reported to be 'unfit for infantry work in the line' and recommended for transfer. The War Diary of the 23rd Manchesters records that the battalion was inspected by Haldane on 18 December and that he marked down 166 men as 'unfit'. By 21 December Haldane had personally inspected those recommended for rejection twice over. Philip Gibbs wrote: 'General Haldane, as commander of the 6th Corps, paraded them, and poked his stick at the more wizened ones, the obviously unfit, the degenerates, and said at each prod, "You can go ... You ... You ..."'[8] In order to get authority to purge so many men from the division, Haldane arranged for the 'combed out' rejects to be inspected by Allenby, GOC of the Third Army. In his autobiography, Haldane described how he 'took care to stage-manage' Allenby's inspection:

> The men who had been combed out were therefore drawn up in line by companies along some steeply sloping ground and care was taken that the army commander, who was not lacking in inches, should view them from above not below. On the flank of certain companies were disposed a few files of tall cavalrymen – Royal Dragoons and Scots Greys – who had been sent to fill vacancies. Thus, when the inspection took place, the Bantams looked at from above seemed more of the dimension of young chickens than dwarf poultry.[9]

Apparently one brigade commander spoke up in the Bantams' defence ('which almost upset my carefully arranged plan'). 'Before he had committed himself too deeply,' Haldane wrote, 'he got a gentle reminder by a kick on the shins that he was spoiling sport.'

Haldane conceded that his zeal for the combing-out process did occasionally cause his judgement to misfire. 'I myself made a bad shot', he wrote of one occasion, when one of the men he selected for removal turned out to be the feather-weight boxing champion of the division. 'This produced such a protest from the brigade commander that it led to his exemption from the rubbish heap.' The choice of terms speaks loudly of Haldane's opinion of the rejected men. He went on: 'It was observable that the man in question appeared to be glad to remain, although most of the others who did not come up to the standard were genuinely pleased to be cast.'[10]

Their officers, though, were not all entirely pleased by the process. It is clear that a lot of the officers who had served with the division for some time felt defensive of the Bantams' record and their pride. Sandilands wrote:

> We who had served with the old original Bantams used to feel very sorry for them. It is a matter of common knowledge within the Division that until the Armistice in 1918 we never attacked without one of the old original Bantams distinguishing himself, and there has never been a medal parade in this Brigade without one at least of them being present.[11]

But the thing was done. On 22 January 1917 the War Diary of the 23rd Manchesters records that the division was now officially 'de-Bantamized'. Emphatically signalling the change in its character, the symbol of the 35th Division, a bantam cock, was scrapped and replaced with a design of seven interlocking fives.

With large numbers of new men coming in (and many of them from Yeomanry regiments rather than infantry), the brigades shifted to the west of Arras, ostensibly for a period of training. The War Diary of the Manchesters indicates, though, that much of this time was spent supplying working parties; with the battalion based around Beaufort-Blavincourt at the end of December, a party of 112 men were sent to work on the railway at Blavincourt and another sixty-two to work on the railway at Wanquetin. Severe frosts set in just after Christmas 1916 and the weather became worse as the month went on. Snow fell at intervals, hampering work. It was 'beastly cold', as one of the men would write. The start of January saw a working party (of 7 officers and 189 other ranks) moving north to Fleury to work with the Heavy Branch of the Machine Gun Corps (i.e. tanks).

Throughout January more new drafts (men of average height and over) were arriving. On 16 January 200 men joined the 23rd Manchesters, ninety-four on the 21st and another thirty on the 23rd. The 'combing out' continued too: on 24 January twenty-four 'unfit' men were sent to the 181st Tunnelling Company (such transfers tended to be former miners), while, on the next day 163 men left for the 23rd Labour Company in Boulogne and the 30th Infantry Base Depot.[12] A total of 187 men ultimately left the 23rd Manchesters, then – roughly one in five men thus having been declared 'unfit'.

One of the new drafts who arrived in January 1917 was Private George Barker. He had been called up under the Derby Scheme and passed fit in August 1916. 'I have never for once dreamed that at the age of forty I should be needed,' Barker recalled. As an average-height man, joining the just de-Bantamized battalion, Barker found his new comrades rather curious. 'They seem to be all small men,' he wrote. 'I, amongst many others, was tall, and it seemed rather peculiar to see tall and short men marching together.'[13]

There was some change now at command level too. On 16 January Montgomery left to take up a new post – effectively a promotion – as a general staff officer (Grade 2) in the 33rd Division. Major General Pinney had left to take command of the 33rd Division in September 1916 and it seems likely that he requested that Montgomery move over with him. Montgomery was succeeded by Major C.H.F. Metcalf, who would remain in the position until July 1917.[14]

The division had been told that they would be given a break from front-line service for two months while the men were trained and organised, but it was not to be. The War Diary of the 23rd Manchesters notes that during January training was carried out when possible, 'but was seriously interfered with, owing to detached working parties, the arrival of drafts and departure of "unfits"'. In the end they would just get one month out of the line. At the end of January the 104th Brigade received orders that it was to take over the French line in the area of Rosières.

The Divisional History concluded the end of the Bantam battalions thus:

It was a period of regret, for great expectation had been entertained of the success of the enterprise. The ultimate result was not the fault of the officers and men of the original battalions, who all went into battle with high hopes and desire for action, and, as one of their officers once remarked, 'They were little men but had big hearts'. But war is no respecter of hopes or theories, and it was to war, and war alone, that the arbitrament of their case was entrusted. The project failed, but the failure was not due to the men who gave their lives in the earlier battles, or to their comrades who survived and who took an honourable part in the succeeding years of warfare.[15]

Chapter 9

'A Strange Adventure, Fantastic as a Dream': Mud and then Movement

In January 1917 the *Manchester Evening News* was quoting General Nivelle, the newly promoted French commander-in-chief on the Western Front and the 'hero of Verdun'. Nivelle had just written, 'We shall soon obtain a complete victory over our detested enemy', and the *Evening News* was investing some faith in that statement. 'We are now enduring unparalleled horrors,' the newspaper wrote. 'The continuation of these horrors may be long or may be short. There are signs that, after all, they may be short.'[1]

Proposing a 'decisive battle' in the Aisne sector, Nivelle now wanted the British to relieve a length of the front presently held by the French. He was confident that he had found the means of breaking through the German defences; he was convinced that a massive artillery bombardment, followed by a large scale infantry assault, would enable his troops to achieve a decisive 'rupture'. In Nivelle's plans, British and French forces would undertake preliminary attacks between the Oise and Arras to pin down German reserves, while the French would deliver the main blow on the Aisne, with a mass of twenty-seven divisions. His offensive could only go ahead, though, if the British allowed French forces to be freed up to deliver that decisive blow.

Nivelle's plans had been approved, in principle, by the French government on 20 December 1916 and, the next day, Nivelle approached General Sir Douglas Haig (shortly to be promoted to the most senior rank of field marshal). Haig refused to concede to a request that he saw as compromising his offensive capability.

In January Nivelle travelled to London to sell his project to Lloyd George. He made a favourable impression. Despite Haig's reservations, there were elements of Nivelle's 'one single, grand battle' plan that Lloyd George found appealing. First, with British troops playing only a subsidiary role, the grand scale losses of the Somme looked unlikely to be repeated. And, secondly, if Nivelle's plan for the spring failed, there was still plenty of time and scope to plan another offensive later in the year.

The British finally agreed to relieve French forces in the southern half of the Somme, as far south as the Amiens–Roye road. Thus, in February 1917, IV Corps began to take over a length of front formerly held by the French.

The start of the month, therefore, saw the 23rd Manchester Battalion marching south. 'We commence marching with the Colonel at our head', new recruit George Barker wrote, 'passing through many villages on our way until it becomes dusk.' On 6 February they marched from Beaufort-Blavincourt to Bouquemaison (around 10 miles), on to Amplier (another 9 miles or so) on the 7th and then on to Naours (11 miles) on the 8th. 'Thank

Heaven our Colonel is human, and orders us to take off our packs and rest every now and then,' reflected George Barker. But the combination of the cold and the mileage seems to have been testing the men's mood.

> As we march on, occasionally joking and singing, the cold seems to become more intense. Our breath is freezing as it comes from our mouths and nostrils. The sergeant by my side draws the officer's attention to my moustache, and it seems that my walrus-like excretion was one mass of ice, with icicles to the left and the right of it. We all laugh, but we still plod on. In a few minutes we halt and relieve ourselves, but dare not stand about too long. We again fall in and continue marching. One man takes an orange from his pocket and tries to bite it, but in his disgust he throws it to the ground; it sounds like a stone dropping, then he stamps on it, and it breaks into pieces of ice.[2]

Eventually they got to Naours, where they would remain, in training, for the next nine days. Here platoons were reorganised 'under the new Trench method', as the War Diary of 17th Lancashire Fusiliers explained: 'Providing that specialists be abolished and every man be capable of using effectively every infantry weapon.' The winter of 1916/17 was a period of change in British methods and equipment. The supply of weapons and munitions improved and a new infantry training manual had been introduced. According to the new system, each platoon was now to be self supporting, at least as far as small arms goes, with dedicated bombing, Lewis gun, rifle grenade and riflemen sections. The idea was that the infantry was no longer to advance shoulder to shoulder – rather smaller, self sustaining fighting units could manoeuvre with more independence. Sandiland's wrote that the training for the new system caused 'great excitement'.[3] The 35th Division was now under the control of IV Corps and, on 12 February, the Corps Commander visited Naours and inspected the training.

On 16 February there was another accident during bombing practice. Second Lieutenant Barker was wounded and one man killed.

Private James Alfred Johnson died on 13 February 1917. He was from Salford. He is buried in St Pierre Cemetery, Amiens.

Private Henry Lytham died on 16 February 1917. He seemed likely to have been the man who was killed in the bombing practice accident. He was aged 25 and from Southport. He is buried in Naours Churchyard.

On 17 February the 104th Brigade entrained towards the east of Amiens and then marched to the camp at Wiencourt-l'Équipée, where they were accommodated in huts. They were just some 8 miles or so behind the lines now. For George Barker it was the first time that he had heard the noise of the guns at the front. He wrote:

> We begin to hear the booming of guns, and we know we are gradually getting nearer the lines of action. As a recruit I feel slightly nervous and cannot sleep at night. I

seem to feel that the shells are going to blow me up, and my nerves are soothed by an old-timer who tells me that they are many miles away. Still I cannot sleep.[4]

On the 19th they marched to Camp des Ballons, a former French army camp, just to the west of Rosières-en-Santerre, where again they slept in huts. 'By no means ideal,' was Brigadier-General Sandilands verdict on Camp des Ballons, but 'a very pleasant change from the mud of the so-called trenches.'[5]

George Barker's recollections of the camp perhaps shed some light on what Sandilands' diplomatic 'by no means ideal' alludes to. Unable to sleep, Barker sees 'dark bright eyes looking at me, then a screaming noise and something scuttling about'. He goes on:

I light a match, and to my horror there are hundreds of rats running around us; they are after the crumbs of cheese and biscuits lying about. I declare, on my honour, that some of these pests were as big as small dogs.

In the morning, when we finish our crude toilet, we take a walk and observe several dung-heaps outside our huts; we poke these with sticks and the fun begins. Talk about rats, there were battalions of them! We strike left and right with our sticks, they squeak and snarl, and the more we kill the more seems to come from the heaps. This is my first killing in France.[6]

From here the 35th Division would take over the French line facing the village of Chaulnes. The series of diagrams overleaf show how the French campaign to the south of the River Somme had come to a halt around Chaulnes by November 1916.

French graves in the Bois de Chaulnes, 1919. Photograph from the *Illustrated Michelin Guides to the Battle-Fields (1914–1918): The Somme, Volume 1*, p. 129

AU SUD DE LA SOMME.

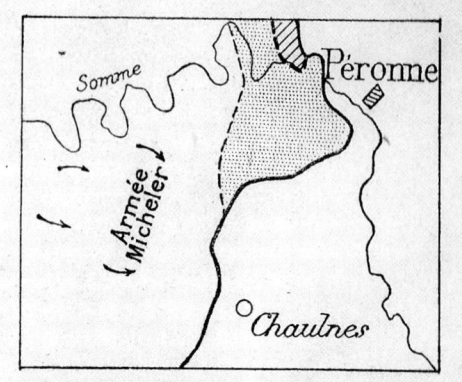

La 6ᵉ armée (Fayolle), gênée par les marais de la Somme, consolide ses nouvelles positions. La 10ᵉ armée (Micheler) se rassemble au sud de la Somme.   Août-septembre.

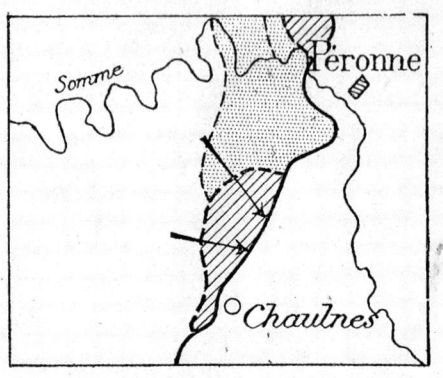

La 10ᵉ armée élargit le front de l'offensive et attaque. Après de brillants succès, sa progression est arrêtée par le gros centre de résistance de Chaulnes.
Septembre-octobre.

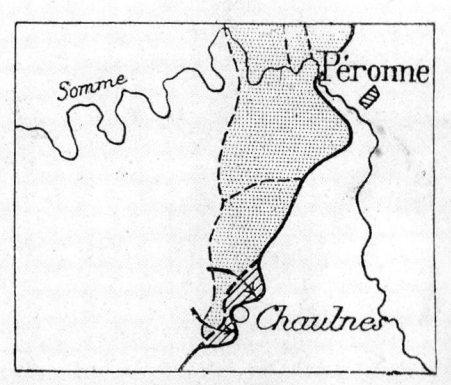

La 10ᵉ armée tente vainement d'enlever Chaulnes où l'ennemi, à moitié encerclé, réussit à se maintenir. Elle s'installe solidement sur ses nouvelles positions.
Octobre-novembre 1916.

A series of diagrams showing the phases in the French campaign. Taken from *Illustrated Michelin Guides to the Battle-Fields (1914 – 1918): The Somme, Volume 1*, p. 13.

A German pillbox in the Chaulnes woods.

Bois Triangulaire.

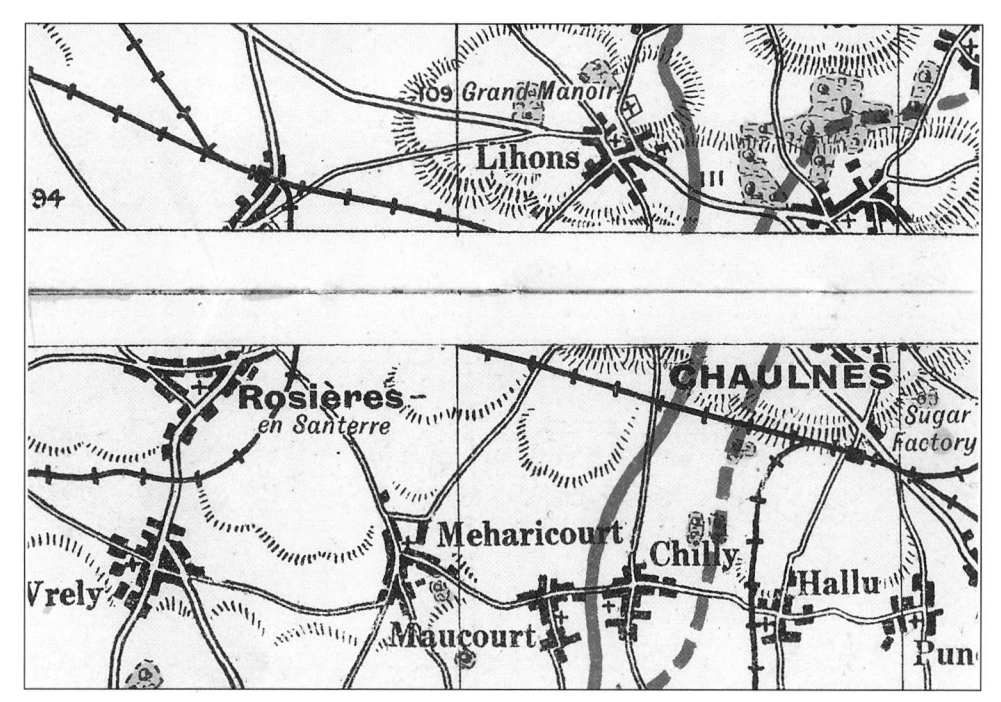

Map showing the location of the woods around Chaulnes. The solid line represents the front on 1 July 1916 and the broken line the front on 1 December. From *The western front at a glance: a large-scale atlas of the Allies fighting line in the west* (George Philip & Son, Ltd, London, 1917).

Chaulnes was an important centre for both road and railway junctions and the Germans were determined to hold it. The front line in 1916 ended up half encircling Chaulnes, but stubbornly stuck there. By the winter of 1916 Chaulnes had been turned into a fortress, with defensive works protecting its flanks. The woods to the north and west were full of trenches, wire entanglements and machine-gun posts. The large numbers of French graves in the Bois de Chaulnes were testament to their costly efforts to capture the wood in October 1916.

The 35th Division was now taking over the front running from Bois Triangulaire (the woodland in between Lihons and Chaulnes) as far as the village of Chilly, to the south. Each brigade would hold approximately 2,000 yards of the front. On 20 February 1917 the 23rd Manchesters marched to Rosières-en-Santerre and then on to the Lihons sub sector, facing Chaulnes. They were heading towards Bois Triangulaire. By now a thaw had set in. There was mud everywhere.

Lihons-en-Santerre, just 2 miles distant from Chaulnes, had been bombarded by the enemy guns since the line settled between the two villages in October 1914. The shelling of Lihons intensified in 1916, as it served as the base of French operations in the Bois de Chaulnes. In July 1916 the church of Lihons was still identifiable, albeit it had already lost its tower and roof. By October, it would be nothing but a pile of debris. When the Manchesters arrived in Lihons, the 'village' was a series of ruins.

Lihons-en-Santerre.

The photographs opposite, taken in 1915 and then into 1916, illustrate the progressive impact of artillery on Lihons.

The 23rd Manchesters had been ordered to take over a length of trenches from the 2nd Battalion of the French 414th Infantry Regiment. The relief started at 7.00 am and French guides came out to direct them into the line. Passing through the ruins of Lihons, the Manchesters entered the communications trenches in single file. 'Orders are given that we must go as silently and as cautiously as possible,' George Barker wrote. It was a slow struggle, more so because the mud was getting worse. George Barker's account goes on:

> To our horror we see ahead of us masses of churned mud. We have to go through this, we sink up to our knees, and every step we take seems to be hard work for us. Our legs get weary and hot, the load on our backs is telling, but we don't give in – as we have the determination to go on at any price. As we go forward the mud becomes deeper, some of us are sinking to our hips, and as we pull out one leg after the other our joints seem to give way. Men are shrieking, crying, becoming hysterical, the torture is terrible. The poor lads carrying Lewis guns are slithering here and there, and with agonised cries, 'I can't go on,' yet somehow they move. They don't want to be left to die in the mud. The anguish of mud is terrible, we become half delirious and half crazy; we use our hands by placing them on the sides of the trenches, and with superhuman strength we pull ourselves out of the sticky quagmiry mess.[7]

Lihons-en-Santerre.

These twin photographs show the same street corner in June 1916 and 1928. *Twenty Years After – The Battlefields of 1914–1918: Then and Now* (1928).

Photograph, taken in September 1916, showing the condition of the roads around Lihons. By February 1917 they were even worse. From *Twenty Years After – The Battlefields of 1914–1918: Then and Now* (1928).

French troops digging trenches through the centre of Lihons, 1916.

Word then comes along that the French guide has lost his way. The men start to speculate. The guide is suspected of being a spy.

Barker wrote that it was dawn by the time that the Manchesters reached the trenches that they were destined to take over. Officially, though, the relief was completed at 12.15 pm. The formal line was that the guides had missed their way in the dark (the words 'unreliable and misleading' are deleted – perhaps a polite afterthought? - in the battalion War Diary). What is certain is that the men were exhausted by the time that the relief was completed.

Stereoscope image of the communications trenches leading from Lihons, 1916.

The French had informed the British that the trenches in this sector were in reasonable condition; they were about to find out that this was not the case. After the severe frosts of early February, a rapid thaw had now set in, causing the trenches to flood and the sides of many of the communication trenches to collapse. The average depth of water in the trenches was two feet (this according to the War Diary of 18th Lancashire Fusiliers). 'Such trenches as still existed were nothing better than ditches full of mud and water,' Sandilands recorded. They were 'extraordinarily bad'.[8] According to George Barker, the French troops that they were relieving had evacuated the trenches, preferring to take their chances sitting on the parapet: 'As we are wading through this filthy muck, we look up and see them sitting on top, exposing themselves to Jerry's fire. But no wonder: it seemed they preferred being killed to standing in this. When the French soldiers see us they run like rabbits in their joy at being relieved from this hell-hole.'[9]

Given the conditions in the trenches, it seems a mercy that enemy activity was slight over the next few days. With parapets crumbling and the mud thigh-high in places, it was found that the only way to bring rations and ammunition up to the front line was over the top during the night or early morning. Often the rations did not make it up at all. George Barker resorted to eating dirty biscuit crumbs out of the corners of his pocket linings. Water was everywhere, but there was soon no water to drink. According to George Barker the men started to debate which would be the riskier option: drinking the filthy water that flooded the trenches – or their own urine.

On 23 February the calm ended. There was suddenly something more pressing to worry about than hunger and thirst. Between 7.45 am and 9.00 am the British front and support lines were heavily bombarded. Three men of the Manchesters were reported killed and two wounded.

> Lance Corporal Harry Lees was killed in action on 23 February 1917. He was aged 32 and from Watersheddings, Oldham. He is commemorated on the Thiepval Memorial.
>
> Lance Corporal Laurence Woodward was killed in action on 23 February 1917. He was from Tyldsley. He is commemorated on the Thiepval Memorial.
>
> Lance Corporal Arthur Whitelegg died of wounds on 24 February 1917. He was aged 24. He is buried in Cerisy-Gailly Military Cemetery. Gailly, to the south-west of Albert, was the site of the 39th and 13th Casualty Clearing Stations.

The grimness of this time in the line is reflected in a note in the Manchesters' War Diary on 25 February: 'One man wounded (self-inflicted)'.

It was with a truly almighty relief, then, that the battalion began to make its way out of the Lihons trenches on 26 February. They struggled back through those flooded and crumbling communication trenches. 'The agony and strain is telling greatly upon us,' George Barker wrote, 'our overcoats are becoming more heavy and caked with mud, my brain is giving way, and my thirst is nearly unbearable.'[10]

They were moved back to Rosières. Sandilands recalled, 'In spite of everything we could do for them, the men suffered badly from the conditions'.[11] Cases of frostbite and trench foot were recorded. 'Our feet were swollen and our legs were blue with cold,' Barker wrote. 'Men were crying and sobbing.' Sandilands noted that this was the last time that the 104th Brigade ever wore their greatcoats in bad trenches; 'When a man took his greatcoat off at Rosières, it was as much as he could do to lift it off the ground, owing to the weight from the plastered mud.' The Divisional History relates that a medical officer in Rosières weighed the uniform of one casualty brought in at this time – 'They were clogged with mud and water and turned the scale at 90lb.'[12] On 27 February the battalion moved back to the Divisional Reserve at Camp des Ballons, where a week of training commenced.

On 6 March, with snow falling, the Manchesters marched back into the line, taking over the Chilly left sub sector from the 16th Cheshires. This section of the line had, over

The village of Chilly.

the previous week, been subject to heavy bombardment and enemy raids. Raiding would continue over the next week. On the 7th, after a bombardment, a twenty-strong enemy party forced their way into a sap, north of La Demi Lune (the section of trenches to the 23rd Manchesters' left), and captured five prisoners of the 17th West Yorkshires; seven Manchesters were wounded. The battalion spent much of its time on patrols during this tour (and was complimented by the divisional commander for the way that these were conducted). It seems likely that this vigilant patrolling prevented more enemy raids. Whilst patrolling the enemy wire, on 9 March, Second Lieutenant C.R. Chaffey was mortally wounded by an enemy sentry. Eight other men were injured.

> Second Lieutenant Charles Russell Chaffey died of wounds on 10 March 1917. According to family records, after being severely wounded, Chaffey was picked up and taken into the enemy lines where he died the next day. His grave was eventually discovered in a German cemetery; the cross, marked with his name and rank, also had the words: 'He Died For His Country'. Today he is commemorated on a memorial in the Fouquescourt British Cemetery, just to the south of Lihons. The cemetery was created after the Armistice when graves were brought in from the battlefields in the surrounding area.
>
> Chaffey was born in Adelaide, South Australia, but moved to Canada as a young man and studied at McGill University in Quebec. He enlisted in August 1914 and served as a private in the Canadian Expeditionary Force before being wounded at Festubert in May 1915. He subsequently obtained a commission in the 23rd Manchesters, becoming a temporary second lieutenant in December 1916. He had only just returned to France in February 1917. He was aged 28.

On 10 March the Manchesters were relieved and began their journey back, through that glutinous mud once again, to Brigade Reserve at Vrely, just to the south of Rosières. Repeated freezing and thaws had turned the roads behind the lines into mudslides and, according to George Barker, the men were 'about done up' by the time that they reached their destination – a waterlogged field full of bell tents. But there were some comforts. They warmed their hands on mugs of hot tea and ate 'bread and margarine, with a little of Tickler's jam'. Barker went on: 'How we should appreciate our mothers, or wives to place our wet clothing near the fire, but we have to be content to let them dry on our backs.'[13]

> Private Gordon Williamson died on 6 March 1917. He was aged 30 and a law stationer's clerk from Pendleton. He is buried in Pendlebury (St John) churchyard.
> Private Joseph Robert Harding died of wounds on 13 March 1917. He was from Shaw. He is buried in Cerisy-Gailly Military Cemetery.

After another cold and wet stint in the trenches down towards Chilly (how apt that name must have seemed), with the enemy noticeably quiet, the Manchesters were moved back to Rosières on 16 March, where they began to prepare for a diversionary attack on the enemy trenches south of Hallu, in support of a 'great offensive' by the French to the south. The game was about to change, though.

> Private William Henry Gregory died on 16 March 1917. He was aged 36 and from Stockport. He is buried in St Sever Cemetery Extension, Rouen.
> Private Fred Tetlow was killed in action on 16 March 1917. He was from Manchester. He is commemorated on the Thiepval Memorial.

'Throwing up the Sponge'
A footnote in the Divisional History notes that, on 7 March, when the enemy party raided the sap north of La Demi Lune, one of the Germans was reported to have shouted in English, 'Don't worry, we are throwing up the sponge in a fortnight'.[14] Were these words taken seriously at the time? It was evidently regarded with sufficient significance that it was written down. Certainly there seems to have been a sense that something was afoot. Fires were observed behind the German lines. Counter-battery fire was noted to have diminished. Patrols were still sighted, though, and field guns continued to shell the British lines.

The Manchesters had heard rumours of a withdrawal back in Arras in October; activity could be seen beyond the enemy lines on the high ground to the rear and there was talk that something significant was in the planning for the spring. Since then air reconnaissance, agent reports and gleanings from prisoners had made it increasingly clear that an enemy withdrawal was possible. Now it seemed that it was true. Over the winter of 1916 the German troops in the rear had been preparing the new Hindenburg Line, selected for its tactical advantages, rather than being imposed by events. Deep dugouts and concrete defences had been built. A network of railways had been laid behind. The

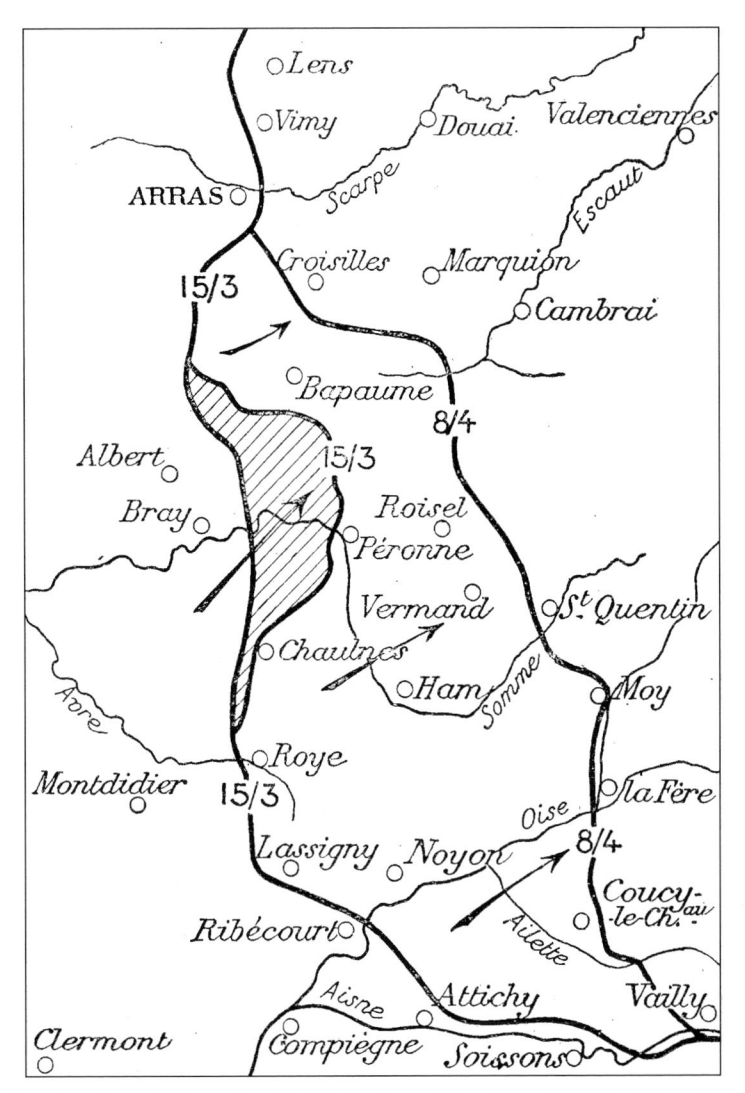

Illustration showing the withdrawal to the Hindenburg Line. Map from the *Illustrated Michelin Guides to the Battle-Fields (1914–1918): The Somme, Volume 1*, p. 29.

new German front would be 25 miles shorter and could be defended more easily by fewer troops. The withdrawal was about to upset Nivelle's game. The main German withdrawal to the Hindenburg Line commenced on 16 March. The salient that Nivelle had intended to exploit decisively was suddenly no longer there.

On 17 March the French attack south of Hallu went ahead. An intense bombardment opened on the enemy trenches at 7.00 am. There was no reply. The British, north of Hallu, advanced. At 2.30 pm the 17th West Yorkshires entered the enemy trenches. They were empty.

Patrols now pushed forwards and the artillery limbered up and began to roll east. The reporter Philip Gibbs, following the advancing British troops, wrote:

The whole of the old German line south of Arras, strong as one vast fortress, built by the labour of millions of men, dug and tunnelled and cemented and timbered, with thousands of machine-gun redoubts, with an immense maze of trenches, protected by forests of barbed wire, had slipped away as though by a landslide, and the enemy is in rapid retreat to new lines some miles away.[15]

On the 17th the Manchesters moved forward to Meharicourt, where they spent the night in cellars, and then, the next morning, they marched east, on to Fonches, crossing the former enemy lines. There was great eagerness to see where the enemy had been and what he had left behind. With what fascination did they peer into the trenches that had faced them? What thoughts occurred as they stared at gun emplacements, dugouts and enemy sign posts? How odd did it feel to march along roads that just days earlier had been behind the enemy lines?

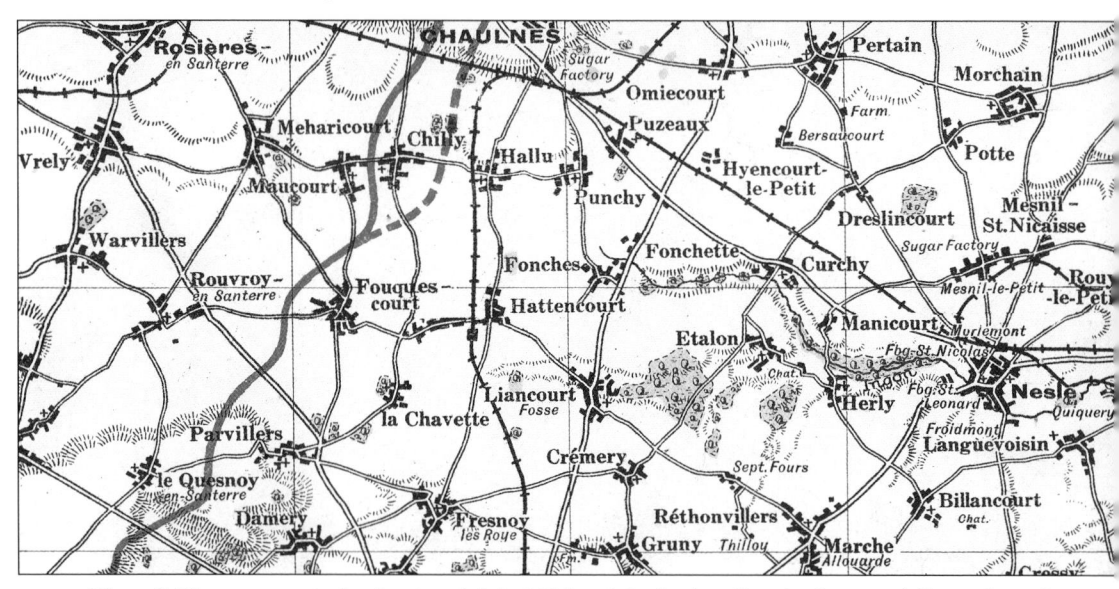

The solid line represents the front on 1 July 1916 and the broken line the front on 1 December of that year. Map from *The western front at a glance: a large-scale atlas of the Allies fighting line in the west* (1917).

At first they moved with some trepidation, not knowing how far back the Germans had gone, or whether this was a ruse that would lure them into a trap, but then other emotions seem to have taken over. Captain G.K. Rose, moving forward with the 2/4th Oxfordshire and Buckinghamshire Light Infantry, part of the advanced guard, wrote of the 'pleasing novelty' of these days:

> To us Infantry this advance was a sort of holiday from the real war. It was like going behind the scenes at a pantomime and discovering the secrets of the giant's

make-up . . . Strong moral and political effects accompanied. Trenches and dugouts, which in some sectors had been visited and revisited with changeless repetition for thirty months, lost their sense of eternity.[16]

A similar mood seems to have been prevalent amongst the Manchesters. Sandilands wrote:

The advance had a wonderful effect on the men, who appeared entirely to forget the wretched conditions under which they had been living. The situation was so novel that many had visions of marching straight into Germany, and ending the war. To march along real roads and across real grass fields was a pleasant change for everyone.[17]

Captain G.K. Rose arrived in Chaulnes on 22 March:

That village, damaged by our artillery, had been finally wrecked by the departing enemy, whose rude notices were scrawled on any walls still standing. 'One million tons of English shipping sunk in the month of February,' said one more polite than others. In spite of all that the Germans had done, quite good accommodation was found for all ranks, and its improvement by old doors, shutters, and selected débris from other ruins provided much amusement. Father Buggins and the Doctor, with a wheelbarrow, were to the fore collecting armchairs covered in red velvet. Stoves and fuel were abundant, and at this time booby-traps were few.[18]

The Manchesters found themselves moving into a strange landscape now. The enemy had left behind a devastated area. Everything of any strategic value had been systematically destroyed. Bridges had been blown up, large craters were left at crossroads, trees were felled and all buildings demolished.

'No list of things destroyed could lend any conception of the wholesale massacre by the Germans of all objects both natural and artificial,' Captain G.K. Rose recorded. He went on:

Château and cottage, tree and sapling, factory and summer-house, mill race and goldfish pond were victims equally of their madness. Hardly the most trivial article had been spared. The completeness of the work astonished. Yet withal our discomfort was slight. It was the French civilians, whose lives and homes had been thus ruined, that such Prussian methods touched.[19]

Photographers and journalists followed the Allied advance through the '*Régions Dévastées*'. It made strong copy. Here, just at a time when the certainty and energy of the Allied cause needed a boost, was more evidence of German 'barbarity'. Philip Gibbs wrote:

Ruins of Chaulnes photographed shortly after the Germans withdrew.

The ruins of Chaulnes, 1917 – the site of the Hôtel de Ville (top), the Rue du Moulin (middle) and the remains of the church (bottom).

AROUND CHAULNES
Then and Now

The twin photographs above show Chaulnes in June 1917 and 1928. Images from *Twenty Years After – The Battlefields of 1914–1918: Then and Now* (1928).

For several days now I have been going with our advancing troops into towns, villages, and country abandoned by the enemy in his retreat. It has been a strange adventure, fantastic as a dream, yet with the tragedy of reality . . . German sentry-boxes still stand at the cross-roads. German notice-boards stare at one from cottage walls, or where the villages begin. Thousands of coils of barbed wire lie about in heaps, for the enemy relied a great deal upon this means of defence, and in many places are piles of shells which he has not removed. Gun-pits and machine-gun emplacements, screens to hide his roads from view, observation-posts built in tall trees, remain as signs of his military life a mile or two back from his front lines, but behind the trenches are the towns and villages in which he had his rest billets, and it is in these places that one sees the spirit and temper of the men whom we are fighting.[20]

Gibbs was fascinated by the thickness of the belts of German wire, by the depth of the enemy trenches and the strong and sophisticated construction of their dugouts. He asked: 'Why has he abandoned such formidable strongholds?' The advancing troops must have been asking it too. Gibbs' answer has a ring of the official journalist about it: 'It seems to me that there is only one answer,' he wrote. 'It is because they had to go and not because they wanted to go. It was because they have no longer the strength to hold their old line against the growing gun-power and the growing man-power of the British Armies.'[21]

Trees sawed and ready to be felled in the anticipation of the withdrawal to the Hindenburg Line.

Trees felled along the road between Noyon and Roye.

On 18 March orders were received by the 35th Division ('much to everybody's disappointment') that halted their push forwards. Attention was now to be turned to repairing the infrastructure of the newly gained territory. Craters needed to be filled, roads had to be made serviceable and safe, railway tracks must be laid, communications *must* function. For the next week the 104th Brigade would be occupied in providing working parties. There was plenty to do. Sandilands wrote: 'The number and size of the craters were enough to make even a perfect optimist despair of ever getting the work completed.'[22]

On 19 March the 23rd Manchesters moved south to Parvillers, where they were attached to the 32nd Division and set to work road repairing in the Damery area. This work, the Divisional History records, was 'uncongenial', but it was 'well and expeditiously carried out, and praise was given for the spirit and energy displayed'.[23] The weather was cold but fine. Soon roads were becoming passable again and there was a strong sense that the war was on the move.

On 28 March the Manchesters marched to Fonches and billeted. From there, the next day, they were moved eastwards, further into the former enemy territory, to work on the roads between Matigny, Toulle and Voyennes.

Philip Gibbs had passed through Voyennes on 25 March. He wrote:

I went into the ruins of the church. It was easy to see how the flames had licked about its old stones, scorching them red, and how the high oak roof had come blazing down before the walls and pillars had given way. Everything had been licked down by flame except one figure on an encalcined fragment of wall. Only one hand of the Christ there had been burned, and the body hanging on the Cross was unscathed, like so many of those Calvaries which I have seen in shell-fired places.[24]

Gibbs interviewed the village curé, who told him of the hardships of the people of Voyennes over the past year, with food supplies extremely restricted and enforced labour for the occupying Germans. Over the past few weeks, then, an orderly destruction had been carried out. Houses were burned, orchards cut down and the church bells taken away for scrap metal. The curé, Monsieur Caron, went on:

> 'Last Sunday, a week ago, at this very hour when the people were all in their houses under strict orders, and already the country was on fire with burning villages, a group of soldiers came outside there with cans of petroleum, which they put into the church. Then they set fire to it, and watched my church burn in a great bonfire. At this very hour a week ago I watched it burn. . . . That night the Germans went away through Voyennes, and early in the morning, up in my attic, looking through a pair of glasses I saw four horsemen ride in. They were English soldiers, and our people rushed out to them.'[25]

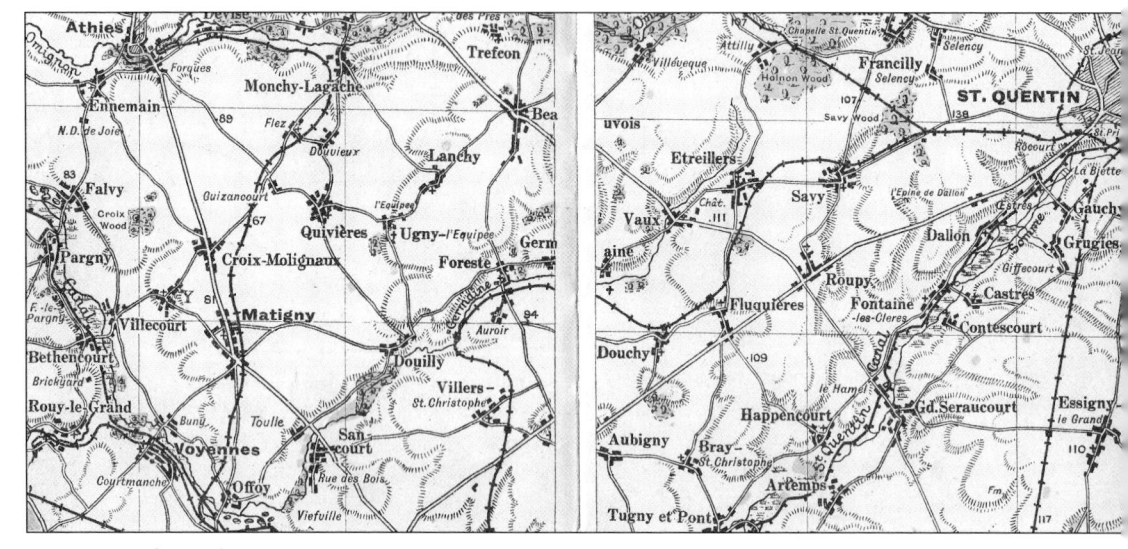

Map from *The Western Front at a Glance* (1917).

On 1 April the 23rd Manchesters marched north to Beauvois, where they were put to work filling craters and repairing roads. The weather was wet and cold at the start of April and on the 4th it turned to snow. 'The weather during this time was most inclement,' records the Divisional History, with typical restraint. It goes on:

> As soon as the German lines were crossed, snow fell, and, from this date until the April 20th, there was a continuous repetition of frost, snow, sleet, and rain, which would have been unwelcome even to those who could house themselves in comfort, and who did not require to spend their lives in the open air. Owing to the

LES DÉVASTATIONS ALLEMANDES EN FRANCE. — ETREILLERS (Aisne).
Abri allemand construit avec le cadran de l'église paroissiale.

A German shelter, constructed from, among other things, the former church clock face, in the ruined village of Étreillers.

wholesale destruction of the countryside, very few villages afforded any shelter at all for the advancing troops until they had leisure to provide some for themselves.[26]

After the initial thrill of crossing the German lines, it was clearly becoming rather bleak.

On 6 April the battalion marched further east to Douilly and then on to Vaux. The next few days would be spent filling craters around Vaux and Étreillers.

Whatever the pleasures for the individual infantryman of moving forwards, the German retreat had put the Allies on the back foot. British and French now had to venture across this dangerous territory towards the new, well-fortified German lines, obliged to reestablish their own front lines and the logistics to support them. Everything had changed – apart from Nivelle's plans. Haig, Robertson and several French generals now foresaw that Nivelle's grand war-finishing plan was unachievable. Faced with dissenting voices, Nivelle threatened to resign. But the French public and Lloyd George, still supported him. And that was enough.

On 9 April the attack at Arras, Britain's part in the Anglo-French offensive, was launched. It began well; Canadian troops took Vimy Ridge (one of the few areas of high ground on the French Flanders plain) and there were greater advances astride the Scarpe River. But, with terrible weather, communications problems and difficulties in moving artillery forward, the initial gains could not be exploited. With a delay in the follow up, the Germans had time to regroup. Reserves were pulled in, and, over the next few weeks the enemy line would consolidate, thicker and more impenetrable than before.

On 16 April Nivelle's attack went ahead on the Aisne. The Germans knew it was coming and had concentrated manpower on the front accordingly. The preliminary artillery bombardment failed to have the desired effect; behind the lightly held German front line trenches there were all-too-intact nests of machine guns, and behind them a great depth of defence. Instead of the first-day advance of 6 miles that Nivelle had promised, the line barely managed to advance 600 yards. But Nivelle could not admit that he had failed.

The *Manchester Evening News* editorial of 7 May was headlined 'Successes in France.' It ran:

> The Hindenburg line, it is obvious from the restrained but exhilarating reports which Generals Haig and Nivelle issue, is yielding and bending in places, and in other places is only maintained at huge sacrifice of human life. How long the Germans will be able to bear this expense cannot be foreseen, but expert opinion inclines to the view that it is of such a terrible nature that it cannot be borne indefinitely. On our own side too, the losses are heavy, as the long list of casualties which we publish from day to day pitiably and painfully proves, but there is at least a little consolation in the knowledge that, owing to the artillery superiority which we have clearly established, backed by the excellent work of our fearless airmen, our losses are much fewer than those of the enemy. Our considerable advantage in numbers over our foes is thus becoming more marked day by day.[27]

It was all about the numbers. The BEF suffered 158,660 casualties over the thirty-nine days of the Arras campaign; a daily rate of over 4,000 men – almost twice the daily losses sustained on the Somme or at Passchendaele. It is estimated that around 30,000 French men were killed and at least 100,000 were wounded during Nivelle's April campaign. At the start of May the French 2nd Division refused to take orders and mutiny quickly spread through the army. The French offensive was suspended on 9 May and Nivelle would be replaced by General Pétain within the week. In the courts martial that followed, 23,385 men would be convicted of mutinous behaviours. At least forty would be executed.

Chapter 10

Saint-Quentin – Finding the Line

For three weeks the 35th Division had been occupied with road repairs. They must have wondered if they had been reconstituted as a pioneer battalion. The war seemed to be happening somewhere else. But then, on Easter Monday, 9 April, as the British offensive at Arras began, the division received orders to shift north-east, towards the enemy held town of Saint-Quentin.

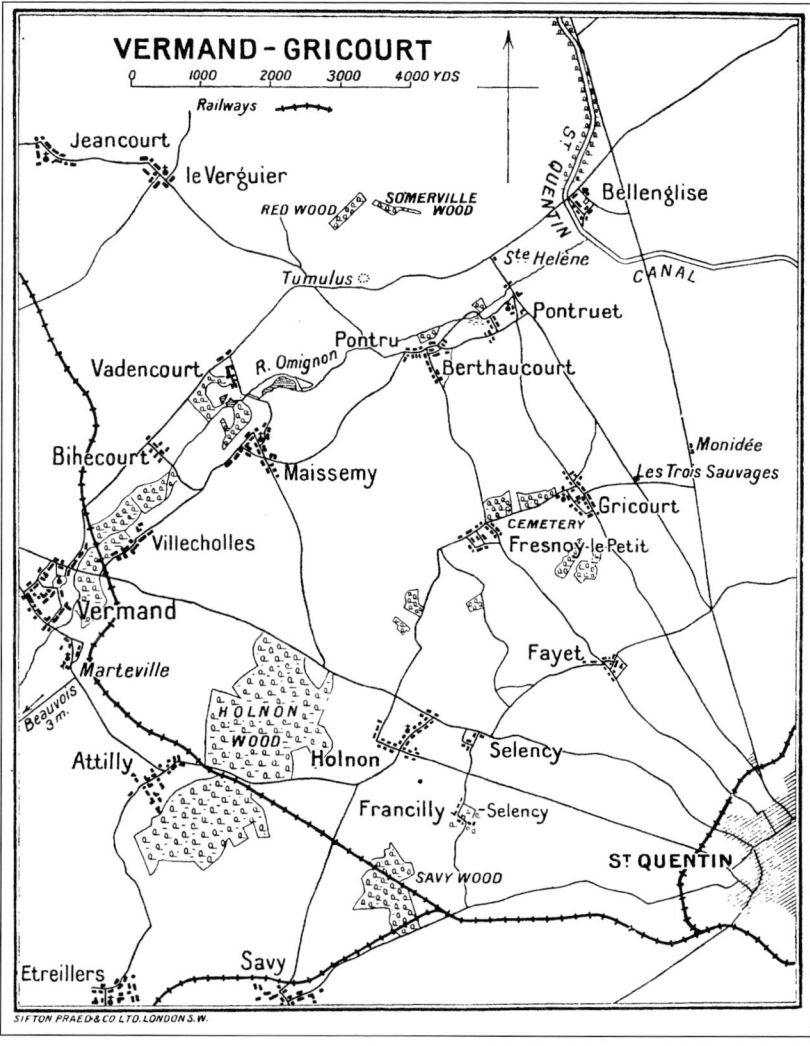

Map from Davson, *The History of the 35th Division*, p. 103.

'*La Picardie Historique et Pittoresque*': the River Omignon at Maissemy.

The British had advanced, in the wake of the German retirement, as far as the River Omignon, a tributary of the Somme, which meandered its way through countryside to the west of Saint-Quentin. The valley of the Omignon, picturesque and peaceful, was a place where weekenders dabbled in the marshes and fished in the ponds, where people from the town took picnics and messed about in boats. In the first week of April 1917, though, the British and Germany armies were facing off around Maissemy and Fresnoy-le-Petit. By the end of that week the 61st Division was digging trenches and erecting wire in front of Maissemy and, on 11 April, those new lines of trenches were being handed over to the 35th Division. The 104th Brigade was now ordered to take over the line from Fresnoy to the River Omignon.

On 10 April the 23rd Manchesters marched from Étreillers, where they had been filling craters, due north some 5 miles to Villecholles. Here they relieved the 2/6th Royal Warwicks in brigade reserve. Passing by Vermand, they saw more signs of the recent German retreat; the roads around Vermand had been mined and the bridges across the Omignon were blown. The front line now, though still in the process of settling down, circled around the west side of Saint-Quentin and then cut north-west towards Pontruet.

At this point 'Official Kinematographer' Geoffrey Malins was also travelling in the direction of Saint-Quentin, hoping to film 'the triumphant entry of the troops' into that town. ('It would be the first film actually showing the point of "liaison" with the French and their subsequent advance – making it, from an historical, public, and sentimental point of view, a film *par excellence*.') Getting as far as Vermand, he observed:

> The same desolation and wanton destruction was everywhere in evidence; but the most diabolical piece of vandalism was typified by the once beautiful Chateau of Caulaincourt, which was an awful heap of ruins . . . The wonderful paintings and tapestries in the library of the Chateau had been destroyed. As I wandered among the ruins, filming various scenes of our engineers at work sorting out the debris, I noticed many things which must have been of inestimable value. Every statue and ornamentation about the grounds was wilfully smashed to atoms; the flower pots which lined the edges of the once beautiful floral walks had been deliberately crushed – in fact a more complete specimen of purposeless, wanton destruction it would be impossible to find.[1]

The following day the Manchesters moved up to the newly dug trenches, relieving the 2/8th Royal Warwicks at Maissemy. It was snowing again. The village of Maissemy had been systematically destroyed in February. Having felled all the trees, and stripped away anything from the village's fabric that could usefully be employed elsewhere the Germans had brought Maissemy to the ground. The buildings that had not been dynamited had been set alight.

From the eastern side of Maissemy the troops could see the skyline of Saint-Quentin – the shape of its factory chimneys and the distinctive profile of the Basilica (from the tower of which, it was said, the Germans were watching over everything). They could

CHATEAU DE CAULAINCOURT (Aisne)
construit en 1772
détruit à la dynamite par les Allemands
en dehors de tout combat en 1917

Postcard showing images of the Chateau of Caulaincourt before the war and after, having been dynamited by the Germans.

also see the town's approaches being shelled. And they were being shelled again too. Their war had emphatically re-started.

> Private Amos Leang died of wounds on 10 April 1917. He was from Manchester. He is buried in Bois-Guillaume Communal Cemetery Extension.
> Lance Corporal James Burns died of wounds on 14 April 1917. He was aged 38 and from Salford. He is buried in Ennemain Communal Cemetery Extension.

Panorama, taken in 1919, looking out from the top of the Basilica, Saint-Quentin.

The front line was still very much mobile. The 35th Division might be engaging with the enemy again, but this was not the static trench warfare that they had grown accustomed to over the past few months. Posts were being extended forwards now and raids tested the boundaries. The 17th, 18th and 20th Lancashire Fusiliers were winning plaudits for skirmishing against the enemy and capturing ground and prisoners (the 17th Lancashire Fusiliers took fifty German prisoners at Fresnoy – the first batch of which the 35th Division could brag). In view of these successes, it was decided to launch a larger scale raid on Pontruet.

In conjunction with the 20th Lancashire Fusiliers, a raiding party of Manchesters set off from Berthaucourt in the early hours of the morning of 16 April. Under cover of an artillery and machine-gun barrage, nine officers and 160 men advanced on the village. But the village was empty. It seems that the enemy had just left. Sandilands wrote: 'In the sense that Pontruet was swept bare of the enemy, the raid was entirely successful, but it did not result in the capture of prisoners, as the garrison of the village, unfortunately, did not wait for the Manchesters.'[2] A search discovered freshly blood-stained bandages, indicating that the enemy had not long since gone, but there was no engagement. The Manchesters had missed their chance. It seems, though, that the raid was regarded as having been well conducted. Sandilands concluded, 'These operations had a splendid effect on the Brigade, and greatly raised its fighting value.'

> Private James Harry English was killed in action on 16 April 1917. He was from Ashton under Lyne. He is buried in Vadencourt British Cemetery, Maissemy.
>
> Private Robert Marshall was killed in action on 16 April 1917. He was from Ashton under Lyne. He is buried in Vadencourt British Cemetery, Maissemy.
>
> Private Leonard Mottershead died of wounds on 16 April 1917. He was aged 28 and from Manchester. He is buried in St Sever Cemetery Extension, Rouen.
>
> Private Charles Wilson was killed in action on 16 April 1917. He was from Manchester. He is buried in Vadencourt British Cemetery, Maissemy.

Later that day the Manchesters were relieved by the 16th Cheshires and, in foul weather, marched back to billets at Tertry. After the brief excitement of the raid on Pontruet, the following week would be spent back working on road repairs again. An event was arranged, though, to amuse and divert the men: a divisional horse show. Reading Sandilands' description, it does sound as if this perhaps might have been more amusing and diverting for the officers than it was for the men: 'Here a Divisional Horse Show was held, which, as regards the entries, was a great success, though the enthusiasm of the spectators was rather dampened by torrents of rain which fell throughout the day.'[3]

On 23 April the Manchesters were back in trenches, in the line just to the rear of Bihécourt. This stint would, at least, earn the Manchesters some operational plaudits. On the 24th, in conjunction with an action by the 59th Division, they established a post on the high ground ('Lone Tree') just north of Pontru. Then, on the 25th, there was another fruitful patrolling operation: a party of one officer and ten other ranks moved out to a crater to the west of Ste Helène, which, it had been observed, was generally occupied by the Germans at night. They waited. When the enemy arrived the patrol engaged them; one man was killed and the rest of the party driven off. With an identification of the enemy secured (156th IR and 452nd IR, 234th Division[4]) and no casualties sustained, the operation was deemed to be a success. Sandilands wrote that, during this period, the 104th Brigade started to get a good reputation for raiding and patrolling. 'The conditions were ideal for patrolling,' he recorded, 'the weather was good, the going consisted of sound turf, and there were plenty of natural landmarks. It was no uncommon thing for patrols to go for a distance of 1,000 yards beyond the front line posts.'[5] 'Fisher Crater', the object of many skirmishes and raids thereafter, was subsequently so called after the officer of the 23rd Manchesters who first took it.

Two days later, on 27 April, the Manchesters were involved in another raid into the Ste Helène area. Again in conjunction with operations by the 59th Division, a party of three officers and sixty men pushed out towards the enemy trenches around Ste Helène. The defences here were found to be strongly held. In the course of the patrol six men of the Manchesters were wounded and another two were reported as missing.

The next morning the Manchesters were relieved and returned to billets in brigade reserve in Vermand. They would spend the next week providing working parties, first going up to the trenches in front of Bihécourt and latterly up to Vadencourt. The Manchesters' War Diary indicates that both locations were part of the 'Brown Line'. But, as Sandilands wrote, there was some apparent confusion as to where and exactly what the 'Brown Line' was! 'These were great days for the siting and completion of the "Brown Line",' Sandilands recorded. 'Everyone seemed to have a different idea as to where the "Brown Line" was, and as to what it was supposed to be for, but we finally arrived at some sort of conclusion and carried on.'[6]

> Private John Monk was killed in action on 27 April 1917. He was aged 39 and from Pendleton, Manchester. He is commemorated on the Thiepval Memorial.
>
> Private Harry Lea died on 1 May 1917. He was from Wigan. He is buried in Cayeux Military Cemetery.
>
> Private Victor Stanley Johnstone died on 2 May 1917. He was aged 29 and from Didsbury. He is buried in Neslé Communal Cemetery.

Whatever the fatigue of working parties, the weather had at least improved. The first week of May was warm and it seemed generally to boost morale. The Divisional History records, 'The whole aspect of the countryside was altered, as hedgerows and trees burst into leaf. Holnon Wood, St Quentin Wood, and the whole valley of the Omignon from Villeque to Maissemy all at once became green, and the troops awoke to the fact that they were fighting in a really beautiful country.' Davson footnotes that even the trees that had been felled by the enemy in the orchards were suddenly miraculously breaking into bud.[7] Sandilands registered the change of mood that the arrival of spring brought as well:

> Anyone who was at Vermand at this period must remember the first two days of spring, when every tree and flower seemed suddenly to bud, and the whole countryside was changed as if by magic. The change was even more noticeable after a miserable winter, which had seemed to us almost interminable . . . There were times when it was almost impossible to believe that a war was going on.[8]

Sandilands recalled walking amongst the flowers and watching fish in the ornamental ponds of the Chateau de Vadencourt. But the Manchesters were heading back for more raiding.

On 5 May the 23rd Manchesters were ordered to carry out a raid against a wood to the north of Pontru. It would later be marked on maps as 'Somerville Wood', renamed after the officer who led this attacking party. The Wood ('of straggling growth, about half a mile long'[9]) was occupied by the enemy and, angling up a hillside between the two lines, was of 'considerable tactical importance'.[10] The 59th Division had previously assaulted it, but failed to take it.

George Barker was one of these men taking part in the raid. He recalled the moments before it began:

> A tot of rum is given us to revive our spirits, we shake each other by the hand, and wish one another good luck. Our artillery commences a creeping barrage which we have to follow up at a given signal; we crouch down and wait.
>
> In the distance it looks like a firework display; shells are dropping thick and fast amongst the enemy, and every now and then a shell would burst dangerously near us, indicating to our officer that Jerry is trying his range.[11]

The main attacking party – of five officers and 159 other ranks – left the jumping off place ('Purple Copse', to the west of Somerville Wood) at 2.30 am under cover of a heavy artillery barrage. At the same time, a diversionary attack (by one officer and thirty other ranks), with Lewis guns and grenades, was staged against the south-western side of the wood. It seems that this demonstration completely deceived the enemy, allowing the main attacking party to enter the wood from the north-west end, facing only very slight resistance. They bombed all the dugouts and shelters and drove the enemy out of the wood. Four men were taken prisoner.

George Barker's account continues:

> At last our captain decides to move forwards, and with Mills bombs in our pockets, and rifle with bayonet fixed, we came to the enemy's barbed wire. Lads with wire-cutters make a way for us through clouds of smoke. Pieces of shell are flying and dropping with a sting, bombs are bursting right and left, and amidst it all our lads are yelling like mad men. Machine gun nests, and the first line of trenches are being taken, prisoners are surrendering and being marched off at the point of bayonet.[12]

At 3.15 am the party withdrew to their own lines, leaving the 17th Lancashire Fusiliers to man the posts in the wood – and George Barker. He had become disorientated, done a bit of souvenir gathering and then found himself among the Fusiliers. 'I was informed that the attack was very successful,' he wrote. The Manchesters' casualties were nine wounded; sixty dead Germans were found in the wood.

Later that day, at 9.30 pm, the Germans tried to seize the wood back. A party of seventy men were estimated to have attacked and, after hand-to-hand fighting, they drove the Lancashire Fusiliers from their posts. However a counter-attack, around midnight, regained Somerville Wood for the British. According to Sandilands' account, the counter-attack was launched by a working party on their own initiative. The Germans were driven back before orders had been received.

Hugh Somerville. Photograph from *Manchester Courier*, 1 October 1915.

> Hugh Somerville was recognised for his role in the capture of what afterwards was to become known as Somerville Wood. An article in the *Edinburgh Evening News* (19 July 1917) reported that Sir Douglas Haig had mentioned him in his despatches and that he was to be awarded the Military Cross for his part in the raid. The citation for the latter (*London Gazette*, 14 August 1917) reads: 'For conspicuous gallantry and devotion when in charge of a raiding party. By his personal example and courage he was mainly responsible for the success of the raid. He has previously displayed the same sterling qualities.' Lieutenant Somerville would also now be promoted to captain. The *Edinburgh Evening News* stated that he had carried out 'a brilliant piece of tactical work'.
>
> Hugh Somerville was from Edinburgh. He was attending university in his home town when the war broke out, but he enlisted in the 16th Royal Scots ('McCrea's Battalion'). In April 1915 he obtained a commission in the Manchester Regiment. He was promoted to lieutenant in the 23rd Manchesters in November 1915. After the 23rd Battalion was disbanded, Somerville transferred to the 2nd Manchesters and he would be awarded a second Military Cross in 1918 ('For conspicuous gallantry and devotion to duty during an enemy attack. When his company headquarters had been surrounded and only two men were left alive he managed to reach the main body of his company, organize an attack and drive the enemy out. This successful finish was due to his gallantry and determined energy,').[13]

After a couple of days in billets in Vermand, again providing working parties, the Manchesters were back in trenches near Pontru and manning the outposts in Somerville Wood. The weather was warm and reports coming through to the troops told them that the French attack in Champagne was progressing well, with Craonne captured and thousands of enemy prisoners taken.

On 7 May Bernard Montgomery, now with the 33rd Division, took a day's leave and went to visit the 104th Brigade. He wrote to his mother:

> The country where the 104th are is delightful; the Bosche withdrew his lines there very quickly and there was no fighting. It is just like the country in England, not a shell hole to be seen anywhere . . . It was delightful seeing all the old faces in the 104th Brigade; I visited every unit and saw most people. It was a beautiful summer's day and was a real holiday for me.[14]

On 15 May the 23rd Manchesters were relieved by the Canadian Cavalry Brigade (Strathcona's Horse and Royal Canadian Dragoons). The Manchesters marched back to camp in Poeuilly Valley, just to the rear of Vermand.

> Lance Corporal Joseph Smith was killed in action on 15 May 1917. He was from Failsworth. He is commemorated on the Thiepval Memorial.

In Poeuilly Valley military medals were awarded to three men for their conduct during the attack on Somerville Wood. While in camp here Lieutenant Colonel Mills arranged 'a splendid gymkana'. The 18th Bengal Cavalry and Central Indian Horse regiments took part, 'which pleased and interested our men very much,' General Sandilands related. 'Very few in the Brigade had even seen native troops before, let alone really good tent-pegging and trick riding.'[15]

The 35th Division now received orders that it was to shift west. The 104th Brigade was moving towards Péronne and the division would come under orders of XV Corps.

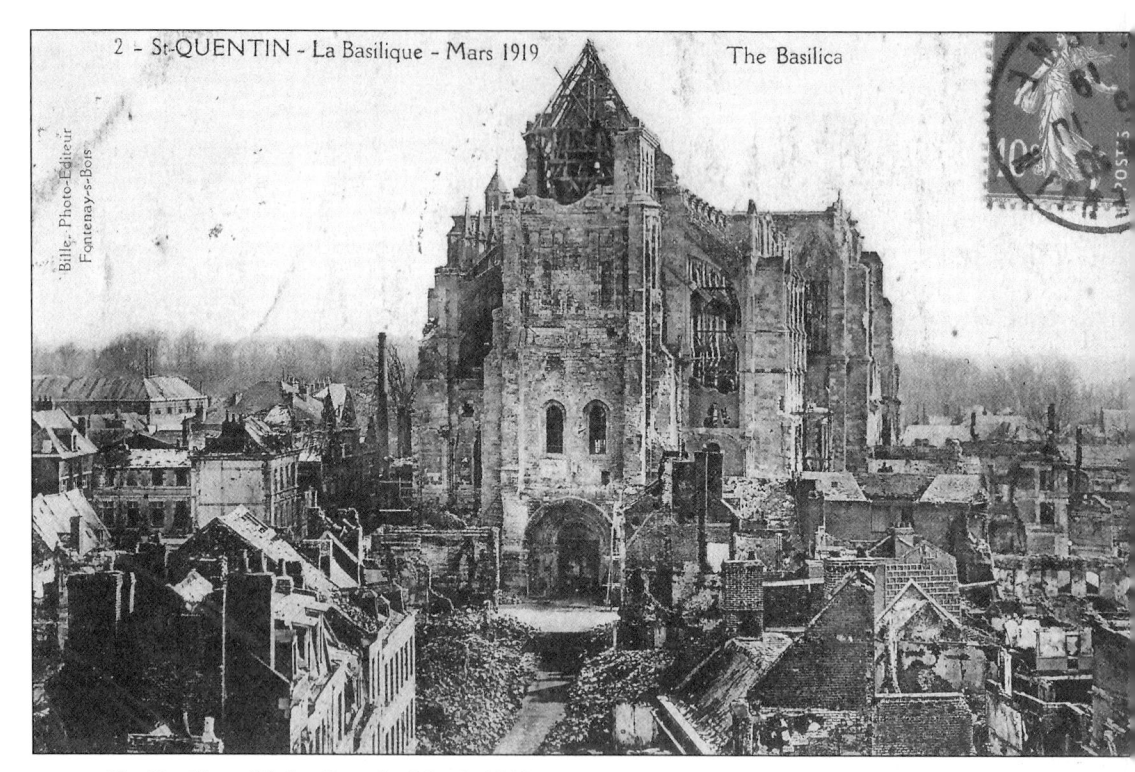

The Basilica of Saint-Quentin, March 1919.

Inside the Basilica of Saint-Quentin, October 1918.

Chapter 11

Péronne and Gauche Wood – Working Parties, Cricket Matches and Plagues of Frogs

On 21 May 1917 the 23rd Manchesters moved north-west, around 9 miles, from the camp in Poeuilly Valley to billets in Péronne. Travellers arriving in Péronne two years later could read in their Michelin *Guides*:

> Péronne a sub-prefecture of the Département of the Somme, was one of the centres of the sugar and hosiery industries in France, with a pre-war population of about 5,000 inhabitants. Built at the junction of the Rivers Somme and Cologne, which form a picturesque girdle of marshes and ponds before the walls of the town, Péronne was formerly a fortified city. Its brick ramparts and moats were being dismantled when the late war broke out.[1]

The advancing Germans entered Péronne in August 1914, but were driven out on 15 September. They reoccupied the town ten days later, though, and would remain there until March 1917. During that time the town was subject to Allied bombardment and then a 'systematic destruction'. In 1919 the evidence of this recent history was striking. The Michelin *Guide* goes on:

> Everywhere pillage preceded destruction. The houses, whose walls (more or less damaged) still remain standing, were completely emptied. The doors, partition-walls, windows and wood-work were taken out and burnt. All the safes, including those of the Banque de France, were broken open. All articles of any value were carried away, and the rest destroyed. In 1917, mattresses ripped open, battered perambulators and cradles, broken furniture, dislocated pianos, even books and family photographs, torn to pieces, were found among the ruins. In the gardens, the fruit-trees were either cut down or hacked at their roots.[2]

At 7.00 am on 18 March 1917 a battalion of the Royal Warwicks of the 48th Division entered Péronne. The French had fought for it for two years. When the British arrived the town was still burning.

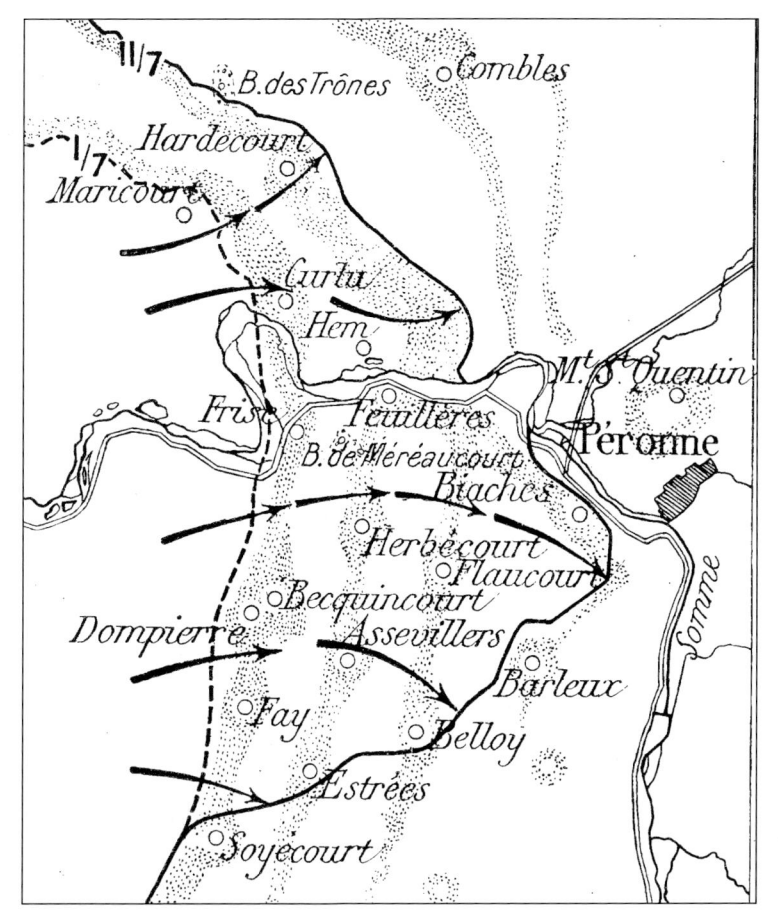

This map shows how the French armies had pushed towards Péronne in 1916 until the town was in sight, but they had not succeeded in taking it. *Illustrated Michelin Guides to the Battle-Fields (1914–1918): The Somme, Volume 1*, p. 17. The grey shading represents 'the German lines of resistance'.

Philip Gibbs got to Péronne the day after the first British troops arrived. The ruins of the town made an impact (and powerful press copy):

Before going, firebrands had been at work, setting alight all the houses not already smashed by shell-fire. They were burning, when I passed them, so fiercely that the hot breath of the flames was upon my face. Even now it was possible to see that Péronne had once been a little town of old-world dignity and charm. Frontages of some of these gutted houses were richly carved in Renaissance style, among them being the ruins of the Palais de Justice and the Hôtel de Ville and the Maison Municipale. Here and there along the Rue St.-Fursy and in the Grande Place was an old French mansion built before the Revolution, now just a skeleton of broken brickwork and timber. Though many houses were still standing enough to see they were houses, there was hardly one that had escaped the wrath of war. It was pitiful to see here and there old signs, showing the life of the town in peace, such as the

Français souvenons-nous !
1509. **La France reconquise** — PÉRONNE - Kultur !
*Les bandits signent leur forfait de cette grossièreté :
Ne vous lamentez pas, souriez !*
Stupidly the bandits from this rudness their crime subscribe :
Not to Cry, to laugh !

Photographs taken when the British arrived in Péronne. The German notice on the building above translates as: *Do not be angry but wonder.*

Français souvenons-nous !
1507. **La France reconquise** — PÉRONNE (Somme)
Place de l'Eglise - Le vol, le feu, puis la dynamite indiquent la rage des boches en fuite
The Church Place - Effect of the retreating German's fury

Français souvenons-nous !
1503. **La France reconquise** — PÉRONNE (Somme)
Les troupes Anglaises à leur arrivée
Arrival of English soldiers

Photographs taken after Péronne was abandoned by the Germans and occupied by the British.

'Librairie Nouvelle', the 'Teinturerie Parisienne' belonging to Mme. Poitevineau, the Notary's house, full of legal books and papers scattered on a charred floor beneath a gaping roof, a shop for 'articles de chasse' kept by one Monsieur Bourdin. Those signboards, reminding one of Péronne before the war, were side by side with other signboards showing the way of German life until 6.30 yesterday morning . . .

The only inhabitants of the Grande Place were a big black cat, looking sick and sorry for itself, and a dummy figure dressed as a French Zouave, sprawling below the pedestal of a statue to Catherine de Poix, heroine of the siege of 1870. The statue had been taken away, like that of Faidherbe in the square of Bapaume. On top of the pedestal had been laid the dummy figure in French uniform, but our soldiers removed it. Péronne was a dead town, like Ypres, like Bapaume, like all those villages in the wake of the German retreat.[3]

When the Manchesters arrived Péronne had been in Allied hands for two months. Though destruction was everywhere apparent, it still, in the words of Brigadier General Sandilands, 'looked more or less like a town'.[4] The Manchesters would spend the next two days in Péronne, providing working parties.

On 23 May they moved into camp at Templeux-la-Fosse, some 5 miles or so to the north-east of Péronne. They were in countryside again, and a good 7 miles back behind the front line. The Divisional History described the landscape thereabouts: 'Wide stretches of open grassland interspersed with woods, the remains of important villages, and valleys, which varied in depth from 50 to 300 feet, formed the chief features.'[5] The weather was very hot and there were clearly some pleasant diversions to be had while in camp here. On the evening of 24 May the officers of the Manchesters played the officers of the 20th Lancashire Fusiliers at cricket. The War Diary of the Fusiliers boasts that they won by three overs.

The next day the battalion moved north to Sorel le Grand, where again they were providing working parties on that now not-so-elusive Brown Line. Sports competitions were held in the evenings.

Gauche Wood Sector

On 2 June 1917 the 35th Division came under the command of III Corps (due to the withdrawal of XV Corps from the line) and shifted north-east to the Gauche Wood sector. Gauche Wood ('*Bois Gaucher*') was a small woodland to the rear of the village of Villers-Guislain, north of Épehy. As field guns and reserves tended to be 'hidden' there, it regularly attracted the attention of enemy artillery. The front line in this sector was not continuous and in stretches consisted only of detached posts. As Sandilands put it, 'trenches in the real sense hardly existed'. This area would see fierce fighting at the beginning of December 1917, as the Germans launched a counter stroke in the vicinity in response to the Cambrai offensive. Through the spring and early summer of 1917, though, it was a relatively quiet sector. The main Hindenburg Line ran to the rear of Honnecourt.[6]

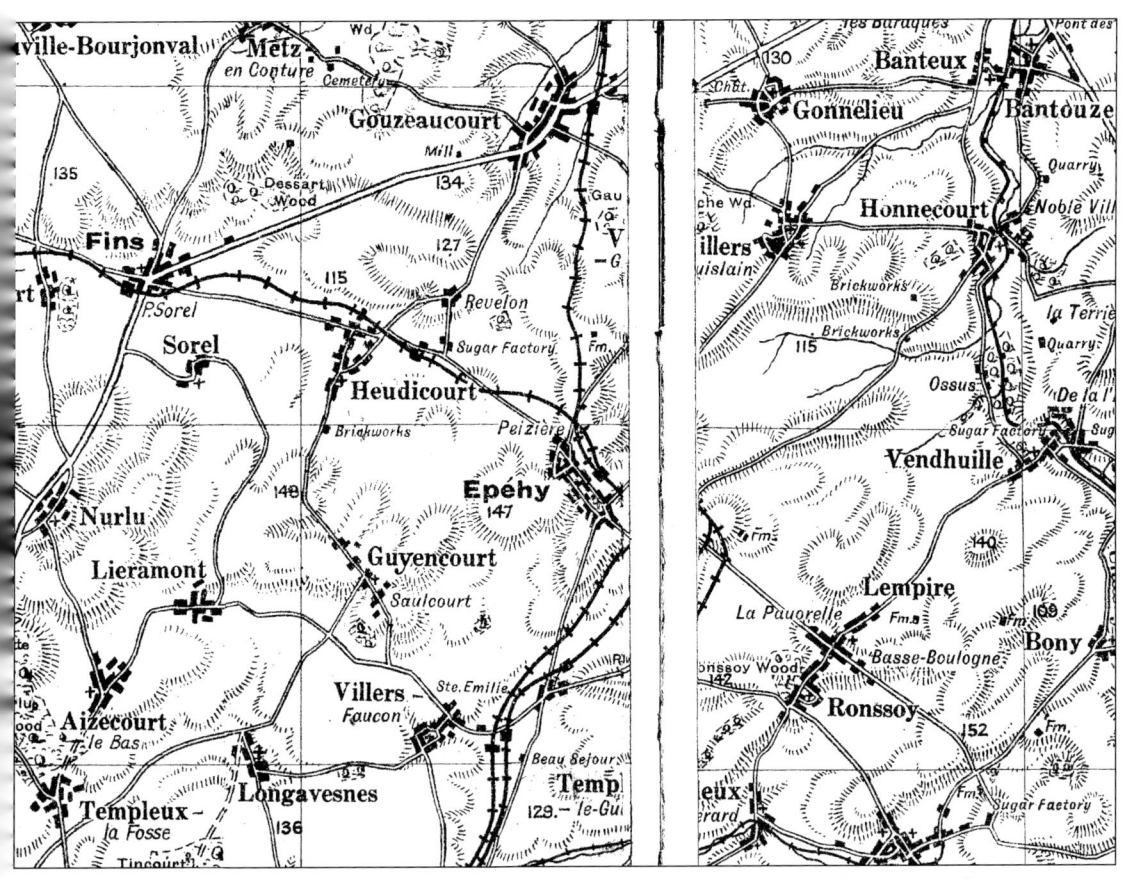

Map extract from *The western front at a glance: a large-scale atlas of the Allies fighting line in the west* (1917).

The Manchesters were taking casualties again, albeit not in large numbers. Having relieved the 17th Lancashire Fusiliers at the front (such as it was), one man was wounded by shell fire and subsequently died. The next day one man was wounded on patrol and later died. But the enemy does not seem to have been actively aggressive here. Sandilands recorded: 'Although the approaches to the front line were fully exposed to view from the enemy trenches, sniping was unknown. Occasionally Villers-Guislain used to be fairly heavily shelled, but taking it all round it was a quiet sector.' The Divisional History notes that senior officers were able to ride most of the way to the front line and to walk over the open to the trenches. It went on: 'During the month of June no operation of importance was undertaken by our troops or by the enemy. Numerous patrol encounters took place, but the Germans showed no desire to prolong the meeting.'[7]

Private Michael Curley died of wounds on 3 June 1917. He was from Ancoats. He is buried in La Chapelette British and Indian Cemetery, Péronne.

Lance Corporal Fred Ashton died of wounds on 4 June 1917. He was aged 22 and from Droylsden. He is buried in Heudicourt Communal Cemetery Extension.

Map showing the location of Gauche Wood and Villers-Guislain, just on the edge of the Hindenburg Line (the black line indicated on the map above). *Liverpool Echo*, 14 April 1917.

Though it therefore does not seem to have been a hostile sector, there is evidence that Gauche Wood was not without its discomforts. The War Diary of the 18th Lancashire Fusiliers notes, 'Trenches wet and muddy. Sleeping accommodation for officers and men poor.'

The 23rd Manchesters remained in the Gauche Wood sector until they were relieved on 10 June and moved back to the camp at Templeux-la-Fosse for another week of providing working parties. 'We again encountered our old friend the "Brown Line",' Sandilands recalled, 'which was just as elusive as before, and to make matters worse a "Green Line" had now been projected by the authorities.'[8] Training was also taking place

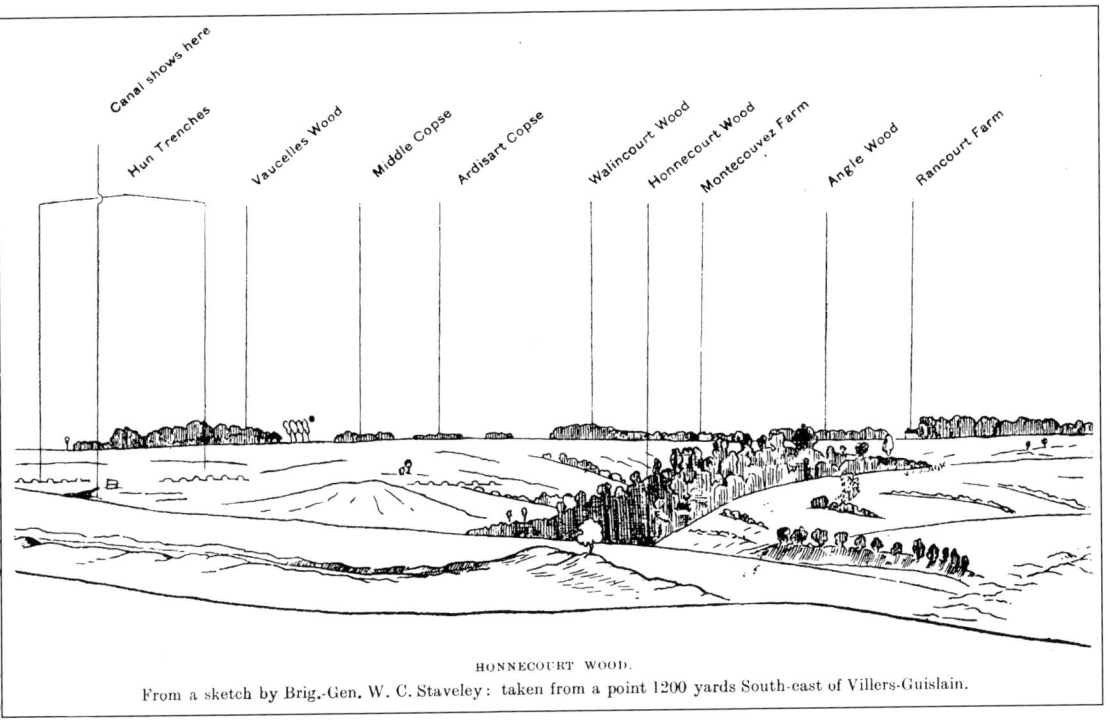

HONNECOURT WOOD.
From a sketch by Brig.-Gen. W. C. Staveley: taken from a point 1200 yards South-east of Villers-Guislain.

Sketch looking towards Honnecourt from Villers-Guislain. From Davson, *The History of the 35th Division*, p. 119.

at this time. On 16 June a brigade attack was practised. The War Diary of the 20th Lancashire Fusiliers notes that the Manchesters had been designated the role of 'moppers up and carriers'.

The pattern continued. On 18 June the Manchesters were in Brigade Reserve in the Villers-Guislain sector, providing working parties for the front line. Sandilands' recollections of such tasks confirm that this was indeed an unaggressive part of the line:

> It was in this sector that we jumped and wired a new front line in one night, which afterwards became known as 'Gardiner's Bank'. The material for putting up an apron fence covering a length of about 1,000 yards was taken up in every available vehicle, including pontoon waggons. These vehicles were actually driven out, and off-loaded in No Man's Land, without interference from the enemy. This incident provided conclusive proof that the enemy had not any very warlike intentions.[9]

It was quite common for men here to work in the open in the early mornings and evenings without attracting hostile attention. They also played football in the rear and had time for nature observations. Sandilands records that around this time a 'plague of small frogs' suddenly appeared in the trenches. 'There were literally myriads of frogs,' he wrote, 'hopping and crawling about in the trenches, and it was impossible to walk a yard without squashing several under foot.'[10] George Barker recalled the same: 'As we take over the front line trenches, we see swarms of small frogs in our path, which we gradually get rid of by sprinkling down a disinfectant fluid every now and then.'[11]

But some more martial occupations were about to come the Manchesters' way. On 26 June they were back in the line again. After several days of concentrated bombardment (five men were killed and four wounded by shell fire on 27 June), an alert was issued on the 29th indicating that the section of line held by the 23rd Manchesters – around the Fawcus Avenue communication trench – was likely to be raided by the enemy. This anticipated raid materialised the next morning. On 30 June, at 6.00 am, an enemy party, of twenty to thirty men, entered Fawcus Avenue under cover of artillery and trench mortar barrage, and taking advantage of a thick mist. Lewis guns, from both flanks, opened on the party and they withdrew. One wounded man was left behind, and subsequently died, but it was believed that other casualties were inflicted. One sergeant of the 23rd Manchesters was captured. He had just joined the battalion the night before.

> Private Harry Bell was killed in action on 27 June 1917. He was from Manchester. He is buried in Villers-Guislain Communal Cemetery.
>
> Private James Leigh was killed in action on 27 June 1917. He was aged 22 and from Moston, Manchester. He is buried in Villers-Guislain Communal Cemetery.
>
> Private Joseph Talbot died of wounds on 27 June 1917. He was from Brown Edge, Staffordshire. He is buried in Fins New British Cemetery, Sorel-Le-Grand.
>
> Private Robert Taylor was killed in action on 27 June 1917. He was from Hulme. He is buried in Villers-Guislain Communal Cemetery.
>
> Private Harry Whitehouse was killed in action on 27 June 1917. He was aged 22 and from Hulme. He is buried in Villers-Guislain Communal Cemetery.

On 2 July the Manchesters were relieved by the 12th Suffolks and moved back again to the divisional reserve at Templeux-la-Fosse. Here they would spend the next fortnight training; musketry was practised on a range, there was instruction in bayonet fighting, company drill and working in Lewis gun teams. There was also a return cricket match; the War Diary of the 20th Lancashire Fusiliers details that the officers of the battalion played a second match against the 23rd Manchesters. This time the Manchesters won.

Chapter 12

'The Birdcage': Fighting for the Higher Ground

In July the 35th Division shifted south and relieved the Cavalry Corps in the Épehy area. As was the case in the neighbouring Gauche Wood sector, the front here was for the most part a series of detached posts. In this sector it was all about fights over posts, over hills and farms and woodlands. In this area in the summer of 1917 the focus was snatching the tactical advantage and improving the tactical position.

The village of Épehy had been taken by the British in April, and, since that date, posts had been gradually pushed out towards the Hindenburg Line, 5 miles or so distant, on the far side of the Saint-Quentin Canal. Arriving in the Épehy sector with the 7th Manchesters in May 1917, Captain S.J. Wilson recorded his impressions of the area:

> The front was just in process of solidifying from the liquid state as a result of the German recent retirement to a safe position. The enemy therefore looked calmly down upon us from his elaborate Hindenburg system of trenches beyond Vendhuile whilst we expanded our isolated outposts into organised continuous lines. He himself, however, was also busy digging a sort of outpost work in advance of the main line of defence, for he had held up any further British advance principally from a bulwark of land mass called the Knoll on the western side of the canal, while his main line was really on the eastern side. Because of the disjointed condition of the front there was always a danger, when going from one company to another, of men wandering into the Boche lines.

All that remained of the main street in Épehy at the end of the war.

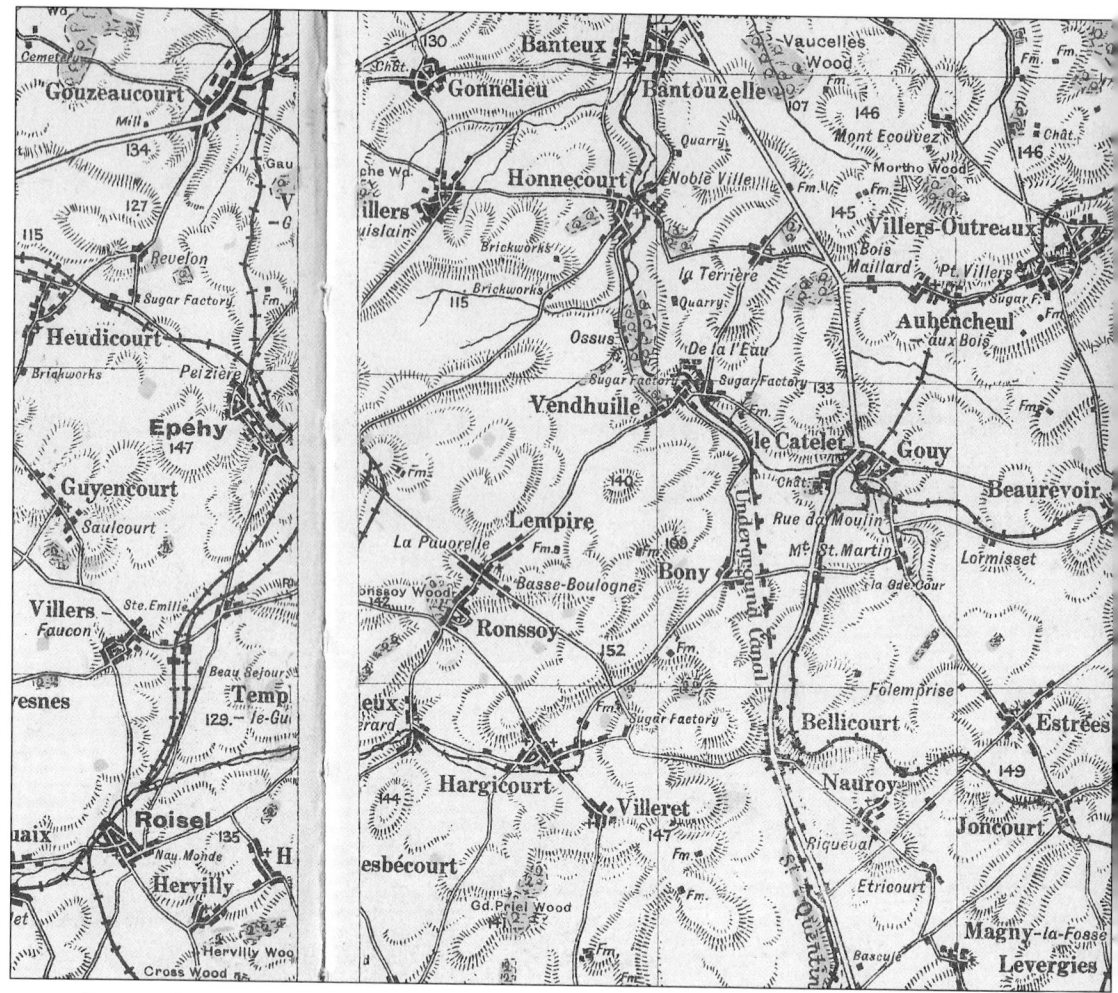

Extract of a map from *The western front at a glance: a large-scale atlas of the Allies fighting line in the west* (1917).

With continuous trenches not, at this time, yet constructed, Captain Wilson noted that there was 'a good deal of digging to be done in this sector'.[1]

By the time that the 23rd Manchesters arrived here in July, some trench systems had been established, but there was still much work to be done in linking up and fortifying positions. 'This period formed one of the most interesting in the history of the Brigade,' Sandilands would recall. 'The weather still held good, and there was always something for everyone to do.'[2]

A series of valleys sloped down towards the Saint-Quentin Canal. The valleys of Ossus Wood and Canal Wood were still being contested and were effectively no-man's-land. Divisional headquarters were based in Villers-Faucon, 2 miles to the south-west of Épehy.

In addition to the Knoll, mentioned by Captain Wilson, the significant features of this sector were Gillemont Farm and the Birdcage.

248

The ruined village of Épehy.

The remains of the school at Épehy after the war, with potential students to its right.

- Gillemont Farm (to the south of sector) was a high point, about 400 feet above the nearest posts. The area around Gillemont Farm was contested by both armies.
- The Knoll (north of Gillemont Farm) was a high point, about 35–40 feet above the nearest posts. It was in the hands of the enemy and commanded a good view of the Allied positions, especially those to the south of it.
- The Birdcage (north of the Knoll, facing the village of Vendhuile, which was in enemy hands) was, in the words of Brigadier-General Sandilands, 'one of the

Panorama looking towards Vendhuile.

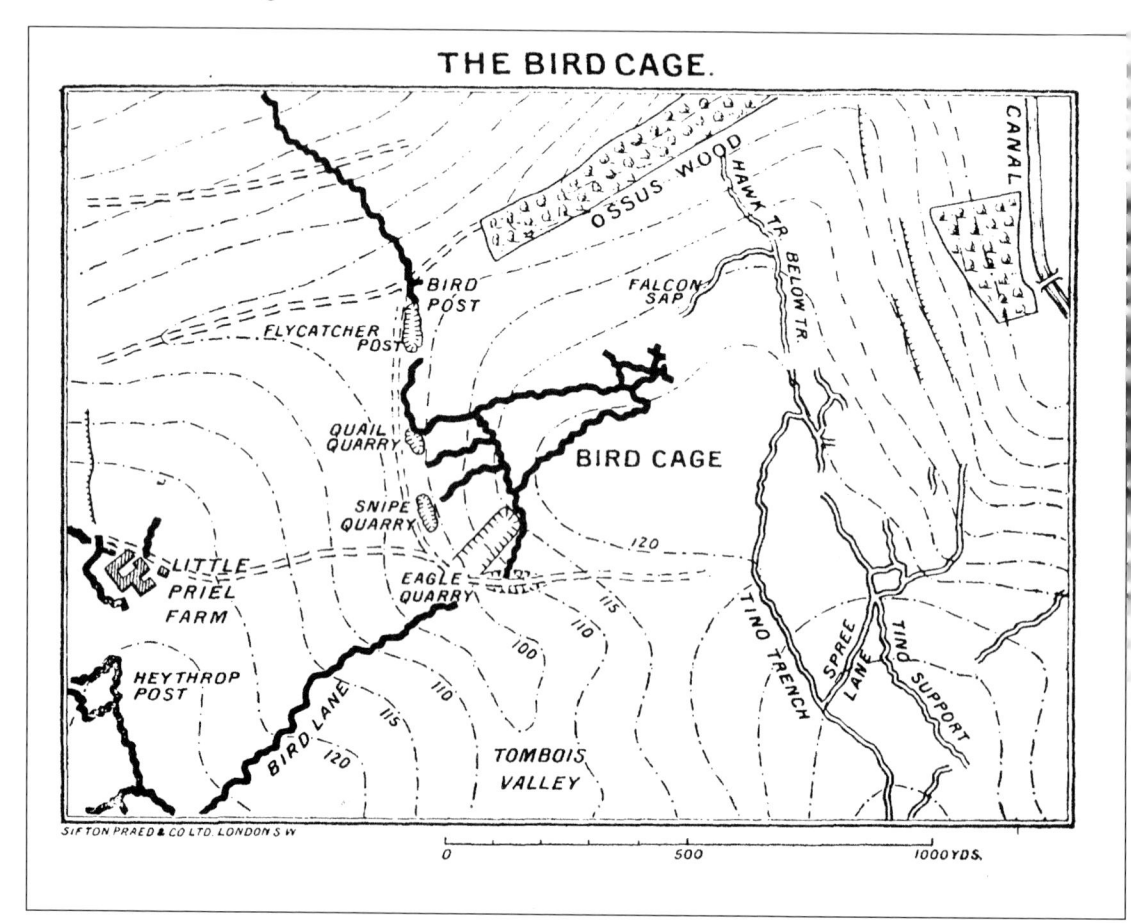

The Birdcage. From Davson, *The History of the 35th Division*, p. 126.

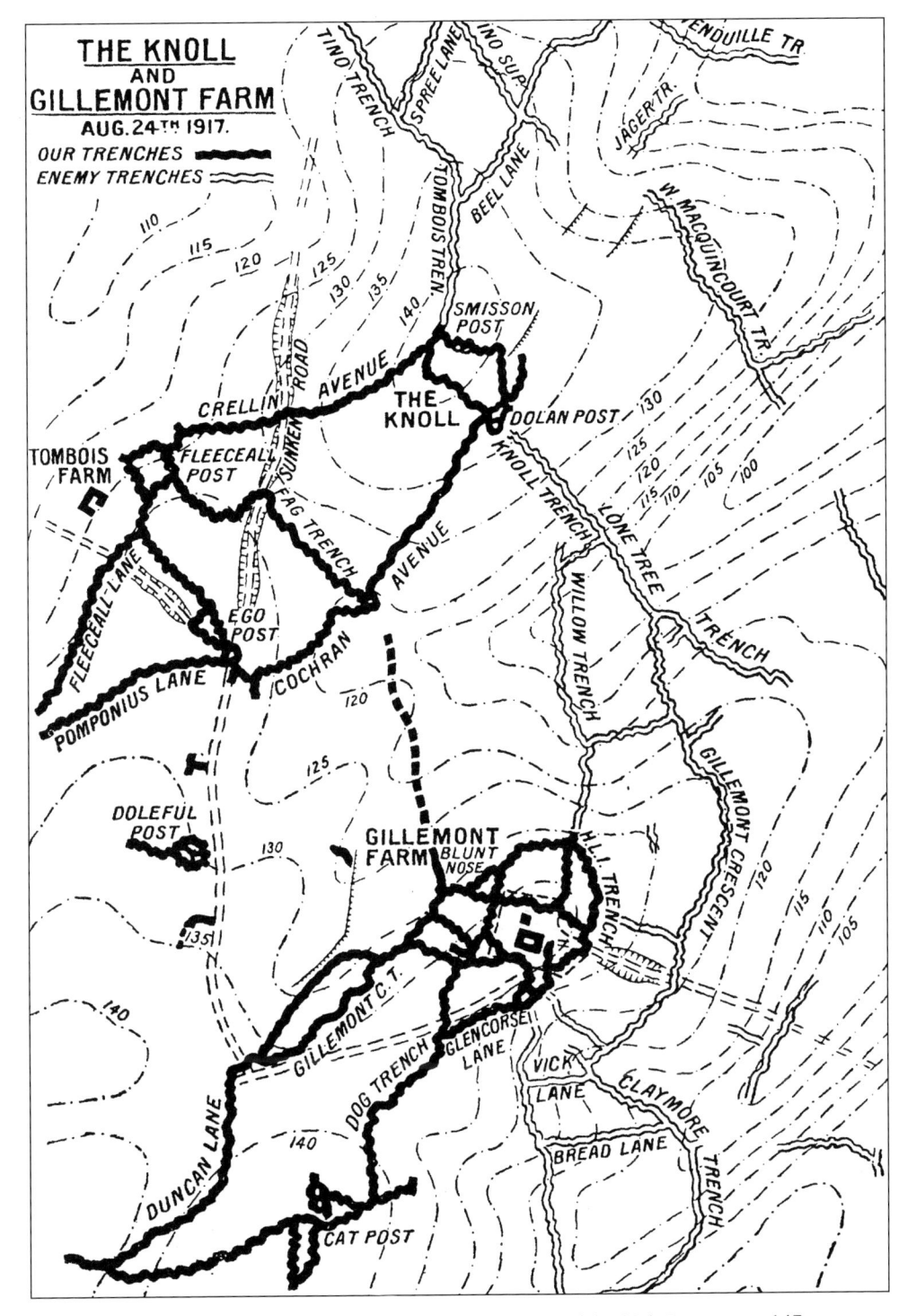

The Knoll and Gillemont Farm. From Davson, *The History of the 35th Division*, p. 147.

freaks of the war'. The Birdcage was a network of trenches on a hillside that sloped down towards the canal. It had originally been a series of saps, constructed in order to obtain a view from the crest of the hill. It had been held by the cavalry and had evolved as a defensive work, the various isolated posts progressively being joined up. The original post was approximately 500 yards ahead of the next defensible line. They were joined by 'one miserable communication trench' (Sandilands), down the forward slope. As the Divisional History puts it, the duty of holding the Birdcage 'was not highly esteemed'. As soon as the 35th Division took over this sector they began work to make this feature more practically defensible. A second communication trench was constructed and then a cross trench (called the Perch). Dugouts were built and the whole thing became more purposeful. As Sandilands put it, 'from being a work which was simply asking for capture, the Birdcage became a regular little stronghold'.[3]

On 15 July the Manchesters relieved the 16th Cheshires in the Catelet Valley section of trenches, just to the north of the Birdcage. The following morning one man of the Manchesters was killed as he returned from a patrol and another man was wounded the next day under similar circumstances. The Manchesters' War Diary indicates that during the course of this week considerable patrolling was being carried out, both by day and by night. Several posts, which it had been assumed were held by the enemy, were found, when visited by patrols, to be unmanned. Much useful information was apparently gleaned from these patrolling activities and the battalion was highly complimented for the way that this work was conducted. These activities seem to have been carried out without too much enemy interference but, around 21 July, the attitude of the enemy seems to have altered. Artillery and machine guns suddenly became much more active.

> Corporal George Ernest Marshall died on 16 July 1917. He was from Plaistow, Middlesex. He is buried in Unicorn Cemetery, Vendhuile.
>
> Private Herbert John Osborn died on 23 July 1917. He was aged 21 and from Attleborough, Norfolk. He is buried in Tincourt New British Cemetery.

On 23 July the Manchesters were relieved and moved back into a support position. For the next few days they would be providing working parties for the front line, and, with enemy bombardment continuing, this was evidently eventful work.

Patrols had indicated for some days that there were signs that an enemy raid was imminent. On the morning of 26 July those expectations were realised. At 4.30 am an enemy artillery barrage began. All units stood to arms. At 6.10 am, then, a raid was launched on the sector of trenches to the Manchesters' left (at the junction of the front line and Fawcus Avenue), occupied by the 13th Yorkshires. The enemy succeeded in entering the trenches and captured several prisoners before retreating. However, as they retired to their own trenches they were caught by a British artillery barrage and rifle fire and several of the prisoners were able to escape.

Three days later the Manchesters would get their chance to do some raiding. On 29

July an operation was launched on Hawk Trench, an enemy advanced line just to the north of Ossus Wood. The raid was preceded by a short, intense artillery bombardment and a machine-gun barrage of five minutes' duration, after which the guns formed a protective barrage round the point of entry. The raiding party, under Captain Gibbons, was divided into four groups, each consisting of one officer and fifteen men. They started off from a position about 400 yards from the enemy line. Nos 1 and 2 groups (under Lieutenants Burkett and Mason) entered the enemy trench at 2.30 am. They reached Hawk Trench without encountering significant opposition, although Lieutenant Burkett's party was delayed by the wire and suffered a few casualties before breaking through. Lieutenant Mason's party had no such difficulty. Party no. 3 covered their right flank and no. 4 group made a diversionary demonstration. On entering Hawk Trench the raiding parties found a machine gun with its crew of four men lying dead beside it. Turning northwards up the trench they counted thirty dead Germans of the 124th Regiment, and at a point about 150 yards on, they secured a second machine gun. Then, at 3.15 am, having bombed a dug-out, they returned to their lines, bringing both machine guns with them. No prisoners were captured nor were any of the enemy seen alive; if any survived the barrage, they had apparently fled. The Manchesters suffered nine men wounded (seven of whom were only slightly injured) and one man was missing.

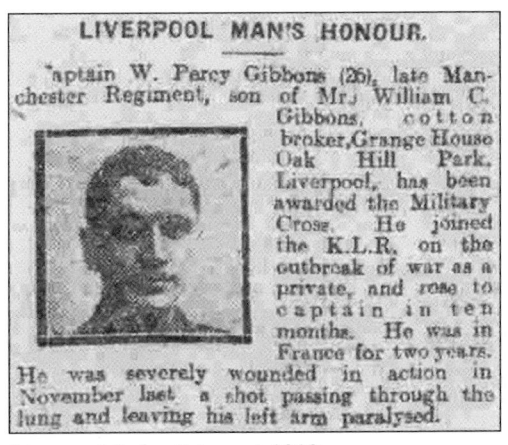

> Private Edward Harold Edwards was killed in action on 29 July 1917. He was from Oldham. He is commemorated on the Thiepval Memorial.

> Captain William Percy Gibbons was one of the battalion's original officers. He was the son of a Liverpool cotton broker and in 1914 was employed in the family firm, Oscar Gantes & Co. At the start of the war he joined the Liverpool Pals as a private, but he took a commission in the Manchester Regiment. He was appointed second lieutenant in the 23rd Manchester Battalion in January 1915, and was soon promoted, becoming a captain by November of that year. He had gone from private to captain in the space of ten months.
>
> **LIVERPOOL MAN'S HONOUR.**
>
> Captain W. Percy Gibbons (26), late Manchester Regiment, son of Mr. William C. Gibbons, cotton broker, Grange House, Oak Hill Park, Liverpool, has been awarded the Military Cross. He joined the K.L.R. on the outbreak of war as a private, and rose to captain in ten months. He was in France for two years. He was severely wounded in action in November last, a shot passing through the lung and leaving his left arm paralysed.
>
> *Liverpool Echo*, 5 August 1918.
>
> Captain Gibbons would be seriously wounded in action in November 1917. A shot passed through his lung and he was left with a paralysed left arm. His war was ended. He relinquished his commission in July 1918. He would be awarded the Military Cross (for 'conspicuous gallantry and devotion to duty' over the course of 1917) and attend the investiture at Buckingham Palace in August 1918. He was still only aged 26.

> Lieutenant Herbert John Mason would subsequently be awarded the Military Cross for his part in the raid on Hawk Trench. The citation reads: 'For conspicuous gallantry and devotion to duty during a raid upon hostile trenches. He led his party through enemy wire with the greatest determination, inflicting loss on the enemy and capturing two machine guns, one of which he carried back himself to the battalion headquarters, which were 1,000 yards away. He set a fine example to all ranks.'[4]
>
> Lieutenant Mason, who was from Watford, died of wounds in December 1918. He was aged 30. He is buried in Great Yarmouth (Caister) Cemetery.

On 31 July 1917 the Manchesters were occupying the front line north of the Birdcage. It began to rain that night. It was to be the start of a week of notably wet weather (the battalion War Diary remarks upon it). This was also the day on which the Third Battle of Ypres was launched. It was raining, too, to the north and it would now rain for almost the whole month – twice the normal average for the time of year.

On 7 August the Manchesters were relieved by the 4th Dismounted Cavalry Brigade, and moved back to divisional reserve at Gurlu Wood. Preparations were now being made for an attack on the Knoll and Gillemont Farm, with a view to preventing the enemy from getting a firm a hold on the high ground. The 35th Division was taken out of the line for ten days in order to practise the attack. The capture of the Knoll had been assigned to the 105th Brigade and that of Gillemont Farm to the 106th Brigade. The 104th was required to make a diversionary raid on a 1,000 yards wide front between Ossus Wood and Canal Wood. The Knoll/Gillemont attack was originally planned for 15 August but, with delays in the arrival of heavy artillery, it was put back until the 19th. During this time a decision was made to scale up the infantry attack, so that the aim was now to capture and hold the enemy trenches facing Gillemont Farm. Preparations for the attack were thorough and detailed; a full-scale replica of the Knoll trenches was dug and the attack was repeatedly practised.

While they were in Gurlu Wood there were also boxing competitions and concerts. On 8 August Brigadier General Sandilands gave a speech about the Battle of Minden. As they had back in Happy Valley in 1916, all ranks of the Lancashire Fusiliers wore red and white roses on their helmets.

On 19 August the Manchesters moved back into the line. Meanwhile, to the south, the attacks on the Knoll and Gillemont Farm had been launched. At 4.00 am the 15th Cheshires and 15th Sherwood Foresters attacked the Knoll. They took the German trenches within 15 minutes. All objectives were gained. For the next few days, though, they would face fierce counter-attacks.

On 21 August a substantial party – fourteen officers and 259 men – of the 23rd Manchesters raided Hawk Trench and Canal Wood trenches in conjunction with the 17th Lancashire Fusiliers (according to Sandilands, still wearing those white and red roses in their helmets). This was a diversionary raid, designed to take pressure off the men defending the Knoll. But, as it happened, the launch of this raid coincided with a renewed enemy attack on the Knoll. As the Manchesters' raiding parties were waiting to head off (zero was 4.25 am), they were subjected to heavy shelling and suffered severe casualties.

Not wanting to give any indication of a planned raid, a decision had been made that no preliminary wire cutting should take place. The raiding party had been told, though, that the wire was thin and that the accompanying artillery barrage would enable them to cross it. However, as it was, they encountered 'formidable wire entanglements'.[5] The need to cut the wire caused sufficient delay that the barrage had lifted off the enemy trenches before the Manchesters had made their way through. The enemy were therefore able to man their parapets and direct fire and bombs at the approaching raiders. In spite of this, the Manchesters succeeded in entering the enemy trenches – 300 metres either side of Catelet Road – at 4.30 am and there a sharp fight ensued. Dug-outs were bombed, casualties inflicted and ten prisoners (belonging to the 10th Bavarian Division) were taken. The party withdrew at 4.55 am. There were four officers of the Manchesters wounded (two slightly), five men were killed, three were missing and forty-four were wounded. With the bombardment at the start, and the unexpectedly thick wire, Sandilands recorded that the Manchesters' raid 'was not as successful as had been hoped'.[6]

Private Arthur Whittaker died on 14 August 1917. He was from Manchester. He is buried in St Sever Cemetery Extension, Rouen. Generally men who had died in the hospitals in the Rouen area were buried here.

Private Herbert Andrew was killed in action on 21 August 1917. He was aged 36 and a cotton piecer from Mossley. He is buried in Épehy Wood Farm Cemetery.

Private Austin Charters was killed in action on 21 August 1917. He was from Manchester. He is commemorated on the Thiepval Memorial.

Lance Sergeant Alexander Cross was killed in action on 21 August 1917. He was from Hurst, Lancashire. He is commemorated on the Thiepval Memorial.

Lance Corporal Alfred Danks was killed in action on 21 August 1917. He was aged 32 and from Kidderminster, Worcestershire. He is commemorated on the Thiepval Memorial.

Private John Hafford was killed in action on 21 August 1917. He was aged 23 and from West Gorton. He is buried in Épehy Wood Farm Cemetery.

Grave of Herbert Andrew, one of the men killed during the raid on 21 August. His family chose the inscription 'Duty Nobly Done'. This British War Graves Photographic Association image was sent to his family.

Private Harry Duckworth Johnson was killed in action on 21 August 1917. He was aged 30 and from Castleton. He is commemorated on the Thiepval Memorial.

Private Wilfred Lawton was killed in action on 21 August 1917. He was aged 20 and from Werneth, Oldham. He is commemorated on the Thiepval Memorial.

Lance Corporal Arthur Wade died on 21 August 1917. He was aged 26 and from Pendleton. He is buried in Épehy Wood Farm Cemetery.

Private Thomas Gallagher died on 23 August 1917. He was aged 39 and from St Helens. He is buried in Abbeville Communal Cemetery Extension.

Corporal Henry Ware died of wounds on 26 August 1917. He was aged 30 and from Sutton, Surrey. Before the war Henry Ware worked as a groom. This perhaps explains why, on the outbreak of war, he joined a Yeomanry regiment – the Duke of Lancaster's Own Yeomanry. During the course of 1916, though, the Duke of Lancaster's Yeomanry was converted to a cyclist unit. Ware qualified as a military cyclist in September 1916; however, by the end of the year, like many men in the under-used Yeomanry units, Ware found himself transferred to an infantry unit as a reinforcement. In December 1916 he joined the 23rd Manchester Battalion in France. A man of 5ft 11in, Ware suddenly found himself in a Bantam battalion. He would be promoted to lance corporal in March and corporal in May 1917.

Corporal Ware was recommended for the Distinguished Conduct Medal for his actions during the August raid. The citation reads:

> For conspicuous gallantry and devotion to duty during a raid on the enemy's trenches. He pushed ahead of the raiding party and started to cut the wire in face of heavy rifle fire and bursting bombs. He was severely wounded, but, flinging himself across the wire, continued to cut it. When the rest of the party reached him he held down the uncut wire and ordered the men to walk over him. Throughout he showed the greatest fortitude, and his self-sacrifice undoubtedly enabled the others to reach the enemy trench.[7]

Having been shot through the thigh, Corporal Ware was evacuated to the 42nd Stationary Hospital at Amiens. He died of his wounds. He is buried in St Pierre Cemetery, Amiens.

On 25 August, after a heavy bombardment, a German attack took back their earlier losses around Gillemont Farm. By the end of that night the situation around Gillemont was back to where it had been a month previously. Then, on the night of 30/31st, with a similarly violent assault, the enemy retook the Knoll. With the 105th and 106th Brigades suffering heavy casualties to the south, the 104th Brigade was obliged to do a long stint in the Birdcage sector.

The Manchesters would remain in the line until 6 September. For most of this time they were occupied in improving the defences to the north of the Birdcage. Sandilands recalled:

'View from the Knoll, looking north' (i.e. towards the Birdcage). Davson, *The History of the 35th Division*, p. 140.

Great improvements were made in the line, and it will always be a source of grief to members of the Brigade who were serving at this time to think that the wonderful catacombs, wells and tunnels which were made with an immense amount of labour in Eagle and Pigeon Quarries fell later into the hands of the enemy during their attack on 1 or 2 December, 1917.[8]

When they were not labouring in the line, they were providing working parties. The battalion seem to have predominantly spent September with a spade in their hands. The sector was quiet. Flowers were picked and decorated dugouts. Vegetables were harvested from the deserted gardens of the surrounding villages. 'The weather is warm and we are nearing the end of September,' wrote George Barker, 'roads are very dusty and all is quiet.'[9] In September 1917 the battalion suffered just one casualty. October 1917 would prove to be a very different month.

Second Lieutenant Eric Tattersall was killed in action on 26 September 1917. He was aged 21 and from Didsbury, Manchester. He is buried in Tincourt New British Cemetery.

The end of September would see the battalion marching back towards Péronne and, from there, they entrained to Arras. On 2 October, they arrived in Hauteville, to the west of Arras. They would remain there for the next ten days, refitting and training. George Barker wrote:

> When we arrive at our destination it is discovered that tents have already been pegged out for us by the advance party, and we soon take possession. Our stay is rather longer here than usual. Square holes are dug in the earth sufficiently large, and filled with water, to enable the lads to have a bath. A change of underclothing is given us and we are newly shod, parcels arrive from home for some of us, and many of them are shared . . . During the day we go through our usual drill and exercises, with occasional inspection of equipment and rifles.[10]

As the Divisional History records, they were now being prepared for 'the conditions prevailing in the battle area of the Passchendaele Ridge, to which the division was now due to proceed'. Training for the Passchendaele sector stressed the difficulty of the terrain. There was instruction in the use of gas masks and lectures about the effects of various gasses. Talks were given on the care of the feet in waterlogged conditions. It was noticed, as the men waited for their next move, that their rations seemed to have been increased. 'What's our fate now?' George Barker wrote. 'We are full of pessimism, and know in our hearts that we are "for it".'[11]

'In the autumn of 1917 the war entered into an autumn, or late middle-age, of its own', the *Manchester Guardian*'s C.E. Montague would reflect. He went on:

> One leaf that had gone pretty yellow by now was the hope of perfect victory – swift, unsoured, un-ruinous, knightly: St. George's over the dragon, David's over Goliath. Some people at home seem to be still clinging hard to that first pretty vision of us as a gifted, lithe, wise little Jack fighting down an unwieldy, dastardly giant. But troops in the field become realists.[12]

Any dreams of 'unsoured, un-ruinous' victory that may have still persisted among the 23rd Manchesters would be severely tested during the month that was to follow.

Chapter 13

Houthulst Forest: 'Practically Annihilated'

On 23 October 1917 the Manchester newspapers carried accounts of 'a new victorious push on the Flanders front'. The *Manchester Evening News* reported that the attack 'aimed at closing in upon the southern part of Houthulst Forest, which the Germans have transformed into a veritable fortress'. The outcome, the paper stated, was 'most satisfactory'.[1]

The reality, for the 23rd Manchester Battalion at least, was not at all satisfactory.

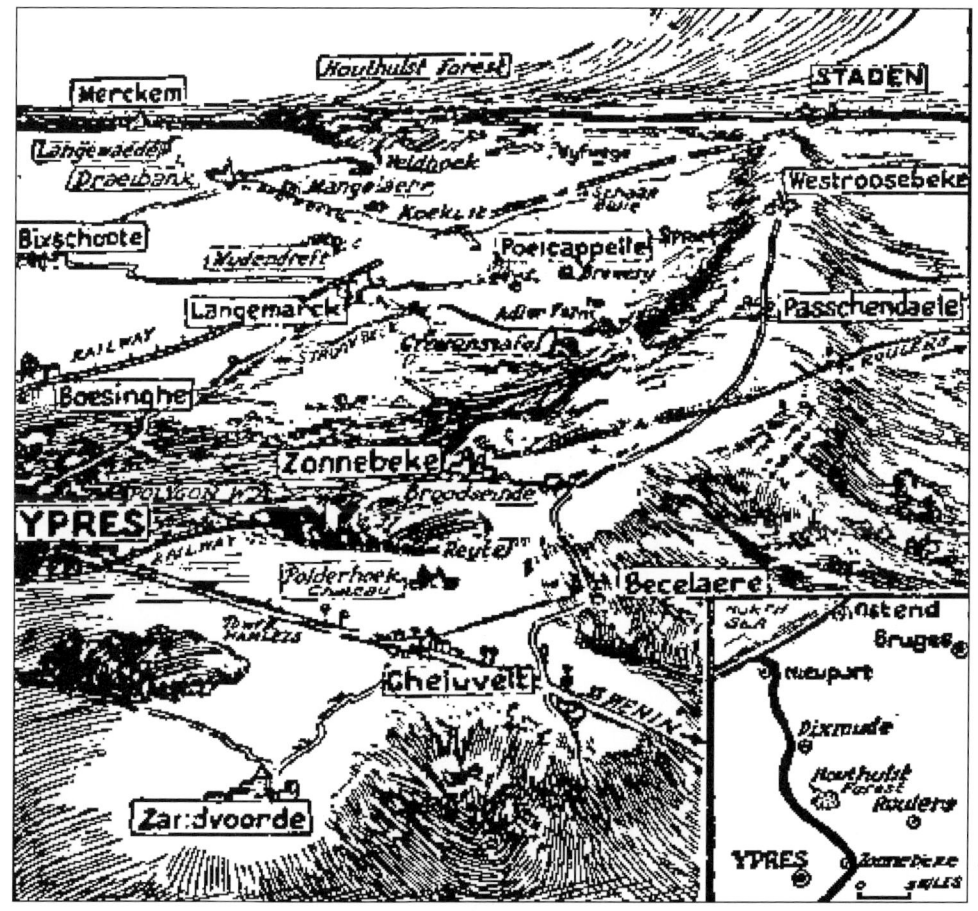

Illustration showing the topography of the Passchendaele ridge. Gibbs, *From Bapaume to Passchendaele*, p. 240.

FIFTH STAGE : THE BRITISH ATTACK HOUTHULST FOREST AND APPROACH PASSCHENDAELE.

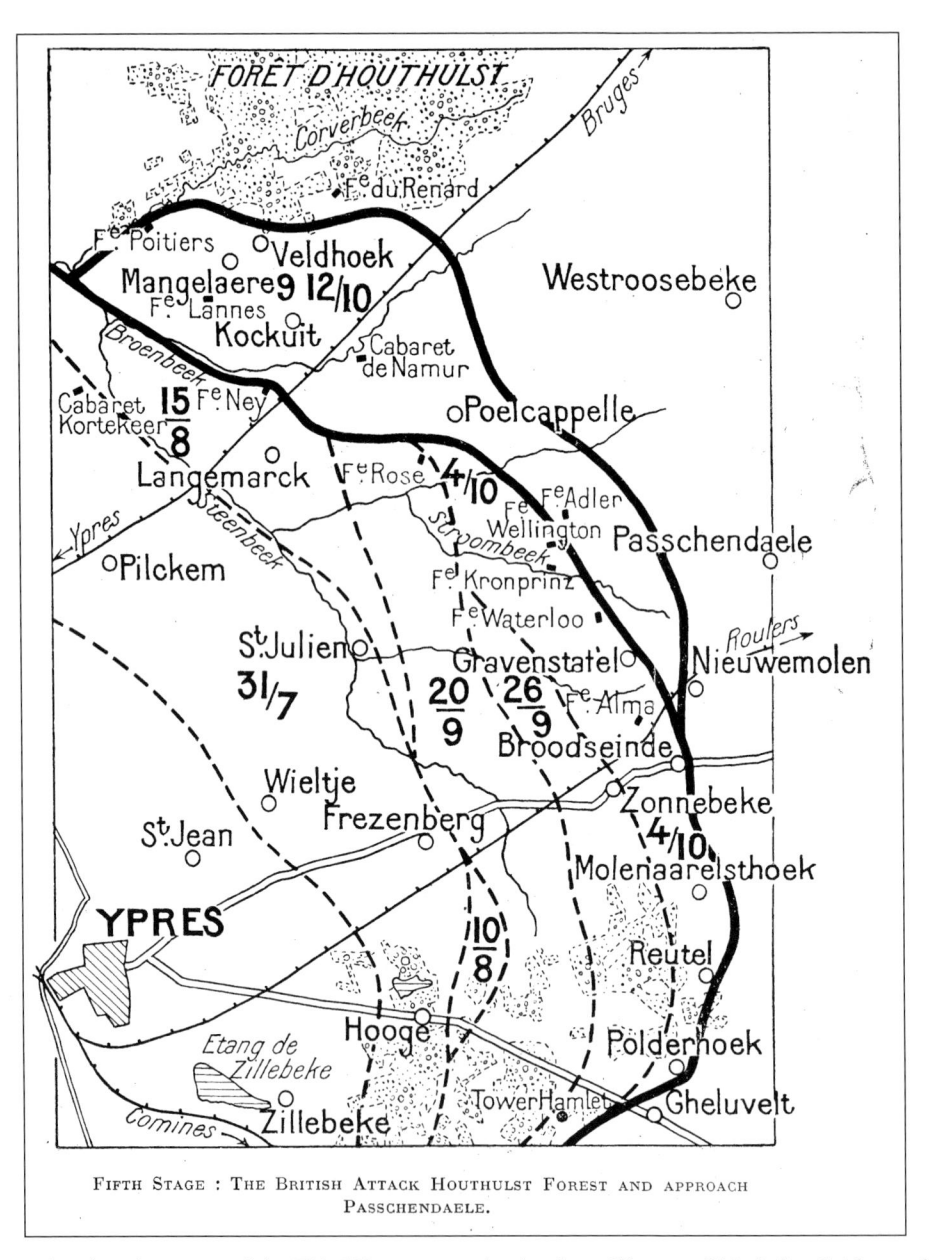

Map showing the stages of the Third Ypres campaign by date. *Illustrated Michelin Guides to the Battle-Fields (1914–1918): Ypres*, p. 33.

By the time that the 35th Division arrived in the sector, the Third Battle of Ypres had already been going on for more than two months. Having secured the Messines Ridge, south of Ypres, in early June, the British had turned their attention to the high ground of the Passchendaele ridge to the north. After initial success at Pilckem Ridge, the weather

260

broke and, through August, the campaign turned into a heavy, muddy slog against well-prepared (and progressively reinforced) enemy defences.

The September and early October phases of the campaign (the battles of Menin Road, Polygon Wood and Broodseinde) were largely successful, showing that well-planned attacks could, with the weather's co-operation, breach the German defences. But, by 9 October, coinciding with the Battle of Poelcapelle, heavy rain returned.

With the rain, the Broembeek brook was transformed into a wide expanse of mud and water. To the north of Ypres troops struggled through a semi-liquid landscape. At a conference of army commanders on 13 October, it was decided that further attacks should be suspended until the weather improved.

The 23rd Manchesters were meanwhile travelling north. With its schooling for the Ypres sector complete, the battalion entrained for Proven, to the north-west of Poperinghe. A network of railway lines met at Proven and thus, it was an important centre for transport and supply storage. Troops were billeted in Proven itself, once not more than a village street with a few farms and barns behind it, and there were also a large number of camps in the surrounding fields. If this was once a sleepy backwater, it was not any longer. The activity around Poperinghe clearly made an impression on the Manchesters. Sandilands wrote: 'The congestion of traffic behind the lines was amazing. A continuous stream of lorries and of all kinds of horse-drawn vehicles moving three abreast passed ceaselessly along the main roads about Poperinghe.'[2]

Proven was usually safe from enemy shelling, hence its use for billeting, for supply depots and ammunition dumps. But by mid October 1917, it was no longer quite so comfortable. Camping at Proven, the 104th Brigade experienced night bombing for the first time. It must have brought home the fact that they were approaching the Ypres front. This was not going to be like anything that they had experienced before.

The next morning, 16 October, they were back in railway carriages again, now destined for Boesinghe. Until July 1917 the village of Boesinghe had directly faced the German front line, across the Yser Canal, but the first stage of the Third Battle of Ypres, the Battle of Pilckem Ridge, had pushed the German line back. The landscape hereabouts told that story. There was nothing left of Boesinghe apart from ruins. Sandilands recorded: 'Although nothing definite was known about the situation, it soon became evident that hard fighting under the very worst conditions was in store for the Brigade.'[3]

'What is this uncanny feeling that comes over men when trouble is brewing?' George Barker wrote. He went on:

The appearance of miles around is of such a devastating character, that the very look of it seems to cause a shudder to run through the body. Nature appears to have been destroyed, eaten, then gulped up again; there was no sign of a tree for miles around, only small broken stumps, churned mud everywhere, shell holes large enough to bury a horse, with pools of water of a dangerous kind.[4]

From Boesinghe the battalion started to head towards the front, north of Langemarck. Beyond Boesinghe, the journey was by duckboard track. The Divisional History recorded:

The ruins of Boesinghe church.

Troops outside a reinforced shelter in the ruined outbuildings of Boesinghe Chateau.

Approach to the front line from the canal was obtained by means of two duckboard tracks known as Clarges Street and Hunter Street, which maintain a devious course between large shell holes filled with water. To step off these usually meant immersion, or at best an extra coating of wet mud, and this accident was by no means rare, as it is not attractive to anyone to maintain a vertical position on a narrow board when shells fall close, particularly at night. These tracks crossed two marshy streams named the Steenbeek and the Broembeek, on which were many of the battery positions. They were persistently shelled with high explosive and gas, especially at the points where the tracks crossed them. These bottoms were full of gas three nights out of four, and it will therefore be deduced that the management of reliefs and supplies to the front line was a matter of some difficulty.[5]

William Collins, who served with the No. 1 Cavalry Field Ambulance of the Royal Army Medical Corps, recalled those difficulties:

We used to go, every morning, up this duckboard track, from below Boesinghe right up to Langemarck. We were stepping over a couple of dead men every morning. They were laid across the track, because they could not be moved into the side. They'd have been sucked into the mud. They were collected by the Pioneer Party and buried. But we stepped over them every morning. We never failed to step over a man and one or two dead men. It was a nightmare because all you had was a couple of duckboards, side by side, and either side of it was about ten feet of mud, with the top of a tank sticking out of it here and there. The tracks stopped at Langemarck . . . There's a memorial on the Menin Gate to 60,000 men whose bodies were never recovered in that small Ypres salient. They were all sucked into the mud.[6]

For three years the front line had pushed back and forth around Langemarck. It had seen hand-to-hand fighting, had had trenches dug around it, bombs dropped on it and had its name made into the stuff of myth. Langemarck had been retaken by the British on 16 August 1917. The capture of the village was one of the few successful outcomes from the costly August phase of the Third Ypres campaign. But Langemarck itself had not survived. William Collins recalled:

The place had been flattened to the ground and there was a board, at the side of the road, propped up, and on it was stencilled: 'This was Langemarck' . . . That was the only evidence there was that the town had ever stood there. Only that board. All the bricks and rubble were laying on the ground. You couldn't see a building or a tree, anything at all. As far as the eye could see, there was nothing. It was completely devastated.[7]

The Manchesters were now taking over front line trenches to the north-east of Langemarck. They were shelled while the relief was being carried out. George Barker wrote:

Sketch looking towards Langemarck from Pilckem, along the duckboard tracks. Davson, *The History of the 35th Division*, p. 158.

Langemarck church in ruins, *c.* 1915.

All that remained of Langemarck church in 1918.

Demons are working at the guns all night through without respite. The continual detonations and bursting of shells, combined with our narrow escapes, makes some of us so nervous that it seems to nearly turn our brain. We crouch and duck, thinking that any moment we may be blown to atoms; spent pieces of shell are dropping on our helmets in large quantities, and confusion is everywhere.[8]

The battalion War Diary recorded that in the course of the move front-wards, four men were killed, two were wounded and two were missing.

> Private Frederick Blanchard Green was killed in action on 16 October 1917. He was aged 30 and from Moss Side, Manchester. He is commemorated on the Tyne Cot Memorial.
> Private James Guest was killed in action on 16 October 1917. He was from Miles Platting. He is buried in Cement House Cemetery, West-Vlaanderen.
> Private William Sillitoe was killed in action on 16 October 1917. He was from Longsight. He is commemorated on the Tyne Cot Memorial.
> Private Robert Taylor was killed in action on 16 October 1917. He was aged 25 and from Salford. He is buried in Cement House Cemetery, West-Vlaanderen.
> Private Fred Williamson was killed in action on 16 October 1917. He was aged 26 and from Hollinwood, Oldham. He is commemorated on the Tyne Cot Memorial.
> Private William McLean died of wounds on 18 October 1917. He was aged 22 and from Bradford, Manchester. He is buried in Harlebeke New British Cemetery, West-Vlaanderen.

The stretch of the front taken over by the 104th Brigade extended from the Ypres–Staden railway to a point 250 yards south-east of the Faidherbe Cross Roads. The 17th Lancashire Fusiliers were in the position on the Manchesters' left and the 21st Northumberland Fusiliers on their right. The area ahead of them was, in the words of the Divisional History, 'a sea of mud, thickly pitted with water-logged shell holes'. The War Diary of the 17th Lancashire Fusiliers noted that conditions were 'extremely bad' in their new sector; from Vee Bend forwards, it was 'a sticky morass of muddy shell-holes with only tapes to show the routes to the forward lines'.

Mud ahead. Mud behind. Everywhere it was mud. 'The general appearance of the country surpassed anything any of us had seen even at the Somme,' Brigadier General Sandilands wrote. He went on:

> The whole place was practically under water and blown to bits; dead men and animals lay about everywhere; the scene was worthy of Dante's inferno. Whenever a heavy shell fell, a column of water, 50 to 100 feet high, was raised, and it was no uncommon thing for dozens of shells to fall in the space of a few minutes within a few hundred yards' radius of the spot where one happened to be. There was no such thing as a safe place in those days; nothing approaching a trench or breastwork existed; duck-board walks on top of the ground were the most luxurious form of communication.[9]

The area was also full of ammunition dumps, Sandilands recorded, and there were guns and howitzers of all sizes. He marvelled at how they kept on working, up to their axles in mud and water. With the difficult terrain it was a challenge to get guns into forward areas, or to bring up the ammunition to supply them. Poor visibility hampered observation and stable platforms could not be secured. Technical problems multiplied. All of these factors would shortly become of significance to the advancing Manchesters.

Here the 104th Brigade saw pill boxes for the first time. It having proved impossible to dig trenches in the waterlogged terrain (any hole that was dug flooded and collapsed), clusters of pill boxes had been built. Sandilands noted, with some surprise, that these were not small shelters as had been supposed, but rather substantial structures with thick concrete walls.

After sleeping a night in the open, George Barker found shelter in the ruin of a farm:

An officer emerges from a pill-box, and with a whisper tells us to make for the distant ruins of a farm. Panting with nervous fear we each make for it, and our steps are shaky as we proceed. I try to run but my limbs are like lead. Plonk-za! – a near shave that time. Some of us manage it, others get hit and join their unfortunate companions in death. Wounded men must make for safety as best they can until stretcher-bearers can get to them. It doesn't seem as if an insect can live in this inferno, and only those of us who have charmed lives can escape.'[10]

Enemy aircraft provided a further novel irritant during this period. Sandilands wrote:

In addition to unlimited shells, low-flying aeroplanes had become very fashionable at this period. After being well machine-gunned by aeroplanes by day in the forward areas, and bombed by a fleet of anything up to a dozen Gothas round about Elverdinghe, the average infantryman used to reflect deeply on the British air superiority; but we were assured that our aeroplanes were doing excellent work at altitudes which rendered them invisible to the naked eye![11]

Barker's account continues:

All at once I hear and see a German aeroplane coming, and one of the lads foolishly goes and exposes himself by standing near the open door. Suddenly the machine turns tail, proving to me that our hiding place has been discovered.

We haven't long to wait before Jerry tries to annihilate us with a terrific bombardment. Shells are bursting all around us every few seconds. One of them comes near me and a fragment hits me like a kick from a horse at the top of my thigh. I am paralysed for the moment and feel I am burning, and in looking down I find my trousers cut and a terrible gash in my flesh. I can see my leg hanging by a sinew with layers of fat and lean showing like the remains of a bullock that has just been killed; then blood flows profusely.[12]

Barker was fortunate to be picked up by stretcher bearers, but as they struggled back through the mud, he was soon pitched off the stretcher and ended up being carried piggy-back by lads who 'shake like a leaf' and who kept falling over themselves. 'There is no god,' one of the stretcher bearers told Barker, 'to allow such torments to come to innocent men like this.'

Orders were received on 17 October that the 104th Brigade was to take part in an attack on the 22nd. Having had a couple of days of fine weather, the enemy was evidently expecting a renewed attack and consequently the shelling had become severe. A decision was therefore made to take the brigade out of the line in order to explain the orders to them. This was evidently a difficult decision; Sandilands recorded: 'It was a choice of evils between remaining in the line or going back for only one complete night; but although the men had a long and tiring march both ways, it at least got them out of the mud and shelling for a few hours.'[13]

On 18 October then the brigade were moved back to De Wippe Cabaret, to the west of Elverdinghe. The 23rd Manchesters suffered twenty-two casualties in the course of the relief. The War Diary of the 17th Lancashire Fusiliers gives some impression of what that day was like:

The shelled village of Elverdinghe.

Relief was reported complete about 10 p.m., but the Companies experienced the greatest hardship in crossing the 1200 yds to VEE BEND, which owing to a steady rain had now become a soggy mass of mud through which the men could move only with the greatest difficulty. A party of Stretcher Bearers carrying a wounded man down from 'Y' Company took nearly 6½ hours to reach VEE BEND and arrived completely exhausted. At about 11 p.m. the enemy commenced a violent gas-shell bombardment with 'mustard gas' shell and all ranks were compelled to put on their Respirators. Even so, many cases of blisters and sores were reported.

Back in the camp, the forthcoming attack was explained. The 35th Division were to take part in a diversionary manoeuvre in order to distract the Germans from the preparations for the main attack on Passchendaele, which was due to start again on 26 October, and to provide a strong left flank to support the main advance. Together with the French, XIV Corps were to advance northwards into Houthulst Forest. The Divisional History describes the topography:

Four miles to the north of Pilckem lay the wooded area known as Houthulst Forest, a domain of irregular shape, extending to about 1,500 acres and composed of enclosures of deciduous trees in various stages of growth and divided by roads, rides, ditches, and fences, into rectangular portions from ten to twenty acres in extent. For the most part these enclosures were covered with thick undergrowth, and movement off the rides was difficult. The infantry of the division were destined to become well acquainted with this.[14]

The Duke of Marlborough is alleged to have said, 'Whoever holds Houthulst Forest holds Flanders'. Certainly the Germans did not mean to let go of it easily. On 23 October Philip Gibbs would write:

Houthulst Forest, in spite of all the gas that has soaked it, was full of German troops of the 26th Reserve Division, under stern orders to defend it to the death, with another division in support, and the Marines on their right. They had many concrete emplacements in the cover of the forest, from which they were able to get their machine-guns into play, and along the Staden railway there were blockhouses not yet destroyed by our bombardment, which were strongholds from which they were not easily routed.[15]

On the 20th the Manchesters moved back up to the front line trenches north-east of Langemarck. There was considerable – and pretty much continuous – shelling on the way in. They were about to play their part in the Third Battle of Ypres.

The Manchesters now occupied the front line position with the 17th Lancashire Fusiliers on their left, the 18th Lancashire Fusiliers in close support, the 20th Lancashire Fusiliers in Reserve and the 34th Division on the Manchesters' right. With the planned lines of advance of the 17th Lancashire Fusiliers and the 23rd Manchesters diverging, it

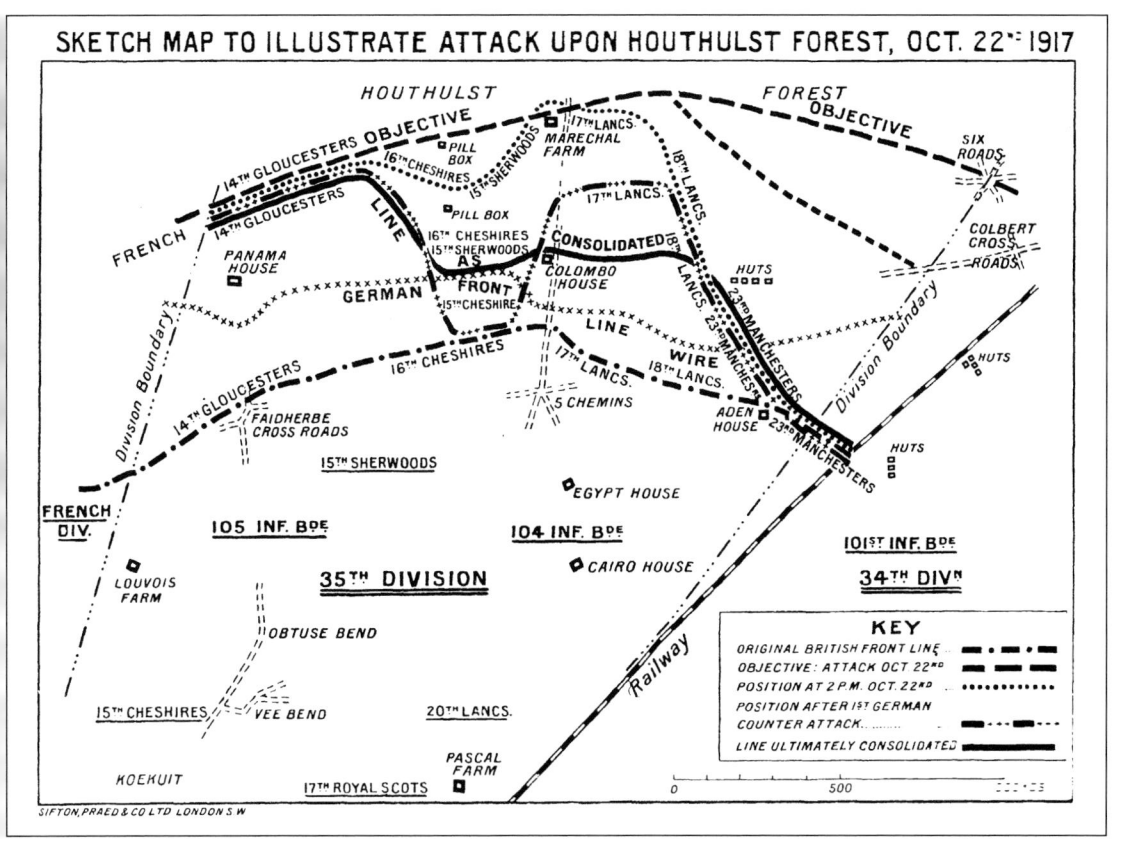

Sketch map of Brigade trenches. Davson, *The History of the 35th Division*, p. 158.

would be the role of the 18th Lancashire Fusiliers to fill up the gap thus formed at the junction of the two forward battalions.

Before the attack, Allied pilots took photos of the ground that the men would have to cross. Philip Gibbs described these images:

> Everywhere the shell-craters show up shinily in the aerial photographs, with their water reflecting the light like silver mirrors. Higher up there are floods about Houthulst Forest extending to the place where the enemy keeps his guns behind the protection of the water, and no lack of rain-filled shell-holes on each side of the Ypres-Staden railway.[16]

Throughout the day of 21 October the Allied artillery put down a heavy bombardment. The enemy artillery replied. While daylight remained the battalions at the front lay low and quiet in shell holes, trying to avoid the attention of the numerous enemy aircraft which were flying over the front. The night of the 21st then was bitterly cold. Rain started to fall about midnight. The shell holes in which the troops were waiting to attack began to flood. The mechanisms of rifles jammed. The Stokes guns that were meant to be being

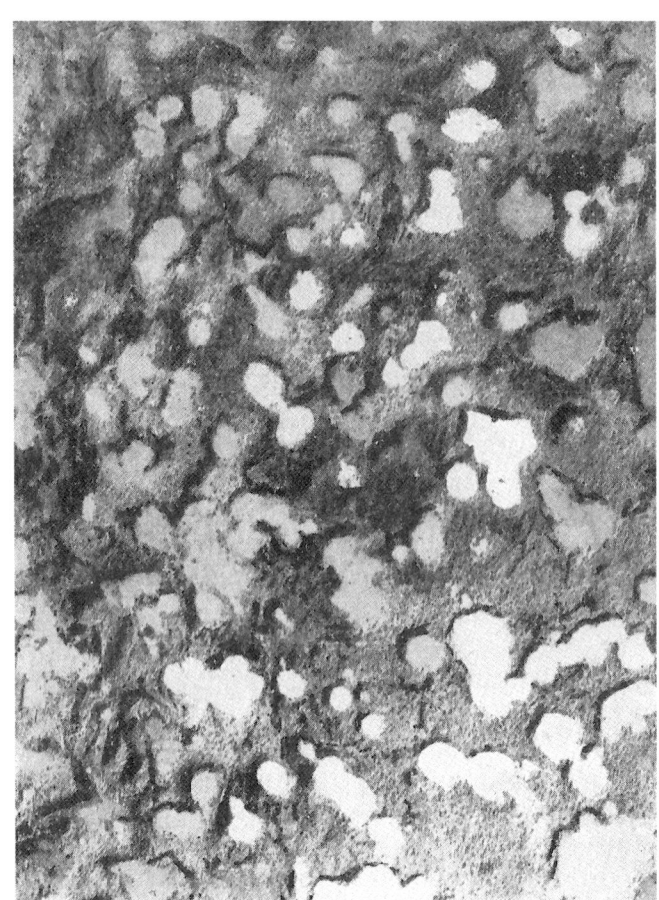

'Part of the ground covered by the offensive seen from an aeroplane'. *Illustrated Michelin Guides to the Battle-Fields (1914–1918): Ypres*, p. 30.

Houthulst Forest.

brought forward could make it through the muddy approaches. As preparations progressed for the attack it became clear that there were going to be issues in communicating from front line to rear.

At 2.00 am on 22 October the battalions formed up on tapes which had been laid in advance of the front line. The final objective, about 1,000 yards from the forming-up position, was the line ending at the Six Roads junction. The target line was about 500yd wider than the line that the troops were to set off from, and so this necessitated a fan-shaped advance. Though the officers had a reasonable idea of direction, it seems that the men were less well informed. The enemy began to put down a light barrage on the area between the forward positions and Egypt House.

As zero hour approached patrols were sent out to link up with the 16th Royal Scots, who were supposed to be to the 23rd Manchester's right flank. This proved impossible. 'This unfortunate accident had a serious influence on the succeeding operations', the Divisional History records.[17]

The attack was launched at 5.35 am. The troops advanced behind a creeping barrage at the rate of 100 yards per 8 minutes. The slow rate of advance had been determined in order to give the men time to move over what was known to be difficult terrain. But it seems that it was too slow. The War Diary of the 18th Lancashire Fusiliers recorded:

At Zero hour 5.35 a.m. Battalion moved off keeping close to our barrage which was found too slow (8' for 100y) and in consequence we suffered several casualties. In addition the barrage was very ragged, one shot in four falling short. This was probably due to the bad gun platforms. Lts PRITCHETT & BOWERS were conspicuous in their efforts to keep their men back.

In the opinion of Brigadier General Sandilands, the slow rate of advance of the creeping barrage was a significant factor in the attack's outcome. He wrote: 'Let anyone try to take eight minutes to walk 100 yards, and then form an opinion as to what his feelings would be in taking part in a great and glorious advance.'[18] To make matters worse, enemy aircraft were now passing repeatedly overhead, spraying the advancing troops with machine-gun fire.

Having advanced about 400 yards, the Manchesters reached their first objective. They had, thus far, suffered only slight casualties. 'From this point however,' the War Diary records, 'the resistance was more stubborn and very heavy rifle and machine gun fire was experienced from both flanks.' Things were about to go badly wrong. As they crested a small rise, resistance was about to become very stubborn. The War Diary of the 18th Lancashire Fusiliers details:

Shortly after the attack started the MAN. R. suffered very heavy casualties and were held up. Our line continued to advance but owing to its right flank being unprotected began to suffer heavy casualties. At about 6.15 a.m. Capt M. R. WOOD M.C. who was in command of the two leading coys realised, that he had worked too far over to the left., so moved his own coy (X) back a short way and then over to the right in order to try and re-establish touch with the MAN. R. but moved forward to attack the wood under very heavy M.G. and rifle fire from his front and right flank.

About 600 yards on from their starting position, the Manchesters now found themselves exposed to heavy machine-gun fire. With their right flank and rear exposed by the failure of the 16th Royal Scots' attack, the Manchesters were now targeted by machine guns from the direction of the railway and the huts just beyond it. With the 18th Lancashire Fusiliers' attack having drifted too far to the left, the Manchesters also now found themselves facing fire from the huts on their left flank and rear. There was also heavy machine-gun fire from the direction of Six Roads and Colbert cross roads, ahead of the 23rd's attack. It was coming at them from every angle.

All of the Manchesters' officers who took part in the attack (with one exception, who was acting as liaison officer with the 34th Division) and a large proportion of the NCOs were either killed or wounded. Without leadership, uncertain as to the direction they should be heading, and facing severe resistance, the men floundered. As the Manchesters' War Diary puts it (with characteristic under-statement) 'the Battalion was unable to make further progress'.[19] Brigadier General Sandilands recalled:

It had been realised that the Division on our right had made some mistake in their orders, as before zero no trace of them could be seen. What actually happened to this Division has never been discovered, but their failure to start in close touch with the 23rd Manchester Regiment was the cause of that Battalion being practically annihilated, as their right flank was completely in the air, and fully exposed to the most devastating machine-gun fire. Through no fault of their own the Manchesters were brought to a complete standstill.[20]

By 6.50 am the 17th Lancashire Fusiliers had reached their objective, but the 18th Lancashire Fusiliers and the 23rd Manchesters – or what remained of them – had swung back to their starting positions. The survivors, about fifty men under the command of a sergeant-major, eventually made it back to the original line. The surviving Manchesters withdrew to the vicinity of Egypt House. The War Diary of the 17th Lancashire Fusiliers documented their arrival there. It records:

Battn. H.Q. at EGYPT HOUSE became aware of a straggling crowd of men falling back on them from the direction of the YPRES–STADEN Railway. The officers at H.Q. immediately turned out and stopping the rot, put the men – a mixture of Manchesters, and 16th Royal Scots from the Division on our right – into a shell-hole line immediately covering EGYPT HOUSE. From what could be learnt from these men, it appeared that the left of the Right Division had for some reason or other failed to come up, and has consequently left uncovered the Right of the MANCHESTERS, who in their turn went wide and lost touch with the 18th LANCASHIRE FUSILIERS.

By 8.10 am the situation was deemed critical. Two companies of the 4th Salford Pals were ordered up to stabilise the flank between the 18th Lancashire Fusiliers and Aden House.

At 8.38 am the 20th Lancashire Fusiliers, who had been in reserve, received orders to send two companies forward. Captain W.A. Swarbrick, coming up with these companies, reached Egypt House at 10.15 am. There he was told that the Manchesters had suffered severe casualties and that nothing was known of the brigade which was meant to have advanced to the Manchester's right. The two companies of 20th Lancashire Fusiliers now moved forward facing heavy hostile fire.

The blockhouses and pill boxes to the rear were soon full of casualties. Many of the wounded were brought back to Egypt House, a group of small pill boxes which had been designated as the Battalion H.Q. Being in a conspicuous position, though, and with constant movement visible around it, this locality was heavily shelled. Alan MacIver, Assistant Brigade Major of 104th Brigade, would recall:

> I went up to combined Battalion headquarters to see my Brigade Commander, on the morning of the attack, and the situation was quite horrifying. They couldn't get the wounded out and when they got them out they were very heavily shelled and the place was full of dying wounded people who had been hit again. The Battalion commanders were almost in tears and there was simply nothing one could do.[21]

Sandilands' account conveys that frustration:

> It was almost impossible for anyone to come out of Egypt House to help the wounded, and it was not possible to carry a stretcher through the narrow door-way. It was a ghastly scene; dozens of men – dead, mutilated, or dying – were lying round the walls. Such a sight one would think was calculated to drive a young boy fresh from home clean out of his mind, and one marvels that this was not the common result.[22]

But the men that made it back to Egypt House were the lucky ones. The War Diary of the 17th Lancashire Fusiliers records:

> There were still large numbers of wounded lying out as the supply of stretcher bearers was lamentably inadequate and continual sniping during daylight made the collection of the wounded exceedingly difficult. Advantage was taken of the darkness to bring in a number of these men . . . Some of the men were so exhausted however by the frightful conditions of wet and cold, that they could scarcely be got out of the line.

A party made it up with rations as darkness fell. A rum ration was issued and, getting a mention in the Divisional History and battalion War Diaries, that rum was clearly very welcome. The War Diary of the 17th Lancashire Fusiliers notes: 'The men also each received a ration of rum, the value of which can be understood when it is realised that they had lain all day in shell holes up to their waists in water.'

That night the remaining men of the 23rd Manchesters were relieved by the 4th Salford Pals. They moved back to Pascal Farm. At the end of the day the battalion War Diary recorded that eight officers had been killed, five were wounded and one missing; twenty men were killed, 115 wounded and fifty-five missing. The final figures would be higher. Ultimately ten officers and sixty-six other ranks from the battalion were recorded as having died on 22 October and another nine died of wounds over the following few days. A total of seventy-four of them, having no known grave, are commemorated on the Tyne Cot Memorial.

Why was there a gap on the Manchesters' right flank? Sandilands asserted that the 34th Division's did not show up on account of 'some mistake in their orders'. The 16th Royal Scots seem rather to get the blame for not being there to defend the Manchesters' right flank. But accounts from the 34th Division, show that the Scots *were* there, albeit in depleted numbers and under extremely trying circumstances. Robert Johnston was a second lieutenant with the 16th Royal Scots; he wrote: 'On the way up the line we were shelled and driven off the duckboard track on several occasions, finding it again with difficulty in the light of shellfire and German Verey lights. It took us four hours to cover about two miles to the Ypres–Staden railway line.' Then, as they approached the front, the Allied barrage was falling on their positions too. While forming up, the 16th Royal Scots 'were heavily shelled by the enemy, and also coming under our own barrage (due

Approaches to Houthulst Forest.

Shelters in Houthulst Forest.

to the difficulty in forming up correctly already alluded to)'. According to Second Lieutenant Johnston, SOS rockets were sent up 'without, however, any effect'. They suffered heavy casualties – sufficient that only enough men remained for one wave, 'but these advanced at zero, in line with the Manchesters of the 35th Division, and the left companies, "C" and "D", reached the final objective – the pill boxes about Six Roads – where they came under heavy machine gun fire'. Johnston wrote:

> The confusion and fog of war was never more marked due to the condition of ground and weather. There was a complete absence of landmarks and communications, while neither the Battalion Commander nor the Brigadier were able to control the battle. Just junior leaders, young officers and N.C.O.s and men sticking it out without hope of survival . . . When the attack commenced we were all tired, dispirited and exhausted men without hope of victory. Our morale was very low, no jokes or singing in the ranks, a feeling of dumb despair, strangely enough accepting our position without thought or questions . . . The common denominator for the infantry soldiers in this battle was misery.[23]

The sketch map overleaf shows how the barrage line and the 16th Royal Scots' starting line overlapped.

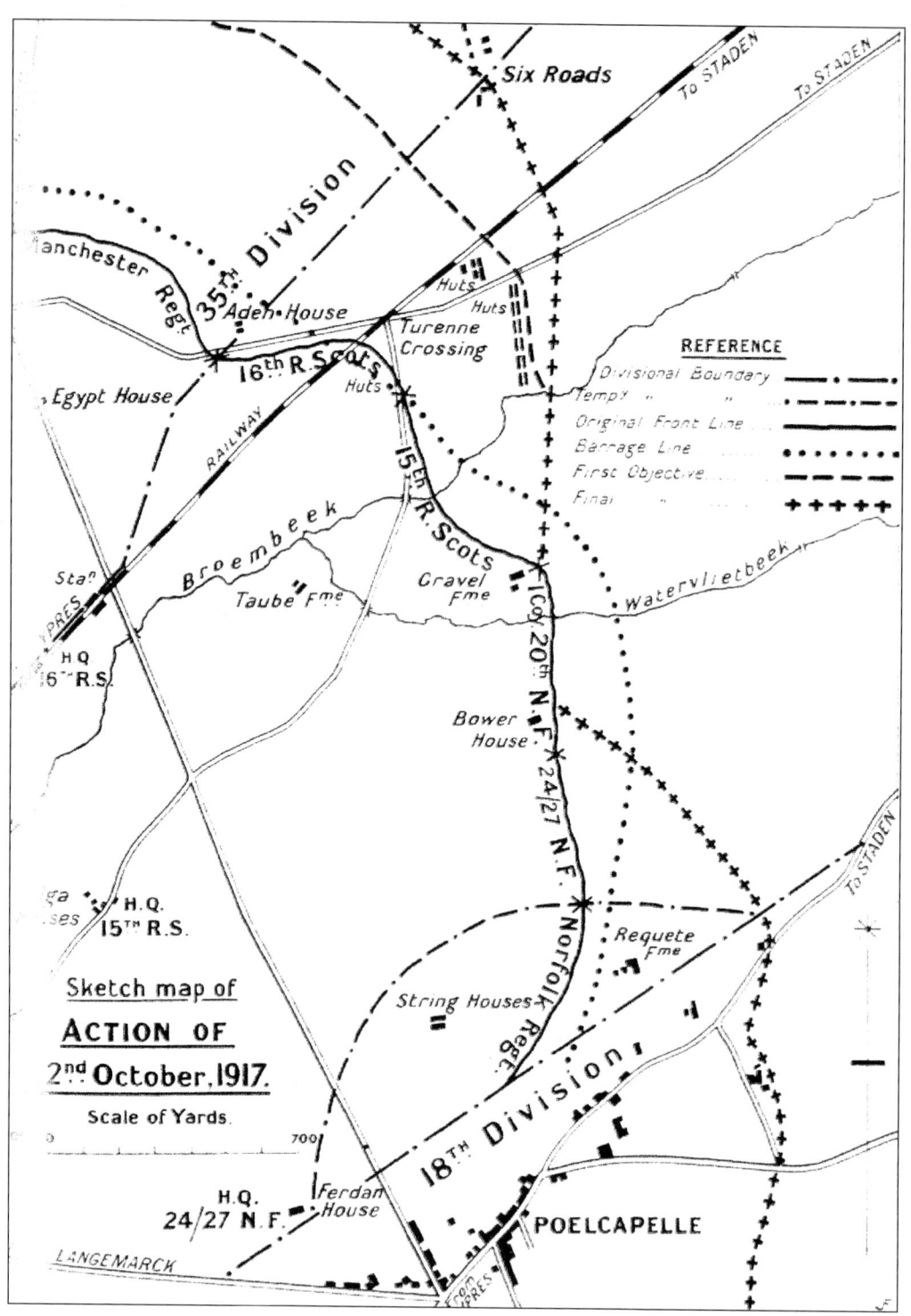

Lieutenant Colonel J. Shakespear, *The Thirty-Fourth Division, 1915–1919* (1921), p. 164.

One of the roads through Houthulst Forest.

A combination of factors (the challenging terrain, the strength of the enemy's defences, the rate and accuracy of the creeping barrage, the lack of cover on their right flank etc.) contributed to the failure of the attack. What resonates most powerfully from accounts of that day is a terrific sense of confusion. On 23 October the War Diary of the 18th Lancashire Fusiliers recorded a series of 'Remarks', reflecting on what went wrong with the attack and what could be learnt from it. It concluded: 'The importance of keeping direction in the attack cannot be overestimated and every possible precaution must be taken to ensure this such as laying tapes, taking compass bearings, noting landmarks etc. Special parties should be detailed in each coy to ensure that direction is kept.'

After 22 October it is clear that many of those involved questioned the astuteness of their superiors. The experience seems to have rather shaken the faith of both men and officers. Alan Squarey MacIver, the Assistant Brigade Major and Intelligence Officer of 104th Brigade, afterwards reflected:

One could not understand why the higher command continued to attack during this period because any attack was absolutely certain to fail – the troops could not advance more than a few yards in the mud and every attack which was made was disastrous. The men were extremely gallant. They used to complain a good deal, but they never failed to do what they were told.[24]

Second Lieutenant Robert Johnston, of the 16th Royal Scots (later to rise to lieutenant colonel), wrote that the attack was 'a complete disaster'. He went on:

The Poelcapelle road through Houthulst Forest.

The ground was a morass without shelter or landmarks other than enemy pillboxes. We had no guides, no communications, hot meals or rations. One Company of my Battalion lost its way on the approach march, and did not partake in the battle. My C.O. was gassed and the second in command shell-shocked. Two Company Commanders and half the Platoon Commanders were killed. Only the walking wounded managed to get back . . . The Generals who ordered us forward for this attack, on 22nd to 26th October 1917 astride the Ypres–Staden railway at Poelcapelle Stop, should have been sacked. I look back in anger at those responsible.[25]

> Private Cecil Ashton was killed in action on 22 October 1917. He was from Hindley, Wigan. He is commemorated on the Tyne Cot Memorial.
> Private William Thomas Ball was killed in action on 22 October 1917. He was aged 28 and from Salford. He is commemorated on the Tyne Cot Memorial.
> Lance Corporal Joseph Beazley was killed in action on 22 October 1917. He was aged 20 and from Hindley, Wigan. He is buried in Poelcapelle British Cemetery.
> Private William Henry Beeley was killed in action on 22 October 1917. He was aged 24 and from Stalybridge. He is commemorated on the Tyne Cot Memorial.
> Lance Corporal William Bishop was killed in action on 22 October 1917. He was aged 31 and from Aldershot, Hants. He is commemorated on the Tyne Cot Memorial.
> Private Watts Chadwick was killed in action on 22 October 1917. He was from New Mills, Derby. He is commemorated on the Tyne Cot Memorial.

Private Edward Chapman was killed in action on 22 October 1917. He was from Salford. He is commemorated on the Tyne Cot Memorial.

Private John Henry Clift was killed in action on 22 October 1917. He was from Bridgnorth, Shropshire. He is commemorated on the Tyne Cot Memorial.

Private William Theobald Cooper was killed in action on 22 October 1917. He was from Bangor in Wales. He is commemorated on the Tyne Cot Memorial.

Lance Sergeant Albert Cornthwaite was killed in action on 22 October 1917. He was from Moston, Manchester. He is commemorated on the Tyne Cot Memorial.

Private James Ernest Courtman was killed in action on 22 October 1917. He was aged 31 and from Hulme, Manchester. He is commemorated on the Tyne Cot Memorial.

Lance Corporal Frederick Victor Crispin was killed in action on 22 October 1917. He was aged 20 and from Didsbury. He is commemorated on the Tyne Cot Memorial.

Private John Dalgliesh died of wounds on 22 October 1917. He was aged 22 and from Moss Side, Manchester. He is buried in Dozinghem Military Cemetery.

Private Thomas George Davies was killed in action on 22 October 1917. He was from Leominster, Herefordshire. He is commemorated on the Tyne Cot Memorial.

Private John Donoghue was killed in action on 22 October 1917. He was aged 22 and from Collyhurst, Manchester. He is commemorated on the Tyne Cot Memorial.

Private Patrick Duffy was killed in action on 22 October 1917. He was from Ballaghdoreen, County Mayo. He is commemorated on the Tyne Cot Memorial.

Private John Eaton was killed in action on 22 October 1917. He was aged 37 and from Denton, Manchester. He is commemorated on the Tyne Cot Memorial.

Lance Corporal Solomon Edelstone was killed in action on 22 October 1917. He was aged 21 and from Hightown, Manchester. He is commemorated on the Tyne Cot Memorial.

Private William Gee was killed in action on 22 October 1917. He was from Crewe, Cheshire. He is commemorated on the Tyne Cot Memorial.

Private Francis Graham was killed in action on 22 October 1917. He was from Manchester. He is commemorated on the Tyne Cot Memorial.

Private Alfred Green was killed in action on 22 October 1917. He was from Droylsden. He is commemorated on the Tyne Cot Memorial.

Private Charles Albert Greenacre was killed in action on 22 October 1917. He was aged 21 and from Manchester. He is commemorated on the Tyne Cot Memorial.

Private John Henry Griffiths was killed in action on 22 October 1917. He was aged 42 and from Manchester. He is commemorated on the Tyne Cot Memorial.

Private Thomas William Harding was killed in action on 22 October 1917. He was from Failsworth. He is commemorated on the Tyne Cot Memorial.

Private John Henry Harrison was killed in action on 22 October 1917. He was aged 20 and from Blackley, Manchester. He is commemorated on the Tyne Cot Memorial.

Private Richard Harrison was killed in action on 22 October 1917. He was from Salford. He is buried in Poelcapelle British Cemetery.

Private Joseph Hennessey was killed in action on 22 October 1917. He was from Chorlton-on-Medlock. He is commemorated on the Tyne Cot Memorial.

Private Richard Hornby was killed in action on 22 October 1917. He was from Salford. He is commemorated on the Tyne Cot Memorial.

Private James Horrocks was killed in action on 22 October 1917. He was from Littleborough. He is commemorated on the Tyne Cot Memorial.

Private James Henry Howarth was killed in action on 22 October 1917. He was from Stockport. He is commemorated on the Tyne Cot Memorial.

Private John Hoyle was killed in action on 22 October 1917. He was from Hurst, Lancashire. He is commemorated on the Tyne Cot Memorial.

Private John Humphreys was killed in action on 22 October 1917. He was aged 32 and from Walsingham, Norfolk. He is commemorated on the Tyne Cot Memorial.

Private George William Jones was killed in action on 22 October 1917. He was aged 29 and from Failsworth. He is commemorated on the Tyne Cot Memorial.

Private Gwylim Victor Pennant Jones was killed in action on 22 October 1917. He was aged 27 and from Rhyl. He is commemorated on the Tyne Cot Memorial.

Private Richard Kearns was killed in action on 22 October 1917. He was aged 37 and from Hulme, Manchester. He is commemorated on the Tyne Cot Memorial.

Private John Kelly was killed in action on 22 October 1917. He was aged 23 and from Manchester. He is commemorated on the Tyne Cot Memorial.

Sergeant William Kirkham was killed in action on 22 October 1917. He enlisted in Southport. He is commemorated on the Tyne Cot Memorial.

Private Charles Knight was killed in action on 22 October 1917. He was from Ardwick. He is commemorated on the Tyne Cot Memorial.

Private John Loughrey was killed in action on 22 October 1917. He was from County Down. He is commemorated on the Tyne Cot Memorial.

Private Arthur Marshall was killed in action on 22 October 1917. He was from Wakefield and had been awarded the Military Medal in July 1917. He is commemorated on the Tyne Cot Memorial.

Private Thomas Martin was killed in action on 22 October 1917. He was from St Helens. He is buried in Cement House Cemetery, West-Vlaanderen.

Private Frank McCormick was killed in action on 22 October 1917. He was aged 32 and from Old Trafford, Manchester. He is commemorated on the Tyne Cot Memorial.

Private John McDonald was killed in action on 22 October 1917. He was aged 24 and from Manchester. He is commemorated on the Tyne Cot Memorial.

Private Christopher Mee was killed in action on 22 October 1917. He was aged 23 and from Wolstanton, Staffordshire. He is commemorated on the Tyne Cot Memorial.

Lance Corporal Robert Milne was killed in action on 22 October 1917. He was from Dundee. He is commemorated on the Tyne Cot Memorial.

Private William Moores was killed in action on 22 October 1917. He was from Manchester. He is commemorated on the Tyne Cot Memorial.

Private Harvey Morris was killed in action on 22 October 1917. He was aged 39 and from Oldham. He is commemorated on the Tyne Cot Memorial.

Lance Corporal Albert Mottershead was killed in action on 22 October 1917. He was aged 33 and from Longsight, Manchester. He is commemorated on the Tyne Cot Memorial.

Sergeant Joseph Nolan was killed in action on 22 October 1917. He was from Manchester. He is commemorated on the Tyne Cot Memorial.

Private James Edward Parker was killed in action on 22 October 1917. He was from Ancoats. He is commemorated on the Tyne Cot Memorial.

Private William Nuttall Pollard was killed in action on 22 October 1917. He was aged 26 and from Stockport. He is commemorated on the Tyne Cot Memorial.

Private Walter Prince was killed in action on 22 October 1917. He was aged 20 and from Buxton. He is commemorated on the Tyne Cot Memorial.

Sergeant Stephen Pritchard was killed in action on 22 October 1917. He was aged 20 and from Salford. He is commemorated on the Tyne Cot Memorial.

Private George Reeve was killed in action on 22 October 1917. He was from Leicester. He is commemorated on the Tyne Cot Memorial.

Corporal John Regan was killed in action on 22 October 1917. He was from Miles Platting. He is commemorated on the Tyne Cot Memorial.

Private William Shaw was killed in action on 22 October 1917. He enlisted in Preston. He is commemorated on the Tyne Cot Memorial.

Private Albert Edward Smith was killed in action on 22 October 1917. He was from West Gorton. He is commemorated on the Tyne Cot Memorial.

Private Francis Sullivan was killed in action on 22 October 1917. He is commemorated on the Tyne Cot Memorial.

Private John Joseph Talbot was killed in action on 22 October 1917. He was aged 20 and from Leigh, Lancashire. He is commemorated on the Tyne Cot Memorial.

Private David Thomas was killed in action on 22 October 1917. He was from Bolton. He is commemorated on the Tyne Cot Memorial.

Private Charles Thorpe was killed in action on 22 October 1917. He was from Stockport. He is commemorated on the Tyne Cot Memorial.

Private Harry Turner was killed in action on 22 October 1917. He was aged 25 and from Stockport. He is commemorated on the Tyne Cot Memorial.

Private William Thomas Tyrer was killed in action on 22 October 1917. He was from Wigan. He is commemorated on the Tyne Cot Memorial.

Private Wilfred Ewart Wall was killed in action on 22 October 1917. He enlisted in Southport. He is commemorated on the Tyne Cot Memorial.

Private Nelson Wilde was killed in action on 22 October 1917. He was aged 31 and from Stalybridge. He is commemorated on the Tyne Cot Memorial.

Corporal Alfred Wilson was killed in action on 22 October 1917. He was aged 21 and from Longsight. He is commemorated on the Tyne Cot Memorial.

Captain Arthur Thomas Abraham was killed in action on 22 October 1917. He was aged 32 and originally from Suffolk. As a young man he had moved to New Zealand to farm, but by 1914 he was living in British Columbia, Canada. At the outbreak of war he joined the Canadian infantry as a private and he was in France by early 1915. He was badly gassed at Ypres. Recovering, he returned to the front, remaining there until he received a commission in the Manchester Regiment. He was awarded the Military Cross in June 1917 and was promoted to lieutenant in July. He was promoted, to captain, ten days before he was killed. (*Auckland Weekly News*, 24 January 1918.) He is commemorated on the Tyne Cot Memorial.

Second Lieutenant Alfred Wraith Bellamy was killed in action on 22 October 1917. He was aged 23 and from Withington, Manchester. Bellamy enlisted in November 1914 with the 1/7th Manchesters, and served in Egypt and at Gallipoli. He returned to England in January 1916, where he was treated in hospital for enteric fever (typhoid). He was posted to the 3rd Manchesters in December 1916, transferred to the 19th Battalion in France and then was commissioned, in the 20th Battalion in May 1917. He was reported missing on 22 October 1917 while attached to the 23rd Manchesters. He is commemorated on the Tyne Cot Memorial.

Second Lieutenant Cecil Haddon Cook was killed in action on 22 October 1917. He was aged 21 and from Belleville, Barbados, British West Indies. In 1914 he was studying medicine at Edinburgh University, but left to join the Inns of Court OTC. He was commissioned in January 1917. He is commemorated on the Tyne Cot Memorial.

Second Lieutenant John William Dixon was killed in action on 22 October 1917. He was aged 28 and from Oldham. He enlisted in May 1915 and served sixteen months with the Royal Welsh Fusiliers before he was commissioned. Prior to joining the army he was works manager at Oldham Corporation Central Gasworks. He is commemorated on the Tyne Cot Memorial.

Captain Joseph Leonard Milthorp Morton was killed in action on 22 October 1917. He was aged 22 and from Wolverhampton. He was studying at Christ Church College, Oxford, in 1914 but left, in April 1915, having secured a commission with the 23rd Manchester Battalion. His obituary in the school magazine (the 'Wulfrunian') of Wolverhampton Grammar School reads,

His death on October 22nd 1917, was due to an act of manly devotion. He had led his own company well forward, when he saw that the company on his right, its officers all down, was in difficulties. Though already hit twice, he went to pull things together and was killed on the way. Colonel, Company Commander, Chaplain and others unite in speaking of him as a fearless soldier and a gallant gentleman, whose loss would be acutely felt by the whole Battalion.

He is commemorated on the Tyne Cot Memorial. (Quotation and photograph reproduced with the kind permission of Wolverhampton Grammar School.)

Captain George Edward Simpson was killed in action on 22 October 1917. He was aged 24 and from Liverpool. He is commemorated on the Tyne Cot Memorial.

SIMPSON.—October 22, aged 24 years, Captain GEORGE E. SIMPSON, S.B., Manchester Regiment, dearly-loved and only son of Mary E. and the late George A. Simpson, 10, Duncan-street, Liverpool. Fell whilst nobly doing his duty.
   Loved and respected by all who knew him.
           Liverpool Masonic Lodge (No. 1547).

Manchester Evening News, 3 November 1917.

Second Lieutenant Harold Thomas Styles was reported missing (presumed killed) on 22 October 1917. He was aged 23 and from Craven, North Yorkshire. His wife wrote to fellow officers to try to get news of him, but to no avail. In May 1918 the War Office notified his family that he had now officially been registered as killed in action. A letter from B.C. Thompson, a private in Second Lieutenant Styles' Company, was published in the *Craven Herald* on 24 May 1918. It reads:

About October 22nd at Houthulst Wood we were going over between 5-30 and 6 a.m., my section being led by this officer, when, having got to the edge of the wood, he was shot and died instantly. I myself shouted something to him about some Germans retiring, and getting no answer went over to him and found him on his knees quite dead. I touched him to make sure and then went back to my Lewis gun. I myself was wounded very soon afterwards.

The local paper said 'His loss will be greatly felt in the village, as he was a very popular and sociable lad, and the heartfelt sympathy of the people of Austwick and district are extended to his relatives in the sad loss.' Even four years on, Harold Styles' wife continued to place missing notices in the newspapers.

Harold Styles had been a butler before the war. He volunteered in 1914 and served as a private in the Cheshire Regiment. He had not been long in the army, though, before he was promoted to lance corporal, and subsequently attained the position of company sergeant major. He was offered a commission with the Manchesters in January 1917 and after training returned to France in July 1917. He was recommended for the Military Cross 'following gallantry and soldierly conduct in a very successful attack on the Western Front between the 18th and 22nd August'. He is commemorated on the Tyne Cot Memorial.

> STYLES.—In proud and loving memory of my dear husband, Lieut. H. T. Styles, M.C., who was missing in France (presumed killed), October 22, 1917. "His toil is past, his work is done, and he is fully blest; he fought the fight, the victory won, and entered into rest."—From his loving wife and child.

Tamworth Herald, 22 October 1921.

Lieutenant William Logan Weir was killed in action on 22 October 1917. He was aged 23 and lived in Lanarkshire. He is commemorated on the Tyne Cot Memorial.

Lieutenant Henry Lowes Willey was killed in action on 22 October 1917. He was aged 24 and from Haltewhistle, Northumberland. He was commissioned into the Manchester Regiment in August 1915 and promoted to lieutenant in May 1917. He is commemorated on the Tyne Cot Memorial.

Second Lieutenant William Arnold Wilson was killed in action on 22 October 1917. He was aged 23 and from Moss Side. Having joined the Manchester Regiment as a private at the start of the war, he served in France for fifteen months before he was offered a commission early in 1917. Prior to the war he worked for a firm of chartered accountants in Manchester. He is commemorated on the Tyne Cot Memorial.

Manchester Evening News, 31 October 1917.

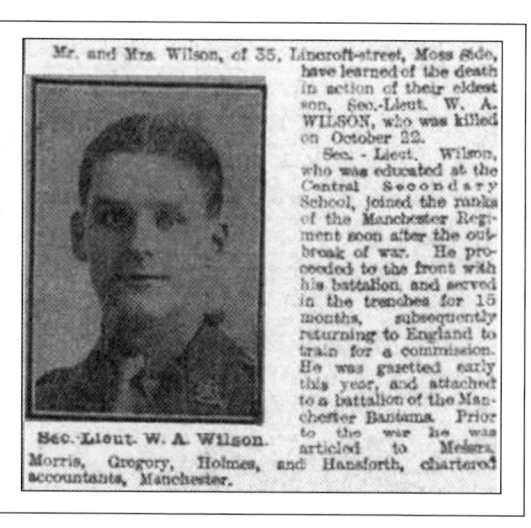

> Mr. and Mrs. Wilson, of 35, Lincroft-street, Moss Side, have learned of the death in action of their eldest son, Sec.-Lieut. W. A. WILSON, who was killed on October 22.
> Sec.-Lieut. Wilson, who was educated at the Central Secondary School, joined the ranks of the Manchester Regiment soon after the outbreak of war. He proceeded to the front with his battalion, and served in the trenches for 15 months, subsequently returning to England to train for a commission. He was gazetted early this year, and attached to a battalion of the Manchester Bantams. Prior to the war he was articled to Messrs. Morris, Gregory, Holmes, and Hansforth, chartered accountants, Manchester.

On 23 October the surviving Manchesters moved back to De Wippe Cabaret. A church parade was held. A band played the 'Funeral March'. The 'Last Post' was sounded. That same day Brigadier General Sandilands ordered a raid, to be undertaken by the 20th

Lancashire Fusiliers, on the enemy pill boxes to the north of Aden House. It was from these positions that most of the fire that concentrated on the 23rd Manchesters had originated. With the surprised enemy sending up the SOS, an artillery barrage opened on the attacking party. The party of Fusiliers withdrew, but not before they had suffered significant casualties.

Private William Barber died of wounds on 23 October 1917. He was aged 29 and from Rochdale. He is buried in Solferino Farm Cemetery.

Private Albert Henry Huddleston was killed in action on 23 October 1917. He was aged 30 and from Longsight, Manchester. He is buried in Dozinghem Military Cemetery.

Private William Andrew died of wounds on 24 October 1917. He was aged 29 and from Oldham. He is buried in Étaples Military Cemetery.

Private Robert Hurst died of wounds on 24 October 1917. He was from Wigan. He is commemorated on the Tyne Cot Memorial.

Private Frank Rhodes died of wounds on 27 October 1917. He was from Beswick, Manchester. He is buried in Dozinghem Military Cemetery.

Private John Worrall died of wounds on 30 October 1917. He was aged 33 and from Middleton. He is buried in Étaples Military Cemetery.

Private Joseph Burns died of wounds on 3 November 1917. He was aged 20 and from Ancoats. He is buried in Dozinghem Military Cemetery.

Private Ellis Nixon died of wounds on 5 November 1917. He was aged 35 and from Beswick, Manchester. He is buried in Mendinghem Military Cemetery.

Lance Corporal Herbert Brooks died of wounds on 6 November 1917. He was aged 22 and from Bolton. He had previously been wounded in July 1916. He is buried in Étaples Military Cemetery.

On 30 October the Manchesters marched to Larry Camp, near Elverdinghe. During the first few days of November there was heavy enemy bombardment (with gas shelling through the night and high-explosive bombardment taking over at dawn) and, providing working parties on the light railway in the forward areas, the Manchesters continued to suffer casualties.

It was probably with some relief then that they marched to Elverdinghe station on 3 November and entrained away from the front. That night they were back in Privett Camp, at Proven, north of Poperinghe. The next day the battalion was inspected by the Divisional Commander.[26] These days at Privett Camp were spent training. On 6 November the news came through that Passchendaele had finally fallen to the Canadians. Though it was now just a ruin of a village the strategic (and psychological) significance of taking the crest of the ridge was substantial.

'What is Passchendaele?' Philip Gibbs wrote on 6 November 1917.

As I saw it this morning through the smoke of gun-fire and a wet mist it was less than I had seen before, a week or two ago, with just one ruin there—the ruin of its

'What was once Passchendaele' reads the caption. In 1919 the Michelin *Guide* to Ypres advised travellers: 'Passing through shell-torn country. Passchendaele – now razed to the ground – is reached. All that remains of the church is the mound seen in the background of the photograph.' *Illustrated Michelin Guides to the Battle-Fields (1914–1918): Ypres*, p. 64.

Tyne Cot cemetery and memorial photographed in the 1920s.

church—a black mass of slaughtered masonry and nothing else, not a house left standing, not a huddle of brick on that shell-swept height. But because of its position as the crown of the ridge that crest has seemed to many men like a prize for which all these battles of Flanders have been fought, and to get to this place and the slopes and ridges on the way to it, not only for its own sake but for what it would bring with it, great numbers of our most gallant men have given their blood, and thousands—scores of thousands—of British soldiers of our own home stock and from overseas have gone through fire and water, the fire of frightful bombardments, the water of the swamps, of the beeks and shell-holes, in which they have plunged and waded and stuck and sometimes drowned . . . Passchendaele is but a pinprick on a fair-sized map, but so that we should not take it the enemy had spent much of his man-power and his gun-power without stint, and there have flowed up to his guns tides of shells almost as great as the tides that flowed up to our guns, and throughout these months he has never ceased, by day or night, to pour out hurricanes of fire over all these fields, in the hope of smashing up our progress. A few days ago orders were issued to his troops. They were given in the name of Hindenburg. Passchendaele must be held at all costs, and, if lost, must be recaptured at all costs. Passchendaele has been lost to the enemy to-day, and if we have any fortune in war, it will not be retaken.[27]

German graves in the remains of Houthulst Forest.

Chapter 14

'The Beginning of the End'

In November 1917 Philip Gibbs wrote:

> It is a dreary and tragic landscape, and though I have seen four autumns of war and the long, wet winters of this Flemish country, the misery of it and the squalor of it struck me anew to-day, as though I saw it with fresh eyes. In all this country round Ypres, still the capital of the battlefields, holding in its poor, stricken bones the soul of all this tragedy, and still shelled—yesterday very heavily—by an enemy who even now will not let its dust alone, there is nothing but destruction and the engines of destruction. The trees are smashed, and the ground is littered with broken things, and the earth is ploughed into deep pits and furrows by three years of shell-fire, and it is all oozy and liquid and slimy.
>
> Our Army is like an upturned ant-heap in all this mud, and in the old battle-grounds they have dug themselves in and built little homes for themselves and settled down to a life of industry between one shell-crater and another, and one swamp and another, for the long spell of winter warfare which has now enveloped them, and while they are waiting for another year of war, unless Peace comes with the Spring.[1]

On 20 November the 23rd Manchester Battalion was heading back to the front. Heavy rain was falling as they marched towards Poelcapelle. The village had been fiercely fought over since early October and, by the end of that month, it was a 'scrap-heap village', nothing more than a pile of stones. 'Poelcapelle, except for the pill-boxes, was hardly recognisable as the remains of a village,' Brigadier General Sandilands observed, 'and was even worse than Langemarck, which at least possessed a mound of white stone which had once been the church.'[2]

The Manchesters moved up to front-line trenches to the right of the divisional sector. Called the Paddebeek sector, it took the name of the stream that in normal times flowed quietly past Goudberg. This was not normal times. The Paddebeek sector was now 'a morass', a 'horrible swamp'. Conditions here, and the state of communications, were just as bad as they had been on the edge of Houthulst Forest.

On the evening of 21 November an SOS signal was sent up by the 18th Lancashire Fusiliers, manning the length of trenches to the Manchesters' left. A patrol had spotted an estimated 250 Germans advancing on Tracas Farm, south-east of Poelcapelle. The Very lights revealed the enemy advancing in several waves. Preparations were made for

German troops outside Poelcapelle church in the early stages of the war.

A road near Poelcapelle in 1918.

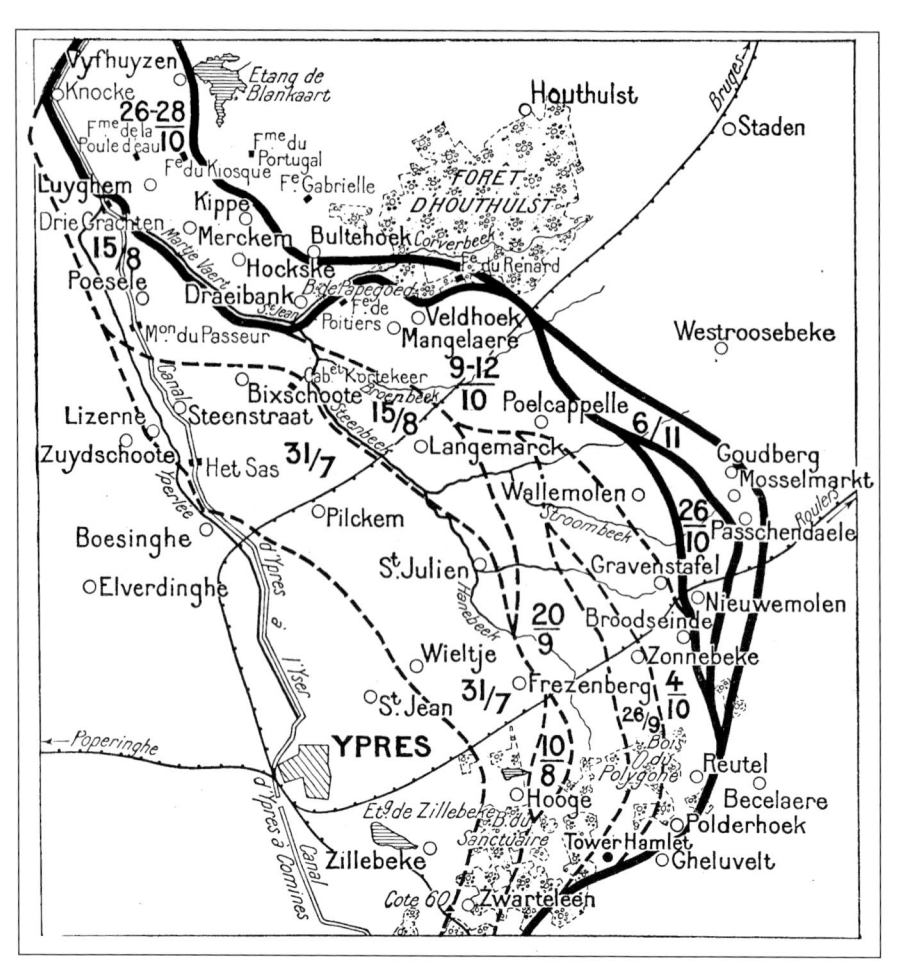

Map showing the stages of the Third Ypres campaign. *Illustrated Michelin Guides to the Battle-Fields (1914–1918): Ypres*, p. 34.

an attack. Fire was withheld until the attacking troops were within close range. 'Then,' the Divisional History records, 'rapid fire from machine guns, Lewis guns and rifles threw the enemy into utter confusion'. The attacking troops withdrew, but not before they had suffered a large number of casualties. There were fifteen enemy dead counted in no-man's-land the following morning.[3]

The days were wet and misty. On 22 November gas was released by the enemy, and three men were treated for its effects. Later that day, though, the Manchesters were relieved by the 17th Lancashire Fusiliers and moved back into brigade reserve at 'canal bank', a camp to the east of Brielen (south of Boesinghe) on the Yser–Ypres canal.[4]

On the 24th they moved back into the divisional reserve. Battalion headquarters and two companies moved to camp at Kempton Park, described by the Divisional History as 'a collection of Nissen Huts at a road junction midway between Wieltje and Pilckem'. Kempton Park was close enough to the front to be in range of the enemy guns. Indeed,

Dugout in the Poelcapelle sector, 1918.

Destroyed waggons and a large bunker, Poelcapelle, 1918.

The remnants of a farm near Poelcapelle, 1918.

just a few days earlier, it had been targeted by a high-velocity gun. One shell had scored a direct hit on the brigade office hut and a dud buried itself under the hut where the officers of the 18th Lancashire Fusiliers had been sleeping. It was a 'memorable night', Sandilands recorded. Here the Manchesters were now occupied providing working parties for the Royal Engineers. The other two companies and the battalion transport moved to P Camp, in the Peselhoek area, to the north of Poperinghe. On the 28th Battalion headquarters and the two companies who had been in Kempton Park moved by rail to P Camp. There they would remain, training, until 1 December.[5]

> Private Arthur Ferguson Millar died on 30 November 1917. He was aged 19 and from Cheetham, Manchester. He is buried in the Mendinghem Military Cemetery.

On 2 December the Manchesters moved back to brigade reserve at Canal Bank. On the 4th, they were back in the front line in the Poelcapelle–Paddebeek sector. One officer (Second Lieutenant Gray) and one man were reported to have been killed during the course of the relief and six wounded. At least this time it was dry in the trenches. The rain had now ceased and the weather had become colder. The enemy was also quieter. It was still, though, a difficult and depressing place to be. 'Although the weather had become dry, a fog generally hung over the country,' the Divisional History recorded, 'and the atmosphere in that desolate region was depressing.' It goes on:

Frequent reliefs were a necessity, but the infantry, in carrying them out, had to walk long distances on duckboard tracks and men entering the line had, generally, no better billet to look forward to than a damp and chilly shell hole. The ground became hard, and digging was toilsome. It was hoped, chiefly by those who did not know Flanders, that better conditions would prevail when the division next took over the line.[6]

Second Lieutenant Charles W. Gray was killed on 4 December 1917. The *Manchester Evening News* recorded that 'Mr Gray before the war was a well-known and highly respected Manchester pressman'. He was, for several years, on the editorial staff of the *Daily Mail* (northern edition) and later worked for the *Manchester Courier* and *Manchester Weekly Times*. Gray enlisted as a private with the Royal Warwickshire Regiment (he was originally from Birmingham) early in 1916. In October 1916 he had written an article for the *Manchester Weekly Times* ('Office to Trench in Ten Weeks') in which he described his experience of volunteering alongside Derby recruits ('I am not a "Derbyite" . . . but I was sent to my depot with a party comprised almost entirely of "Derbys"'). Gray wrote: 'We were not harshly treated, but we were in no danger of forgetting that we were "Derbys". One bold youth complained on a certain morning that the breakfast tea was cold. "No wonder", rejoined the orderly sergeant, "it's been waiting for you for eighteen months."' While serving in France, Gray was recommended for a commission. He proceeded for training at St John's College, Cambridge, and after passing his exams was gazetted to the 23rd Manchester Battalion.

He left a widow and five young children. He is buried in St Julien Dressing Station Cemetery.

Manchester Evening News, 13 December 1917; *Manchester Weekly Times*, 15 December 1915 and 28 October 1916.

> Private Joseph Cecil Squier died of wounds on 6 December 1917. He was aged 27 and from Bulphan, Essex. He is buried in Mendinghem Military Cemetery.

On 6 December the Manchesters were relieved by 106th Brigade and returned to P Camp. From there, then, on the 8th they were transferred by train to rest camp in the Corps Reserve Area near Houtkerque (to the west of Poperinghe). 'Here,' Sandilands wrote, 'in spite of the very cold weather, the men enjoyed themselves and got plenty of amusement combined with a minimum of training.' Kit was cleaned, there were baths and changes of clothing, there were church parades and football matches, there was some training – but mostly there was rest. A whole glorious month of it.[7]

On 11 December the battalion moved by road to rest billets at Nouveau Monde, near Herzeele. Christmas Day was given as a holiday and a brigade dinner was served in Houtkerque. Sandilands fondly recalled the gastronomic attractions of that locality: 'The officer's restaurant just behind the church at Houtkerque probably forms the outstanding feature of December, 1917, in the recollection of many second lieutenants, and, perhaps, even in that of those of more exalted rank.' On 28 December a brigade boxing competition began (with Sergeant Sheppard of the 23rd Manchesters beating Private Casey of the 18th Lancashire Fusiliers in the Lightweight category) and on the next day there were more brigade sports (the 23rd Manchesters won the 'Marching and shooting competition'). The new year opened with an 'Assault at Arms' on 3 and 4 January – a divisional tournament in which military skills were tested, competed for and trumpeted. The weather was fine and frosty and some fun was had.[8]

> Private Edmund Knowles died of wounds on 14 December 1917. He was aged 30 and from Oldham. He is buried in Ste Marie Cemetery, Le Havre.

All too soon, though, it was back to the mundane and muddy business of war. On 7 January 1918 the Manchesters were moved by rail to Bridge Camp near Elverdinghe. The next day they were moving forward into a support position in the Langemarck area. Sandilands remarked that conditions had 'changed a good deal since the Houthulst days'. Gone was the chaos in the back areas and the system of duckboard tracks had been improved, now leading almost up to the front-line posts. There were other challenges, though; it had snowed heavily and was bitterly cold. It made the move forward hard going.[9]

On 10 January the Manchesters moved into a forward position in the Poelcapelle sub sector. For the next few days they would back and forth with the 17th Lancashire Fusiliers, alternately in support trenches and at the front. Battalion war daries note that these were 'very quiet' days in the line. There was little shelling and few casualties. Sandilands recalled:

> Owing to the state of the ground, even patrolling was difficult, and raids were out of the question. Most of the men were employed on large working parties, making

corps lines, deep dug-outs and strong points, which were never used, and which were eventually abandoned after the German offensive in March.[10]

There was some accommodation in the broken down pill boxes and shelters all about. Headquarters, too, were in pill boxes. Though they might offer reasonable protection, their comforts were not extolled. Sandilands wrote: 'Unless one had lived in a pill-box it is difficult to imagine the discomfort which it may entail. It was common to find a commanding officer with the whole of his Battalion staff, including signallers, runners, pigeon flyers, wireless operators and cooks, living in perhaps two or three small rooms, each about 10 feet square.'[11]

Concrete shelters in the Poelcapelle area, 1918.

Snow fell again on 14 January, and two days and nights of heavy rain followed and then it snowed again. 'Needless to say,' the Divisional History recounts, 'the Steenbeek immediately rose in flood and washed away the bridges. B/159 Battery was once again flooded, and dead horses were washed down into the gun position. The roads were submerged, and many of the duckboards of the tracks were displaced.'[12]

On 16 January the Manchesters were relieved and moved back to the divisional reserve at Canal Bank (Brielen). Here three companies were attached to 255 Tunnelling Company of the Royal Engineers. On the 24th they were back in the support trenches and, on the 26th, they returned to the front line in the Poelcapelle sub sector. The War Diary of the

18th Lancashire Fusiliers, manning the trenches to the Manchesters' right, notes that this was another 'very quiet' stint, but the Manchesters were about to get some excitement on 27 January, the Kaiser's birthday. At about 6.00 am, under cover of thick fog, a party of about twenty enemy crept up and rushed one of the Manchesters' posts from the rear. They succeeded in capturing a sergeant and three men. As the party was retreating, though, a Lewis gun was opened on them from the next post and one of the prisoners escaped. The day also saw one officer and two other ranks wounded by machine-gun fire while wiring the support line. On the first of February the Manchesters were relieved and returned to the Divisional Reserve at Kempton Park.

> Private William Smith died of wounds on 8 January 1918. He was from Ashton under Lyne. He is buried in Cement House Cemetery, West-Vlaanderen.
> Private Joseph Pearson was killed in action on 15 January 1918. He was aged 27 and from Audenshaw, Manchester. He is commemorated on the Tyne Cot Memorial.
> Private William Everett died of wounds on 18 January 1918. He was from Norfolk. He is buried in Mendinghem Military Cemetery.
> Private John Hanson died of wounds on 30 January 1918. He was aged 25 and from Oldham. He is buried in Cement House Cemetery, West-Vlaanderen.
> Private Arthur Harrison died on 1 February 1918. He was aged 28 and from Nottingham. He is commemorated on the Tyne Cot Memorial.

By the end of 1917 severe tensions were developing between senior military and politicians as the army called for new manpower to replace the significant numbers lost during the Third Battle of Ypres. The Army Council had, through the second half of the year, repeatedly informed the government that the manpower deficit needed to be resolved. Replacement drafts were not keeping up with losses and, by October 1917, the shortfall was about 75,000 men in the infantry alone. However, in November, the War Office informed Haig that it would not be possible to provide reinforcements on the scale that he required. Indeed, he was told that the shortfall was likely to expand, approaching an estimate of 259,000 men by late 1918. Haig protested that this deficiency would significantly impact flexibility, but the government was resolute; the War Cabinet had no intention of intensifying recruitment to replace Haig's losses. With manpower thus restricted, the army had little choice but to review its limited resources and accordingly restructure. A decision was therefore taken to scale back the size of infantry divisions, disbanding 134 battalions and consolidating those that remained by redistributing men.

At the start of February 1918 the 23rd Manchesters were officially notified that it was to be one of those battalions that were to be broken up. With a stroke of a pen units of men who had joined and served together for the past two years simply ceased to be. The frustration at this decision is evident in the recollections of brigade and divisional commanders. The Divisional History records: 'Under instruction from the Army Council divisions were changed from a 13 battalion to a 10 battalion basis and this necessitated the breaking of many ties of mutual admiration and friendship which bound together

Image captioned 'Flanders Battlefield in Winter'. *Illustrated Michelin Guides to the Battle-Fields (1914–1918): Ypres*, p. 19.

units which had been fighting side by side for years.' Sandilands went further: 'It was with a feeling of intense regret that we finally had to take leave of two battalions who had played such a conspicuous part throughout the career of the Brigade in France.'[13]

On 4 February the Manchesters were back in those Nissen huts at Kempton Park. Instructions had been received that the men of the 23rd Manchesters were to be redistributed as reinforcements between the other Manchester battalions. Thus seven officers and 150 men were to be transferred to the 2nd Manchesters, twelve officers and 250 men to the 11th Battalion and twelve officers and 230 men to the 12th Battalion.

With the decision to disband having been announced, it was quickly enacted. On 6 February those men who had been allocated to the 2nd Manchesters left. The following day, the remainder of the 23rd Manchesters moved to G Camp, near Poperinghe. From there, they were marched to Poperinghe Station on 11 February and the parties of men allocated to the 11th and 12th Battalions departed. There was evidently some sadness as men went their separate ways. Sandilands reflected: 'There was never a happier family than the 104th Infantry Brigade. We all knew each other, and had a certain way of doing things, possibly not the best way, but at any rate one which we all understood and had got used to.'[14]

On 16 February the 'surplus', those men who had not yet been reassigned to other battalions, moved back by lorry to the II Corps Reinforcement Camp at Merckeghem (between Saint-Omer and Dunkirk). The next day orders were received for the formation of Entrenching Battalions and so, on 20 February, Entrenching Battalion Number 12 was officially formed, under the command of Lieutenant Colonel L.M. Stevens, with all of the surplus personnel of the former 23rd Manchesters duly incorporated as part of it. Thus it was, on 20 February, that Stevens signed the War Diary of the 23rd Manchester Battalion for the last time.

Entrenching battalions had existed earlier in the war, being temporary units formed as pools of men from which drafts of replacements could be drawn by conventional infantry battalions. They had ceased to exist by the autumn 1917, due to manpower shortages, but were now revived. In February 1918 twenty-five entrenching battalions were set up. It was envisaged that they would be employed on repair work and trench digging in the forward area. They could be used as a reserve force if needed but, not really being intended to serve as fighting units in their own right, they were not equipped with light artillery or signals. Despite these limitations, the 12th Entrenching Battalion would shortly find itself holding off the German advance in the vicinity of Tergnier-Quessy (south of Saint-Quentin) while in support of the 58th Division.

Thus it ended for the 23rd Manchesters, just as the war was about to enter a new phase. At 4.40 am on 21 March a terrific enemy bombardment would begin along a front of more than 50 miles (from Arras to south of Saint-Quentin). An infantry assault followed at 9.40 am. The *Manchester Guardian* reported: 'After several hours of this hurricane shelling, in which it is probable that a great deal of gas was used with the intention of creating a poison-gas atmosphere around our gunners and forward posts, the German infantry advanced and developed attacks against a number of strategical points.'[15]

With large numbers of troops now transferred from the Russian front, the Germans had the numerical advantage and the morning's foggy conditions served in their favour. 'The attack already appears to be on a formidable scale,' the *Guardian* went on, 'with a vast amount of artillery and masses of men, and there is reason to believe that it may be indeed the beginning of the great offensive.' The report continued: 'If so, it is a bid for a decisive victory on the western front at no matter what sacrifice and with the fullest brutalities of every engine of war . . . At the present moment our troops are fighting not only for their own lives but also for the fate of England and all our race.'[16] By the end of the day the British had suffered around 38,500 casualties, of whom 7,500 were killed and 21,000 were taken prisoners of war. Over 98 square miles of territory had been lost.

'We stand, then, at the opening of critical days,' the *Manchester Guardian* editorial recorded on 23 March. But it chanced to spy some glimmer of hope in the situation:

> None of us can say how long the crisis now opening may last, for we know neither

how long the present battle may be pressed nor what part it is meant to play in the entire German schemes. One thing only we are entitled to hope. The resort to a great offensive, with its doubtful chances of success and its certainties of immense cost in life, indicates strong pressure in Germany to bring the war to an end . . . The coming of the Americans casts its shadow before and we may allow ourselves the hope that, if this offensive follows the course of other offensives on the west, it will prove to be the beginning of the end.[17]

It was not quite the end. By late March, the 2nd and 12th Manchesters were engaged against the German advance on the Somme. All three of the battalions that the 23rd Manchesters had been redistributed to would be involved in the German Spring Offensive of 1918. The Entrenching Battalions were disbanded in April 1918 and the men were transferred to other battalions to replace men lost during the March offensive.

> Second Lieutenant Thomas Clarkson was killed in action on 22 March 1918. He was from Stockport. Mobilised as a Territorial in 1914, he went to France with the 6th Battalion, Cheshire Regiment. He was the battalion's colour sergeant and quartermaster. When his contracted service as a Territorial expired, he re-enlisted into the Cheshires and, in October 1916, he re-joined the battalion as its regimental sergeant major. In December 1916 he was offered a commission and returned to England for training; he was gazetted to the 23rd Manchesters in May 1917. After the disbanding of the 23rd Battalion, Clarkson was transferred to the 12th Manchesters. On 22 March the 12th Manchesters were near Havrincourt, just to the south of Cambrai. There were four successive enemy attacks in the vicinity and the village of Havrincourt was lost. Lieutenant Clarkson was one of the 12th Manchesters' thirty-one casualties in the register that day. He is commemorated on the Arras Memorial, where he is identified in the register as a member of the 23rd Manchesters.

> Lieutenant Dirk Jacobus Kruger was killed in action on 2 April 1918. He was aged 29 and from Cape Colony, South Africa. A private in the South African Infantry from September 1915, Kruger obtained a commission in the 23rd Battalion in August 1917. He is buried in the Warloy-Baillon Communal Cemetery Extension. Though the battalion had already been disbanded by April 1918, his gravestone identifies him as a member of the 23rd Manchesters.

> Private John Hadfield was killed in action on 1 April 1918. He was from Stalybridge. He is commemorated on the Pozières Memorial. A former member of the 23rd Battalion, he was attached to the 7th Battalion Queen's Own (Royal West Kent Regiment) at the time of his death. He is identified in the memorial register as a member of the 23rd Manchesters.

Sergeant Robert Brunt was killed in action on 4 April 1918. He was from Buxton, Derbyshire. He is commemorated on the Pozières Memorial. Like Private Hadfield, he was attached to the 7th Battalion Queen's Own. He is identified in the memorial register as a member of the 23rd Manchesters.

Private Frank Carter was killed in action on 4 April 1918. He was from Oldham. He is buried in Caix British Cemetery. His gravestone identifies him as a member of the 23rd Manchesters.

Private George Park was killed in action on 4 April 1918. He enlisted in Failsworth. He is buried in Crucifix Corner Cemetery, Villers-Bretonneux. His gravestone identifies him as a member of the 23rd Manchesters.

Sergeant William Henry Green was killed in action on 24 April 1918. He was aged 29 and from Salford. He was a recipient of the Military Medal and was one of the original 1914 Manchester Bantams. He is commemorated on an Addenda Panel of the Tyne Cot Memorial, where he is identified in the register as a member of the 23rd Manchesters.

Private Ernest Leigh was killed in action on 23rd August 1918. He was from Oldham. He is buried in Dernancourt Communal Cemetery Extension. His gravestone identifies him as a member of the 23rd Manchesters. In effect he was the last '23rd Manchester' – or the last man to be identified as such – to be killed in action.

Chapter 15

'Honour the Dead Remember the Living'

News of the imminent Armistice reached Manchester just after ten on the morning of 11 November 1918. With an official announcement expected, there had been an all-night vigil in the newspaper offices. All wires had been cleared in anticipation. And then, by 10.25 am flags were being unfurled at the offices of the *Guardian* and the *Evening News*. With the presses already set up and ready to roll, it was only a short matter of time before newspaper carts, also decked in patriotic colours, were carrying the hot-off-the-press headlines all over the city. Suddenly factory sirens were sounding and all across Manchester people were flinging open their windows. 'It was as though people had heard the news and wanted to breathe it,' the *Manchester Guardian* observed. 'It seemed just what occurs after a long and heavy thunderstorm, when people may be seen opening their windows as though some welcome release had come.'[1]

Soon people were on the streets. At 11.00 am, as the Armistice was being enacted,

Albert Square at noon on 11 November 1918. *Manchester Guardian*, 12 November 1918.

people crowded into Albert Square. There was a momentary stillness as the crowd watched a flag being hoisted over the Town Hall. There seems to have been a feeling of shock more than joy in this instant. There was a sense of solemnity. People cried rather than cheered.

The mood shifted over the course of the day, though. Tears turned to joyous laughter and by the afternoon the predominant tone was one of jubilation. The munition workers broke out, shops, offices and warehouses closed and a holiday was declared at the grammar school. By 1.00 pm, the streets were packed:

> Along all the main roads into the city, along Ashton Old Road, along Stockport Road and Hyde Road, work-girls poured in hundreds, gathering as they went flags and the other patriotic symbols which had been so suddenly rushed out of obscurity of the hawker's warehouse. They clambered on town-going lorries. In Market Street one saw a cart, drawn by the tiniest of donkeys, with seven or eight sturdy girls in overalls, cheering and flag-waving... The girls – for the first crowds were mainly girls – flocked in their workclothes, shawls over heads, or in the light trousered overalls of the munition works. They shouted and cheered, breaking up now and then to do a few steps of a wild fox-trot.[2]

The bells of the Town Hall clock were ringing and the tugs in Salford Quay were sounding their horns. People were trimming their hats with red, white and blue. The newspaper reports of the day emphasise the sudden loudness and colour of all of this jubilation – a wild breaking out of vitality after the long, stifling wait of war. As night fell, the city lit up. After so long an age of stumbling through dimmed streets, suddenly every lamp in the city seemed to be burning brightly. There was a 'feverish energy' now, wrote the *Manchester Guardian*:

> It was given point and direction by bugle bands and drums. In almost every main street at any time during the evening one could see such a band, with its flag-waving leader and its long straggling tail of men and girls linking arms across the street. They marched quickly and unimpeded through the crowded streets, for there were no tramcars to break their ranks. It was, indeed, a wonderful contrast with the days that are just behind us – streets with lights but no traffic, crowds that moved about us as if they had no care and no thought beyond the burning joy of the moment.

The night's celebrations were exuberant and spontaneous and raucous - and extended into the early hours of the morning. The *Manchester Guardian* editorial observed: 'Long pent-up reserves of nervous energy and high spirits took long to work themselves out.'[3]

It was a gloriously happy moment for Manchester – and one that newspaper columns would recall in coming years with a fond but melancholy note. Through the 1920s Manchester would continue to see demonstrations on its streets. The tone of them, though, would be quite different.

Bringing the men home
The physical demobilisation of the armed services (some 3.5 million men at the end of the war) was a huge administrative and logistical undertaking. During the General Election that followed the Armistice Lloyd George made promises of immediate demobilisation. These were vote-seeking, impractical promises and they would have the effect, over the next year, of dangerously weakening the discipline of the men who were still awaiting their release.

The demobilisation scheme had been drawn up by Lord Derby, as Secretary of State for War, back in 1917. The order of release was formulated with a view to getting industry back onto a peacetime footing as quickly as possible, but the scheme took little account for the weariness and frustrations of those who had served a long time. The order of demobilisation was thus: first 'pivotal' men ('an officer or soldier required in a civil capacity immediately on the cessation of hostilities for the purposes of national reconstruction') were to return to civilian life; then 'contract' men (who had had formal offers to resume their pre-war employment) would be let go; then 'slip' men (men who had been issued with a release slip by the Ministry of Labour, having been deemed likely to be 'assured' of employment in civil life); and lastly 'general demobilisation' would follow.[4] It was widely perceived as unfair that men who had only recently joined up (and who were likely therefore to be conscripts) could be released before those who had served for four years. And, in practice, the scheme was made worse by bureaucratic bungling. There was delay and confusion and inconsistency. Heightening the dissatisfaction and men's desire to be released was the prospect of being sent to fight against the Bolsheviks in Russia. Though the official line was that only volunteers would be posted to Russia, it was widely believed that unwilling conscripts were being sent in that direction.

Already, by early January 1919, frustration with this scheme was amply apparent. There was agitation in Folkestone, Dover and Southampton, as men who had been home on leave demonstrated their reluctance to return back across the Channel. Servicemen picketed the docks.[5] Through January disturbances broke out throughout the country. Men were voting with their feet and army discipline was crumbling fast. There was concern in the War Office about how far this unrest would extend. One of the first actions of Winston Churchill, after he was appointed Secretary of State for War in January 1919, was to introduce a revised demobilisation scheme. By the end of January 1919 around 750,000 men had already been released. Under the new scheme the remaining 2,750,000 would first be reduced to 1,300,000 by allowing home all men aged over 37, or who enlisted before 1916, or who had been wounded more than twice. The numbers would then gradually be reduced by first letting men aged over 36 go; then men over 35; then those who had been twice wounded; and then men over 34. 'Perfect or imperfect,' the *Manchester Guardian* reflected, 'it will bring a million and a half officers and men home within three months, and there is a fine volume of human happiness assured in that.'[6]

In the process of being released from the army and returning home, men's ideals and expectations, however tested they had been overseas, were bolstered. Newspapers reminded them of the debt that society owed them. Crowds applauded their sacrifices. Politicians talked of making a land fit for heroes to live in. They were encouraged to recall the principles that they had been defending. They were told that the fruits of victory would be theirs. All of this set them up to be disappointed.

Peace Day, 19 July 1919

With the treaty negotiations at Versailles finally complete and peace signed at the end of June 1919, a national celebration – 'Peace Day' – was fixed for 19 July 1919. Plans were announced to light a chain of bonfires down the country (acknowledging the beacons that were lit to warn of the approach of the Spanish Armada on 19 July 1588) and a grand Victory Parade was being prepared for in London.

From the outset, though, there seems to have been some disquiet and confusion as to what 'Peace Day' was meant to represent – and whether it ought to be a jubilant celebration or a solemn commemoration. Its reporting in the Manchester papers reflects this ambiguity and the mixed enthusiasm for the project. 'Anyone who goes outside his house and garden ought to be able to see by this time that the country as a whole is not in the mood for a huge bout of dear and noisy merry-making,' a *Manchester Guardian* editorial considered. It went on:

> Men and women are learning, each with his own measure of bitterness, the element of disillusion that there is in nearly all success. You fight the good fight, and, lo! the prize itself has changed while you fought, and alloy has crept into the gold. You finish the long race, and only then you find that the 'you' who has won it is not the same 'you' who once had it to win. Everywhere, in all classes, you find a vague disappointment that the victorious England is not the same England of August 4, 1914, simply with her desire attained . . . something seems to be lost in the spirit which fired us then, and we cannot get it back any more than the parents can get back their sons.[7]

In some parts of the country veteran associations took a decision to boycott Peace Day and it appears that there was not much enthusiasm for it in Manchester either. The 'apathetic' response from ex-servicemen in Manchester seemed to surprise and disappoint the City Council. Advertisements had been issued in May, inviting ex-combatants to participate in a civic reception but, by 5 June, only 3,000 men had accepted.[8] A letter to the *Manchester Evening News* reflects why enthusiasm might have been somewhat lacking:

> Sir,
> I am sure the title Peace Day will send a cold shiver through the bodies of thousands of 'demobbed' men who are walking about the streets of Manchester looking for a job. Could a term be found that would be more ironical for such men? Perhaps, after the Manchester and Salford Corporations have celebrated this 'Peace' and incidentally will have wasted the thousands of pounds which it will cost, they will devote their spare time to alleviating the 'bitterness' and 'misery' which exist in the body and mind of the unemployed ex-soldier.
> It is high time some very forcible and active measures were taken. Many Manchester businessmen refuse to employ the ex-soldier on the grounds that he

has lost four years of experience in this line or that line of business through being in the army. What a splendid and patriotic retort to make to the men who were chiefly instrumental in saving their business from being in the possession of the Hun.[9]

The programme caused Manchester City Council some consternation and, in the end, official arrangements were low key: a dozen bands were engaged to play in the parks, the Town Hall bells were rung and the Lord Mayor and the City Council travelled through the city in an illuminated tramcar. There was no official scheme of street decoration - though companies and individuals ultimately took on that task and the streets were accordingly 'gay with bunting and flags'.[10]

As it was, the people of Manchester themselves seem to have determined the character of the city's Peace Day celebration. While young people enjoyed boisterous festivities (already by the night of the 18th they were spilling out into the streets, playing instruments and dancing 'the latest American "jazzes" and "cake walks"' in Albert Square), gangs of children gleefully banged on tin drums and begged coins from the crowds and 'hundreds of skylarking mill girls romped about the streets in khaki'.[11] The *Manchester Guardian* observed, though, that the festivities lacked the 'sparkle of spontaneity'. The city could not recapture the delirious joy of 11 November 1918. 'That was the sudden release of a long confined effervescence of feeling. It burst with explosive force without any official drawing of the cork.' The *Guardian* reported:

> Thousands of people collected in the streets and walked about aimlessly inspecting the unsatisfying decorations and looking for something more exciting to happen. This constrained and awkward situation was saved by the youthful and (if a plain word may be used) the rowdy elements in the population, whose sportive activities in public are usually regarded by the police with an unfriendly and repressive eye.

There is an implication that, in the evening, the tone of the celebrations was, here and there, tinged with something darker.

> The 'mafficking' in the streets reached its highest pitch of extravagance after sundown. Albert Square, which is always a focussing point for any unusual agitation of public feeling, was filled with a merrily turbulent crowd – dancing, singing, blowing paper horns, beating drums and tin cans, and occasionally letting off fireworks with a high power of detonation. The restraints usually imposed on public life in the streets were swept away, with results not always pleasant. There were many signs of a liberal use of intoxicants. Occasional fighting marred the prevalent merriment and good humour.[12]

'Honour the dead, remember the living'
On 19 July 1919 it was not just a time of giddy (or rowdy) mafficking; in Manchester the day was also marked by a protest march. In the afternoon a procession of unemployed ex-

servicemen moved through the streets of the city centre. It was reported that the column of men, walking four abreast, many of them wearing their medal ribbons, stretched nearly the whole length of Oxford Street. They carried banners which bore the words 'Justice', 'Employment', 'Work, not charity' and 'Honour the dead, remember the living'.

The demonstrators marched to Platt Fields, where a meeting had been convoked. By the time that the procession reached that locality its numbers had swelled and the men were 'a battalion strong and more'. Before the speeches began the Last Post was sounded.

The Chairman of the meeting, Mr Fred Cox, told the crowd that 'they had fought for freedom, but the freedom they had won was the freedom to starve'. He went on:

> To give a man 29*s*. a week was destructive work. It resulted in the breaking up of homes, in the under-nourishment of children, and the loss of efficiency in all directions. Employment ought to be found immediately on housing, roads, and every kind of public work, and the Government dole of 29*s*. could be paid to municipalities to help them to bear the cost of the schemes. It was work they wanted, not doles. They had been asked to save the country; now they asked the country to save them from poverty and degradation.

Mr W. Richards, who had organised the meeting, proposed that 'failing a reasonable reply from the Government within a reasonable time' the unemployed ex-servicemen of Lancashire should march to London. 'Winter was coming,' he threatened, 'and winter, with its cold and hunger, meant riots. That was why something must be done soon.'[13]

Unemployment

The golden age of 'Cottonopolis' had been coming to an end in 1914. Changes were already then making Manchester's confidence creak. The war would exaggerate and speed up both the internal and external forces of change – so that the Manchester the demobbed soldiers came back to was not the Manchester of their childhood.

Over the course of the last four years Manchester had firmly moved onto a war footing. Factories and warehouses had been turned over to munitions production. By 1917 Manchester was producing 2,000 4.5in shells per week. Elsewhere engineering works shifted to producing aircraft parts and dye plants converted to produce explosives. Already by 1916 a commentator could write: 'It has been said that the present war constitutes a definite fissure in the modern world's continuity – a sort of geological "fault" in the stratification of time. Already Manchester is becoming acclimatized to war and "twelve months ago" begins to look antiquated, almost antedilivian.'[14] That 'fissure' was definite and irreversible. In 1919 it was not just the immediate challenge of converting manufacturing premises back to peacetime production lines that Manchester faced. The markets that Manchester's goods served before the war had changed fundamentally and forever.

The decline of Lancashire's textile industry began during the war, as the supply of raw cotton was disrupted. At the end of the war the industry experienced a brief recovery; there was again the shipping capacity to bring raw cotton in and domestic demand was healthy. In 1920 textile manufacturers made good profits. It was a brief glimmer, though.

The following year was a terrible one for the cotton trade. And, though exports would start to pick up through the first half of the 1920s, they remained well below pre-war levels. Between 1920 and 1926 organised short-time would become the general rule in Lancashire cotton spinning. During this period most operations turned over just two-thirds of normal activity levels. By 1928 export figures were heading down again. As the market share figures overleaf show, Britain's dominance in that market was finished. Some of the markets that Lancashire had traditionally supplied contracted after the war and other competitor countries (which had the advantage of cheaper labour costs and were closer to the supply of the raw materials) had carried on developing and meeting the demand of their domestic and export markets. By 1930 British exports would have waned to almost a third of what they had been in 1913. Lancashire's position was slipping. British cotton exports went into a long enduring decline.

The Pals battalions had been promised that their jobs would be waiting for them when they got home – but, in so many cases, employers would prove unable, or unwilling, to honour that undertaking. In November 1918 around 1,000 people were registered with the Openshaw Employment Exchange as being unemployed. By January 1919 3,000 men were registered as unemployed in the district and 6,500 women. Around 50 per cent of the unemployed women were former cotton operatives who had become munition workers and now found themselves without work. As the numbers of demobilised men increased, the severity of the problem would grow.[15]

Various veterans associations were formed by early 1919 to represent the interests of the jobless ex-servicemen. The National Federation of Discharged and Demobilised Sailors and Soldiers (NFDDSS) was established in 1917 by London based veterans groups.[16] In 1919 its Manchester branch articulated the grievances of local veterans. In February it convened a public meeting at the Co-operative Hall, Downing Street, in Manchester. Several hundred men were reported to have attended. Mr Paley, vice president of the Manchester branch of the NFDDSS, forecast 'very grave trouble' ahead unless the needs of veterans were addressed.[17]

The *Manchester Guardian*'s leader writer, C.E. Montague, took a keen interest in the welfare of ex-servicemen. His editorials for the *Guardian*, from the time of his own demobilisation in 1919 until his retirement in 1925, give an insight into the difficulties being experienced by both returning ex-combatants and by the city that was taking them back. In March 1919 the *Guardian*'s editorial would be reflecting on a recent demonstration by the NFDDSS. 'A disposition to chafe is showing itself among a growing body of unemployed ex-sailors and soldiers in Manchester,' the paper's leader article began. It was now estimated that there were around 11,000 unemployed ex-servicemen in the Manchester district, around 6,000 of them being in receipt of the Out of Work Donation.[18] In a meeting with the Lord Mayor, a deputation from the NFDDSS articulated concern that employers were exploiting veterans' need to find work:

Many employers, it is said, welcome their former workmen back at the pre-war rate of wages 'What is the use of 45s. a week to me?' asked a demobilised man yesterday. 'It is not a living wage for a man with six children. I get 50s. out-of-

Year	Cloth exports – millions of yards	Year	Britain's share of worldwide cotton exports (%)
1913	7075	1829-31	70
1914	5736	1882-84	82
1915	4749	1910-13	58
1916	5254	1926-28	39
1917	4978	1936-38	28
1918	3699	1953-55	12
1919	3524		
1920	4435		
1921	3038		
1922	4313		
1923	4329		
1924	4585		
1925	4637		
1926	3923		
1927	4189		
1928	3968		
1929	3765		
1930	2491		
1939	1426		
1955	534		

Source: Lars G. Sandberg, *Lancashire in Decline: A Study in Entrepreneurship, Technology, and International Trade* (1974), pp. 4, 141, 176, 213.

work benefit for six months, and I will continue to draw it until something much better turns up.' That is a common attitude. The men have in mind the substantial wages earned by civilians during the war, and they have a feeling that theirs is the only labour which, apparently, has not gained in value.[19]

The pride of ex-servicemen was smarting. They clearly felt degraded and in some respects cheated by the country that they had fought for. This didn't feel like being treated fairly.

By August the Manchester papers were reporting that 'a grand route march' was being planned, from Manchester to London 'as a means of drawing attention to the lack of work'. The *Manchester Guardian* lamented that it was a 'depressing spectacle' that men who had fought for their country had reason to complain that 'they are not given a chance of earning a living in it'.[20]

'Peterloo, 1819: Labourloo, 1919'
In 1819 people had crowded onto St Peter's Field, Manchester, to hear the famed orator

Henry Hunt speak against the Corn Laws and in favour of political reform. The meeting had been progressing peaceably, but with so many people assembled (an estimated 60,000–80,000), the magistrates were afraid that there could be a disturbance. An arrest warrant was issued for Hunt and, in the panic that followed, the Yeomanry drew their swords and started to lash out at the surrounding crowds. There were fifteen lives lost, and of the 654 recorded casualties, at least 168 were women. The 'Peterloo Massacre' instantly became a sensation and it would cast a long shadow.

The centenary of Peterloo, in August 1919, focused thoughts on the defence of principles and on how the lot of the average Mancunian had changed over the past hundred years. Its commemoration was also a high profile event that provided a platform on which current grievances could be voiced.

'The battle still goes on,' the *Manchester Guardian* recorded, 'Saturday's demonstrators evidently see the situation to-day very clearly as a battle, and as nothing less. As much was said in a dozen speeches and written on no few banners.'[21] Among the slogans on those banners was: 'Peterloo, 1819: Labourloo, 1919'.

Before the public meeting, on Platt Fields, that had been convened to commemorate the anniversary, a procession moved through the streets of the Manchester. The piquancy of this spectacle was not lost on the watching journalists:

> With bands playing and banners flying, on foot or in waggonettes, men, women and children moved southwards down Peter Street. The red bonnet carried on a long pole that came at the head of the procession stopped when the demonstrators were ranged along the Prince's Theatre and the Free Trade Hall. Here, on the very ground where, a century before, the horror of Peterloo was at that moment being enacted, heads were bared and the 'Marseillaise' was sung, and 'We'll wave the scarlet banner high' went up from a thousand throats.[22]

The day also saw a mass meeting in the Free Trade Hall, convened by Manchester and Salford Independent Labour Party. Philip Snowdon, of the ILP, told the crowd, 'In 1914 your country needs you. In 1919 nobody wants you.'[23]

'Women dilutees'

A further source of ill feeling was female employment. Lancashire had for a long time bucked national norms in its mass employment of female labour. But even here, during the war years, employment opportunities for women would expand and change. It was not just a matter of the transition from textile work to munitions; by 1918 Manchester women were working in skilled occupations in engineering and manufacturing and as clerks in warehouses, banks and insurance companies. They were in commercial and professional roles and widely employed by the local authorities. They were clearly performing these roles proficiently and when, at the end of the war, employers did not see fit to terminate their service, this became a source of resentment to returning servicemen. This grievance surfaces again and again at meetings of veterans associations.

In April 1920 a committee representing the various veterans associations met with representatives of the Manchester Employers' Federation. At this meeting 'women dilutees' were identified as being responsible for the fact that disabled ex-servicemen were struggling to find employment. The figure of the down-on-his-luck ex-serviceman was an emotive symbol; but the disabled veteran was even more potent. Speakers at this meeting 'felt very strongly on this subject' and a resolution was unanimously passed 'urging that it was the sacred duty of all employers to reinstate their pre-war employees whether fit or disabled, and that female labour which could be carried out by the disabled ex-service men should be replaced.'[24]

'The promise is not quite fulfilled'
In September 1920 there were estimated to still be at least 3,000 unemployed ex-servicemen in Manchester. The *Manchester Guardian*'s C.E. Montague took the opportunity to remind employers of their pre-war promises:

> In the first months of the war we took it upon ourselves here to say things, in the name of all Manchester business men, which must have increased the assurance of many volunteers for the famous 'Pals' battalions that after the war they would not be left to walk the streets. There was no word of complaint then that we promised too much. But till each of those three thousand men has got at least the offer of a decent job the promise is not quite fulfilled.[25]

The situation was not to improve though over the next year. With recession beginning to bite, the 'Out of Work Donation' scheme would be extended again for ex-servicemen to March 1921. In November 1921 Edwin Stockton, President of Manchester Chamber of Commerce and Chairman of the 'Debt of Honour Committee', wrote to the *Manchester Guardian* warning that, at the third anniversary of the Armistice, 'vast numbers of the gallant men who achieved victory for us were in the most unhappy circumstances of employment and consequent deprivation'. And those unhappy circumstances seemed likely to develop into something challenging. Stockton went on:

> The ex-service men feel they have very special claims upon the community, and in view of the services they have rendered to humanity they do not consider their present position to constitute even justice, nor to speak of gratitude. This feeling of soreness may be a source of grave danger to the social structure of our country.[26]

There was clearly a very real sense that this 'soreness' could break out in dangerous directions. The government feared civil disorder. Between 1919 and 1921 Home Office correspondents monitored the major industrial centres and delivered secret 'Reports on Revolutionary Organisations'. Fear of the radicalisation of ex-servicemen was evidently prominent in the thinking of those tasked with assisting to find them employment in Manchester. In March 1922 a representative of the Labour Ministry's Appointments Department advised Manchester employers that every man given a job 'became a contented worker, and the nation could not afford to drive anyone into the Bolshevik ranks'.[27]

Other agencies were working to address and appease veterans' resentments too. In July 1921 the National Federation of Discharged and Demobilized Sailors and Soldiers merged with its rival National Association of Discharged Sailors and Soldiers, plus the more conservative Comrades of the Great War and the Officers' Association, forming the British Legion. While still energetically representing ex-servicemen's interests, with a particular focus on employment and pensions, and addressing their welfare issues, in this new guise the voice of veterans would lose its radical edge. The British Legion's first-stated principle was that it was 'democratic, non-sectarian, and non-Party politically'. The Legion was created to 'inaugurate and maintain comradeship' and to 'inculcate a sense of loyalty and service'.[28] Coinciding with Armistice Day 1921, a letter from the British Legion was published in the Manchester papers. It stated the organisation's aim: 'The British Legion exists as the league of brotherhood of all ex-servicemen, and we are pledged to make every sacrifice in our power to aid our less fortunate comrades.' In the winter of 1921 it was the immediate objective of the Legion to set up two feeding centres in Manchester. To that end, street collections were to be organised following Armistice Day and an appeal for gifts of food, clothing and boots was issued. The letter from the British Legion emphasised, though, that it could offer comradeship and companionship, not just emergency assistance for the destitute. 'Our centres are in effect poor men's clubs,' it explained, 'for last winter dozens of voluntary concerts were arranged in the dining halls in the cold evenings. It was a great benefit for men down and out to bring their wives to such cheery surroundings.'[29]

The first-stated objective of the British Legion, though, was to 'perpetuate the memory of those who died in the service of their country'.[30] With the British Legion as the veterans' mouthpiece there would also now be more focus on remembrance and commemoration.

'The spirit of memory'
In 1920 a report in the *Manchester Guardian* detailed how the city chose to commemorate 11 November. At the approach of 11.00 am a crowd packed into Albert Square, the newspaper noted, 'tiered itself up on monuments and anything that could be climbed, and was prolonged as far as one could see at every approach and in every window and on all the roofs'. With the last strike of the Town Hall clock, a bugle sounded and then silence descended. 'The effect upon the people was curious,' the newspaper observed:

> Everyone stood very still; no one sought his neighbour's eye or passed remark. The stress of movement had passed from the street and given way to the stress of emotion – emotion displayed awkwardly, perhaps, but deeply felt. The hush deepened. It had spread over the whole city and become so pronounced as to impress one with a sense of audibility. It was a silence which, in the words of an Italian poet, 'had its language and its prayers' – a silence which was almost pain. Market Street seemed to have become transfigured into a cathedral nave in which women and men were offering an unspoken devotion. And the spirit of memory brooded over it all.[31]

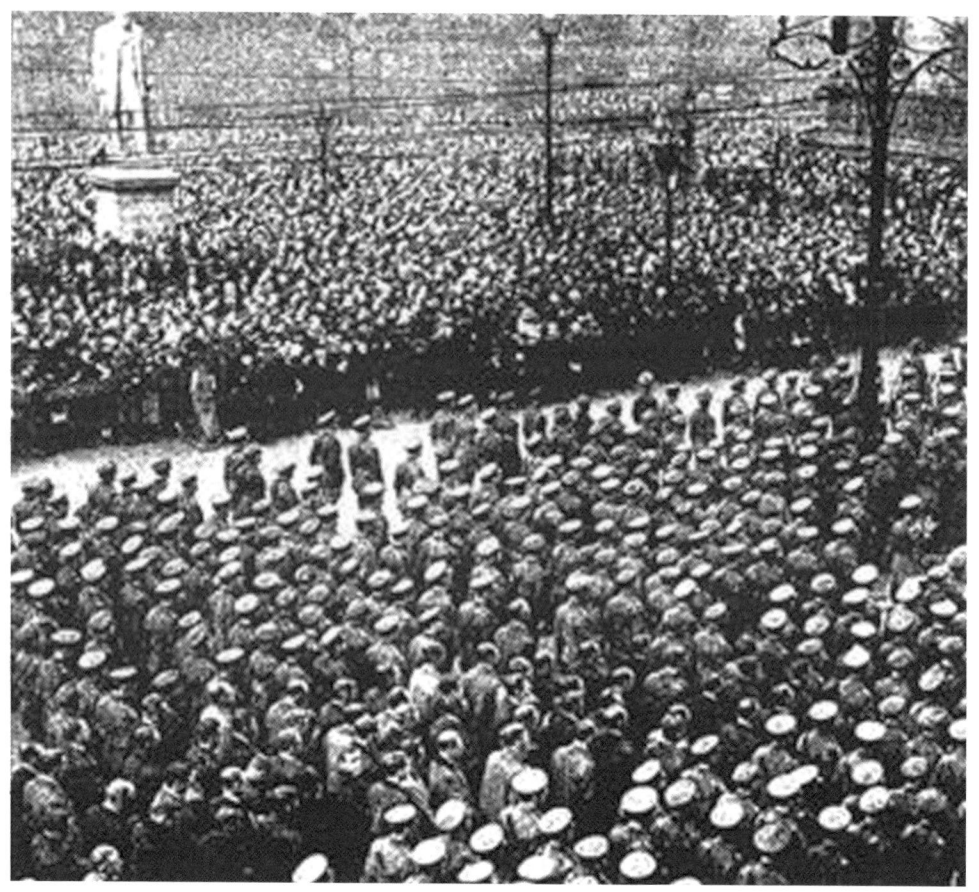

Armistice Day scene in Albert Square. *Manchester Guardian*, 12 November 1921.

After the service, the crowds cheered as the men of the Manchester battalions marched past. It was at this point that many women in the crowd wept, the *Guardian* observed – 'The marching tunes were so unbearably jolly'.

Though the service of remembrance was held in Albert Square, the two minutes silence was observed throughout Manchester:

> In the mills of Manchester there was the abrupt cessation of the whirr and din of the looms and the silence of the weaving sheds as men and women stopped work to think what might have been, and the quick resumption as if nothing had happened. In the municipal schools children and teachers stood in silence, with bowed heads and hands together . . . In public places of business, such as the General Post Office, there was the same curious effect, as of a clock being stopped and then, after a spell beginning again.[32]

Whatever the financial strains of the 1920s, and the disenchantment of the ex-servicemen, Armistice Day continued to be widely respected and participation was numerous. In 1922 it was estimated that 50,000 people observed the two minutes silence in central Manchester.[33]

'A permanent place of honour and remembrance'
After the Manchester battalions marched through Albert Square they moved on to St Ann's Square, where wreaths were laid on the South African War Memorial. 'The St. Ann's Square statue to the Manchesters who fell in the South African War is the only appropriate central position for this annual tribute,' the *Manchester Guardian* observed, 'and it is not unnaturally felt that the vastly greater sacrifice of 1914–18 deserves its own permanent place of honour and remembrance.'[34] This opinion was widely shared, it seems, but this aim would not be realised until 1924.

In November 1921 a letter was published in the Manchester papers, signed 'Lest we forget'. It asked: 'As Armistice Day draws near I would like again to inquire the reason why Manchester has not erected a city cenotaph in commemoration of its lives given and sacrificed?'[35] A response would be published from E.D. Simon, the Lord Mayor of Manchester. He stated that, as a result of the representations made to him 'by many sections of the community', he had brought the question of a memorial before the City Council.

In August 1922 a War Memorial Committee ('consisting of members of the City Council, together with representatives of different aspects of Manchester Business, of the

The South African war memorial in St Ann's Square, 1919. William Hamo Thorneycroft's 'The Last Shot', which had been dedicated in 1908, represents a soldier of the Manchester Regiment, a wounded comrade at his feet, standing with bayonet fixed.

military forces, and of other sections of Manchester life') was appointed to debate and advance the matter. In October it reported its decision that a 'suitable monument' should be erected 'on the best available site in Manchester', but at no greater cost than £10,000. As the memorial was to commemorate all of Manchester's lost – 'drawn from all sections of the community' – the Committee stated that it felt strongly that the memorial should 'be the gift not of a comparatively few individuals but of the city as a whole'. A public subscription was thus opened and it was emphasised that the smallest contributions would be welcomed.[36]

The scheme soon, however, began to be contentious. Both the question of the site and the question of design would be controversial. The Committee initially recommended that the memorial should be sited in Albert Square – the 'pivot' and 'first position of honour in the city'. It was proposed that all existing statuary be removed from the square, including the Albert Memorial, in order that the war memorial would be the one dominating feature. To that end, an approach had been made to the King who duly consented to the re-siting of the Albert Memorial.[37] The *Manchester Guardian*'s C.E. Montague applauded this bold plan – and the King's 'handsome assent' to it:

> If our common memorial were not as close to the city's very heart as the dead in the war remain to the hearts of the living, we all should feel that a false sense of values was disfiguring our streets. The site of the Albert Memorial is the only possible site, especially since the remarkable character and profound appeal of the annual service on Armistice Day have consecrated the square, at least for one day of each year, into a kind of memorial chapel.[38]

Not only was this the principal civic space in the city, this was the location where many men had volunteered their services for the Pals battalions and where they had paraded in front of Kitchener in 1915.

However not everyone was quite so convinced of the appropriateness of this site – or of the plan to remove the existing statues. By March 1923 letters were appearing in the Manchester papers articulating arguments against the choice of Albert Square and, throughout April, critics vociferously made their case. The volume and the tone of the letters, for and against, make it clear that this issue was provoking strong feelings. The arguments against the Albert Square site were on the basis of aesthetics (would the new memorial jar against the square's Gothic architecture?), precedent (if statues could so easily be removed, what was to stop a future generation doing away with the war memorial?) and cost (the city architect estimated that removing and re-siting the existing statues would cost around £8,400).[39]

Some of the parties objecting to the reconfiguring of Albert Square were influential people. When the City Council came to debate the issue, the arguments against moving the statues were loudly and apparently convincingly voiced. The council voted – by seventy-one votes to thirty – that Piccadilly would be a more appropriate site. The old Manchester Infirmary had just been demolished in Piccadilly and Manchester's Art

Albert Square, *c.* 1910.

Piccadilly, prior to the demolition of the old Manchester Royal Infirmary in 1909.

Gallery Committee supported the idea of the memorial being constructed in the open space thus created. The Council referred the matter back to the War Memorial Committee for further consideration.[40]

But, within a month, the Piccadilly proposal would be rejected too. The issue of what to do with the old infirmary site had been being debated since 1912 (should it remain an open space, or could an art gallery, a library or another public building be constructed on the site?), and it was still beset by disagreements. On 4 May the War Memorial Committee met and decided to recommend to the City Council that St Peter's Square should instead be the site of the memorial. This choice was duly endorsed by the Council on 17 May 1923.[41]

The suitability of the St Peter's Square site would continue to be questioned. Many felt that St Peter's Square was not quite right – it did not have the central status of Albert Square, it was slightly off-centre, already cluttered and felt crowded when people gathered there. It seemed like a second-best option. When the memorial was finally unveiled, in July 1924, the *Manchester Guardian*'s editorial would lament that 'The Unknown Warrior is the Defrauded Warrior too': 'Our Manchester war memorial has been given a secondary site in the city, the best one being still dedicated to the memory of an estimable German who had the good fortune to marry a young English queen . . . We have honoured our dead substantially but not surpassingly.[42]

The site was now fixed, but the controversy was not yet over. Next design of the memorial – and the method of its selection – was also to prove contentious. The initial plan was that the design should be selected by open competition. To that end, in June 1923, advertisements were placed inviting proposals. However, just a month later, this method of choosing a design was abandoned – due to, in the Lord Mayor's words, 'certain insuperable difficulties'. Argument seemed to have developed over who should have the final say over the design. A subcommittee was thus appointed instead and instructed to approach an artist 'who can be trusted to prepare a suitable design'. Another flurry of letters to the papers followed, debating how a decision on such a matter should be made, and expressing disappointment over the War Memorial Committee's seemingly arbitrary and arrogant stance.[43]

That architect chosen was Sir Edwin Lutyens, designer of the Whitehall cenotaph, and in September 1923 his proposed design was finally revealed in the Manchester newspaper.[44] Lutyen's Manchester cenotaph was to be built in Portland stone and would be described in the official dedication programme thus:

> The main feature consists of a pylon, rising to a height of 32 feet from the ground level, surrounded by a moulded and carved bier upon which is laid to rest the figure of a fighting man with equipment at his side and feet and a greatcoat thrown over the whole, conveying to those who stand below no individual identity and so in truth 'every mother's son'.

Its creator designed it with the aim of expressing, 'the triumphant end of the war as well as the sadness and sorrow it entailed'.[45]

The memorial was finally consecrated on 12 July 1924. The act of unveiling was carried out by Lord Derby and a Mrs. Bingle, 'a citizen of the working-class district of Ardwick, whose three sons were killed in the war'. When the red, white and blue drapery fell away, and the memorial was revealed for the first time, it seemed 'to offer itself to those in front as an imposing open-air temple, roofless and without walls, but none the less certainly entombing the great host of Manchester's dead'.[46] The most poignant and impressive moment, though, in the opinion of the *Manchester Guardian* journalist who observed the scene, was when the dignitaries stood aside and the bereaved families were allowed to place wreaths on the memorial:

> A stream of women flowed between the obelisks and covered the great expanse of stone with flowers. The crowd felt a quick sense of community with these mourners, and the flowers they left lying in the sunshine made together a brightness so vast and intense that it outshone in significance the glint of steel and brass and gold lace on the military background.[47]

Lord Derby then gave an address. The memorial was 'something more than a tribute to the dead', he said. His speech went on:

> 'It is an example, and at the same time a warning, to the living. It is an example in that it will show for all time that in her country's need Manchester came forward to do its part, and her citizens, counting not the cost, laid down their lives that we and those who come after us might live in a free country. It is a warning in that it will show to future generations yet unborn what the cost of war is, and will teach them that though they must always be prepared for war the very worst way of settling difficulties is by war.'[48]

Members of the Manchester battalions paraded and then, the official ceremony complete, the public were permitted to move towards the memorial. The number of people wanting to approach the cenotaph was so great that police had to marshal the queue. They would still be doing so at 10.00 pm. Thousands paid their respects.[49]

Lutyens designed a series of cenotaphs after the Whitehall model (in chronological order – Southampton, Rochdale, Derby and finally Manchester). On all of them a soldier rests at the top of the plinth. Manchester's soldier, the last in the series, differs from those that preceded him, though. While the others rest their heads on a wreath or cushion, and are draped in a cloak or shroud, Manchester's soldier is rather more authentically a soldier of the First World War. His head rests on a kitbag and he is covered with a trench coat. At his feet there is a rucksack and his helmet. There is less classicism and heroism to the styling of Manchester's soldier; he is more distinguishably a son of the city. 'Manchester comes into possession to-day of one of the few fine war memorials in the country,' the *Manchester Guardian* wrote.

The War Memorial, with wreaths, in the 1920s.

The subject would seem at first sight to leave the artist little scope; the recumbent figure, of a fighting man, all his equipment about him and an overcoat as a shroud. And yet, in this case, the general impression, for what it may be worth, is that Sir Edwin Lutyens has given a realistic effect, a nobly harmonious form. The overcoat, as it is flung over the figure, is first realistic and then, as if by a natural accident, beautiful.[50]

The first Armistice Day ceremony at the new War Memorial. *Manchester Guardian*, 12 November 1924.

In 1924 the crowds that gathered to honour the war dead on Armistice Day were reported to be bigger than ever before. 'Six years – in some cases even ten – have not given life, with all its insistent urgency, time enough to obliterate under vivid new impressions the sorrows that came of the war,' the *Manchester Guardian* reflected. The sight of the survivors too struck the journalist with sadness. Watching as the men of the Manchester Regiment marched past to wartime tunes, he recorded:

> These lively tunes had a special poignancy of their own. It was to these tunes that so many men had marched away. The appearance of many of the ex-servicemen yesterday was not such as to check emotion. Some of those who went by were crippled so badly that they hopped rather than marched in step; one assisted himself to the quick pace of his companions with a pair of crutches; and many more showed by unmistakeable signs that they had had no luck in their return to normal life.[51]

Disbanded battalions also continued to march together. A Pathé newsreel survives, from 1926, showing that year's Armistice Day Parade. Some thirty-odd men represent the 23rd Manchesters. Some tall men, possibly officers, lead the column and some are clearly the former Bantams. Some wear their medals. All of their eyes turn to salute the cenotaph. They walk behind a banner that reads '23rd Bantams'.

'Innumerable thousands' of people made their way, in the rain, to Albert Square to mark the tenth anniversary of the end of the war. Watching a newsreel of that day, it's the size of the crowds that pack the pavements and the long lines of men on crutches and in wheelchairs that are striking. After the silence, the rain falling more heavily now, the people watched the march-past. 'Company after company came the ex-servicemen,' the *Manchester Guardian* recorded:

> Grey-haired men, disabled now from physical smartness, hurried by with the lame and the injured; old uniforms mocked at the uneven array of hats and caps. Some companies passed the Cenotaph bare-headed, the water streaming off the brims of their hats; some saluted only in the manner of soldiers, their eyes upon the white pillar. For three-quarters of an hour the detachments turned into Oxford Street, and at the end of it the Bishop and the Lord Mayor led a company of soldiers and sailors and councillors to lay a wreath upon the Stone of Remembrance.[52]

George Barker gives a personal insight into what the Cenotaph meant to the Manchester men who had served, and lost friends, in France and Belgium. His recollections of his time with the 23rd Manchester Battalion finish with an account of walking through St Peter's Square, in the early hours of the morning, one day in 1928. Barker finds himself drawn towards the Cenotaph. He wrote:

> Past memories float through my brain. As I look upon the monument of stone, old sympathies are re-kindled. I am again in the trenches, happenings are going through my mind like a kaleidoscope working. Absent-mindedly I go forward and turn to

The march-past, 1928. *Manchester Guardian*, 12 November 1928.

my left, facing the coat of the warrior, and I seem to be glued to the ground. I look to my left, then to my right, and every time I turn my head I see hundreds of small lights, which gradually become larger, and in each of these appear familiar faces, nodding and smiling as if they want to be recognised. I can hear myself shouting 'Jim', 'Bill', 'George', and all manner of names known to me on the battlefields. They all seem to be a happy family, and I feel I want to be with them.[53]

The Pals battalions were still marching behind their banners after Manchester had been through another world war. A report of the Armistice Day parade of 1952 observed the lines of old soldiers: 'The pavement crowds between whom they passed seemed to have the habit of remembrance; they kept their warmest handclaps for the oldest and most reduced of the local Old Comrades' Associations, among them the indomitable handful of the 'Bantams'.'[54]

Postscript
In January 1921 the colours of the Pals battalions were deposited in Manchester Cathedral. It was an occasion of ceremony and display, of pride and also of mourning. Strong contingents of the battalions marched alongside as the flags were carried through the streets of the city. The Lord Mayor gave an address to the men, speaking of the need 'for preserving the spirit of comradeship which had carried them through the trials of war'. As the colours were received by the Dean, the congregation in the cathedral sang: 'Clear before us through the darkness/Gleams and burns the guiding light:/Brother clasps the hand of brother,/Stepping fearless through the night.'[55]

In 1936 the Derby Chapel in Manchester Cathedral was re-dedicated as the chapel of the Manchester Regiment. An appeal had funded the printing of memorial books, in which the names of the 14,209 dead of the Manchester Regiment were recorded, and the carving of a shrine to house them. The carvings on the shrine worked together the Lancashire rose and the Flanders poppy.

The chapel was dedicated on 11 November 1936. The cathedral was packed with members and former members, of the Manchester Regiment. It was a day of great pageantry and solemnity. A *Manchester Guardian* journalist attending the ceremony wrote that it was like a scene from Thomas Hardy's *Dynasts*, the atmosphere 'charged with the stuff of which many a scene in the great epic-drama is made'.[56]

The drama, though, was not yet over.

In the early hours of the morning of 23 December 1940 there was an air raid on Manchester. A bomb fell on the cathedral. The Regimental Chapel took a direct hit. The damage was sufficient that the chapel would have to be substantially rebuilt. Another public appeal was then launched, this time to fund the restoration work. It was initially estimated that it would take five years to repair the damage, but ultimately it would be another decade before work was complete.

The Chapel of the Manchester Regiment was rededicated in November 1951 in a service attended by the Queen. Veterans of both world wars then filled the cathedral. During the dedication service the Queen ceremoniously turned the pages of the new Rolls of Honour. The Last Post was sounded and, after a prayer, Reveille. The Dean, in his address, spoke about sacrifice and memory. '"Do not forget," he concluded, "because they do not forget you, but keep fresh their memory in gratitude."'[57]

The Manchester Regiment chapel, *Manchester Guardian*, 12 November 1936.

Notes

Introduction
1. MS Letters of Eustace Lockhart Maxwell, NAM 1974-02-34-30. The letters of the Maxwell family are reproduced here with the kind permission of the National Army Museum.
2. Quotation from 'The Bantam Soldiers' Ditty', a poem published in the *Morecambe Visitor*, 20 January 1915. Percy Gidley's letter was published in the *Morecambe Visitor* on 13 October 1915. As the Bantams moved on (to Masham, Salisbury Plain and eventually France) Gidley continued to correspond regularly with the paper. All quotations from the *Morecambe Visitor* are reproduced with the kind permission of *The Visitor* (Johnston Press plc).
3. MS Letters of Eustace Lockhart Maxwell, NAM 1974-02-34-31.
4. Diary entries for 20 July 1916 from Major General Reginald John Pinney's Army Book, No. 3. Diaries and papers, IWM Collection 66/257/1. Extracts from Major General Pinney's army diaries are reproduced with the kind permission of Philip Pinney.
5. Both quotes are from articles written by the journalist Philip Gibbs, who took continuing interest in the Bantam battalions. See *Daily Chronicle*, 19 June 1916 and Philip Gibbs, *Now It Can Be Told* (1920), p. 404.
6. Quotation from 'The Bantam Soldiers' Ditty'.

Chapter 1
1. *Manchester Evening News*, 29 June 1914. All images and quotations are reproduced with the kind permission of the *Manchester Evening News*. In her Almanac for 1914, Madame de Thebes predicted the outbreak of a war – detailing that German troops would approach Paris, but not enter it. Several regional papers picked up and publicised these 'prophecies' over the course of 1914. She also forecast that the Kaiser would die on 29 September 1914.
2. *Manchester Courier*, 9 January 1914. The article went on: 'In spite of increased competition, we are still unapproachable in the production of cotton cloth, nor is there any genuine reason to suppose that we are even now nearing the limits of expansion.'
3. Lars G. Sandberg, *Lancashire in Decline: A Study in Entrepreneurship, Technology, and International Trade* (1974), p. 3.
4. *Ibid.*, pp. 141, 142, 167.
5. This interview was printed in the *Manchester Courier* and *Manchester Guardian*, 9 July 1914.
6. See *Manchester Courier*, 8 July 1914. Going on to short-time was the traditional way that Lancashire textile manufacturers responded to a downturn in demand. The strategy was normally supported by employers and trade unions and respected throughout the

industry. Cotton spinning factories had gone onto short-time in 1900, 1903, 1904 and 1910.
7. *Manchester Guardian*, 1 August 1914. Quotations from the *Manchester Guardian* are reproduced with the kind permission of Guardian News & Media Ltd.
8. *Manchester Evening News*, 27 and 28 July 1914.
9. Under Scott's ownership the *Guardian* had rediscovered something of its radical roots. By 1914 it was firmly leaning towards the Liberal left, campaigning for social reform and espousing causes such as women's suffrage, Irish Home Rule and firmly opposing the Boer War (a stance that made a considerable dent in its circulation figures).
10. The *Manchester Guardian*'s non-interventionist argument ran thus: 'We wish Servia no ill; we are anxious for the peace of Europe. But Englishmen are not the guardians of Servian well-being, or even of the peace of Europe. Their first duty is to England and to the peace of England. Let us for a moment drop solicitude for Europe and think of ourselves. We ought to feel ourselves out of danger, for, whichever way the quarrel between Austria and Servia were settled, it would not make a scrap of difference to England. We care as little for Belgrade as Belgrade does for Manchester.' See *Manchester Guardian*, 30 July 1914.
11. The *Manchester Guardian*'s editorials were severely critical of the stance of *The Times*, which had advocated that if Russia came out in support of Serbia, forcing Germany and France into war, 'we must strike as one man'. *The Times* argued that, in the interests of 'fair play', Britain would be compelled to become involved. 'This is mediation with shirt-sleeves rolled up,' said the *Guardian*. See *Manchester Guardian*, 28, 30 and 31 July 1914.
12. *Ibid.*, 31 July 1914.
13. *Ibid.*, 31 July 1914.
14. *Ibid.*, 1 August 1914.
15. *Manchester Evening News*, 31 July 1914.
16. *Manchester Guardian*, 3 August 1914.
17. *Manchester Evening News*, 3 August 1914.
18. *Manchester Guardian*, 3 August 1914.
19. *Ibid.*, 4 August 1914.
20. *Ibid.*, 5 August 1914; *Manchester Courier*, 5 August 1914.
21. On 5 August full-page advertisements for the Neutrality League appeared in the Manchester papers. These appealed to Englishmen to 'DO YOUR DUTY and keep your Country out of A WICKED and STUPID WAR. Small but powerful cliques are trying to rush you into it; you must DESTROY THE PLOT TO-DAY or it will be too late.' The Neutrality League urged the public to write to their local newspapers and MPs, to organise protest meetings, to demand that their trade unions pass resolutions and to encourage their religious ministers to take a firm stance. Signatories of the League's manifesto included, among others, the Lord Mayor of Manchester and C.P. Scott. The Neutrality League had been established, in late July 1914 by pacifism proponent Norman Angell. Angell had been arguing for several years (with the moral and financial support of the Conservative Garton Foundation) that war with other industrialised nations could not be

in Britain's economic interest. The League contested that there was 'no reason to suppose' that Germany would attempt to annex any part of Belgium, fearing rather the influence that a European war would give Russia: 'If we took sides with Russia and France, the balance of power would be upset as it has never been before. It would make the military Russian Empire of 160,000,000 the dominant Power of Europe. You know what kind of country Russia is.' The Neutrality League disbanded on 5 August 1914. In its short existence it spent nearly £1,300 on advertising. See *Manchester Guardian*, 3, 5 and 8 August 1914; *Manchester Courier*, 5 August 1914; *Manchester Evening News*, 5 August 1914.

22. *Manchester Courier*, 5 August 1914.
23. *Manchester Evening News*, 3 August 1914; *Manchester Guardian*, 3, 4 and 5 August 1914.
24. *Manchester Courier*, 5 August 1914.
25. *Manchester Guardian*, 5 August 1914; Robert Roberts, *The Classic Slum: Salford Life in the First Quarter of the Century* (1971), p. 186.
26. *Manchester Courier*, 5 August 1914.
27. *Ibid.*
28. *Ibid.*
29. *Manchester Guardian*, 6 August 1914.
30. Roberts, *The Classic Slum*, p. 187.
31. See *Manchester Evening News*, 3 August 1914; *Manchester Guardian*, 3 and 4 August 1914. These reader letters also loudly express Liberal England's repugnance for Russia. It was perceived as an autocratic regime, a persecutor of democrats. Good Liberals could not stomach the idea of fighting on the same side as the Czar. One correspondent wrote: 'It is unthinkable that we should be plunged into war to assist that priest-ridden, monk-ridden autocratic reactionary despot who, more than any other, has brought about this calamity of a European War'. There was a prevalent opinion that Russia wished to use a European war to seize Persia and convert it into a Russian province. This was then perceived as a threat to India. Russia is seen as the oppressive 'other', far more of a natural foe than our German cousins with whom we can do business. The papers also carried letters from representatives of the churches. Prayers for peace had been offered in Manchester's churches in the first week of August – and resolutions had issued from them, urging the government to retain a neutral stance. At Manchester Cathedral the Dean had taken the sermon on 2 August. 'Let us pray that we may not be drawn into a conflict which is properly no affair of ours,' he had preached.
32. *Manchester Guardian*, 4 August 1914. The *Manchester Courier* took a similar tone. 'If the interference should continue for a prolonged period we may once more have conditions in Lancashire resembling those of the Cotton Famine,' it warned on 5 August.
33. *Manchester Guardian*, 4 August 1914.
34. *Ibid.*, 5 August 1914; *Manchester Courier*, 7 August 1914.
35. *Manchester Courier*, 8 August 1914.
36. *Manchester Guardian*, 5 August 1914. 'A little more knowledge, a little more time on this side, more patience, and a sounder political principle on the other side would have

saved us from the greatest calamity that anyone living has known. It will be a war in which we risk almost everything of which we are proud, and in which we stand to gain nothing,' Scott wrote. 'Some day we shall all regret it.' The article goes on to predict that the war would be over 'in two months or three months at the outside'.

37. *Manchester Courier*, 22 September 1914.

38. C.E. Montague, *Disenchantment* (1940), p. 109. Recruited by C.P. Scott to write for the *Manchester Guardian* in 1890, C.E. Montague effectively became the paper's editor. He also married Scott's daughter in 1898. Though he had argued against Britain becoming involved in the conflict, and despite the fact that he was aged 47 in 1914, Montague would shortly enlist. He dyed his white hair black in order to convince the army to take him, prompting fellow journalist H.W. Nevinson to comment: 'Montague is the only man I know whose white hair in a single night turned dark through courage'. He would serve as a private in the front line and, from July 1916, after having been injured, was an officer in GHQ's Intelligence Department, where his responsibilities included escorting VIPs visiting the battlefields. Montague published his reflections on the conflict, *Disenchantment*, in 1922.

39. *Manchester Guardian*, 26 August 1914.

40. *Ibid.*, 23 September 1914.

41. *Manchester Courier*, 26 September 1914.

42. *Ibid.*, 29 September 1914.

43. *Ibid.*, 4 September 1914.

44. The *Manchester Courier* of 1 August 1914 estimated there to be 4,000 Germans living in Manchester and its surrounding towns.

45. *Manchester Courier*, 4 August 1914.

46. Roberts, *The Classic Slum*, p. 181.

47. *Manchester Courier*, 4 August 1914.

48. *Manchester Guardian*, 8 August 1914.

49. *Manchester Courier*, 13 and 18 August 1914. 'The penalties for any breach of the Order or of the regulations made under it are immediate arrest without warrant, a fine of £100, and six months imprisonment with hard labour,' recorded the *Manchester Guardian*, 13 August 1914.

50. *Manchester Courier*, 4 September 1914; *Manchester Guardian*, 4 September 1914; *Manchester Evening News*, 5 September 1914.

51. *Manchester Guardian*, 5 September 1914. The *Guardian* (9 September 1914) made some objection to the use of manacles: 'Considering the strength of the escort, and the futility of any attempt to escape, the need for this was not obvious. It should be borne in mind that these men are untried, that they are arrested on suspicion at the discretion of the Chief Constable, and that, though there may be good ground for their detention, there is none for degrading them.'

52. *Manchester Guardian*, 10, 11, 12 and 14 September 1914.

53. *Manchester Courier*, 30 September 1914.

54. *Manchester Courier*, 12 May 1915. Of the twenty-one defendants who appeared before Manchester City Police Court on 12 May, thirteen were women. For more details

see Panikos Panayi, 'The Lancashire Anti-German Riots of May 1915', *Manchester Region History Review II*, no. 2 (1988/9).

55. The phrase is taken from a leaflet canvassing for recruits that was issued in Manchester in November 1915, Cited in the *Manchester Courier*, 15 November 1915.

56. *Manchester Guardian*, 17 August 1914.

57. *Ibid.*, 27 August 1914. Not all shared the enthusiasm to enlist, though. Recalling the first week of the war, Albert Hurst, later of the 17th Manchesters, remembered the general attitude of his work colleagues: 'They thought that anybody that joined up was a bloody fool!' (IWM interviews, Albert Hurst, catalogue number 11582).

58. *Manchester Evening News*, 21 August and 1 December 1914.

59. Roberts, *The Classic Slum*, p. 189.

60. Winnie went on: 'The dear lad was always cheering us up. 'They'll never take you,' my Dad said, 'You're not the height of two-penny-worth of coppers!' But he was big enough for the Bantams, and lay dead in France less than two years later.' Quoted in Sidney Allinson, *The Bantams* (2009), p. 28.

61. *Manchester Evening News*, 28 August 1914.

62. There is an assumption implicit in these terms that the war would not be of long duration. *Manchester Evening News*, 26 August 1914; *Manchester Guardian*, 27 August 1914.

63. *Manchester Evening News*, 28 August 1914.

64. *Manchester Courier*, 28 August 1914.

65. In Manchester the 'Pals' battalions were also to be variously referred to as the 'Chums' and the 'City's Own' battalions. *Manchester Evening News*, 2 September 1914.

66. *Manchester Guardian*, 31 August 1914.

67. *Manchester Evening News*, 29 August 1914.

68. *Manchester City Battalions' Book of Honour* (1916), p. xiv. All quotations from the *Book of Honour* are reproduced with the kind permission of the Manchester & Lancashire Family History Society. The reports in the local papers note some frustration among those queuing to enlist. Clearly the authorities had underestimated the appeal of the Pals battalion and were significantly overwhelmed. 'The irritation caused among those who offered themselves for enlistment by the delays and what looked like the rebuffs arising from the inadequacy of the recruiting staff found emphatic expression yesterday. Men who had been appealed to by huge advertisements in the papers, by their employers, and by public speeches to come to the aid of their country were surprised to find that their endeavour to respond to the appeal was met with apparent indifference. They were kept waiting in queues in a narrow street outside the artillery depot in Hyde Road for half a day and longer, only to be told at the end that they could not be seen till the morrow. And on the morrow the process was repeated . . . Patience broke down upon the strain. Early in the afternoon it was decided to form a massed deputation to the Lord Mayor. About 600 men marched to the Town Hall to demand a redress of their grievances.' *Manchester Guardian*, 1 September 1914.

69. *Manchester Courier*, 2 and 3 September 1914; *Manchester Guardian*, 3 September 1914. *Manchester City Battalions' Book of Honour*, p. xv.

70. *Manchester Courier*, 11 September 1914.
71. *Manchester Guardian*, 9 September 1914.
72. *Ibid.*, 15 and 21 September 1914. It should be noted that in 1914 the average Englishman had a height of 5ft 6in, a chest girth of 36.5in and weighed 10st 10lb. See Journal of the Royal Sanitary Institution, Volume XXXVI, No. 3, April 1915, p. 106.
73. *Manchester Courier*, 14 November 1914.
74. *Manchester Evening News*, 13 November 1914.
75. To the *Manchester Guardian* these patriotism measuring 'devices' were 'Recruiting thermometers'.
76. *Manchester Evening News*, 13 November 1914.
77. *Manchester Courier*, 23 November 1914.
78. *Ibid.*

Chapter 2

1. *Manchester Courier*, 24 April 1915.
2. *Manchester Evening News*, 21 August 1914.
3. *Ibid.*, 7 September 1914.
4. *Ibid.*, 6 November 1914.
5. *Manchester Courier*, 17 November 1914. F.E. Smith MP, later 1st Earl of Birkenhead, was a lawyer and politician. In 1914 he was in charge of the Government Press Bureau with responsibility for newspaper censorship. Alfred Hopkinson, formerly Vice Chancellor of the University of Manchester, was on the Committee on Alleged German Outrages in Belgium.
6. H.M. Davson, *The History of the 35th Division in the Great War* (1926), p. 1.
7. *Manchester Guardian*, 20 November 1914.
8. *Ibid.*
9. *Manchester Evening News*, 23 and 24 November 1914.
10. *Manchester Guardian*, 25 November 1914; *Manchester Evening News*, 25 November 1914; *Manchester Courier*, 25 and 26 November 1914; *Manchester Evening News*, 5 December 1914.
11. *Manchester Evening News*, 26 November 1914. There are repeated indications in the local press that the men objected to the term 'Bantam'. They preferred to be called 'Bobs' Own'.
12. *Manchester Evening News*, 27 November 1914; *Manchester Courier*, 27 November 1914.
13. *Manchester Guardian*, 27 November 1914.
14. *Manchester Courier*, 28 November 1914; *Manchester Evening News*, 28 November 1914; *Manchester Guardian*, 28 November 1914.
15. *British Medical Journal*, 28 November 1914.
16. *Manchester Courier*, 30 November 1914; *Manchester Evening News*, 30 November 1914.
17. *Manchester Courier*, 2 December 1914; *Manchester Evening News*, 1, 2 and 3 December 1914; *Manchester Guardian*, 3 December 1914.

18. *Manchester Courier*, 4 December 1914; *Manchester Guardian*, 4 December 1914. Recruiting was completed for the reserve company of the 8th City Battalion in early January 1915.
19. *Manchester Courier*, 5 December 1914.
20. *Morecambe Visitor*, 4 and 25 November, 9, 16 and 23 December 1914. It was reported, at the start of November, that Lord Derby had been in communication with the War Office on Morecambe's behalf, 'but there was no chance for Morecambe as there were not local facilities, as at Southport, for training a division'.
21. *Manchester Evening News*, 30 December 1914. The 20th and 21st Battalions headed to Morecambe on 30 December, with the 22nd and 23rd following on 2 January 1915.
22. *Manchester Guardian*, 4 January 1915.
23. *Manchester Evening News*, 2 January 1915.
24. *Ibid.*, 2 January 1915.

Chapter 3

1. *Manchester Guardian*, 5 January 1915.
2. *Morecambe Visitor*, 23 December 1914.
3. *Ibid.*, 30 December 1914, 6 January 1915.
4. *Ibid.*, 30 December 1914, 6 and 20 January 1915.
5. *Manchester Evening News*, 14 and 30 December 1914; *Manchester Guardian*, 5 January 1915.
6. *Manchester Guardian*, 5 January 1915.
7. *Manchester Evening News*, 30 December 1914.
8. *Morecambe Visitor*, 30 December 1914; *Manchester Courier*, 2 January 1915; *Manchester Guardian*, 5 January 1915.
9. *Manchester Guardian*, 5 January 1915.
10. *Manchester Evening News*, 30 December 1914 and 10 February 1915; *Manchester Courier*, 2 January 1915; *Manchester Guardian*, 5 January 1915. The 91st Brigade's billeting in Morecambe evidently made it something of an attraction, according to a *Manchester Guardian* report of 13 January 1915. The reserve companies were at this time being recruited and the figures seemed to demonstrate that 'preference was again shown for the battalions which are training at Morecambe, and apparently the nearness of Heaton Park to the homes of the men is not regarded as an advantage great enough to counterbalance the attractions of the seaside . . . The four battalions in the watering-place only need 201 men now, while 853 are wanted for those in Manchester.'
11. *Manchester Courier*, 2 January 1915.
12. *Morecambe Visitor*, 30 December 1914.
13. *Manchester Evening News*, 10 February 1915. C.E. Montague, of the *Manchester Guardian*, commented on the 'immense simplification' that civilian men's lives underwent when they became soldiers. This 'second boyhood' – and its accompanying removal of responsibilities – had its attractions. 'All his maturity's worries and burdens seemed, by some magical change, to have dropped from him; no difficult choices had to be made any longer; hardly a moral chart to be conned; no one had any finances to mind;

nobody else's fate was put in his hands, and not even his own. All was fixed from above, down to the time of his going to bed and the way he must lace up his boots. His vow of willing self-enslavement for a season had brought him the peace of the soldier.' Montague, *Disenchantment*, p. 17.
14. *Morecambe Visitor*, 20 January 1915.
15. *Ibid*., 6 January 1915.
16. *Manchester Evening News*, 10 February 1915.
17. *Manchester Guardian*, 5 January 1915. C.E. Montague of the *Manchester Guardian* later observed, 'Drill, to the average recruit, was like some curious game or new dance, various and rhythmic, and not very hard: it was rather fun for adults to be able to play at such things without being laughed at.' Montague, *Disenchantment*, pp. 14–15.
18. *Morecambe Visitor*, 6 January 1915.
19. *Ibid*., 23 December 1914.
20. *Ibid*., 24 February 1915.
21. Fields at Bare and Torrisholme were made available to the Brigade on the proviso that 'no entrenching will be carried out on the land'. *Morecambe Visitor*, 23 December 1914 and 24 February 1915.
22. *Morecambe Visitor*, 28 April and 6 May 1915.
23. *Manchester Guardian*, 5 January 1915.
24. *Morecambe Visitor*, 21 April 1915.
25. *Manchester Guardian*, 13 March 1915; *Manchester Evening News*, 12 March 1915.
26. *Manchester Evening News*, 10 February 1915.
27. *Morecambe Visitor*, 6 January 1915. The *Manchester Evening News*, 6 January 1915, noted that footballs were being sent to the men in Morecambe. 'One of the Morecambe battalions had a slice of luck the other day. They made a request from a member of the committee for forty footballs. By accident the order was duplicated, and they got eighty.'
28. *Manchester Evening News*, 8 March 1915.
29. *Ibid*., 8 April 1915; *Morecambe Visitor*, 14 April 1915.
30. *Morecambe Visitor*, 14 April 1915.
31. *Ibid*., 23 December 1914 and 5 May 1915.
32. In January 1915 the local paper reported that 130 men had signed up for Monsieur Ménétrière's French evening classes ('the fee is very low – 1d per session'), held weekly in the Soldiers' Institute at the Green Street Wesleyan School. In February 100 more were attending the YMCA's free classes in conversational French. *Ibid*., 20 January and 24 February 1915.
33. *Ibid*., 10 February 1915. Lieutenant Bertram Noble, from Blackburn, transferred to the 16th Lancashire Fusiliers prior to being posted to France in March 1916. Having come through the Somme, Lieutenant Noble drowned while swimming in the sea off Hardelot Plage in August 1916.
34. *Ibid*., 28 April 1915.
35. It is not clear whether Gidley ceased to write them after that date – or whether the paper chose to stop publishing his poems. Percy Gidley's medal card indicates that he later transferred from the Manchesters to the Tank Corps.

36. *Manchester Evening News*, 10 February 1915.
37. *Morecambe Visitor*, 10 February 1915.
38. At the Quarter Sessions, Edward Hanson, a printer from Manchester and a private in the 23rd Battalion, pleaded guilty. He was sentenced to three months' hard labour. *Ibid.*, 10 March and 7 April 1915.
39. *Ibid.*, 10 February 1915.
40. IWM interview with W. Hunt. Catalogue number 24873.
41. *Morecambe Visitor*, 5 April 1915.
42. *Manchester Evening News*, 10 February 1915.
43. *Manchester Evening News*, 9 and 30 December 1914 and 25 January 1915; *London Gazette*, 10 December 1912.
44. *Manchester Guardian*, 3 February 1915; *Manchester Courier*, 2 February 1915; *Manchester Evening News*, 25 January 1915.
45. *Morecambe Visitor*, 6 January 1915.
46. *Manchester Courier*, 20 March 1915.
47. IWM interviews. Catalogue number 24873.
48. *Manchester Guardian*, 19 September 1914; *Manchester Evening News*, 12 February 1915; *Manchester Courier*, 22 March 1915. In terms of the army providing work for the textile industry, some specialist areas found advantages; companies that could make webbing for belts, bandoliers and linings were suddenly doing well. Apart from these small specialist areas, though, there were few knock-on benefits for Lancashire's cotton trade.
49. *Manchester Courier*, 22 March 1915.
50. *Manchester Guardian*, 22 March 1915.
51. *Ibid.*, 22 March 1915.
52. *Manchester Evening News*, 22 March 1915.
53. Sidney Allinson, *The Bantams* (2009), p. 68.
54. *Manchester Evening News*, 22 March 1915. The song, 'I Do Like A S'nice S'mince S'pie' is everywhere in 1915, and seems to have been a particular favourite among the Manchesters, who are also reported as singing it in Morecambe.
55. *Manchester Guardian*, 22 March 1915.
56. *Ibid.*, 15 April 1915.
57. *Manchester Evening News*, 16 March 1915.
58. *Ibid.*, 4 May 1915; *Manchester Courier*, 5 May 1915.
59. *Morecambe Visitor*, 28 April and 5 May 1915.
60. See letters and notes in the Imperial War Museum's Bernard Law Montgomery Archive: IWM, BLM 1/28, 1/29 and 1/30. The citation for the DSO, published in the *London Gazette* in December 1914, reads: 'Conspicuous gallant leading on 13th October, when he turned the enemy out of their trenches with the bayonet. He was severely wounded.' He was actually shot through the right lung. His injuries were sufficiently serious that a grave was dug for him. He spent two months in the Herbert Hospital, Woolwich. Montgomery's letters are reproduced with the kind permission of the Imperial War Museums.

61. IWM, BLM 1/30 and 1/32. The 112th Brigade was originally established in January 1915 and, at that time, comprised the 11th East Lancashires, the 11th South Lancashires, the 24th Manchesters and the 17th Lancashire Fusiliers. It was headquartered at the King's Hotel, Oxford Road, Manchester. The original Brigade Major was Major J.A. Nixon, but having been badly wounded in the early months of the war, he was replaced by Montgomery. The 112th Brigade carried out some initial training in north Wales, but in March 1915 it was broken up and its battalions reallocated. Brigade HQ were then ordered to Chester and informed that they were to be reconstituted as a Bantam brigade.
62. IWM, BLM 1/30.
63. IWM, BLM 1/31.
64. *Morecambe Visitor*, 26 May and 2 June 1915.
65. *Manchester Evening News*, 21 June 1915.
66. *Morecambe Visitor*, 7 July and 13 October 1915.
67. *Ibid.*, 20 January 1915.
68. *Burnley Express*, 11 August 1915; *Burnley News*, 18 August 1915.
69. MS Letters of Eustace Lockhart Maxwell, NAM 1974-02-34-18.
70. Davson, *The History of the 35th Division in the Great War* (1926), p. 5.
71. Interview with John Duffield, Catalogue number 4411, IWM.
72. Diary entries for 28 June 1915 from Pinney's Army Diary, No 2. Private papers of Major General Sir Reginald Pinney, IWM 66/257/1.
73. IWM, BLM 1/32.
74. *Morecambe Visitor*, 1 September 1915.
75. *Ibid.*
76. *Manchester Courier*, 11 December 1915.
77. Montague, *Disenchantment*, p. 84.
78. Interview with John Duffield, Catalogue number 4411, IWM.
79. Conscientious objectors were sent to Parkhouse later in the war, employed there making mailbags. Through 1917 the camp would variously be used as a depot for the Australian Imperial Force and as a Convalescent Training Depot for soldiers with syphilis and gonorrhoea. After the war the site became derelict and local children played in the practice trenches that had been dug by the troops. Most of the structures on the site had been demolished by 1923.
80. *Manchester Evening News*, 10 February 1915.

Chapter 4

1. *Manchester Evening News*, 29 January 1916.
2. The steamer seems likely to have been *Mona's Queen*. Launched in 1885, she was sailing the route between Fleetwood and Douglas in 1914. Continuing her troop carrying duties until the end of the war, she was returned to the Steam Packet Company in 1920 and remained in service until 1929.
3. Interview with John Duffield, Catalogue number 4411, IWM.
4. *Ibid.*
5. The area that HMS *Viking* entered was known by the French to contain a German

minefield. But *Viking*'s charts were not accurately marked. The destroyer was towed cautiously back to port. It was eventually repaired and its duties as part of the cross channel patrol continued until the end of the war.

6. Interview with John Duffield, Catalogue number 4411, IWM.
7. *Morecambe Visitor*, 16 February 1916.
8. IWM, BLM 1/34.
9. MS Letters of Eustace Lockhart Maxwell, NAM 1974-02-34-24. Maxwell was a Major with fellow Bantam battalion the 19th Durham Light Infantry in February 1916.
10. Davson, *The History of the 35th Division*, p. 9.
11. IWM, BLM 1/35.
12. Diary entries for 11 February 1916 from Major General Reginald John Pinney's Army Book, number 3. Diaries and papers, IWM Collection 66/257/1.
13. Edmund Blunden, *Undertones of War* (1928), p. 9.
14. Quoted from J.W. Sandilands, *A Lancashire Brigade in France* (1919), p. 9.
15. Blunden, *Undertones of War*, pp. 36–7.
16. Sandilands, *A Lancashire Brigade in France*, p. 10. According to Sandilands, reports of 'crowing' circulated but 'the accuracy of this statement was never verified'.
17. W Company was assigned to the 10th (1st Rhondda) Welsh Regiment, X Company to the 13th (2nd Rhondda) Battalion, Y Company to the 14th (Swansea) Battalion and Z Company to the 15th (Carmarthenshire) Battalion, all service battalions, and part of the 38th Division's 114th Infantry Brigade. See 'Account of the 23rd (Service) Battalion's service in France and Flanders' (typescript), MR1/3/1/49, Tameside Local Studies and Archives.
18. Though he was the first man to die on active service, Martin Cunningham was actually the 23rd Battalion's sixth bereavement; Charles Ferguson died in January 1915 and is buried in Manchester Southern Cemetery. James Riley, Peter Bowen and Ralph Smith all died while the battalion was training in Morecambe, respectively in January, March and May 1915. All three are buried in Torrisholme Cemetery. Robert Wilson died in Manchester in November 1915 and is buried in Gorton Cemetery. All of the men who died during the battalion's training period have CWGC headstones.
19. *Manchester Evening News*, 16 March 1915 and 6 March 1916; *Aberdeen Journal*, 6 March 1916.
20. MS Letters of Eustace Lockhart Maxwell, NAM 1974-02-34-24. Steel helmets had first appeared in the French army during the spring of 1915. The French design, resembling the helmet of the *sapeur-pompier*, is attributed to Intendant-General August-Louis Adrian – and hence was called the 'Casque Adrian'. Britain's War Office Invention Department was ordered to assess the French design and to develop a British equivalent. A design patented in 1915, by John Leopold Brodie of London, stronger than the French equivalent and more straightforward to manufacture, was ultimately adopted.
21. *Nottingham Evening Post*, 7 March 1916; *Manchester Evening News*, 17 March 1916.
22. *Manchester Evening News*, 30 March 1916.

Chapter 5

1. Davson, *The History of the 35th Division*, p. 12.
2. IWM, BLM 1/38.
3. Montague, *Disenchantment*, p. 49.
4. IWM, BLM 1/39.
5. Interview with John Duffield, Catalogue number 4411, IWM.
6. Davson, *The History of the 35th Division*, p. 14.
7. Diary entries for 24 March and 2 April 1916 from Major General Reginald John Pinney's Army Book, number 3. Diaries and papers, IWM Collection 66/257/1.
8. IWM, BLM 1/40.
9. Montague, *Disenchantment*, p. 71.
10. MS Letters of Eustace Lockhart Maxwell, NAM 1974-02-34-28.
11. Diary entry for 1 April 1916 from Major General Reginald John Pinney's Army Book, number 3. Diaries and papers, IWM Collection 66/257/1.
12. IWM, BLM 1/40.
13. IWM, BLM 1/41.
14. Davson's *The History of the 35th Division*, p. 15.
15. IWM, BLM 1/41.
16. Sandilands, *A Lancashire Brigade in France*, p. 11.
17. IWM, BLM 1/41.
18. IWM, BLM 1/40.
19. IWM, BLM 1/30.
20. Sandilands was originally commissioned in the Manchester Regiment in 1895. In 1897 he transferred to the Queen's Own Cameron Highlanders. He fought in the Sudan campaign and was Mentioned in Despatches. He then served in the Second Boer War and was again Mentioned in Despatches.
21. IWM, BLM 1/42.
22. *Ibid*.
23. Diary entries for 30 April 1916 from Major General Reginald John Pinney's Army Book, number 3. Diaries and papers, IWM Collection 66/257/1.
24. A footnote in Davson's *The History of the 35th Division* (p. 18) adds that during this night the enemy put up a board in no-man's-land announcing the fall of Kut-al-Amara, and the loss of 15,000 prisoners. The siege of the British-Indian garrison in the town of Kut, 100 miles south of Baghdad, by the Ottoman army had ended on 29 April. The garrison surrendered after a siege of 147 days. Around 13,000 Allied soldiers survived to be made prisoners.
25. Recalled in the magazine *Twenty Years After – The Battlefields of 1914–1918: Then and Now* (1928).
26. IWM, BLM 1/43.
27. *Ibid*. 'Ne'er cast a clout till May be out' is an old English proverb; a 'clout' variously (and debatably) meaning either a clod of earth or a fragment of clothing.
28. Diary entry for 7 May 1916 from Major General Reginald John Pinney's Army Book, number 3. Diaries and papers, IWM Collection 66/257/1.

29. Diary entry for 9 May 1916 from Major General Reginald John Pinney's Army Book, number 3. Diaries and papers, IWM Collection 66/257/1; Davson, *The History of the 35th Division*, p. 18.
30. Gidley wrote an account of the raid which would later be published in the *Morecambe Visitor*, 19 July 1916.
31. *Ibid.*
32. For reports in local press, see *Manchester Evening News*, 26 June and 11 August 1916 and *Manchester Guardian*, 27 June 1916. Arthur Hare was killed in action on 23 July 1916. He is commemorated on the Thiepval Memorial. Andrew Lee would finish the war in the Labour Corps. William Townley remained in the Manchester Regiment until 1918.
33. Diary entry for 13 May 1916 from Major General Reginald John Pinney's Army Book, number 3. Diaries and papers, IWM Collection 66/257/1.
34. Personal papers of James O'Connor, Tameside Local Studies and Archives Centre. Reference: MR4/17/282.
35. 'Recollections of Active Service with the 2/5th Gloucester Regiment in France and Flanders, 1915–1918'. Typescript memoir of Francis Charles Lewis, transcribed from the diaries that he kept during his service. IWM catalogue number: Documents 16506.
36. Diary entries for 19 May 1916 from Major General Reginald John Pinney's Army Book, number 3. Diaries and papers, IWM Collection 66/257/1.
37. MS Letters of Eustace Lockhart Maxwell, NAM 1974-02-34-30.
38. Maxwell was sorry to leave the Durhams, with whom he had been for six months. He wrote: 'I have been feeling very homesick for them, and am hoping that the Manchesters will prove to be of the same quality.'
39. MS Letters of Eustace Lockhart Maxwell, NAM 1974-02-34-18.
40. *Ibid.*
41. *Ibid.*
42. Letter reproduced in Davson, *The History of the 35th Division*, p. 328.
43. MS Letters of Eustace Lockhart Maxwell, NAM 1974-02-34-18.
44. *Ibid.*
45. MS Letters of Eustace Lockhart Maxwell, NAM 1974-02-34-31. The chaplain was John Duffield. The second-in-command was Major Charles Grimshaw. Though Maxwell was rather dismissive of his army record, Grimshaw had previously seen service in the South African War ('for which he holds medal and clasps'). After volunteering for the 1st City Pals in September 1914, he had been given a commission in the 7th City Battalion in December 1914 and was promoted to captain in February 1915. He subsequently transferred to the Bantams and was promoted to major in December 1915. This 'case of very rapid promotion' attracted the attention of the local newspapers. Taken out of the line suffering from shellshock on 20 July 1916, Grimshaw would be in hospital in Britain for the next two months. *Manchester Evening News*, 23 August 1916.
46. *Ibid.*
47. Diary entry for 12 June 1916 from Major General Reginald John Pinney's Army Book, number 3. Diaries and papers, IWM Collection 66/257/1.
48. MS Letters of Eustace Lockhart Maxwell, NAM 1974-02-34-31.

49. *Ibid.*
50. *Ibid.*
51. *Ibid.*
52. *Ibid.*
53. *Ibid.*
54. Diary entry for 2 July 1916 from Major General Reginald John Pinney's Army Book, number 3. Diaries and papers, IWM Collection 66/257/1.
55. Diary entries for 19 June 1916 from Major General Reginald John Pinney's Army Book, number 3. Diaries and papers, IWM Collection 66/257/1.
56. Blunden, *Undertones of War*, p. 59.
57. MS Letters of Eustace Lockhart Maxwell, NAM 1974-02-34-33. In March 1918 the artillery bombardment of Béthune intensified and in April the civilian population was evacuated. Subject to terrific bombardment between 13 and 18 April 1918, Béthune was effectively razed to the ground.
58. MS Letters of Eustace Lockhart Maxwell, NAM 1974-02-34-33.
59. Diary entries for 23 June 1916 from Major General Reginald John Pinney's Army Book, number 3. Diaries and papers, IWM Collection 66/257/1.
60. MS Letters of Eustace Lockhart Maxwell, NAM 1974-02-34-31.
61. IWM, BLM 1/46.
62. MS Letters of Eustace Lockhart Maxwell, NAM 1974-02-34-33.
63. *Ibid.*
64. *Ibid.*
65. Laurence ('Law') Lockhart Maxwell was a brigadier general with the 1st Indian Cavalry Division in France. MS Letters of Eustace Lockhart Maxwell, NAM 1974-02-34-34.
66. Diary entries for 24 June 1916 from Major General Reginald John Pinney's Army Book, number 3. Diaries and papers, IWM Collection 66/257/1.
67. MS Letters of Eustace Lockhart Maxwell, NAM 1974-02-34-33.
68. Diary entries for 28 and 30 June 1916 from Major General Reginald John Pinney's Army Book, number 3. Diaries and papers, IWM Collection 66/257/1.

Chapter 6

1. *Manchester Evening News*, 1 July 1916.
2. *Ibid.*, 6 July 1916.
3. The French 39th Division were advancing to the right of the British 30th Division. They succeeded in their objective of capturing Bois Favières (to the south-east of Montauban).
4. Quoted in Everard Wyrall, *The History of the King's Regiment (Liverpool), 1914–1919* (1930), Vol. II, p. 274.
5. *Manchester Evening News*, 10 July 1916.
6. *Illustrated Michelin Guides to the Battle-Fields (1914–1918): The Somme, Volume 1. The First Battle of the Somme (1916–1917) (Albert–Bapaume–Péronne)*(1919), p. 63. Quotations and images from the Michelin *Guides* are reproduced with the kind permission

of Michelin Tyre PLC.
7. MS Letters of Eustace Lockhart Maxwell, NAM 1974-02-34-35.
8. IWM, BLM 1/47.
9. *Ibid.*
10. MS Letters of Eustace Lockhart Maxwell, NAM 1974-02-34-35.
11. MS Letters of Eustace Lockhart Maxwell, NAM 1974-02-34-34.
12. *Manchester Evening News*, 6 July 1916.
13. Trônes Wood was called Bois des Troncs before the war – a British cartographer misspelled it and the name seemed to stick.
14. Wyrall, *The History of the King's Regiment*, Vol. II, pp. 274–5. The locality that became known to the British as Maltz Horn Farm was previously called Maltzkorn Farm.
15. Geoffrey H. Malins, *How I Filmed the War: A Record of the Extraordinary Experiences of the Man who Filmed the Great Somme Battles Etc* (1920), pp. 184, 189, 190, 192, 193.
16. MS Letters of Eustace Lockhart Maxwell, NAM 1974-02-34-35.
17. *Ibid.*
18. IWM, BLM 1/49. Montgomery used a series of code numbers in his letters to his mother to refer to place names.
19. IWM, BLM 1/49.
20. Diary entries for 10 and 12 July 1916 from Major General Reginald John Pinney's Army Book, number 3. Diaries and papers, IWM Collection 66/257/1.
21. MS Letters of Francis Aylmer Maxwell, NAM 1974-02-31. Letter of 15 July 1916.
22. Davson, *The History of the 35th Division*, p. 27.
23. MS Letters of Eustace Lockhart Maxwell, NAM 1974-02-34-36.
24. Diary entries for 14 July 1916 from Major General Reginald John Pinney's Army Book, number 3. Diaries and papers, IWM Collection 66/257/1.
25. *Manchester Evening News*, 14 July 1916.
26. MS Letters of Eustace Lockhart Maxwell, NAM 1974-02-34-36.
27. The account of the events of 20 July is put together from: Davson, *The History of 35th Division*, pp. 34–6; Sandilands, *A Lancashire Brigade in France*, pp. 13–14; War Diary of 23rd Battalion Manchester Regiment (WO 95/2484); War Diary of 15th Battalion Notts and Derby Regiment (Sherwood Foresters) (WO 95/2488); 'Account of the 23rd (Service) Battalion's service in France and Flanders'; diary entries for 20 July 1916 from Major General Reginald John Pinney's Army Book, number 3. Diaries and papers, IWM Collection 66/257/1.
28. 'First Report of Operations 20-07-16', War Diary of the 15th Battalion Notts and Derby Regiment (Sherwood Foresters), WO/95/2488, p. 143.
29. By 6.20 am the French, whose attack coincided, had succeeded in taking Maltz Horn Farm. Over the course of the day the French right flank advanced around 2,500 yards.
30. Interview with John Duffield, Catalogue number 4411, IWM.
31. A sad adjunct to this history is that a corporal of the Sherwood Foresters, Jesse Wilton, was executed by firing squad on 17 August 1916. Wilton had been given the task of occupying a forward post near Arrow Head Copse in the early hours of 19 July. Having

been subjected to prolonged shelling and machine-gun fire, with no rations for three days and fearing an imminent German attack, Wilton's party of seven returned to their own lines at 10.00 pm on 20 July, six hours earlier than had been ordered. Wilton was found guilty of quitting his post. There is evidence that when Wilton and his men returned to the lines a panic ensued, which could have triggered a widespread retreat. Officers drew revolvers to steady the situation ('Colonel Gordon feared for the steadiness of his battalion') and, with concerns as to discipline, it was deemed that Wilton had to be seen to be being punished. For a fuller account see Peter Simkins, '"Each One a Pocket Hercules": The Bantam Experiment and the Case of the Thirty-fifth Division', in Sanders Marble (ed.), *Scraping the Barrel – The Military use of Substandard Manpower 1860–1960* (2012), p. 86; and Julian Putkowski and Julian Sykes' *Shot at Dawn: Executions in World War One by Authority of the British Army Act* (1998), pp. 101–2.

32. Diary entries for 20 July 1916 from Major General Reginald John Pinney's Army Book, number 3. Diaries and papers, IWM Collection 66/257/1.
33. 'First Report of Operations 20-07-16', War Diary of the 15th Battalion Notts and Derby Regiment (Sherwood Foresters), WO/95/2488, p. 144.
34. Quoted in a letter, dated 28 July 1916, from Baron Rothband, Jack's brother; reproduced in Michael Stedman's *The Manchester Pals* (2004), p. 143.
35. Extract from the journal of Francis Aylmer Maxwell. MS Letters of Eustace Lockhart Maxwell, NAM 1974-02-34-40.
36. MS Letters of Eustace Lockhart Maxwell, NAM 1974-02-34-40.
37. Note written by Francis Aylmer Maxwell. MS Letters of Eustace Lockhart Maxwell, NAM 1974-02-34-41.
38. Sandilands, *A Lancashire Brigade in France*, p. 13.
39. Wyrall, *The History of the King's Regiment*, Vol. II, p. 292.
40. *Ibid.*
41. *Ibid.*, pp. 292–4.
42. IWM, BLM 1/48.
43. Congratulatory message reproduced in the War Diary of the 18th Battalion Lancashire Fusiliers, WO/95/2484, p. 113.
44. IWM, BLM 1/51.
45. Diary entries for 29 July 1916 from Major General Reginald John Pinney's Army Book, number 3. Diaries and papers, IWM Collection 66/257/1.
46. For a detailed account of the 30 July attack see Michael Stedman's, *The Manchester Pals* (2004) pp. 147–153.
47. Diary entries for 30 July and 2 August 1916 from Major General Reginald John Pinney's Army Book, numbers 3 and 4. Diaries and papers, IWM Collection 66/257/1.
48. IWM, BLM 1/52.
49. Diary entries 30 July 1916 from Major General Reginald John Pinney's Army Book, number 3. Diaries and papers, IWM Collection 66/257/1.
50. IWM, BLM 1/52.
51. IWM, BLM 1/53.
52. *Ibid.*

53. Diary entries for 17 August 1916 from Major General Reginald John Pinney's Army Book, number 4. Diaries and papers, IWM Collection 66/257/1; IWM, BLM 1/54.
54. IWM, BLM 1/55.
55. Sandilands, *A Lancashire Brigade in France*, p. 15.
56. *London Gazette*, 20 October 1916.
57. *Manchester Guardian*, 10 October 1916.
58. *The Times*, 19 April 1978.
59. Davson, *The History of the 35th Division*, pp. 50, 51; diary entries for 23 August 1916 from Major General Reginald John Pinney's Army Book, number 4. Diaries and papers, IWM Collection 66/257/1; Sandilands, *A Lancashire Brigade in France*, p. 15.
60. Diary entries for 24 August 1916 from Major General Reginald John Pinney's Army Book, number 4. Diaries and papers, IWM Collection 66/257/1; IWM, BLM 1/39 and 61.
61. *Ibid*.
62. IWM, BLM 1/55.
63. *Manchester Guardian*, 29 August 1916.
64. *Ibid*, 16 August 1916.
65. Diary entries for 28 August 1916 from Major General Reginald John Pinney's Army Book, number 4. Diaries and papers, IWM Collection 66/257/1.
66. Davson, *The History of the 35th Division*, pp. 52, 53.
67. Diary entries for 31 August 1916 from Major General Reginald John Pinney's Army Book, number 4. Diaries and papers, IWM Collection 66/257/1.
68. Wyrall, *The History of the King's Regiment*, Vol. II, p. 321.
69. Malins, *How I Filmed the War*, p. 236.
70. *Illustrated Michelin Guides to the Battle-Fields (1914–1918): The Somme, Volume 1*, p. 84.

Chapter 7

1. Walter Hale, *By Motor to the Firing Line: An Artist's Notes and Sketches with the Armies of Northern France, June–July 1915* (1916), pp. 136, 139.
2. Philip Gibbs, *From Bapaume to Passchendaele, On the Western Front, 1917* (1918), p. 41.
3. Hale, *By Motor to the Firing Line*, pp. 142, 143. At the time that Walter Hale was in Arras, in July 1915, the Allied and enemy trenches at Blangy had been closer than anywhere else along the front – just 20 yards apart in places.
4. Sandilands, *A Lancashire Brigade in France*, p. 17; Davson, *The History of the 35th Division*, p. 57.
5. Sandilands, *A Lancashire Brigade in France*, pp. 17, 18.
6. Davson, *The History of the 35th Division*, p. 65.
7. Diary entries for 21 and 22 September 1916 from Major General Reginald John Pinney's Army Book, number 4. Diaries and papers, IWM Collection 66/257/1.
8. Captain J.C. Dunn, *The War The Infantry Knew: 1914–1919: A Chronicle of Service in France and Belgium* (1938), p. 260. Landon's health seems to have been a persistent

issue. He was sent back to England in September 1915 due to ill health, but had returned in the October. In July 1917 he would return to England again, his health finally forcing him to retire from active service.

9. Sandilands, *A Lancashire Brigade in France*, p. 18.

10. *Ibid.*, pp. 18, 19; Davson, *The History of the 35th Division*, p. 66. At 7.30 am on 6 October the gas discharge was ordered to take place at 9.30 pm. At 9.10 pm the discharge was cancelled, but the counter order was not received by 104th Brigade until 9.22 pm, by which time gas was already being discharged in front of Blangy. With the wind against them, the men in the front line had already withdrawn, but eight of them later had to be treated for gas inhalation. At 11.42 pm a new order was received, directing that the gas should be discharged at 1.00 am (on the 7th). At 12.50 am this order was cancelled. At 6.10 pm the discharge was ordered for 8.15 pm, but at 7.30 pm this order was cancelled. The Divisional History notes that 106th Brigade were 'mystified by these proceedings'. No wonder.

11. War Diary of 17th Battalion Lancashire Fusiliers, Catalogue Reference: WO/95/2484, p. 76.

12. *Ibid.*

13. Davson, *The History of the 35th Division*, pp. 75, 76.

14. Sergeant Stones would later claim that he was unable to fire his rifle because the safety catch was on and the cover was over the breech. He therefore wedged it across the trench in order to slow the advance of the raiding party. Stones also maintained that Mundy had ordered him to head back to the support line to raise the alarm.

15. The person who shouted this instruction was never identified. The account of the night's events in Sandilands' *A Lancashire Brigade in France* (p. 19) states that 'the raiding party was composed entirely of English-speaking men' – and so there has been some suggestion that the command might have come from the enemy.

16. Davson, *The History of the 35th Division*, p. 80. There is a detailed account of the night's events in John Sheen's *Durham Pals: 18th, 19th, and 22nd (Service) Battalions of the Durham Light Infantry in the Great War* (2006), pp. 127–32.

17. The court heard that Lance Sergeant Stones was in a heightened nervous state when he reported the enemy incursion and, by this point, was struggling even to walk. Despite testimonies to his good character and hitherto unblemished fighting record (his commanding officer stated: 'He is the last man I would have thought capable of any cowardly action'), Stones received the death penalty.

18. Quoted in Peter Simkins, '"Each One a Pocket Hercules": The Bantam Experiment and the Case of the Thirty-fifth Division', in Marble (ed.), *Scraping the Barrel*, p. 91.

19. Ernest Thurtle was a Labour MP. After serving in the war, he campaigned for the abolition of the death penalty for cowardice or desertion in the British army. Thurtle first introduced the measure for abolition in 1924. It became Labour Party policy in 1925 and was eventually approved by the House of Commons in 1930. His 2d pamphlet *Shootings at Dawn: The Army Death Penalty at Work*, published in 1929, collected together a series of letters giving evidence relating to the Military Death Penalty.

20. Gibbs, *From Bapaume to Passchendaele*, p. 44.

Chapter 8

1. Variant on the common soldiers' corruption of 'The Church's One Foundation' ('Fred Karno's Army'), as sung by the Bantams.
2. Sir James Aylmer Lowthorpe Haldane, *A soldier's saga: the autobiography of General Sir Aylmer Haldane* (1948), pp. 335–6.
3. The anecdote, retold in Haldane's autobiography, was recounted in full in Philip Gibbs' *Now It Can Be Told* (1920), pp. 402, 404.
4. Haldane, *A soldier's saga*, p. 335.
5. Davson, *The History of the 35th Division*, p. 5.
6. *Ibid.*, p. 5.
7. Sandilands, *A Lancashire Brigade in France*, p. 19.
8. Gibbs, *Now It Can Be Told*, p. 404.
9. Haldane, *A soldier's saga*, pp. 335–6.
10. *Ibid.*
11. Sandilands, *A Lancashire Brigade in France*, pp. 19–21.
12. The Labour Corps was formed in January 1917. The Labour Companies, being reorganised at this time, were manned by officers and men who had been medically rated below the A1 condition required for front line service.
13. George Barker wrote, and published, an account, *Agony's Anguish* (1931), of his experiences with the 23rd Manchesters. Under the Derby Scheme men who voluntarily registered their name would be called up only when it was deemed necessary; the process grouped them by age and marital status. Married men, as Barker was, were told that they would be called up only once the supply of single men was exhausted. The scheme was superseded by the Military Service Act in March 1916, which introduced conscription for all unmarried men aged 18 to 41 years. With liability for military service extended to married men in May 1916, and the upper age limit increased to 51 in 1918, Barker probably would not have escaped military service. Barker, *Agony's Anguish,* pp. 8, 19.
14. Alan MacIver, the Assistant Brigade Major, related that Simmons and Montgomery had not got on. 'He and Monty never liked each other,' MacIver recalled. But, then, MacIver does not seem to particularly have been a fan of Montgomery. He described him as, 'A pretty cold fish, but very efficient'. See interview with Alan Squarey MacIver, staff officer at HQ 104th Brigade, IWM sound recording, catalogue reference 33051.
15. Davson, *The History of the 35th Division*, p. 6.

Chapter 9

1. *Manchester Evening News*, 20 January 1917.
2. George Barker, *Agony's Anguish*, pp. 21–3.
3. Sandilands, *A Lancashire Brigade in France*, p. 22.
4. Barker, *Agony's Anguish*, p. 21.
5. Sandilands, *A Lancashire Brigade in France*, p. 22.
6. Barker, *Agony's Anguish*, p. 21–2.
7. *Ibid.*, pp. 24–5.
8. Sandilands, *A Lancashire Brigade in France*, p. 21.

9. Barker, *Agony's Anguish*, p. 26.
10. *Ibid.*, pp. 32–3.
11. Sandilands, *A Lancashire Brigade in France*, p. 21.
12. Davson, *The History of the 35th Division*, p. 89.
13. Barker, *Agony's Anguish*, pp. 42–3.
14. *The History of the 35th Division*, p. 91,
15. Gibbs, *From Bapaume to Passchendaele, 1917*, p. 77.
16. Captain G.K. Rose MC, *The Story Of The 2/4th Oxfordshire and Buckinghamshire Light Infantry* (1920), pp. 78, 80, 88.
17. Sandilands, *A Lancashire Brigade in France*, p. 24.
18. Rose, *The Story Of The 2/4th Oxfordshire and Buckinghamshire Light Infantry*, pp. 78–9.
19. *Ibid.*, p. 80.
20. Gibbs, *From Bapaume to Passchendaele*, pp. 82–3.
21. *Ibid.*, p. 92.
22. Sandilands, *A Lancashire Brigade in France*, p. 24.
23. Davson, *The History of the 35th Division*, p. 101.
24. Gibbs, *From Bapaume to Passchendaele*, pp. 93–4.
25. *Ibid.*, pp. 93, 96.
26. Davson, *The History of the 35th Division*, p. 101.
27. *Manchester Evening News*, 7 May 1917.

Chapter 10
1. Malins, *How I Filmed the War*, p. 294–5.
2. Sandilands, *A Lancashire Brigade in France*, p. 26.
3. *Ibid.*
4. A note in the Divisional History details that the facing German division contained a large proportion of young soldiers. They were apparently nicknamed 'the rabbits' by the 35th Division. 'They were somewhat lacking in warcraft,' Davson commented in *The History of the 35th Division*, p. 106.
5. Sandilands, *A Lancashire Brigade in France*, p. 28.
6. *Ibid.*
7. Davson, *History of the 35th Division*, p. 108.
8. Sandilands, *A Lancashire Brigade in France*, p. 27.
9. Davson, *The History of the 35th Division*, p. 108.
10. Sandilands, *A Lancashire Brigade in France*, p. 28.
11. Barker, *Agony's Anguish*, p. 50–1.
12. In Barker's account, in *Agony's Anguish*, it is Captain J.S. Foulkes, Somerville's senior officer, who leads the raid. Barker writes of Foulkes: 'a better officer you could not meet in the army. There was no fear in this man – cool, collected, brave, and with the courage of a lion, but above all he was human to the last degree; we all loved him and would follow him to hell if need be.'
13. *London Gazette*, 29 November 1918.

14. IWM, BLM 1/60.
15. Sandilands, *A Lancashire Brigade in France*, p. 29.

Chapter 11
1. *Illustrated Michelin Guides to the Battle-Fields (1914–1918): The Somme*, Volume 1, p. 97.
2. *Ibid.*, p. 99.
3. Gibbs, *From Bapaume to Passchendaele*, pp. 80–1. Catherine de Poix (also known as 'Marie Fouré') was actually the heroine of the siege of 1536, when the Spanish, under the leadership of the Prince of Orange, besieged Péronne for thirty consecutive days. A statue of General Faidherbe, commemorating his victory over the Germans in 1871, had been removed in Bapaume. When the British arrived there in 1917 the bronze statue of Faidherbe had been replaced by 'an enormous stove-pipe'.
4. Sandilands, *A Lancashire Brigade in France*, p. 29.
5. Davson, *The History of the 35th Division*, p. 118.
6. *Ibid.*, p. 120; Sandilands, *A Lancashire Brigade in France*, p. 30.
7. Sandilands, *A Lancashire Brigade in France*, p. 30; Davson, *The History of the 35th Division*, p. 121.
8. Sandilands, *A Lancashire Brigade in France*, p. 30.
9. *Ibid.*
10. *Ibid.*, p. 31.
11. Barker, *Agony's Anguish*, p.49.

Chapter 12
1. Captain S.J. Wilson, MC, *The Seventh Manchesters, July 1916 to March 1919* (1920), pp. 34–6.
2. Sandilands, *A Lancashire Brigade in France*, p. 32.
3. *Ibid.*, p. 32; Davson, *The History of the 35th Division*, p. 127.
4. *London Gazette*, 8 January 1918.
5. According to the War Diary of the 17th Lancashire Fusiliers, they encountered three belts of wire, the first two of which were thick. The Fusiliers set off from Lone Tree (see plan on p. 251) and attacked a section of the Canal Wood trenches, just to the north of the Manchesters' attack.
6. Sandilands, *A Lancashire Brigade in France*, p. 33.
7. *London Gazette*, 25 January 1918.
8. Sandilands, *A Lancashire Brigade in France*, p. 34.
9. Barker, *Agony's Anguish*, p. 56.
10. *Ibid.*, pp. 56–8.
11. *Ibid.*, p. 64.
12. Montague, *Disenchantment*, pp. 147, 149.

Chapter 13
1. *Manchester Evening News*, 23 October 1917.

2. Sandilands, *A Lancashire Brigade in France*, p. 36.
3. *Ibid.*
4. Barker, *Agony's Anguish*, p. 66.
5. Davson, *The History of the 35th Division*, p. 159.
6. Interview with William John Collins, who served with No. 1 Cavalry Field Ambulance, Royal Army Medical Corps, attached to 1st Cavalry brigade on the Western Front and in Germany, 1915–19. IWM Sound Recordings, Catalogue number 9434.
7. Interview with W.J. Collins. IWM Sound Recordings, Catalogue number 9434. Langemarck fell into German hands again in the spring of 1918. It was finally recaptured by the Belgian army in September 1918.
8. Barker, *Agony's Anguish*, p. 68.
9. Sandilands, *A Lancashire Brigade in France*, pp. 37–8.
10. Barker, *Agony's Anguish*, p. 68–9.
11. Sandilands, *A Lancashire Brigade in France*, p. 38.
12. Barker, *Agony's Anguish*, p. 71.
13. Sandilands, *A Lancashire Brigade in France*, p. 37.
14. Davson, *The History of the 35th Division*, p. 158.
15. Gibbs, *From Bapaume to Passchendaele*, pp. 426–7.
16. *Ibid.*, p. 426.
17. Davson, *The History of the 35th Division*, p. 161.
18. Sandilands, *A Lancashire Brigade in France*, p. 40.
19. It seems that a small group of Manchesters did make it as far forwards as Six Roads, where they were witnessed attacking the pill boxes; a group of 16th Royal Scots gave rifle fire support to this group, but any further advance was held up by the enemy wire. 'For some of the time the gallant little party of Manchester men and Scots held on,' a history of the 34th Division records, 'but they suffered heavily, and at last the survivors had to give way, retiring sullenly to a position east of Egypt house.' Lieutenant Colonel J. Shakespear, *The Thirty-Fourth Division, 1915–1919* (1921), p. 161.
20. Sandilands, *A Lancashire Brigade in France*, pp. 38–9.
21. Interview with Alan Squarey MacIver, staff officer at HQ 104th Brigade, IWM sound recording, catalogue reference 33051.
22. Sandilands, *A Lancashire Brigade in France*, p. 40.
23. Private Papers of Lieutenant Colonel R.W.F Johnston CMG CBE MC TD. Typescript memoir. IWM, catalogue reference: Documents 4474.
24. See interview with Alan Squarey MacIver, staff officer at HQ 104th Brigade, IWM sound recording, catalogue reference 33051.
25. Private Papers of Lieutenant Colonel R.W.F Johnston CMG CBE MC TD. Typescript memoir. IWM, catalogue reference: Documents 4474.
26. July 1917, Major General George McKenzie Franks had assumed command of the 35th Division (replacing Major General H.J.S. Landon).
27. Gibbs, *From Bapaume to Passchendaele*, p. 452–4.

Chapter 14
1. Philip Gibbs was writing on 7 November 1917. *From Bapaume To Passchendaele*, p. 461–2.
2. Sandilands, *A Lancashire Brigade in France*, p. 44.
3. Davson, *The History of the 35th Division*, p. 175.
4. It was in the French lines opposite Brielen that gas had first been used as a weapon in the Ypres Salient, back in April 1915.
5. Davson, *The History of the 35th Division*, p. 173; Sandilands, *A Lancashire Brigade in France*, p. 41.
6. Davson, *The History of the 35th Division*, pp. 176–7.
7. Sandilands, *A Lancashire Brigade in France*, p. 41.
8. *Ibid.*, p. 42; Davson, *The History of the 35th Division*, p. 180.
9. Sandilands, *A Lancashire Brigade in France*, p. 43.
10. *Ibid.*
11. *Ibid.*, p. 44.
12. Davson, *The History of the 35th Division*, p. 181.
13. *Ibid.*, p. 183; Sandilands, *A Lancashire Brigade in France*, p. 44.
14. Sandilands, *A Lancashire Brigade in France*, p. 82.
15. *Manchester Guardian*, 22 March 1918.
16. *Ibid.*
17. *Ibid.*, 23 March 1918.

Chapter 15
1. *Manchester Guardian*, 12 November 1918.
2. *Ibid.*
3. *Ibid.*; *Manchester Evening News*, 11 and 12 November 1918.
4. In March 1919, in a House of Commons debate, Winston Churchill was asked to define what the various categories meant. See Hansard, HC Deb 20 March 1919, Vol. 113 cc2262-5W; *Manchester Guardian*, 17 December 1918.
5. *Manchester Guardian*, 6 January 1919.
6. *Ibid.*, 30 January 1919.
7. *Ibid.*, 27 June 1919.
8. It was finally decided that this official 'Welcome Home' for the troops should take the form of a series of receptions ('treats') to be held in Belle Vue Gardens. Men were to be given 'a suitable meal' and an address from the Lord Mayor. *Ibid.*, 5 June, 4 and 19 July 1919.
9. *Manchester Evening News*, 10 July 1919.
10. *Manchester Guardian*, 19 July 1919.
11. *Ibid.*, 19 and 21 July 1919.
12. *Ibid.*, 21 July 1919.
13. *Ibid.*, 21 July 1919.
14. H.M. McKechnie, *Manchester in 1915: Being the Handbook for the Eighty-Fifth Meeting of the British Association for the Advancement of Science, Held in Manchester,*

September Seven to Ten, 1915 (1916).
15. *Manchester Guardian*, 30 January 1919.
16. The NFDDSS was founded in January 1917, initially with the aim of articulating opposition to the Review of Exceptions Act, which made it possible for men who had formerly been discharged from the army on medical grounds to be re-conscripted.
17. *Manchester Guardian*, 25 and 26 February 1919.
18. The 'Out of Work Donation' scheme was introduced in November 1918, offering emergency financial assistance to both unemployed ex-servicemen and civilians. It originally provided men with a weekly 'dole' of 24*s*, and 20*s* for women. Ex-service personnel could claim it for a maximum of twenty-six weeks, during the twelve months following demobilisation, and civilians could receive it for thirteen weeks, during the six months following the scheme's inception. The number of ex-servicemen claiming state assistance peaked in May 1919. In Lancashire and Cheshire 73,732 men were claiming at this time. *Ibid.*, 22 November 1919, 21 September 1920.
19. *Ibid.*, 19 and 20 March 1919.
20. *Ibid.*, 14 August 1919.
21. *Ibid.*, 18 August 1919.
22. *Ibid.*
23. Philip Snowden, formerly the ILP MP for Blackburn, had campaigned against conscription during the war. He lost his seat in the 1918 General Election, but would be re-elected in 1922 (to represent Colne Valley). *Ibid.*, 18 August 1919.
24. *Ibid.*, 30 April 1920.
25. *Ibid.*, 21 September 1920.
26. *Ibid.*, 8 November 1921.
27. *Ibid.*, 17 March 1922.
28. As stated in the *British Legion Pilgrimage Handbook* (1928).
29. *Manchester Guardian*, 11 and 12 November 1921.
30. As stated in the *British Legion Pilgrimage Handbook* (1928).
31. *Manchester Guardian*, 12 November 1920.
32. *Ibid.*
33. *Ibid.*, 11 and 13 November 1922.
34. *Manchester Guardian*, 12 October, 11 and 13 November 1922; 31 March, 10 and 12 November 1923.
35. *Ibid.*, 7 November 1921, 12 October 1922.
36. *Ibid.*, 11 and 12 October 1922.
37. *Ibid.*, 7 February 1923.
38. *Ibid.*
39. *Ibid.*, 31 March, and 9, 10, 11 and 12 April 1923.
40. *Ibid.*, 12 April 1923.
41. *Ibid.*, 5 May 1923; 17 May 1923.
42. *Ibid.*, 14 July 1924.
43. *Ibid.*, 5 June, 3, 12 and 13 July and 20 September 1923. A further point of controversy was the means of the cenotaph's construction. Instead of employing local men, as had

been one of the original ideals of the committee, Lutyens used the London-based Nine Elms Stone Masonry Works. *Ibid.*, 8 July 1924.
44. *Ibid.*, 20 September 1923.
45. *Ibid.*, 8 July 1924. The final cost of the memorial was £6,490. The unspent balance of the money subscribed – £4,082 – was used to provide beds (to be called the 'Manchester War Memorial Beds') in local hospitals for the dependents of servicemen who died in the war. *Ibid.*, 28 April 1925.
46. *Ibid.*, 14 July 1924.
47. *Ibid.*
48. *Ibid.*
49. *Ibid.*, 11, 12, 14 and 15 July 1924.
50. *Ibid.*, 12 July 1924.
51. *Ibid.*, 12 November 1924.
52. *Ibid.*, 12 November 1928.
53. George Barker thinks that he sees angels around the Cenotaph and hears a voice telling him: 'Tell the mothers and fathers of this world that their sons who they mourned as lost are much better off that the peoples of the earth; they are now at peace with the Lord, and great happiness is theirs.' The account may sound rather fanciful, but it reflects the depth of emotion with which ex-combatants privately reacted to the Cenotaph – and a solace that some found in it. Barker, *Agony's Anguish*, pp. 93–5.
54. *Manchester Guardian*, 10 November 1952.
55. 'Order of Service: Reception of the colours and memorial service for the 11th, 12th, 13th, 23rd, 51st, 52nd and 53rd Service Battalions and the 1st Garrison Battalion,' 8 January 1921. Tameside Local Studies and Archives Centre, MR3/18/14. *Ibid.*, 10 January 1921.
56. *Ibid.*, 1 July, 11 and 12 November 1936.
57. *Ibid.*, 17 November 1951.

Index

Abraham, Capt Arthur Thomas, 282
Aden House, 273, 285
Albert, 145, 148–9, 155, 173, 180, 214
'Alien enemies', 24–7
Aliens Restriction Act (1914), 25
Allenby, FM Edmund Henry Hynman, 202
Anderson, D.E., 40
Annezin, 134, 136
Armistice, reaction in Manchester, 301–302
Armistice Day, commemoration, 311–14, 318–20
Arras, 185–98, 205, 225–6
Arrow Head Copse, 156–8, 171, 333
Australian army,
  1st Battalion, First Australian Imperial Force, 118, 120
  2nd Battalion, First Australian Imperial Force, 119
Aveluy Wood, 148, 150–1, 153

Bannatyne, Maj James Fitzgerald, 125–7, 129
  Bantam battalions,
  criticism of, 162, 180, 182, 197–8, 199–202
  disbanding, 203
  instigation, 37–46
  rationale for, 37–40
Barker, Pte George, 203, 205–207, 211, 213–14, 216, 234, 245–6, 257–8, 261, 263, 265–7, 319–20, 336, 341
Battalions of 35th Division, 80, 84–7, 94, 102, 104, 108, 112, 119, 131, 145, 153, 156, 173, 180, 193–4, 198–200, 203, 206–207, 209, 223, 227, 229, 231, 236, 242, 247, 252, 254, 260, 268
104th Brigade, 80, 84, 94, 110, 116, 118–20, 145, 148, 155, 169–70, 173–5, 178–80, 189, 196, 198, 203, 206, 223, 229, 235–6, 254, 256, 261, 265, 266–7, 273, 277, 297, 335
  17th (Service) Battalion Lancashire Fusiliers, 80, 110, 167, 178, 193–4, 206, 231, 234, 243, 254, 265, 267–8, 272–4, 290, 294
  18th (Service) Battalion Lancashire Fusiliers, 80, 115, 118, 130–1, 160, 168, 213, 231, 268–9, 271–3, 277, 292, 294, 296
  20th (Service) Battalion Lancashire Fusiliers, 80, 128, 189, 192, 231, 242, 245–6, 268, 273, 285
105th Brigade, 84, 156, 158–9, 196, 254, 256
  15th (Service) Battalion Cheshire Regiment (1st Birkenhead), 254
  15th (Service) Battalion Nottinghamshire & Derbyshire Regiment (Sherwood Foresters), 130–1, 156–60, 254, 333
  16th (Service) Battalion Cheshire Regiment (2nd Birkenhead), 214, 232, 252
106th Brigade, 84, 129, 196, 254, 256, 294

17th (Service) Battalion West Yorkshire Regiment, 215, 217
19th (Service) Battalion Durham Light Infantry, 117, 129, 196–7,
Battle of the Somme (film), 147, 180
Belgium,
  atrocities in, reaction to, 22–4
  refugees in Manchester, 23
Bellamy, 2Lt Alfred Wraith, 282
Bernafay Wood, 146, 148, 167
Béthune, 103, 107, 132, 134, 136–8, 145, 332
Bigland, Alfred MP, 39–40, 47
Bihécourt, 232–3
Birdcage, 247–57
Birkenhead, 39–40, 47
Blangy (Arras), 188–91, 335
Blendecques, 101
Blunden, Edmund, 104, 106, 116, 136
Boëseghem, 103
Boesinghe, 261–3, 290
Boulogne-sur-Mer, 99–101
Bouzincourt, 148–9
Brielen, 290, 295, 339
Brigades, of 35th Division *see* Battalions
Briqueterie, 146
British Medical Journal, 45–6

Calonne-sur-la-Lys, 103, 107–108, 110
Canal Wood, 248, 254, 338
Cathedral, Manchester, 320–1
Cenotaph *see* War memorial
Chapel of the Manchester Regiment, Manchester Cathedral, 320–1
Caulaincourt, Chateau, 229–30
Chaffey, 2Lt Charles Russell, 215
Chaulnes, 207–209, 219–21
Chilly, 209, 214–16
Citadel camp, 177, 179
Clarkson, 2Lt Thomas, 299
Clerks and Warehousemen's Battalion, 30
Congreve, Gen Walter Norris, 173
Cook, Lt Col Walter, 73

Cook, 2Lt Cecil Haddon, 282
Cotton trade, 8–10, 12, 21, 306–308, 322, 324
Croix-Barbée, 124–5, 128

De-bantamization, 199–204
Delville Wood, 119, 167
Demobilisation, 303
Derby, Lord (Edward George Villiers Stanley), 30–1, 142, 144–5, 303, 317
Disbanding, of 23rd Manchester Battalion, 296–8
Divisions,
  9th Division, 198
  18th Division, 128, 153, 156
    12th (Service) Battalion, Duke of Cambridge's Own (Middlesex Regiment) 19th Division, 153
  30th Division, 143–4, 146–7, 166, 171, 173, 332
  See also Manchester Regiment and King's Regiment (Liverpool)
  32nd Division, 223
  34th Division, 268, 272, 274
    16th (Service) Battalion (2nd Edinburgh), The Royal Scots (Lothian Regiment), 271–2, 274–5, 277, 339
  38th (Welsh) Division, 104, 330
    10th (Service) Battalion (1st Rhondda), Welsh Regiment, 107, 330
    13th (Service) Battalion (2nd Rhondda), Welsh Regiment, 330
    14th (Service) Battalion (Swansea), Welsh Regiment, 107, 330
    15th (Service) Battalion (Carmarthenshire County Committee), Welsh Regiment, 330
  59th Division, 232–3
Dixon, 2Lt John William, 282
Doidge, Capt Reginald Chamberly, 110
Duffield, Rev John, 85–6, 90, 98–9, 115, 160, 166

Durandeau, 2Lt Richard Frederick, 110–11

Elverdinghe, 266–7, 285, 294
Entrenching battalions, 298–9
Épehy, 242, 247–9, 255–6
Étreillers, 225, 229

Falfemont Farm, 178–9
Favières Wood, 145, 332
Federation of Master Cotton Spinners' Associations, 9–10, 21
Ferme du Bois, 113, 128, 130–2
Folkestone, 98, 303

Gauche Wood, 242–6
German population in Manchester, 24–7
  arrests of, 25–6
  attacks on, 27
Gibbons, Capt William Percy, 253
Gibbs, Sir Philip Armand Hamilton, 135, 186, 198–200, 202, 217–19, 222–4, 239, 268, 269, 285–6, 288
Gidley, Pte Percy, 6, 70, 81–3, 86–9, 91–2, 99–100, 125–7, 322, 328, 331
Gillemont, 248–9, 251, 254, 256
Goggins, L/Cpl Peter, 197
Gordon, Lt Col R.H.S., 158–60, 162–3
Gosling, Capt Frederick William, 160, 164
Goudberg, 288
Gray, 2Lt Charles W., 292–3
Guillemont, 6, 146, 156, 159, 166–7, 169–72, 177–9, 181–4
Gurlu Wood, 254

Haig, FM Sir Douglas, 86, 131, 205, 225–6, 235, 296
Haking, Gen Sir Richard Cyril Byrne, 102, 128, 135
Haldane, Gen Sir James Aylmer Lowthorpe, 199–200, 202
Hale, Walter, 186, 188–9, 335
Happy Valley, 156, 173–4, 177, 254
Hare, Sgt Arthur, 126–7, 135, 167, 331

Heaton Park, 47–8, 75, 79
Height, minimum requirement for infantry, 33
Herzeele, 294
Hill, Lt Col Sir Henry Blyth, 68, 72–4, 81, 91
Hindenburg Line, 216–17, 222, 226, 242, 244, 247
Honnecourt, 242–5
Houthulst Forest, 259, 268–84, 287–8, 294
Houtkerque, 294

Johnston, 2Lt Robert W.F., 274–5, 277–8

Kiggell, Lt Gen Sir Launcelot Edward, 131
King's Regiment (Liverpool), 146
Kitchener, FM 1st Earl Horatio Herbert, 27, 29–30, 34, 69, 74, 76–7, 84, 102, 198, 314
Knoll, 247–9, 251, 254, 256–7
Kruger, Lt Dirk Jacobus, 299

Landon, Maj Gen Herman James Shelley, 193–4, 197–8, 201–202, 335
Langemarck, 261, 263–4, 268, 288, 294, 338
Lee, Pte Andrew, 126–7, 331
Lihons-en-Santerre, 209–15
Liverpool, 21, 30, 115, 143, 146, 164, 253, 283
Lutyens, Sir Edwin Landseer, 316–18, 341

Macara, Sir Charles Wright, 9
MacIver, Assistant Brig Maj Alan Squarey, 273, 277, 336
Mackenzie, Brig Gen Gerald Mackay, 80–1, 119–20
Mackinnon, Gen Sir Henry, 43, 65, 78
Maissemy, 228–9, 232–3
Malins, Geoffrey, 147–8, 180, 184, 229
Maltz Horn Farm, 146, 156–9, 162, 167, 333
Manchester, 8–50, 142, 180, 301–21

349

Manchester Regiment,
  2nd Battalion, 23, 235, 297, 299
  1/6th Battalion (Territorials), 20
  1/7th Battalion (Territorials), 20, 282
  11th (Service) Battalion, 28, 297
  12th (Service) Battalion, 297, 299
  16th (Service) Battalion (1st City), 24, 31–2, 48, 143, 147, 170, 332
  17th (Service) Battalion (2nd City), 31, 48, 143, 147, 170–1, 325
  18th (Service) Battalion (3rd City), 48, 143, 147, 170–1
  19th (Service) Battalion (4th City), 33, 35, 48, 91, 143, 147, 166–7, 170, 282
  20th (Service) Battalion (5th City), 33, 34, 48, 50, 61, 64, 70, 74, 79, 282
  21st (Service) Battalion (6th City), 34, 48, 50, 79
  22nd (Service) Battalion (7th City), 34, 40–1, 46–8, 79, 107, 115, 177, 332
Manchester City Battalions' Book of Honour, 11, 30–2, 44, 72–4, 78–9, 84–6, 89–90, 93–7
Maricourt, 143, 156, 162
Masham, 82–5, 88, 193, 201
Mason, Lt Herbert John, 253–4
Maxwell, Maj Eustace Lockhart, 6–7, 85, 101, 109, 116, 129, 130–4, 136, 138–40, 145, 148–9, 155, 159–60, 165, 329, 331
Maxwell, Brig Gen Francis Aylmer, 153, 165
Maxwell, Brig Gen Laurence Lockhart, 165
McCabe, Sir Daniel, 30
McDonald, L/Cpl John, 197
Merville, 107, 117, 119, 126–7, 129
Minden Day, 173, 254
Monro, Gen Sir Charles Carmichael, 126, 138
Montague, Charles Edward, 23, 90, 114, 116, 258, 307, 310, 314, 324, 327
Montauban, 143–6, 153, 177, 183

Montgomery, Bde Maj Bernard Law, 80–1, 87, 101–102, 112, 114, 116–21, 124, 126, 138, 145, 148, 150–1, 153, 166–7, 169, 172, 174, 179, 203, 235, 328–9, 336
Morecambe, 6–7, 48–85, 88, 92, 94, 99–100, 127, 141, 326–7, 330
Morlancourt, 155
Morton, Capt Joseph Leonard Milthorp, 282–3

Naours, 205–206
National Federation of Discharged and Demobilized Sailors and Soldiers, 311
Neuf-Berquin, 120
Neutrality League, 18, 323
Neuve Chapelle, 104, 120–1, 123, 135
Nivelle, Gen Robert Georges, 205, 217, 225–6

O'Connor, Cpl James, 126, 128, 135
Ossus Wood, 248, 253–4
'Out of Work Donation' scheme, 307, 310, 340

Paddebeek Sector, 288, 292
Pals battalions, instigation, 30–2
Paradis, 116
Parkhouse Camp, 87–91, 94, 329
Passchendaele, 226, 258–60, 268, 285–7
Peace Day (19 July 1919), 304–306
Péronne, 236, 238–43, 258
Pinney, Maj Gen Sir Reginald John, 6, 81, 86–7, 102, 116–17, 121, 125–8, 133, 135, 138, 140, 153, 155–6, 158, 162–3, 170–1, 173–4, 178–80, 182, 193, 203
Poelcapelle, 261, 278, 279, 288–92, 294–5
Pontru, 235
Pontruet, 229, 231–2
Poperinghe, 261, 285, 292, 294, 297
Proven, 261, 285

Quiestède, 101

Rawlinson, Gen Henry Seymour, 167, 179
Recruitment, 27–36, 39–47
Reinforcements, quality of, 174, 179–80, 182, 193, 197, 199–203
Restructuring of infantry divisions, 296–8
Richebourg-l'Avoué, 104, 106, 113–14, 120, 126, 132
Richebourg St Vaast, 104, 106, 126, 128
Roberts, FM Frederick Sleigh, 39–40, 42, 73
Roberts, Robert, 19–20, 25, 29
Rose, Lt Matthew Howard, 118, 125–6, 176–7
Rose, Capt G.K., 218–19
Rosières-en-Santerre, 203, 207, 209, 214, 216
Rothband, Capt Jacob Eustace, 160, 164

Sailly-le-Sec, 167, 173–4
Sailly-sur-la-Lys, 116–17
Saint-Quentin, 227, 229, 231, 236–7, 298
Salisbury Plain, 81, 87–9
Sandilands, Brig Gen James Walter, 81, 120–1, 123, 125–6, 134, 148, 153, 158, 165, 169, 173, 175, 178, 189, 192, 194, 201–202, 207, 213–14, 219, 223, 232–4, 236, 242–5, 248–9, 252, 254–7, 261, 265–7, 271–4, 284, 288, 292, 294–5, 297–8, 331
Scott, Charles Prestwich, 10–12, 16, 22, 322–4
Simpson, Capt George Edward, 160, 164, 283
Smith, Lt Col Reynold Percy, 91, 129
Somme offensive, 6, 142–84, 199, 205, 207, 226, 265
Somerville, Capt Hugh, 233–5
Somerville Wood, 233–6
Stevens, Lt Col Leighton Marlow, 166, 176, 298
Stones, L/Sgt Joseph William, 196–7, 335–6
Styles, 2Lt Harold Thomas, 283–4

Talus Boisé, 156, 160, 166, 168–9, 174
Templeux-la-Fosse, 242, 244, 246
Thiepval Memorial, 160–2, 164–9, 171–2, 175–7, 179–80, 184, 214, 216, 233, 235, 253, 255–6, 331
Touret, Le, 103–104, 114, 129, 132–3
Townley, Pte William, 126–7, 136, 331
Training, 51–94
Trench raids, 121–6, 191, 195, 231–5, 252–6
Trônes Wood, 146, 153–4, 156, 166–7, 169–70, 172, 333
Tyne Cot, Commonwealth War Graves Cemetery and Memorial to the Missing, 265, 278–86, 296, 300

Under-age troops, 85–6
Unemployment, of ex-servicemen, 304–10, 340

Vadencourt, 232–3
Vendhuile, 247, 249–50, 252
Vermand, 229, 233, 235
Vieille Chapelle, 120
Villers-Guislain, 243–6
Voyennes, 223–4

War memorial, Manchester, 313–20
Ware, Cpl Henry, 256
Watson, Lt Frank, 115
Welldon, James Edward Cowell, 24
Wiencourt-l'Équipée, 206
Weir, Lt William Logan, 284
Willey, Lt Henry Lowes, 166, 284
Wilson, 2Lt William Arnold, 284
Women 'dilutees', 309–10

Ypres, 242, 254, 260–1, 263, 282, 288, 296